"In his provocative new book Glenn Davis Stone insists that we misunderstand agriculture.' More than this, he argues that too many luminary analysts – Malthus, Borlaug, Ehrlich – have gotten too many things precisely backwards. Most centrally, the runaway train is not a burgeoning population but an industrial agriculture committed to overproduction. Persuasively illuminating the need to unlearn a variety of agricultural truisms, he shows how a just and regenerative 'Third Agriculture' is being sustained and recreated by peasant farmers and neo-agrarians around the world."

Jack Kloppenburg, *Professor Emeritus, University of Wisconsin-Madison, USA and author of* First the Seed: The Political Economy of Plant Biotechnology, 1492–2000

"Stone combines scholarly precision and compelling prose to shatter the received wisdom that industrial agriculture – patented seeds, mined and synthesized agrichemicals – can ever 'feed the world,' or ever has. An essential book."

Tom Philpott, *author of* Perilous Bounty

"In a magnificent synthesis of anthropology, economics, history and politics, Glenn Davis Stone has traced the arc of why consistently bad questions are being asked of the food system, and consistently bad answers so reliably delivered. In lucid prose, Stone offers a tour of the most important literature, and figures, shaping debates about hunger in the past two centuries. If we are wise, we'll understand why they are poor guides to feeding the planet in the 21st century. And if that happens, it'll be in no small part because of this instant classic, by a scholar writing at the height of his powers."

Raj Patel, *Research Professor, University of Texas, USA and author of* Stuffed and Starved

"With his deft mix of meticulous research and engaging storytelling, Stone reveals how agribusiness has invoked the ghost of Thomas Malthus to impose its technology-obsessed vision of an industrialized agriculture, from Iowa to India to Africa. In the process, he unearths so many deeply rooted myths that we begin again to see our way forward."

Timothy A. Wise, *author of* Eating Tomorrow: Agribusiness, Family Farmers, and the Battle for the Future of Food

"Stone's book is a thoughtful and stinging indictment of the unexamined logics that underlie industrial agriculture. It is a welcome rebuke to the monotonous excuses of big ag, framed in a clear and beautiful reassessment of Malthus. Historians and policymakers will find plenty to chew on here."

Deborah Fitzgerald, *Professor, MIT, USA*

"Stone's new book challenges one of the cherished myths that Western know-how saved the Global South from famine by revolutionizing agriculture in countries like Mexico and India. What that myth obscures is the devastating impact of those policies on small farmers across the globe. The so-called Green Revolution in wheat production, for example, depended on state-subsidized inputs most small farmers could not afford. Big Ag was a myth both capitalists and Marxists promulgated, and it meant that millions of 'peasant' farmers were sacrificed on the altars of industrial agriculture. But as Stone shows in his new analysis of the 'Third Agriculture,' small farms change and evolve."

Tom Sheridan, *Professor, University of Arizona, USA and author of* Where the Dove Calls: The Political Ecology of a Peasant Corporate Community in Northwestern Mexico

"Glenn Stone brings a much-needed critical perspective to the many halos surrounding practices of industrial agriculture. Bringing an anthropologist's eye to new materials and circumstances, Stone challenges core assumptions and theories of demographers and scientists to point towards possible alternatives."

Prakash Kumar, *Associate Professor, Pennsylvania State University, USA*

"In typically forthright style, Stone effectively dismantles the copious mythology that has built up around the Green Revolution project, both past and present. The book marks a must-read contribution for those concerned with the future of global agricultural policymaking."

Marcus Taylor, *Head of Department of Global Development Studies, Queen's University, Canada*

THE AGRICULTURAL DILEMMA

The Agricultural Dilemma questions everything we think we know about the current state of agriculture and how to, or perhaps more importantly how not to, feed a world with a growing population.

This book is about the three fundamental forms of agriculture: Malthusian (expansion), industrialization (external-input-dependent), and intensification (labor-based). The best way to understand the three agricultures, and how we tend to get it wrong, is to consider what drives their growth. The book provides a thoughtful, critical analysis that upends entrenched misconceptions such as that we are running out of land for food production and that our only hope is the development of new agricultural technologies. The book contains engaging and enlightening vignettes and short histories, with case studies drawn from across the globe to bring to life this important debate and dilemma. The book concludes by arguing there is a viable alternative to industrial agriculture which will allow us to meet the world's needs and it ponders why such alternatives have been downplayed, obscured, or hidden from view.

This important book is essential reading for all studying and researching food production and agriculture, and more broadly for all interested in ensuring we are able to feed our growing population.

Glenn Davis Stone is an anthropologist and internationally recognized authority on the history, politics, and ecology of agriculture and food production. He has conducted ethnographic research in Nigeria, India, the Philippines, and Appalachia (US); archaeological research in the Midwestern and Southwestern US; and work in an agricultural biotechnology lab. He has published over 80 academic articles (one of which won the Gordon Willey Prize) and one previous book, and has been awarded fellowships from the School of Advanced Research, the National Endowment for Humanities, and the Guggenheim Foundation. He is currently Professor of Anthropology and Environmental Studies at Washington University in St. Louis.

Earthscan Food and Agriculture

Deep Agroecology and the Homeric Epics
Global Cultural Reforms for a Natural-Systems Agriculture
John W. Head

Fighting for Farming Justice
Diversity, Food Access and the USDA
Terri R. Jett

Political Ecology of Industrial Crops
Edited by Abubakari Ahmed and Alexandros Gasparatos

The Sociology of Food and Agriculture
3rd Edition
Michael Carolan

The Politics of Food Provisioning in Colombia
Agrarian Movements and Negotiations with the State
Felipe Roa-Clavijo

The Governance of Agriculture in Post-Brexit UK
Edited by Irene Antonopoulos, Matt Bell, Aleksandra Čavoški and Ludivine Petetin

The United Nations' Declaration on Peasants' Rights
Edited by Mariagrazia Alabrese, Adriana Bessa, Margherita Brunori, Pier Filippo Giuggioli

The Agricultural Dilemma
How Not to Feed the World
Glenn Davis Stone

For more information about this series, please visit: www.routledge.com/books/series/ECEFA/

THE AGRICULTURAL DILEMMA

How Not to Feed the World

Glenn Davis Stone

To Jason

Glenn

16 Jan 23

Routledge
Taylor & Francis Group
LONDON AND NEW YORK

earthscan
from Routledge

Cover Image: James B. Janknegt

First published 2022
by Routledge
4 Park Square, Milton Park, Abingdon, Oxon OX14 4RN

and by Routledge
605 Third Avenue, New York, NY 10158

Routledge is an imprint of the Taylor & Francis Group, an informa business

© 2022 Glenn Davis Stone

British Library Cataloguing-in-Publication Data
A catalogue record for this book is available from the British Library

Library of Congress Cataloging-in-Publication Data
A catalog record has been requested for this book

ISBN: 978-1-032-26047-1 (hbk)
ISBN: 978-1-032-26045-7 (pbk)
ISBN: 978-1-003-28625-7 (ebk)

DOI: 10.4324/9781003286257

Typeset in Bembo
by codeMantra

For P, A, and J; obvi.

CONTENTS

PREFACE

It is remarkable how many people agree that we need to be worried about our agriculture, while disagreeing on what the worry is.

Agriculture's inability to keep pace with population was one of my first worldly worries. Growing up in the 1960s, I remember being convinced by what I was hearing about the planet being overrun by an unfeedable population. India seemed to be the problem's ground zero, and when scientist Paul Ehrlich assured us – on Johnny Carson's Tonight Show yet – that millions would have to starve there, I knew he was right. Long before I had even heard of Robert Malthus, I was a Malthusian. An actual Malthusian. Many people today don't realize that Malthus was scornful of developing agricultural technologies to feed the populace, reasoning that it would only make more people die in the end; agriculture was by its nature *inherently incapable* of creating enough food. If we're going to have a famine, I thought, let's get it over with and maybe we'll all be better off.

Malthusianism was convenient for the Industrial Revolution's factory owners, as it claimed that if their workers were sick and hungry it was their own fault for having too many babies. But it grew inconvenient as "input industries" – especially fossil fuel-based fertilizers and hybrid seed breeding, and then machinery, pesticides, irrigation, biotechnology, and digital farming – began to ride government support to wealth and influence. Thus came neo-Malthusianism and the dogma that scientists might be able to keep the world fed, if only we got out of their way and let them devise technologies that corporations could roll out. That is what supposedly brought the Indian famine to an end – the neo-Malthusian Green Revolution, the handiwork of "skillful and courageous scientists" (as breeder Norman Borlaug described himself and his colleagues) who understood that the time for the stagnant low-tech farming that activists and romantics love was over. And it goes without saying that more such technologies are needed now more than ever, as we worry about the dilemma of how to feed 9 billion people by 2050.

But I am no longer a Malthusian (or a neo-Malthusian) and that is not our dilemma. After 40 years investigating different forms of agriculture and its social and ecological and political aspects – including ancient cultivation in the prehistoric US, sustainable intensive farming in Africa and the US, semi-industrial agriculture in India and the Philippines, and the history of industrial agriculture – I have come around to a different point of view. Neo-Malthusianism is not only scientifically unsupportable, but *backward*. Our real dilemma is how to unthink the entrenched belief that we will starve without new tricks from scientists and input industries when in reality we have been locked on a treadmill of subsidized over-production for over the last century. When agriculture is industrialized – driven by those input industries and the perennial support and subsidy they need from the public purse – it grows inexorably at the expense of our economy, environment, and health.

And the alternatives are real, not stagnant, traditional, or imagined; they are well described in the scientific literature, although the scholars analyzing them are drowned out by those with vested interests in input industries.

Our agricultural dilemma is that we misunderstand agriculture, and this book is my best shot at rectifying that. Malthus got a lot wrong, but what he got right is the need to go back to first principles to understand how the world works – or at least the part of the world that concerns human numbers and food. Part of this book concerns the way forward, although it is not meant as a how-to guide; more importantly it lays out a case for how modern industrial agriculture came to be as it is – chronically overproducing and dominated by technologies that are not inherently superior, just winners in the sweepstakes for getting government support. I show that this is even true of the technological chapters that wear the biggest halos – fertilizers, hybrid seeds, and the Green Revolution.

This book incorporates much that I have learned from many. Bob Netting was the real scientist of intensive agriculture and I believe the moment when he decided to reboot his research to investigate Kofyar agriculture (described in Chapter 1) was a watershed in human knowledge. Bob was an insightful and honest analyst of agriculture, and many parts of this book grew from seeds planted in conversations with him during our long collaboration. Five other analysts whose work was foundational were Nick Cullather, Deborah Fitzgerald, Timothy Johnson, Jack Kloppenburg, and Michael Pollan. I am also grateful to Marci Baranski, Geoff Childs, Andrew Flachs, Dominic Glover, Jon Harwood, Fred Hebard, Richa Kumar, Frankie Moore Lappé, Robert Mayhew, Raj Patel, Tom Philpott, Colin Renfrew (for assistance and whiskey at Cambridge), Paul Richards, Matt Schnurr, Vandana Shiva, Priscilla Stone, Richard Sutch, Teddy Varno, Tim Wise, and my wonderful students and many research assistants in St. Louis.

1

THREE AGRICULTURES

One Stinking Hot Night in Delhi

One summer night in 1966, a young Stanford biology professor named Paul Ehrlich landed in Delhi. It was his first time in India, and he was accompanied by his wife and young daughter. The family soon found themselves on an unforgettable ride through the bustling Indian capital in an ancient taxi hopping with fleas. Two years later, Ehrlich described his experience on that "stinking hot night in Delhi" on the first page of his best-selling book *The Population Bomb* (1968):

> As we crawled through the city, we entered a crowded slum area. The temperature was well over 100, and the air was a haze of dust and smoke. The streets seemed alive with people. People eating, people washing, people sleeping. People visiting, arguing, and screaming. People thrusting their hands through the taxi window, begging. People defecating and urinating. People clinging to buses. People herding animals. People, people, people, people. As we moved slowly through the mob, hand horn squawking, the dust, noise, heat and cooking fires gave the scene a hellish aspect... since that night I've known the feel of overpopulation.

Some would say that Ehrlich just had a bad reaction to his first brush with the grittiness and bustle of a Third World city; "a hot summer night on Broadway in New York or Piccadilly Circus in London would put Ehrlich in the midst of a far larger crowd," noted Mahmood Mamdani (1972).[1] But Ehrlich was not alone in recoiling from India's cities. A few years later Norman Borlaug, the "father of the Green Revolution" who had bred wheat seeds that would be credited with saving India from starvation, used his Nobel acceptance speech to rage against "the grotesque concentration of human beings into the poisoned and clangorous environment of pathologically hypertrophied megalopolis" (Borlaug 1970).

But Ehrlich (Figure 1.1) was intent on looking beyond the teeming Delhi streets to a larger problem reflected in the crowds. India was in the grip of a drought, had high birth-rates, and was importing millions of tons of American wheat each year. It was time to look

DOI: 10.4324/9781003286257-1

FIGURE 1.1 Biologist Paul Ehrlich in 1970. Photo Credit: Chuck Painter/Stanford News Service.

at things as they are – and as they would soon be. "The battle to feed all of humanity is over," he wrote ominously in *The Population Bomb*. "In the 1970s the world will undergo famines – hundreds of millions of people are going to starve to death in spite of any crash programs embarked upon now" (Ehrlich 1968, 13). The next year he added that by 1985, "enough millions will have died to reduce the earth's population to some acceptable level, like 1.5 billion people." More chilling yet, "[m]ost of the people who are going to die in the greatest cataclysm in the history of man have already been born"; by 1975, "some experts feel that food shortages will have escalated the present level of world hunger and starvation into famines of unbelievable proportions" (Ehrlich 1969, 28).

Some argued that the planet was nowhere near its limits and that food production was growing rapidly, but Ehrlich was not having any of it, insisting instead that overpopulation "will inevitably and completely outstrip whatever small increases in food supplies we make;" soon 100–200 million would be starving yearly (Ehrlich 1970, 293). He sounded like a man with harsh inescapable facts; it was the optimists, with their blindness to the population explosion and naïve belief in technology, who seemed out of touch. The dreamers who refused to recognize the problem of "people, people, people, people" were the real threat to the poor.

Predictions of Third World famine, often citing India, were nothing new. Biologist William Vogt's best-selling 1948 *Road to Survival* bemoaned Indians "breeding with the irresponsibility of codfish" and already being well over a number that could be fed. In the 1950s influential reports from both the Ford and Rockefeller Foundations warned of emergency conditions. Then the 1960s saw a crescendo of these claims. In 1965 predictions of looming Indian famine came from Georg Borgstrom's doomsaying book *The Hungry Planet* and from the young USDA economist Lester Brown, who would go on to a career warning about famines that never came. In 1966 US President Lyndon Johnson repeatedly warned of starvation in India and even used his State of the Union speech to promise an attack on hunger and aid to countries trying to curb their population. Still the *New York Times* chastised him for not showing sufficient alarm about a world where a specter "more terrible than Malthus ever conceived" loomed, and where "famine stalks the great subcontinent of India" (New York Times 1966).[2]

Ehrlich's bomb metaphor was not new either. The Hugh Moore Fund – founded by the Dixie Cup magnate – had been circulating a pamphlet entitled *The Population Bomb* since 1954 (Figure 1.2). The influential report of the Draper Commission on US aid policy was titled "The Population Explosion." Philip Appleman's (1965) *Silent Explosion* had predicted Calcutta's streets would be lined with "ragged skeletons" when they ran out of food.

But none of these earlier warnings caught fire in the public imagination like Ehrlich's did. He was a bold writer, a charismatic speaker, and a Stanford scientist – although many would later suggest that his analysis far exceeded his actual expertise (Merchant 2015, 442). He caught the attention of Tonight Show host Johnny Carson, who invited him on as a

FIGURE 1.2 Left: The Hugh Moore Fund's 1954 Population Bomb pamphlet. Just as Ehrlich's book by the same name would later do, the pamphlet's lurid predictions of an overrun world touched a nerve in readers. A newspaper editor back from a trip to Asia wrote Moore that "the only truly constructive and effective solution I can think of would be for the United Nations to send out a task force to poison village wells" (Merchant 2015, 441). Right: The cover of Environmental Action magazine from 1970, showing the human crowd now so large that people were starting to drop off into space.

guest over 20 times where he delivered compelling accounts of overpopulation and famine in his confident baritone. Ehrlich emerged as the most prolific writer on the population debate in the US (Wilmoth and Ball 1992, 637).

To Ehrlich, the solutions to overpopulation might be disturbing, but the lack of solution was unthinkably worse. He floated the idea of adding "temporary sterilants" to the water with government officials rationing an antidote to let selected people reproduce (1968, 130–131); for India he advocated forced sterilization, but even then it could be a country "we must allow to slip down the drain" (Chase 1977, 398). Ehrlich held that the world should triage the available food when the shortages hit, leading to a massive "die back" and emergence of a world government with strict controls on agriculture and population.

Growing Fears

How these dire predictions could quickly become mainstream is an interesting question.[3] It is true that by the 1960s the baby boom was on and population was growing faster than it had in the past: world population topped 1 billion in the early 1800s, 2 billion by 1930, and 3 billion by 1960. But claims of catastrophic overpopulation had been bandied about when population growth was much lower, as in 1923 when Edward Murray East (who we will meet in Chapter 5) wrote that mankind was threatened by population "advancing in a tidal wave the like of which has never before been seen" (East 1923, 20). Now again we were being told we were overpopulated; but over what? Certainly not over the number that can be fed, as agricultural production had been outgrowing population for over a century and it was growing faster than ever. (As we will see, *overproduction* levels were reaching new heights in the 1960s.) Ehrlich may have felt that India was running out of food, but actually the country was taking land *out* of food production to grow fiber crops, and its agricultural exports were booming (Cullather 2010, 180).

Dread of overpopulation spread anyway. The year 1970 saw the dawn of the modern environmental movement, which was joined at the hip to overpopulation fears. By 1970, Moore's image of landmasses being overrun with people would be updated to show the whole planet being overrun (Figure 1.2). "Few nations," wrote an environmental historian recently, "have been more aware of – and anxious about – population growth than Americans in the late 1960s and 1970s" (Robertson 2012, 1). And not just in the US; the Club of Rome was formed in 1968 by an international group worried about the future of the world, and its 1972 book *Limits to Growth* insisted that population was growing "exponentially" (Meadows et al. 1972). Ehrlich's warnings played perfectly into a social movement then gathering steam.

His warnings were also buoyed by the excitable nature of youth. Ehrlich taught undergraduates at Stanford and he had a knack for captivating their attention. His juggernaut as a public intellectual began with his course on human evolution, to which he added a wildly popular lecture on "where we are going" stressing the impending disaster of overpopulation. This touched a nerve with the baby boomer students of the late 1960s for whom apocalyptic scenarios had been made real by nuclear shelter signs and "duck and cover" drills in grade school. The year after *Population Bomb* appeared, the class valedictorian at Mills College cited Ehrlich in her commencement speech entitled "The Future is a Cruel Hoax":

> Within the next ten years, we will witness widespread famines, and possible global plagues raging through famine-weakened populations. Soon we may have to ask

ourselves grisly questions like 'Will I be willing to shoot my neighbor if he tries to steal my last loaf of bread? Will I be forced to become a cannibal?'

(Mills Quarterly 1969)[4]

I was one of those baby boomers, a teen-ager living in an Ohio college town in 1968, and I remember being riveted by Ehrlich pontificating on the Tonight Show. Here was a charismatic scientist who seemed to be pulling back the curtain on an unfolding cataclysm. I remember discussions with similarly alarmed friends. It was as if the apocalyptic fears of a generation taught to run to the fallout shelter had transferred focus from the nuclear bomb to the population bomb.

But the concerns were just as real among adults, indeed among leaders. In 1974, the US House of Representatives issued a report that spoke of "a potentially devastating crisis is on the horizon," asking

Will America allow a food shortage to surprise us ... and only then react after we find people standing in line from 7 a.m. to 9 a.m. on Tuesday and Thursday mornings waiting to get into their local grocery store to buy a limited quantity of food?

(US House of Representatives 1974)

Dissent

There were dissenting voices at the time, even if they were fewer in number and less riveting than Ehrlich. Some contested whether world population was anywhere near the limit that could be well fed on the planet, a theoretical number that scientists had a long history of estimating. In *How Many People Can the Earth Support?* (1998) demographer Joel Cohen pointed to over 60 independent estimates, ranging from under 1 billion to more than a trillion. The year before *Population Bomb* appeared, there had been two scientific estimates of the number of mouths the earth could feed: one was 157 billion, the other 38–48 billion. At the time, world population was just under 3.5 billion.

Some physical scientists took issue with Ehrlich's predictions. John Maddox, physicist and editor of *Nature*, produced a 1972 book entitled *The Doomsday Syndrome* that disparaged the "prophets of doom." Maddox insisted that famine was receding rather than growing, and that the problems of the 1970s and 1980s could be "how best to dispose of food surpluses in countries where famine has until recently been epidemic."

The challengers to Ehrlich who attracted most media attention were conservative pundits, cornucopians who thought that capitalism and science would feed the world. One was commentator Ben Wattenberg who rebutted Ehrlich with a *New Republic* essay entitled "The Nonsense Explosion";[5] economist Julian Simon, originally a population alarmist who had morphed into a free-market capitalist cornucopian, engaged in heated arguments in print with Ehrlich, who repeatedly called him an imbecile. Imbecilic Simon would later have the last laugh in winning a very public bet with Ehrlich on resources running out (Sabin 2013), but for the most part Simon held forth on limited venues like William F. Buckley's conservative talk show Firing Line while Ehrlich basked in the enormous audience of the Tonight Show and garnered a MacArthur "Genius Award."

But it was those who warned of problems with agricultural surpluses who history proved right, even though abundance did not end hunger. The problems lay with the ability and motivation of those who produced and managed agricultural products to feed the hungry. While hundreds of millions would not starve due to underproducing agricultural systems, tens of millions would struggle to feed themselves even in the presence of overflowing granaries. Even in the US, well over a tenth of the population would continue to be food insecure despite the record surpluses pouring out of heavily fertilized, watered, and pesticide-sprayed fields.

The Original

Ehrlich's followers credited him with "insight" but there was little new about his population alarms – except for his bold predictions of famine that never came to pass. Belief in population growth as an inexorable and catastrophic force, ever threatening not only India but the planet, is an old idea, given shape in Western thought by another young man's uncomfortable brush with the poor.

The script from which Ehrlich was reading was an anonymous booklet published in London in 1798, offering a cheeky assault on the optimistic social philosophers of the day and insisting that overpopulation and misery were inexorable facts of nature. The booklet "went viral," quickly gathering both enthusiastic supporters and livid detractors. The author soon revealed himself, his previously unknown name immediately becoming synonymous with overpopulation: Robert Malthus.[6] Malthus was almost exactly the same age as Ehrlich had been that night in Delhi, and he too was fresh from a disquieting experience in an alien environment where the people had given him the "feel of overpopulation." But his encounter had been far from the teeming streets of Delhi; it was in the backwoods of Surrey, in the impoverished community of Okewood. He had grudgingly taken a job as pastor at the chapel there after a luxurious post-college year in his wealthy parents' house. Life in Okewood was a real step down and he had trouble relating to the farmers and laborers in his parish. He slipped back to his parents' house regularly, where conversations with father Daniel became increasingly contentious. Daniel Malthus was a vocal admirer of contemporary "Enlightenment" thinkers and their sanguine theories of the perfectibility of man and society. This clearly grated on the young pastor; the Okewood peasants didn't seem perfectible at all, and he began to see the philosophers as unrealistic dreamers. He soon quit his post at the Okewood chapel and turned his attention to writing, his frustrations pouring out in the book *An Essay on the Principle of Population as It Affects the Future Improvement of Society with Remarks on the Speculations of Mr. Godwin, M. Condorcet, and Other Writers*. Although the booklet was an artifact of a particular moment in history – a diatribe against Enlightenment ideals and England's welfare policies – it was also timeless. It has been brought back over and over in the years since 1798, sometimes unchanged but often tweaked, adjusted, and deployed to serve new sets of interests.

Some of the day's most influential philosophers provided wonderful foils for his arguments. William Godwin, in the book's title, was a particularly juicy target. Godwin was a fervent utopian, anarchist, and social philosopher whose ideas often pushed the boundaries with his idealized vision of a future society with no need for sex, sleep, or conflict. The odd vision of man besting nature particularly rankled the cynical young Malthus, who prided himself on seeing "things as they are" (Crowther 1974). Like Ehrlich, Malthus was an engaging and confident writer, and his measured but slightly mocking tone delivered a powerful and starkly different view of humans, nature, and prospects for "future improvement of society." *Get real*, to paraphrase Malthus: population growth and food production are both subject to laws of nature, and nature has a built-in imbalance. The only way to raise food production is to put more acres under the plow; meanwhile, the sex drive is here to stay, and so population can grow exponentially. Population growth must therefore be checked by death – often not by outright starvation, but by indirect means such as conflict, disease, or the "vices" that obsessed Malthus. By the immutable facts of human ecology, misery is inevitable and it naturally operates chiefly among the poor. This would be called Malthus's *Dismal Theorem*, and it was a stab at the optimistic heart of the Enlightenment. "It is undoubtedly a most disheartening reflection," noted Malthus, "that the great obstacle in the way to any extraordinary improvement in society is of a nature that we can never hope to overcome." But gloomy or not, the theory had the ring of hard truth, and a noted economist would later call it "one of the most crushing answers that patient and hard-working science has ever given to the reckless assertions of its adversaries" (Marshall and Marshall 1888, 30).

There are three important points to make about Malthus's *Population*. First is that Malthus's famous analysis was built on a consideration of first principles: he started by identifying the fundamental forces and relationships that drive the world of people and agriculture. Much of Malthus's thinking may have been sparked by what he thought he saw at Okewood, but his theory was not about populations in England's backwoods any more than Newton's theory was about trees or apples. Malthus got a lot wrong – in fact *backward* – but what he got right was the importance of careful analysis of basic underlying principles. What are the fundamental drivers of food production?

Second is that Malthus insisted that the real effects of food-population imbalances are indirect: disease and vices do most of the pruning of population, famine just "stalks in the rear." As we will see, many of his claims about these manifestations were fanciful, and he got the nature of the imbalance wrong (we suffer from inexorable agricultural overproduction), but his concern for the indirect manifestations was well placed, and we will see.

Finally, *Population* was never only a work of science but also a political tract; it was not a neutral account of how problems arise, but a manifesto on how we should understand and respond to social problems. Its key impact on policy came from unflinchingly carrying the basic postulates to their logical extreme: if the laws of nature dictated that population would always be checked by human misery, then feeding the hungry would only make more mouths to go hungry. He illustrated this principle by describing a table serving "nature's mighty feast," at which making room for the hungry only turned order and plenty into misery and dependence.[7] To make room for "intruders" is to disobey the "great mistress of the feast" who "humanely refused to admit fresh comers when her table was already full" (Malthus 1803, 532). The proposition that feeding the hungry only creates more misery was later called Malthus's *Utterly Dismal Theorem*, and it impacted English law even during Malthus's lifetime.[8] The theorem would later have disastrous effects in Ireland and India and it would become a core tenant in eugenics (Ross 1998). It would reverberate into current times; influential social scientists like Garrett Hardin would see it as simple "truth" (Hardin 1993, 163) and would write that in order to help poor countries,

> Clearly the worst thing we can do is send food. The child who is saved today becomes a breeder tomorrow. We send food out of compassion, but … Atomic bombs would be kinder.
>
> *(quoted in Kohl 1975, 332)*

A Strange Evening in Hyderabad

Unlike Paul Ehrlich, I was no stranger to Third World cities when I first landed in India. As an anthropologist I had spent a lot of time conducting research on farmers in developing countries, and I had lived in Mexico City and navigated crowded African metropolises like Kano, Lagos, and Nairobi. But India was a new research venue for me and I was excited to land in the bustling city of Hyderabad in summer of 2000. I was at the start of what would become a long-term research program on the agricultural system that was gearing up for its first genetically modified (GM) crop.[9]

My ride from the airport to my friend's apartment had some similarities with Ehrlich's wild ride. It was a long trip in the night air, and I did see "people, people, people, people" – eating, talking, walking, driving, and clinging to over-crowded buses. I am not sure what Borlaug's term "clangorous environment" means, but I suspect this was one. But unlike Ehrlich, I saw nothing ominous or frightening about the crowded streets and sidewalks of Hyderabad. And as far as all the people went ... well it was a *city*, after all, and a fascinating one: small shops and eateries, open markets, street vendors, elevated freeways, motorcycles with whole families, bicycle rickshaws, yellow autorickshaws, billboards advertising Bollywood movies and cell phones, a vast lake with a stone Buddha statue. There were plenty of urban aromas, but it hardly stunk.

On this evening in 2000, the Hyderabad metropolitan area had close to 6 million people; Delhi had 15.7 million, over five times its population on Ehrlich's memorable night; and India's total population was up 106%, topping 1 billion. Ehrlich's nightmares about India's population had come true; however all of his predictions about food shortages had flopped spectacularly. Foodgrain production had been rising much faster than population (Figure 1.3) and India was suffering from its own perverse version of what had plagued the US for decades: *too much food* – at least by some key measures.

The next evening I met with two leading agricultural scientists. Sitting in a restaurant sipping chai, they shared their anxieties over India's grain surplus. In the US we are used to the reality of agricultural surplus; our government pays farmers to not grow crops, and much of our major harvests are not even used for food. But we do not expect surpluses in India, which has long been the poster child for population outracing agriculture. But India's food production was already growing faster than its population before 1965, and that year the government started buying and storing unlimited amounts of wheat and rice in buffer stocks. The government sets "norm" levels for the stocks, above which grain is undesirable and often even unstorable, but it keeps on buying even after stocks exceed norms. Procurement of wheat in particular had for years greatly exceeded norms, and by 2000 the stocks were well beyond what the system could handle. Millions of tons were rotting in the granaries, and that year a parliamentary committee recommended dumping grain into the sea to make room for the next round of purchases (The Hindu 2000). India increased its food exports but the surpluses kept climbing. By 2002 – the same year that India approved its first genetically modified crop, amid global hand-wringing about feeding the developing world with GM crops – the buffer stocks would hit a record of 42 million tons over the norm. Unstorable surplus had become India's new normal (AP 2012, Waldman 2002).

Of course this did not mean that all Indians were well fed. In 2000, India had more hungry people than any other country; their hunger just had nothing to do with agriculture falling behind population growth. India was on the verge of becoming the world's leading

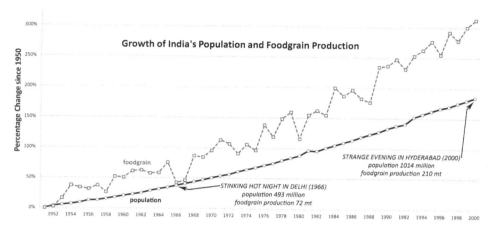

FIGURE 1.3 Lines compare percentage change in population and foodgrain production in India since 1950.

exporter of rice (Workman 2016) and, strangely enough, beef (Krishnakumar 2015). What had happened to Ehrlich's predictions?

The first thing that had happened was that those predictions were based on a thorough misunderstanding of India's situation. India was importing a lot of US wheat when Ehrlich visited, not because of overpopulation but because India wanted cheap food for urban workers and the US wanted to dump its enormous grain surplus. But Indian agriculture was also on the verge of becoming *industrialized* – meaning converted to heavy dependence on external inputs. Industrialized grain production, powered by new types of seeds, government subsidies for the fertilizer industry, aquifer-draining irrigation, and pesticides, was about to be brought to India's wheat farms in the "Green Revolution." The timing of Ehrlich's alarm about India was bizarrely off-target because the real explosion the year that *Population Bomb* appeared was in the wheat fields of the Punjab where a record harvest was coming in. Ehrlich had been scornful at the time, claiming that the "clowns who are talking of feeding a big population in the year 2000 from make-believe 'green revolutions'... should learn some elementary biology, meteorology, agricultural economics and anthropology" (Paddock 1970, 901). But after his predictions of India running out of food bombed, Ehrlich shrugged it off by saying maybe the Green Revolution had actually kept the country fed after all, at least for a while.

The Green Revolution quickly grew into a legend of India averting mass starvation and saving a "billion lives," its chief architect Norman Borlaug being heralded as a "wizard" who had shown a hungry planet the way forward (Mann 2018). The legend deftly turns a brazen failure of Malthusian prediction as somehow proving Malthusian theory – "You see, a billion people *almost* starved!"

Actually we will see that Green Revolution didn't feed anybody who would have otherwise starved. It was not even intended to produce more *food* than would have been produced otherwise (Harwood 2019), just more fertilized, irrigated, and pesticide-sprayed wheat as opposed to low-input rice, sorghum, and healthy legumes. It *industrialized* Indian agriculture, setting Indian farmers on a path toward ever-climbing input costs even as the government subsidized the input industries.

Industrial agriculture arose with contributions from various parts of the world, but it was specifically in the US that it came into full flower. We will see that at its core it is a system for corporations to milk value from the government, and that it has the intrinsic tendency to grow unchecked – as Malthus thought population did. "Overpopulation" is not an actual problem, at least not if "over" means too many people for agriculture to keep up with; but "over-production" is a very real problem if "over" means production that is far above food and fiber needs and that causes economic, environmental, and public health problems. What had happened in the Green Revolution was not humanitarian wizards creating more food, but rather the US exporting the runaway train of subsidized, chemical-intensive agriculture to the Global South. The overproduction that I heard scientists fuming over in an air conditioned Hyderabad hotel three decades after Paul Ehrlich thought he saw unstoppable over-population on Delhi's streets was not a fluke, but a classic feature of industrial agriculture.

A Happy Year on the Jos Plateau

Sitting under a mango tree in Doemak village talking with the local Kofyar chief, Robert Netting realized he had a serious problem. He had been in Nigeria just a few weeks, having arrived on the day in 1960 of independence for the British colony. A PhD student in the University of Chicago's famous anthropology department, he had come to conduct research for a dissertation on how Nigerian independence affected village politics. His focus was on Nigeria's Middle Belt, known for its dozens of diverse ethnic groups. Netting's advisors and funders had judged the topic important, timely, and doable. But once in the Middle Belt he quickly found that local politics were still quite divorced from the political changes in the capital. His research question about the effect of independence on village politics here had a one-word answer: "none." The conversation with the Kofyar chief, sitting together on a mat and sipping millet beer from a calabash, was only confirming this. For an anthropology graduate student, to arrive in the field and immediately learn your whole dissertation project was a bust was a nightmare.

But as he sat there in dismay, something in the landscape caught his attention. Doemak village is nestled on the alluvial plain at the foot of the Jos Plateau, the enormous platform of Paleozoic granite that dominates central Nigeria. The village was surprisingly densely settled, and the adobe residential compounds continued up the rocky and jagged plateau escarpment. Looking at the escarpment, Netting made out rock terraces by the hundred, tidy strips of healthy green crops behind each one. It looked like someone had dragged an enormous comb across the hillside. Every square inch of the landscape seemed to be in production, in a tight and intricate arrangement of ridges, mounds, and terraces, with each compound surrounded by high crops and oil palm trees (Figure 1.4). It seemed like an enormous and complicated garden. Shifting the topic of discussion, he asked the chief about the strange and manicured landscape. "We farm this way because we are crowded," the chief explained. "How else would we farm?" Remarkable, thought Netting.

Over the next few days Netting examined and talked with people in Doemak and other Kofyar villages, becoming increasingly fascinated by what he saw. The Kofyar landscape was indeed crowded, but contrary to the common belief that population pressure caused food shortages and degraded landscapes, this agriculture appeared to be highly productive and stable, despite using only very simple technology. The field surrounding each compound was kept in annual cultivation with grains, legumes, and root crops growing together

FIGURE 1.4 The Kofyar homeland in 1984. The residential compound in the foreground is surrounded by a well-manured field of pearl millet, sorghum, cowpeas, and vegetables. The entire hillside has been terraced for growing various grain and root crops. Photo by G. Stone.

in various combinations. Each household kept a small herd of goats and sheep, stall-fed for enough of the year to produce manure compost for fertilizer. Fields were thoroughly tilled with steel hoes and made into a waffled surface that completely checked erosion.

Netting soon set up residence in a picturesque plateau village called Bong and immersed himself in a completely reinvented dissertation project. He now set out to document and understand this production landscape and the social institutions that made it work. He would spend a year moving among the Kofyar villages and doing ethnographic research, never ceasing to be awed by the mixture of natural and human-made beauty of the landscape. It would be one of the most rewarding times of his life, and it would launch a highly successful career as an analyst of population and smallholder agriculture.

He knew that the project was propelling him into uncharted intellectual territory. Kofyar population densities turned out to be over 500/km^2 yet their agriculture was not only environmentally benign, but landscape-enriching. They were practicing what he would later call *intensive sustainable farming* (although this phrase had not yet come into being), a kind of farming that was scarcely known and certainly not understood. It was jarringly inconsistent with the European colonial image of African farming as backward, destructive, and needing remediation, and its reliance on no more advanced technology than hoes was baffling from the modernist American certainty that food production was increased only by professional agricultural science.[10]

Kofyar agriculture was also dynamic; the fact that the technology was simple did not mean that the farming was unchanging or "stagnant" (the common slur on technologically simple farming). Netting found that once you looked closely, you saw experiments and innovations everywhere. In fact many households were taking advantage of available land on a frontier to the south to open up new farms, growing a new roster of crops and completely transforming their techniques. These people were practicing what is often called subsistence agriculture but that too was misleading: they did provide for their own subsistence but also sold goods in local markets, including livestock and palm oil, and on the frontier farms they were planting rice and yams for sale to help feed Nigeria's growing cities.

Even the fact of the Kofyars' "poverty" was misleading. Extreme poverty is often treated as an objective condition, defined today as "living on less than $1.25/day" (World Bank 2015). By that definition even those selling cash crops on the frontier were extremely poor. And yet most had access to exactly what they needed to farm – a patch of land, hoes, household labor, and livestock. It was the "wealthier" farmers in India who were on a path that lead to debt and suicide (Vasavi 2012), not the "poor" Kofyar.

Netting (Figure 1.5) completed his dissertation in 1963, joined the faculty at the University of Pennsylvania, and began a book on Kofyar agriculture. But before it was finished, a Danish development economist named Ester Boserup published a small book entitled *The Conditions of Agricultural Growth: The Economics of Agrarian Change under Population Pressure*. Netting read it with excitement: it laid out a general theory of agriculture and population that explained much about why the Kofyar farmed as they did and those in less crowded areas farmed as they did. In one of the most influential books ever written on agriculture, Boserup showed how smallholder agriculture was highly elastic, never producing at its maximum intensity unless forced to do so by population pressure, but capable of high productivity when needed. In a sense, Malthus had the causal arrow backward: agriculture did not determine population but population determined agriculture. Boserup's theory helped make the Kofyar fall into place, as Netting wrote in his book *Hill Farmers of Nigeria* (1968), a path-breaking study of nonindustrial intensive farming.

FIGURE 1.5 Robert Netting talking with a Kofyar elder, 1984. Photo by G. Stone.

Netting would conduct research on intensive farmers for the rest of his career. In 1993 he published *Smallholders, Householders: Farm Families and the Ecology of Intensive, Sustainable Agriculture*, a masterful and carefully documented synthesis of research showing the efficiency and productivity of intensive farming around the world and explaining the key social institutions that made the system work.

Boserup's theory and Netting's work were on *intensive agriculture* but that term is used too loosely. Boserup and Netting were describing high productivity from labor and locally developed technologies rather than external, manufactured, "scientific" inputs. The term *intensive* is also applied to *industrial agriculture*, but that is based on external manufactured inputs and which follows a wholly different logic. Of course you can find instances where the two agricultures overlap, but they are fundamentally different in their first principles. The contrast between them is heightened by the frequent attacks by those connected to industrial agriculture on intensive sustainable (smallholder) agriculture as stagnant and its advocates as unscientific and romantic. But as we will see, there is a sound and unromantic science to this dynamic form of farming that may be our best hope for a sustainable food future.

The Dilemma: Three Agricultures

This book is about the three fundamental forms of agriculture that were reflected in the vignettes, and it has something heretical to say about each. The best way to understand the three agricultures, and how we tend to get it wrong on all three, is to consider what drives their growth.

Malthusian Agricultural Growth

Malthusian agricultural growth refers to both a process and a theory. The process is simply using more land to increase production, and the theory is that this is the only way agriculture can grow. To Malthus it was obvious; there was no way that "two ears of grain could grow where only one had grown before" and the key to the human condition was "the absolute impossibility, from the fixed laws of our nature" that agriculture could keep abreast of population growth (Malthus 1798, 23). This intrinsic food gap supposedly reverberates throughout society, causing all manner of problems. This later spawned "neo-Malthusian" schools of thought that agree about the threat of overpopulation but diverge on other points such as the merits of birth control (which Malthus opposed) and, most importantly, on the promise of agricultural technology. Malthusianisms have dominated thinking, discussion, and policy setting on agriculture for centuries – despite their astonishingly poor track record of fitting what actually happens in the world – from the causes of poverty at Okewood, to Paul Ehrlich's blown predictions to famine, to current debates about solutions to world hunger.

Consider a few basic numbers on world population and food production since Malthus put forward his "laws" on why agriculture could never keep pace with population. Since 1798, world population has risen just over sixfold (from around 1 to 6 billion) while agricultural production has risen around tenfold (Federico 2005). Obviously, per capita production has soared. And yet by demographic and nutritional standards, average human well-being has improved, and the years of fastest population growth (like the mid-20th century baby boom) have been marked by particularly rapid improvements in living conditions. Between the early 1950s and the early 1990s, worldwide life expectancy at birth rose from 46 to 64 years, and the developed world's life expectancy advantage dropped from 26 to 12 years (Cohen 1998). Of course many still go hungry and die young, but not because of overpopulation.

And in its race with population, agriculture is pulling farther and farther pulling away: between 1961 and 2005, the world's population increased by 111% while crop production rose by 162% (Burney, Davis, and Lobell 2010).[11] In 1997, an article in a major scientific journal (ironically, a special issue devoted to the question of whether we were "on the edge of a Malthusian precipice") pointed out that not only had world food production been outpacing population growth but that it had been increasing *exponentially* since 1960 (Evans 1997, 901). We pay farmers not to grow; we use vast amounts of farm produce to produce fuel; we burn up much of its food value by feeding animals in factory farms. We throw away and waste a full third of our food globally (Gustavsson et al. 2011). India's idea of dumping grain into the sea was not as perverse as it seems; it was actually quite typical of the world today. But year in and year out, the specter of Malthusian agriculture is used to obscure this reality. This is not an accident; the theory of Malthusian agriculture is needed to justify the second agriculture.

Industrialized Agriculture

Some will tell you the distinctive feature of industrial agriculture is that it is modern, or high-producing, or *efficient*, but the real key is that it runs on *external inputs* created by off-farm industries and sold to the farmer. This changes everything; Malthus said we have to go back to first principles to understand our agricultural situation and I agree. We will look more carefully at industrial agriculture but let us introduce it here by sketching its three fundamental elements.

1 **Appropriations**. Industrial agriculture's dependence on external inputs changes the interests driving the system. External inputs are not simply additions to agriculture; they are the result of industry appropriating processes within farm production and selling them back as inputs (Goodman, Sorj, and Wilkinson 1987; Guthman 2011, 58). If we actually lived in a Malthusian world where farms were locked in a perpetual scramble to meet food needs, then the key difference between fertilizer from a cow and fertilizer from a bag would be that the stuff in the bag is more concentrated and might feed more people. But our world is not Malthusian and the key difference is that the bag of fertilizer is part of the livelihood of the store that sold it, the truck that delivered it, the barge that moved, the factory that made it, the pipeline that brought the gas it is made from, the mine that extracted the gas, the research laboratory that studied its mode of action, and on and on. Each of those nodes has its own vested interests apart from the farmer. This is true of all external inputs, from machinery to pesticides to irrigation to commercial seed to genetically modified traits to remote sensing data.

But while the external inputs are generally made in factories, most forms of agriculture have resisted being completely factorified. Industrial factories override most effects of physical environment, while agriculture unavoidably requires intimate interaction with the environment of the *agri* (field). So industrial inputs have worked their way into agriculture piecemeal. Instead of its own "industrial revolution," agriculture has undergone separate appropriations of various aspects of production, always brought about by new technologies resulting from external scientific research. New technologies are fetishized as if they bring a self-contained power to the farmer's field, but they are actually vehicles for capturing resources from off farm, always benefiting off-farm interests. Each such appropriation tends to open the door for another, in a process that shows no sign of stopping; contrary to Malthus's belief that agriculture was inelastic, agriculture is extremely elastic, with a seemingly unlimited ability to incorporate external inputs.

2 **Harvesting public value.** The second feature has to do with that "efficiency" issue. New agricultural technologies are invariably presented as inherent boosters of productivity and efficiency. But what all major appropriative technologies share is that their development and use is only profitable because of government subsidy. Subsidy comes in two forms. *Upstream subsidy* refers to public funds paying for research, providing logistical and legal aid, and promoting the technology. *Downstream subsidy* refers to government allowing industrial agriculture to pass off – *externalize* – its costs to the environment and human health. This means getting someone or something else to absorb the indirect costs of using the technology, and this pernicious aspect of industrial agriculture is facilitated by so many of the costs being distant, delayed, and diffuse – which helps input industries evade responsibility. Downstream subsidy also includes paying to protect farmers from their own overproduction.

Endless subsidy for industrial agriculture is criticized by liberals and conservatives alike, but it benefits many key players in the economy, including government and corporate interests and the scientific establishment. Ironically, it does not in general benefit the farmers and the public. Of the many vested interests that lead government to subsidize agri-capital, the most prevalent is that it makes both the inputs and the farm outputs artificially cheap, which leads to other methods of production being displaced. Of course those whose interests are tied to industrial inputs see this as progress. Norman Borlaug, who earned fame for his role in spreading chemical-intensive wheat to India, said that "Of course farmers can use barnyard manure, but there is never enough," as if chemical fertilizer is a needed *addition*. But chemical fertilizer *replaces* manure, and then the manuring system breaks down, and the fertilizer industry becomes essential and develops political power. In the early 20th century, a USDA leader promised a future in which chemical fertilizer would be a supplement, "subordinate to the use of animal and green manures in staple crop production" (Johnson 2016, 213). Instead, the US government would pour all manner of subsidy into the fertilizer industry and use of chemical fertilizer would skyrocket, and along with it grain surpluses that would eventually be fed to confined animals who produced vastly more wasted manure.

3 **Overproduction.** The third key feature is that the development of industrial agriculture sets up conditions that promote overproduction which can become catastrophic and seemingly unstoppable. Since governments have interests in supporting industrial inputs, since corporations want to sell as much of each input as they can, and since agriculture is highly elastic, industrial agriculture has an inexorable tendency to produce beyond the actual demand for food and fiber. Malthus got this backward too: population isn't, by its nature, the runaway train, but industrial agriculture is.

Agricultural overproduction is often noted but it is not generally understood how entrenched and serious the problem is. Michael Pollan's (2006) best-selling book *The*

Omnivore's Dilemma describes how post-World War II developments in the US led to industrial overproduction of corn. But Pollan's account of farmers adopting increasingly expensive inputs to grow more corn – despite the devastating effects of corn surpluses – is just one example of a process that has played out over and over. Rather than emerging only after World War II, input-dependent industrial farming is the culmination of a 100-year battle over the shape of farming in the US (Giesen and Hersey 2010, 295). The history of agriculture over the last century is often told as a procession of inventions, each one improving efficiency, productivity, and the life of the farmer and allowing agriculture to keep abreast of population growth. This history needs to be rewritten to show how the development and spread of each new external input benefits vested interests in the commercial and political spheres, while maneuvering farmers to buy more external inputs while overproducing.

Let me illustrate with a quick tour of the US history of agricultural technologies:

- In the US, the first surge in mechanization occurred in the late 19th century when steam-powered tractors and combines proliferated across the Midwest. This put farm hands out of work, made jobs in factories, and exacerbated a growing problem with grain overproduction. Farmers established cooperative marketing arrangements to try to prop up prices, but agricultural prices continued to plummet until the trough of a depression in 1897 (Cochrane 1993, Guthman 2011, 56).
- In the 1920s, US farm commodity prices crashed and farm economies were in crisis. Historians agree on the cause: "overproduction" (Danbom 1979, 132; Fitzgerald 2003, 30). Farmers knew their collective productivity was their worst enemy, but didn't want to limit their own individual output. By the 1920s nearly a quarter of the wheat harvest was going unsold. With too little money in their pockets and too much grain in their fields, the last thing American farmers needed was for government to subsidize a chemical fertilizer industry. But that is precisely what the US government did in the 1920s, and as a final twist of the knife, much of the cost of the subsidy was from farmers' taxes.
- In the 1930s, the problem of farm surplus was still so severe that one congressman suggested that we should stop funding research to combat crop diseases and start funding programs to spread them. But President Franklin Roosevelt's attempts to scale back government agricultural research were met with threats of political retaliation from input companies and others benefiting from overproduction. By the mid-1930s, there was so much excess beef that government agents were buying cows and shooting them on the spot. Meanwhile in England they were killing pigs, in Brazil they were shoveling coffee beans into boilers of locomotives, and in France and Argentina tens of millions of bushels sat in silos (Cullather 2010). But this is when US farmers got government-supported new hybrid corn and a nitrogen fertilizer industry.
- In the 1950s, with a flood of fertilizer pouring from new and re-purposed factories, seed breeders developed new grain varieties to be close-planted and heavily fertilized. Coupled with government price supports, this led to enormous stockpiles of subsidized crops. Although much of the surplus was shipped to developing countries – often with problematic impacts on farmers there – storage costs for the unnecessary grain were staggering. In 1962, Rachel Carson's *Silent Spring* pointed out that

We are told that the enormous and expanding use of pesticides is necessary to maintain farm production. Yet is our real problem not one of overproduction? Our farms, despite measures to remove acreages from production and to pay farmers not to produce, have yielded such a staggering excess of crops that the American taxpayer in 1962 is paying out more than one billion dollars a year as the total carrying cost of the surplus-food storage program.

By the end of the decade the government was still spending a half-billion dollars yearly on storage (Cullather 2010, 142). But this was precisely when the new seeds and inputs regime spread most rapidly, exacerbating the problem of overproduction.

- In the 1970s, University of California scientists announced the breakthrough of a new tomato, with thick skin and hard flesh suitable to be harvested by mechanical harvesters (Hightower 1972, 18). The harvesters were also developed by scientists at a public university, and university officials touted the need to feed growing populations. But at the same time, California growers were systematically plowing under excess crops to keep prices up (Schrag 1978, 29).
- In the 1980s, partly government-sponsored researchers developed a method of genetically engineering bacteria to produce bovine growth hormone, which was hoped to boost milk production by 41%. Monsanto licensed the technology and applied to sell it to dairy farmers who were suffering from a milk glut so serious that the USDA was paying farmers $1.8 billion to slaughter their cattle and get out of the dairy business (Tangley 1986, 590). (The technology appeared on the market in 1994 under the brand name of Posilac and received a cool reception from consumers.)

In every case, developers and sellers claimed the agricultural inputs were what farmers were clamoring for; after all, why else would farmers adopt them? If this were true then we must have emerged from a dark agricultural past into a Golden Age of agriculture in the last century. Yet the opposite is true: it was the early years of the 20th century, just *before* these technological revolutions began, that is called the "golden age of agriculture" (Gardner 2002, 1) and the "age of prosperity" on the American farm (Hurt 1994, 221). Bruce Gardner – not a romantic farm nostalgic but a distinguished agricultural and resource economist – writes that

> The farm economy has never regained the sustained optimistic tone of the first fifth of the century. Nor has farming ever fully regained the significance it had at that time in the national economy. Since 1920 the United States has lost two-thirds of its farms and, in the course of that decline, helped to populate many urban neighborhoods with its refugees.
>
> *(2002, 2)*

And no less of an authority than Willard Cochrane – former head economist in the US Department of Agriculture – concluded that for the vast majority of American farmers, "the agricultural development process based on rapid and widespread technological advance has been a nightmare" (Cochrane 1993, 388). Industrial agriculture has also brought the death of the family farms, most striking in the US where the number of farms dropped from over 6 million in 1935 to under 2 million today. Farms continue to go bankrupt by the tens of thousands each year and it is not a coincidence that farm debt is at an all-time high.

How did we get here? My hope is to provide an answer that will make sense of this strange, maladaptive, and dangerous situation we have gotten ourselves in. It was certainly not inevitable. And it is not the only form of agricultural growth; there is a third agriculture.

The Third (Intensive) Agriculture

The Kofyar were not a fluke. On the contrary, they fit neatly into a pattern of agricultural change in response to population density that Boserup, Netting, and dozens of other economists, anthropologists, geographers, and others have studied. It is powered primarily by human labor and creativity rather than purchased external inputs. Intensive farmers are not a distinctly bounded category but rather a continuum; some will buy external inputs. But if we define intensive farmers as high-producing farmers without heavy dependence on inputs and with a significant nonmarket component to their operations, there are hundreds of millions of intensive farmers today. It is a dynamic type of agriculture and we will see that it includes many "neo-agrarian" farmers in the US and Western Europe.

Intensive agriculture is not the central focus of this book; there is more to be said about industrial agriculture, which is profoundly misunderstood. But just as industrial agriculture cannot be understood apart from Malthusian agriculture – which justifies, supports, and excuses it – it cannot be understood apart from intensive agriculture which offers a realistic viable alternative and gives the lie to the claims that only industrial agriculture can feed the world.

A Look Ahead

We first need to slip back that moment when young Robert Malthus stepped into the Okewood chapel to understand the theory that took shape there. His remarkable little book would wield extraordinary influence over thought and policy up to the present day, despite how much it got wrong and even backward. But it contained a fascinating set of ideas that are essential to understanding the other two forms of agricultural growth. Chapter 2 examines Malthusian theory and the "neo" version of it that is tremendously influential today.

Chapter 3 turns to industrial agriculture, and asks how we ended up with our profoundly maladaptive and overproducing system particularly in the US (and partly exported to other parts of the world). Like Malthus, we go back to first principles to understand industrial agriculture. We can make sense of it by following the advice of The Dude (in *The Big Lebowski*) and "following the money." The "appropriations" that characterize industrial agriculture have huge beneficiaries, and not a hungry population hoping for new farm technologies to feed them.

We then turn to the two key stories in the process of industrializing agriculture. There have been many of the "appropriations" introduced above. As Richard Lewontin points out,

> farmers used to grow their own seed, raise their own horses and mules, raise the hay the livestock ate, and spread manure from these animals on the land. Now farmers buy their seed from Pioneer Hybrid Seed Co., their "mules" from the Ford Motor Company, the "hay" to feed these "mules" from Exxon, and the "manure" from Union Carbide.
>
> *(1982, 13)*

Each of these is a story in its own right but there are good reasons for focusing on fertilizers and seeds. These two inputs are the core drivers of industrial agriculture and also the most misunderstood because they have the biggest halos. Chemical fertilizer is routinely credited with keeping half the planet alive, and discussions about feeding the poor almost always turn to fertilizer; seed breeding is always thought of as inherently beneficial, and the development of *hybrid crops* is saluted as one of science's greatest achievements.

In his essential study *First the Seed* (a title snitched from the motto of the American Seed Trade Association), Jack Kloppenburg treats seeds as the "irreducible core of crop production" and the fundamental point of entry for agricultural capital. But actually it makes more sense to say "First the Fertilizer." The process of undermining mixed crop-livestock farming and replacing animal manure with factory-produced chemicals was the first major incursion of state-subsidized external inputs and it has had the most profound ripple effects through agriculture. Chapter 4 covers the odd story of how industrial (and especially nitrogen) fertilizer came to be, featuring a US presidential State of the Union speech on bird droppings and three larger-than-life European scientists – one irascible, one tragic, and one racist. It then follows the modern story of fertilizer, featuring an obscure government lab in the inter-war years that changed the course of history, a barnstorming tour by Henry Ford and Thomas Edison, an astonishing corporate windfall after World War II, and a country's unending battle with its problem of overproduction.

Chapter 5 tells an equally odd but crucial story of industrial seed breeding, and the period of US history that saw breeders go from working to help farmers to essentially conducting product development research for private seed companies. This story revolves around hybrid corn, which was indeed one of the century's most important inventions, but not because it helped feed the world; its real importance was to maneuver farmers into buying commercially bred seed instead of producing their own seed as they had always done before.

Chapter 6 explores how these two key inputs were brought into the developing world in the "Green Revolution" that I saw some lasting results of in Hyderabad. This dramatic episode in India has become the ultimate neo-Malthusian myth of industrial agriculture but we will see that it is profoundly misunderstood. New analyses show that India's food problems had little to do with overpopulation, that agriculture was growing faster than population despite major headwinds, and that – shockingly – the Green Revolution did not speed up food production at all. It just made it more input-dependent.

Finally we turn to the obvious question of whether viable alternatives exist to industrial agriculture, the answer being a resounding *yes*. Chapter 7 explores the world of intensification, the "third agriculture." This agriculture is much more widespread and productive than most people understand, and it is vastly less ecologically damaging than its industrial counterpart. It is not "romantic" or "stagnant" – industrial agriculturalists' favorite slurs – and we will see that scientific study of it turns Malthusian theories on their head. We explore what makes this form of agriculture tick, using the Kofyar farming introduced above, and then looking at contemporary variants including North American neo-agrarians.

Notes

1 The previous summer saw rioting in Watts which delayed the shipping of a major load of wheat seeds to India, leading a Delhi newspaper to dub Los Angeles "an overcrowded and poverty-ridden area" (Times of India 1965).

2 William and Paul Paddock's 1967 bestseller *Famine 1975!* predicted that only US wheat could mitigate rampant starvation and even then only for parts of the world selected through triage.

3 For more on the surge in population fears, see Mayhew (2014, 195–215), Robertson (2012), and Connelly (2008).

4 The image of humans having to eat other as food ran out had appeared before, including warnings from a physics Nobel laureate (Cullather 2010, 223). The film Soylent Green, in which the Charlton Heston character discovers that the dietary staple by that name is made of people, came out in 1973.

5 Wattenburg's position on population was better informed than Ehrlich's, but he insisted that positions on overpopulation were "liberal" or "conservative." Conservative politician Newt Gingrich wrote that "Wattenberg highlights the intellectual dishonesty of the Paul Ehrlich, left-wing environmentalists and their factual mistakes over the last generation."

6 Not only was the problem of population named for this man, but this man was named for population: Robert was known as "Population Malthus" (James 1979). He normally went by Robert and not Thomas.

7 This passage appeared in the second edition of *Population* (Malthus 1803) and was later removed.

8 The law eliminated "outdoor relief," forcing the poor to either accept low-paying factory work or enter workhouses (Merchant 2015, 52). It is now widely understood to have been based on the interests of the industrial elite (Meek 1971, 8).

9 First marketed in the mid-1990s, GM crops are created by the laboratory alteration and transfer of DNA between organisms and between species.

10 This was two years before Rachel Carson's *Silent Spring* would begin to question this view.

11 Between 1960 and 1986, world population rose by 67% while production of wheat, rice, and maize rose by 94%, 56%, and 82%, respectively (Evans 1997, 902).

References

AP. 2012. "India's Bumper Crops of Wheat Rot in Open Fields Due to Lack of Storage." *Washington Post*, 10 May.

Appleman, Philip. 1965. *The Silent Explosion*. Boston, MA: Beacon.

Borlaug, Norman E. 1970. "The Green Revolution, peace, and humanity." In *Nobel Lectures in Peace 1951-1970*, edited by Frederick W. Haberman, 445–480. Singapore: World Scientific Publishing.

Burney, Jennifer A., Steven J. Davis, and David B. Lobell. 2010. "Greenhouse Gas Mitigation by Agricultural Intensification." *PNAS* 107 (26):12052–12057.

Chase, Allan. 1977. *The Legacy of Malthus: The Social Costs of the New Scientific Racism*. New York: Alfred A. Knopf.

Cochrane, Willard W. 1993. *The Development of American Agriculture: A Historical Analysis, 2nd ed.* Minneapolis: Univ. of Minnesota.

Cohen, Joel E. 1998. "How Many People Can the Earth Support?" *New York Review of Books*, 8 Oct. https://www.nybooks.com/articles/1998/10/08/how-many-people-can-the-earth-support/

Connelly, Matthew. 2008. *Fatal Misconception: The Struggle to Control World Population*. Cambridge MA: Harvard Univ. Press.

Crowther, J. G. 1974. "Malthus: The Founder of Population Theory." *New Scientist*, 10 January:74–76.

Cullather, Nick. 2010. *The Hungry World: America's Cold War Battle against Poverty in Asia*. Cambridge, MA: Harvard Univ. Press.

Danbom, David B. 1979. *The Resisted Revolution: Urban America and the Industrialization of Agriculture 1900–1930*. Ames IA: Iowa State University.

East, Edward Murray. 1923. *Mankind at the Crossroads*. New York: Scribner.

Ehrlich, Paul R. 1968. *The Population Bomb*. New York: Sierra Club/Ballantine Book.

Ehrlich, Paul R. 1969. "Eco-catastrophe." *Ramparts* 8:24–28.

Ehrlich, Paul R. 1970. An Interview with Ecologist Paul Ehrlich. *Mademoiselle*, April:188–189, 291–293.

Evans, L. T. 1997. "Adapting and Improving Crops: The Endless Task." *Philosophical Transactions: Biological Sciences* 352 (1356):901–906.

Federico, Giovanni. 2005. *Feeding the World: An Economic History of Agriculture, 1800–2000*. Princeton, NJ and Oxford: Princeton Univ. Press.

Fitzgerald, Deborah. 2003. *Every Farm a Factory: The Industrial Ideal in American Agriculture*. New Haven, CT and London: Yale Univ. Press.

Gardner, Bruce L. 2002. *American Agriculture in the Twentieth Century: How it Flourished and What it Cost*. Cambridge, MA: Harvard Univ. Press.

Giesen, James C., and Mark Hersey. 2010. "The New Environmental Politics and its Antecedents: Lessons from the Early Twentieth Century South." *The Historian* 72 (2) Summer:271–298.

Goodman, David, Bernardo Sorj, and John Wilkinson. 1987. *From Farming to Biotechnology: A Theory of Agro-Industrial Development*. Oxford: Basil Blackwell.

Gustavsson, J., C. Cederberg, U. Sonesson, R. van Otterdijk, and A. Meybeck. 2011. *Global Food Losses and Food Waste: Extent, Causes and Prevention*. Rome: FAO.

Guthman, Julie. 2011. "Excess Consumption or Over-production?: US Farm Policy, Global Warming, and the Bizarre Attribution of Obesity." In *Global Political Ecology*, edited by Richard Peet, Paul Robbins and Michael Watts, 51–66. London and New York: Routledge.

Hardin, Garrett. 1993. *Living within Limits: Ecology, Economics, and Population Taboos*. New York: Oxford Univ. Press.

Harwood, Jonathan. 2019. "Was the Green Revolution Intended to Maximise Food Production?" *International Journal of Agricultural Sustainability*. https://doi.org/10.1080/14735903.2019.1637236.

Hightower, Jim. 1972. "Hard Tomatoes, Hard Times: Failure of the Land Grant College Complex." *Society* 10 (1):10–22.

Hurt, R. Douglas. 1994. *American Agriculture: A Brief History*. Ames: Iowa State Univ. Press.

James, Patricia. 1979. *Population Malthus: His Life and Times*. London: Routledge & Kegan Paul.

Johnson, Timothy. 2016. "Nitrogen Nation: The Legacy of World War I and the Politics of Chemical Agriculture in the United States, 1916–1933." *Agricultural History* 90 (2):209–229. doi: 10.3098/ah.2016.090.2.209.

Kohl, Daniel H. 1975. "The Environmental Movement: What Might It Be." *Natural Resources Journal* 15 (2):327–351.

Krishnakumar, P.K. 2015. "We Can't Kill Cows, But Globally Lead in Beef Exports." *Times of India*, 23 April. http://timesofindia.indiatimes.com/business/india-business/We-cant-kill-cows-but-globally-lead-in-beef-exports/articleshow/47023833.cms.

Lewontin, Richard. 1982. "Agricultural Research and the Penetration of Capital." *Science for the People*, Jan–Feb:12–17.

Malthus, Thomas Robert. 1798. *An Essay on the Principle of Population As it Affects the Future Improvement of Society with Remarks on the Speculations of Mr. Godwin, M. Condorcet, and Other Writers*. London: J. Johnson.

Malthus, Thomas Robert. 1803. *An Essay on the Principle of Population, or, A View of its Past and Present Effects on Human Happiness with an Inquiry into Our Prospects Respecting the Future Removal or Mitigation of the Evils Which it Occasions*. London: J. Johnson.

Mamdani, Mahmood. 1972. *The Myth of Population Control: Family, Caste, and Class in an Indian Village*. New York and London: Monthly Review Press.

Mann, Charles C. 2018. *The Wizard and the Prophet, Two Remarkable Scientists and Their Dueling Visions to Shape Tomorrow's World*. New York: Alfred A. Knopf.

Marshall, Alfred, and Mary P. Marshall. 1888. *The Economics of Industry*. London: Macmillan & Co.

Mayhew, Robert J. 2014. *Malthus: The Life and Legacies of an Untimely Prophet*. Cambridge, MA: Harvard Univ. Press.

Meadows, Donella H., Dennis L. Meadows, Jørgen Randers, and William W. Behrens III. 1972. *Limits to Growth: A Report for the Club of Rome's project on the predicament of mankind*. New York: Universe Books.

Meek, Ronald L. 1971. "Malthus Yesterday." In *Marx and Engels on the Population Bomb*, edited by Ronald L. Meek, 3–15. Berkeley, CA: Ramparts Press.

Merchant, Emily R. 2015. "Prediction and Control: Global Population, Population Science, and Population Politics in the Twentieth Century." PhD, History, Univ. of Michigan. https://deepblue. lib.umich.edu/handle/2027.42/113440.

Mills Quarterly. 1969. "Commencement '69." *Mills Quarterly*, 17–19.

Netting, Robert McC. 1968. *Hill Farmers of Nigeria: Cultural Ecology of the Kofyar of the Jos Plateau.* Seattle: Univ. of Washington Press.

Netting, Robert McC. 1993. *Smallholders, Householders: Farm Families and the Ecology of Intensive, Sustainable Agriculture.* Stanford, CA: Stanford Univ. Press.

New York Times. 1966. "Johnson vs. Malthus." *New York Times*, 24 Jan, 29. https://www.nytimes. com/1966/01/24/archives/johnson-vs-malthus.html

Paddock, William. 1970. "How Green Is the Green Revolution?" *Bioscience* 20 (16):897–902.

Pollan, Michael. 2006. *The Omnivore's Dilemma: A Natural History of Four Meals.* New York: Penguin.

Robertson, Thomas. 2012. *The Malthusian Moment: Global Population Growth and the Birth of American Environmentalism.* New Brunswick, NJ: Rutgers Univ. Press.

Ross, Eric B. 1998. *The Malthus Factor: Population, Poverty, and Politics in Capitalist Development.* London: Zed Books.

Sabin, Paul. 2013. *The Bet: Paul Ehrlich, Julian Simon, and Our Gamble over Earth's Future*: Yale Univ. Press.

Schrag, Peter. 1978. "Rubber Tomatoes: The Unsavory Partnership of Research and Agribusiness." *Harper's* June:24–29.

Tangley, Laura. 1986. "Biotechnology on the Farm." *BioScience* 36:590–593.

The Hindu. 2000. 'Dump Rotten Foodgrains into the Sea'. *The Hindu*, 20 December.

Times of India. 1965. "Los Angeles Riots." *Times of India*, 21 Aug, 6.

US House of Representatives. 1974. Malthus and America: *A Report about Food and People.* Washington DC: US Government Printing Office.

Vasavi, A.R. 2012. *Shadow Space: Suicides and the Predicament of Rural India.* New Delhi: Three Essays Collective.

Waldman, Amy. 2002. "Poor in India Starve as Surplus Wheat Rots." *New York Times*, 2 Dec. http:// www.nytimes.com/2002/12/02/world/poor-in-india-starve-as-surplus-wheat-rots.html.

Wilmoth, John R., and Patrick Ball. 1992. "The Population Debate in American Popular Magazines, 1946–90." *Population and Development Review* 18 (4):631–668. doi: 10.2307/1973758.

Workman, Daniel. 2016. Rice Exports by Country. *WorldsTopExports*, https://www.worldstopexports. com/rice-imports-by-country/.

World Bank. 2015. *Ending Poverty and Hunger by 2030: An Agenda for the Global Food System. https:// openknowledge.worldbank.org/handle/10986/21771 License: CC BY 3.0 IGO".* Washington, DC: World Bank.

2
POPULATION MALTHUS

Okewood church sits on a small hill in the center of a dark forest in the Mole Valley in Surrey County. Standing in the churchyard, amid the tilted tombstones, unruly grasses, and scattered flowers, with no sounds except birdsong, you wouldn't know you are only 28 miles from the center of London. The old church with yellow walls, sandstone roof, and thick low door looks much as it did when a young Robert Malthus came here in 1789 to begin his first job.

This corner of England is known to music lovers as the "Surrey Delta" because of its role in turning classic American acoustic blues into modern rock and roll. Jimmy Page (of Led Zeppelin and the Yardbirds), Jeff Beck (of the Jeff Beck group and Yardbirds) and Eric Clapton were all Surrey lads; the Rolling Stones honed their blues a club in the Surrey town of Richmond. Today it is known as part of the "stockbroker belt" with its green spaces, picturesque villages, riding clubs, and expensive residential properties. But in the late 1700s it was a backwater, with relatively poor residents and notoriously heavy clay soils that were kind to neither farming nor travel. Okewood church was built for the scattered rural people "whiche dwell very ffar distant from ye parryshe churches" (Stanway 1940) in large part because of the hard traveling in rainy weather.

St. John the Baptist Church at Okewood (Figure 2.1) was erected in 1220 on the site of a Roman villa, which in turn had been built over the ruins of a Druid temple. It had fallen into disrepair by the 1400s when, according to local legend, it benefited from divine intervention. A wealthy local man named Edward de la Hale is said to have been out with his son hunting near the chapel. They wounded a wild boar, and in the excitement of the hunt the son fell off his horse. As the furious boar charged at him, an arrow appeared out of nowhere and killed the boar. De la Hale was sure the arrow had been sent by God to save his boy's life, and in his gratitude he promised God a portion of his wealth. The nearby chapel being in need of repair, he paid for its restoration and endowed it with lands (Stanway 1940).

The Church remains in use to the present day, and on the Sunday morning in Spring 2013 when I found my way there, a service was planned. But that would be later; I had two hours to explore, photograph, and try to envision late 18th century peasants trudging up

DOI: 10.4324/9781003286257-2

FIGURE 2.1 Left: Detail from 1833 portrait of Thomas Robert Malthus by John Linnell, National Portrait Gallery, London. Malthus resisted being depicted because of his cleft palate; this is the only portrait he sat for. Right: Okewood Church, Surrey, 2013. Photo by G. Stone.

the paths to be met by a novice preacher. Eventually the churchyard began to show signs of human life, and a white-haired elder came to greet me warmly, pointing out enthusiastically that there were several paths leading up the hill just as there are multiple paths to Christ. I told him there were also multiple routes to this little church on a hill, and I would have been lost except for Google Maps' encyclopedic knowledge of the Surrey backroads.

Entering the church you have to duck under wide, heavy, and remarkably short door. The service this Sunday was entirely congregation-led; the minister (who was shared among several such small churches) sat in front of me and did not participate. Several congregants took turns overseeing a program of candle-lighting, prayer, and song following a round of dour gay-bashing occasioned by the same-sex marriage bill being considered by Parliament. It was not the first time that a clear feeling of intolerance had found its way into the little church.

A Different World?

In some ways the world Robert Malthus (Figure 2.1) inhabited seems utterly alien to us today. England was in perpetual war with France, the battles fought with flintlocks. Ladies covered their faces in toxic white powder and young men wore powdered pigtails. England was ruled by a king, people traveled on horseback and wrote letters with quills, and political arguments were often conducted by pamphlets passed out on city streets. Cambridge, far from the august intellectual powerhouse of today, was known for drunken rioting by upper-crust college boys (Pullen 2004).

And yet, beneath the surface, there were parallels with today. The technology was different, but those pamphleteers were not that unlike many bloggers today. The Enlightenment was in full bloom, and it was a particularly lively time for public debate on political philosophy, societal ideals, and mankind's drive to perfection. In 1798 the 32-year-old Robert

Malthus added his voice to the political chatter, writing out his essay on the relationship between population and agriculture published anonymously under the title *Essay on the Principle of Population as it Affects the Future Improvement of Society with Remarks on the Speculations of Mr. Godwin, M. Condorcet, and Other Writers*. *Population* went viral, and "has never been out of the public consciousness for the two hundred years since it was written" (Mayhew 2014, 74). Even today this essay – and the tweaked versions of it we will call neo-Malthusian – provides a basic theory of, and way of thinking about, food and population.

One reason for the enduring power of *Population* is how it has served the interests of a range of individuals, states, corporations, and social movements over the years. When it appeared in 1798 the early Industrial Revolution elites who owned the "dark Satanic mills" (as Blake called them), where desperately poor and underfed children and adults labored, could not believe their good luck: here was a scientific theory attributing poverty and hunger to the reproductive habits of the poor and hungry themselves. As Britain's colonial footprint grew, the theory provided a handy explanation for the poverty and intermittent famines caused by taxation and extraction of food and resources. And it has continued to be a powerful tool for diverting attention from underlying problems over the years, and continues to be so in contemporary attempts to make sense of population and agriculture.

The other reason for the booklet's remarkable impact is that it captured a sense of anxiety about population that has persisted across the centuries. Yet one of the ironies of Robert Malthus is that his actual message was **not** to worry. His argument was that a persistent imbalance in population is dictated by the laws of nature: it will always be the lot of the poor to go hungry, be sick, and lead lives plagued by "vices," and attempts to intervene will only make matters worse. Yet his work has been the cornerstone of history's most pervasive strain of worry and fear of the future. It is difficult to find an era in which these anxieties are lacking. Let us reconstruct the events that led the young man to write a tract that would be such a work of its time and also timeless.

Early Years

Born in 1766, Robert Malthus grew up on a country estate in Surrey. His father Daniel, wealthy by inheritance, was something of an underarchiever: he attended Oxford but left without a degree, and tried his hand at law but abandoned it. His real love seems to have been ideas, and he had assembled a substantial library which occupied much of his time as an avid reader. He was a devoted father and much of his relationship with Robert is fortunately preserved in correspondence (Pullen 1986).

Robert matriculated at Cambridge's Jesus College in 1784. He promptly got into trouble; we are not sure exactly what he did but it must have involved some significant damage, as he wrote to his father "I am glad to hear that the affair in town may be settled by one sum; but I am afraid it may not be a very small one" (Pullen 1986, 138). One Malthus scholar suspects that this affair in town "might conceivably have been related to the etymology ("Malt-House") of his surname" (Pullen 1987). Correspondence from father Daniel during these years reflects affection but also some tension. By his senior year Robert had settled down and was getting good grades; he majored in math, graduating with honors in 1788. Then, having no job, he moved back in with his parents, now living in the Surrey village of Albury.[1]

Back at home, Malthus spent his time socializing and "indulg[ing] his pastimes of walking, riding, hunting, and shooting" (Stapleton 1986, 22). But a letter from his father a few years later reveals that they had been having exactly the same arguments that many young people have today in this situation. There was an intellectual struggle unfolding with his father. Daniel was enthralled with the flood of Enlightenment ideas about the "perfectibility of man" and the optimism about social institutions. Daniel's library included the utopian William Godwin, Marquis de Condorcet, and his favorite political theorist Jean-Jacques Rousseau, to whom he sent fan letters and invitations[2] (James 1979, 10–13, Pullen 2004). Rousseau had a particularly rosy perspective on humanity's place in nature, famously writing that "[N]othing is so gentle as man in his primitive state" (Rousseau 1984 (1754), 115).

Conversations around the Malthus dinner table must have been especially lively in Robert's second year at home: that year saw the outbreak of the French Revolution, animated by many Enlightenment ideas. And again we can see unmistakable reflections of today, with the college graduate back home and feeling a bit crowded by his father's politics. Perhaps it was the problems in the particular ideas being propounded at the dinner table (as discussed below), or perhaps it was just a "typical example of the younger generation reacting against the ideas of the older generation" (Pullen 1986, 138). But it is clear that young Bob's attitude on social issues began to take shape at this time, and the shape was sharply divergent from his father's. When he finally left the house for his first job, it would be to the little country church where his impoverished congregants would serve as muse to theories growing out of the arguments around the Malthus dinner table.

To Okewood

Robert's period of relaxing, arguing, and being urged by his father to get a job came to an end the next summer when Daniel secured him an entry-level job as the curate (sub-priest) at the Okewood chapel. Daniel wrote to tell Robert that "you would find your first beginning extreamly quiet, with very little duty that could be irksome to you" (Pullen 1986, 151). As a curate he would give occasional sermons and tend to baptisms and burials, and he was paid well for his light duties.[3]

Okewood was not very far from Albury, but it was a world apart, a backwoods area inhabited by what one historians called "obscure peasants" (Malden 1900, 203, Mayhew 2014, 61). Most were small farmers or laborers "without a great deal in the way of clothes, clocks, schools, doctors, and news" (Malden 1900, 289). More to the point, they were poorly fed. It was clearly the under-nourished children of Okewood that Malthus was describing a few years later in *Population*:

> The sons and daughters of peasants will not be found such rosy cherubs in real life as they are described to be in romances…the sons of labourers are very apt to be stunted in their growth, and are a long while arriving at maturity. Boys that you would guess to be fourteen or fifteen are, upon inquiry, frequently found to be eighteen or nineteen. And the lads who drive plough, which must certainly be a healthy exercise, are very rarely seen with any appearance of calves to their legs: a circumstance which can only be attributed to a want either of proper or of sufficient nourishment.
>
> *(Malthus 1798)*

Malthus was quite right that taking "a long while arriving at maturity" is a good indicator of chronic malnourishment. What he didn't know was that he was looking across one of the biggest diet gaps in history. Economist John Komlos (2005) has studied heights in history, finding no greater height gap than between rich and poor than in late 18th century England. Height of the poor was declining in the late 18th century while the height of the wealthy held steady. The children Malthus saw at Okewood were shorter for their age than any other recorded European or North American group, even including slaves in the US South: a full 22 cm (8.7″) shorter than elite children at age 16. English elites were surprisingly tall – only 2.5 cm shorter than today's US standards. England at the time had, in Komlos's terms, pygmies and giants. In his first time rubbing shoulders with the poor, it is no surprise that Malthus was taken aback by their size. They must have seemed "like a different race from the lads who played cricket at Cambridge" (James 1979, 43). Visits to parishioners would also have brought the wealthy young Cambridge-educated pastor into dirt-floored waddle and daub hovels for the first time (Malden 1900, 289). To Robert Malthus the culture shock must have been as jarring as Paul Ehrlich's ride in a Delhi taxi, and he was just as intent as Ehrlich on drawing broad conclusions from the experience.

Bit players in history can be in the right place and time to nudge the course of human events. Think of Isaac Newton's apple or the finches that caught Charles Darwin's attention. The small, skinny-legged peasants who were entrusted to this tall and well-fed novice pastor from inherited wealth, coming off of a year of post-Cambridge idleness, were just such players. Their poverty and poor nutrition was clearly striking to the young man who had spent the past year listening to his father's disquisitions on progress in the human condition. And the young pastor's reaction was harsh. While English society would later convince itself that Malthus was a humanitarian – his epitaph in Bath Abbey even comments on his "tenderness of heart" – his basic feeling toward the members of his flock was disdain. He managed to see in the under-nourished farmers a sense of entitlement, begrudging them even the bread they mainly lived on: he would later write that "The labourers of the South of England are so accustomed to eat fine wheaten bread that they will suffer themselves to be half starved before they will submit to live like the Scotch peasants" (Malthus 1798, 42).[4]

He also seemed less concerned about his parishioners' grinding poverty than about the danger that someone might try to help them escape it. He wrote that one "cannot by means of money raise a poor man and enable him to live much better than he did before, without proportionably depressing others in the same class" (Malthus 1798, 25). If the poor had more money, they would only eat some meat, which would lead beef producers to increase their herds, put pressure on the nation's grain supply, and raise the cost of meals for the poor. Warming to his argument, Malthus held that increased earnings would only make people lazy and impoverish the nation:

> The receipt of five shillings a day, instead of eighteen pence, would make every man fancy himself comparatively rich and able to indulge himself in many hours or days of leisure. This would give a strong and immediate check to productive industry, and, in a short time, not only the nation would be poorer, but the lower classes themselves would be much more distressed than when they received only eighteen pence a day.
>
> (Malthus 1798, 25)

Of course, the belief that increased wages caused indolence did not apply to the author himself, who was enjoying a generous salary for little work and seemed principally concerned with his own promotion to the priesthood; a few years later he would move on from

Okewood to a rectorship in Lincolnshire which required almost no work at all (Pullen 2004). The economics for the privileged seemed to work differently than for the poor, and in an unguarded moment he let slip the reason why. In attacking England's Poor Law, he wrote that the food being consumed the poor in workhouses "diminishes the shares that would otherwise belong to more industrious and more worthy members." It was not only industry and worth that the poor lacked, but morality itself, as Malthus made clear in the second (1803) edition of *Population*. In that edition he opined that poverty exerts a "considerable moral degradation of character" and that "moral restraint" had to be taught to the poor (Malthus 1803, 512-516). Throughout history, Malthusian thinking would repeatedly lapse from a purportedly scientific theory about there being too many people to the bigoted conviction that there are too many of certain kinds of people (Chase 1977, Ross 1998); the tendency began with Malthus himself.[5]

But what has been most important to social thinking through the years was Malthus's analysis of why the Okewood peasants were so poor. Thinking like a scientist, he was attempting to build general theory, seeing the thin calves and dirt floors as evidence of general processes. But what processes?

It turned out that Okewood appeared to be in the midst of a tiny population boom. The curate's duties included baptisms and burials, and the spidery writing in the chapel register for 1789–1798 shows a yearly rate of 16 baptisms but only five burials (Stapleton 1986, 27, Surrey Record Society 1927). The Cambridge math major would have had no trouble computing that at the current rate, local population would quickly explode.

Malthus was clearly writing about his flock a few years later in *Population*, even if he does not name Okewood or mention the imbalance in the baptisms and burials he had performed. To one biographer it was clear that "it must have been these poor cottage babies, in the 1790s, who first set the curate thinking about the principle of population" (James 1979, 46). It was clear to the young Malthus, as it would be to the young Paul Ehrlich years later, that the poverty he was seeing was the direct result of the runaway train of overpopulation.

Overpopulation… but *over what*, exactly? In the Delhi taxi, what made Ehrlich uncomfortable was the urban populace bearing in on him and his family, looking and acting differently than him. At Okewood, it was ill nourished lower class peasants having babies in earth floored hovels that pushed Malthus out of his comfort zone. But were they really poor because they were having too many babies?

Why Okewood Peasants Were Poor

Malthus never published an analysis specifically of the Okewood peasants, but he did use the situation there to clarify his thinking about general processes of population and poverty. We can use them for the same purpose – to help us understand poverty and malnourishment.

Most people in this area made their living as laborers or farmers. An account of conditions in Surrey from not long before Malthus arrived at Okewood stated that laborers were particularly poor, while small farmers who could keep cows on the common were better off (Malden 1900, 289). Unfortunately, in the late 18th century common fields were only to be found in the north of Surrey; Okewood, at the southern end of the county, had none (Malden 1900, 292–293).

Moreover, the quality of the land that was available was low. Surrey happened to enclose a remarkable diversity of soil types – "some of the very best and some of the worst lands, not only in England but in the world" (Cobbett 1834 [1984]). Albury, where the Malthuses lived, was located in productive alluvium, but Okewood was in "London Clay" where farming would have been more arduous and less productive.

But to Malthus the local agroecology would have been of little interest; he saw English soil as uniformly poor for farming (Malthus 1798, 59). In the theories Malthus would soon put to paper, underfed populations could arise in any environment, but the plight of these particular peasants would have been attributable to the England's welfare system as encoded in the "Poor Law." As he looked at the baptisms in the Okewood Parish Register and the poorly fed children, he was clearly convinced that the Poor Law was only generating more poverty by caring for the children being born in excessive numbers.

Actually the Poor Law was helping to concentrate poverty in areas like Okewood, but not for the reasons Malthus cited. The law required aid for the poor and indigent to be handled on a parish basis, with each parish setting tax rates to pay for local welfare. But historical records reveal huge differences among parishes, with some showing as much as 40% on welfare and some close to zero. The reason was that the gentry in well-heeled parishes were able to maintain pools of impoverished workers while avoiding the tax burden for their welfare. This was accomplished through the creation of "close" (closed) parishes, where landed magnates would destroy cottages to keep the poor from living there. Meanwhile,

> Other parishes, where land ownership was much divided, found such undertakings well-nigh impossible, and thus tended to become densely populated and heavily pauperised "open" parishes, in contrast to the "close" parishes controlled by one or a few landowners…the great financial advantages of one close parish vis-a-vis a neighboring open parish encouraged the practice of clearing parishes.
>
> *(Brundage 1978, 3)*

Wotton Parish (which contained Okewood) and its adjoining parishes of Abinger and Shere were open parishes, and their welfare rolls had been growing rapidly in the late 1700s. Daniel Malthus, one of the highest taxpayers in Shere Parish, had seen his payments rise by 30% in the 1790s (Stapleton 1986, 31). In short, the same system that helped Okewood peasants stay poor was costing Robert's father a lot of money, and in *Population* he bristled at "the rising poor relief payments and the growing population without attempting any analysis of the structure or causes of poverty" (Stapleton 1986, 33). But Malthus's own analysis of the causes of poverty was remarkably selective, with a complete blind spot for the political underpinnings of poverty and a fixation on the libidos of the lower classes. Nowhere in *Population* is there any recognition of Britain's "large body of impotent poor, the aged, the sick, the widowed and children on whose fate Malthus failed to utter a single syllable" (Stapleton 1986, 33).

But a final point about Okewood is that its apparent population boom was a meaningless blip in a tiny sample of demographic events. Had Malthus taken a serious interest in demographic trends he would have found that Okewood was unusual in its cluster of births; neighboring parishes had a surplus of burials for this period (Stapleton 1986, 27). But ironically, "Population Malthus" showed little interest in such details of demography.[6] Foremost on his mind were the convictions he had reached after showing up at Okewood, with Daniel's discussions of Enlightenment philosophy and human perfectibility still ringing in his ears, and then finding himself among the short, ill-nourished, welfare-dependent parishioners who appeared to be reproducing up a storm. In 1797 he put quill to paper, beginning with "The following Essay owes its origin to a conversation with a friend, on the subject of Mr. Godwin's Essay on avarice and profusion." The "friend" was father Daniel, and Mr. Godwin was William Godwin, arguably England's most discussed social philosopher, and for whom Daniel's enthusiasm had touched a nerve in young Robert.

Malthus's Targets

The Hapless William Godwin

Godwin is an interesting story in his own right. Although he had been known in London's radical circles for years, it was the 1793 publication of his book *An Enquiry Concerning Political Justice* that brought him fame as a public intellectual. *Political Justice* was a rambling 900-page work that pushed the envelope of Enlightenment thinking and laid the groundwork for philosophical anarchism. If Enlightenment texts featured optimism, a focus on reason, and a dedication to improving social institutions, *Political Justice* plotted a path to perfection of mind, body, and society by abolishing or revamping most major social institutions. Among the institutions Godwin slated for removal were government, marriage, gender division of labor, and theater. The triumph of reason would ever mean the vanquishing of sexual passion, and propagation would be ruled by the intellect rather than the libido. As Godwin explained,

> Reasonable men then will propagate their species, not because a certain sensible pleasure is annexed to this action, but because it is right the species should be propagated; and the manner in which they exercise this function will be regulated by the dictates of reason and duty.
>
> *(1793, 229)*

Finally, with his internal reality check in full retreat, Godwin predicted the end of sleep and disease, and asked "why may not man be one day immortal?" (Godwin 1793, 234).[7]

In 1797 he followed this up with a collection of essays entitled *Enquirer*, the source of arguments at the Malthus dinner table. This included the "Avarice and Profusion" essay noted above, in which Godwin proposed that "a state of cultivated equality in that state which, in speculation and theory, appears most consonant to the nature of man" (Bonar 1885, 14).

Oddly, this sort of cheery Enlightenment optimism was in vogue just as the industrial revolution was getting off the ground, with its stupendous accumulations of wealth by the emerging industrial elite while a growing urban underclass grew sicker and poorer (Engels 1993[1845]). Godwin was rhapsodizing about man's tendency to cultivate equality just as exaggerated economic inequality was being normalized, and formulating a philosophy of anarchism just as government reform of workplace exploitation was most needed. Malthus's thesis "seemed to entrench and naturalize rather than ameliorate poverty," write Bashford and Chaplin, "just when a new generation of utopians was imagining a brighter and better future" (2016). Malthus shed no tears for the workers in the dark satanic mills, but he scoffed at Godwin's vision of perfection; his Okewood peasants would always be slave to their libidos. Mustering considerable snark, Malthus skewered Godwin's optimistic utopian vision.

Godwin's initial reaction to being used as punching bag and foil for a much-discussed anonymous booklet was surprisingly mild.[8] He wrote Malthus in 1801 to say that he was proud to have inspired so valuable a treatise[9] and praised the "great foundations of his theory" (James 1979) – leading one to wonder how seriously Godwin took the booklet.

After this Malthus's star rose quickly as Godwin's fell. Godwin's wife – the firebrand social philosopher Mary Wollstonecraft – died after giving birth to the baby known to us today as Mary Shelley.[10] By 1805, following publication of an expanded edition of *Population* and appointment as Professor of History and Political Economy at the East India Company College, Malthus was essentially England's foremost political economist (James 1979, 167); meanwhile Godwin's second marriage was unhappy, his literary work was less successful, and he fell increasingly into debt. Eventually he would become a punchline – "the opponent of marriage who was twice married, the novelist who thought it slavish to read the words of others, and the father of two who had expected the urge to propagate to wither" (Mayhew 2014, 46). He eventually became so reliant on his friends' charity as to be called the "prince of spongers" (James 1979, 382), and eventually accepted a government sinecure, completing the aging anarchist's fall from grace.

Finally, in 1820 he published *Of Population: An Inquiry Concerning the Power of Increase in the Numbers of Mankind, Being an Answer to Mr. Malthus' Essay on That Subject* (Godwin 1820). This bloated, decades-late treatise contained none of Godwin's gentle initial response to his young critic. "I hailed the attack of Mr. Malthus," explained Godwin, because it had been an example of the curiosity he had hoped to incite. He assumed that *Population*, with its "erroneous and exaggerated representations of things," would be easily demolished by younger writers. Yet after many years, no one had properly refuted the principle or the "revolting nature of the conclusions he drew" from it (Godwin 1820, 8). Godwin offered many arguments that modern scholars would find agreeable, admixed with swipes at Malthus (whose theory, Godwin wrote, had "flattered the vices and corruption of the rich and great" to gain their "eager patronage" (Godwin 1820, 7)). But *Of Population* was met with derision in 1820s intellectual circles. "Have you seen Godwin against Malthus?" wrote James Mill to David Ricardo; "To me it appears below contempt" (Rosen 1970, 33). Most painful to Godwin, it was met with silence. Malthus's own comment, published anonymously in one of the scant few notices the book received, was that it was "the poorest and most old-womanish performance that has fallen from the pen of any writer of name" (Rosen 1970, 35). In his sixth and final edition of *Population*, published in 1825, Malthus merely noted that Godwin's book "does not require a reply." Malthus's own copy of *Of Population* is still in the collection in the Old Library at Jesus College. Simply inscribed "From the author," it shows neither signs of use nor liner notes.

Other Targets. Nicolas de Condorcet, although featured prominently in the title of Malthus's pamphlet, received only a fraction of the critical attention given to Godwin. He was a less juicy target. He certainly did not entertain notions of extinguishing sexual passions; he was, after all, French (James 1979, 61). Condorcet had written on math, philosophy, and what is now called political science; Condorcet voting systems are still in use. But most importantly, Condorcet was a robust proponent of science as the engine of societal progress. This was argued mainly in his posthumous *Sketch of an Historical View of the Progress of the Human Mind* (1795), which Malthus seized on.

It was actually Condorcet's analysis of how population could outpace agriculture than had inspired Malthus. But in classic Enlightenment fashion, *Sketch* emphasized the drive toward perfection by reform of social institutions. Condorcet laid particular stress on gender roles, even arguing that women should take up research in the natural sciences – a scandalous position given the prevailing belief that "women would lose their modesty if they were permitted to study subjects like biology" (Groenewegen 2003, 133). The gender issue was linked directly to population growth, as he held that education – especially of women – would lead to lowered birthrates. (This argument, also taken up in Godwin's 1820 *On Population*, has been resoundingly confirmed in subsequent studies.)[11]

A third key writer on population that Malthus took aim at was Richard Price. Like Condorcet, Price combined political philosophy with mathematical analysis (including the rigorous analysis of parish registers noted above). Like many social analysts of the day, he believed that a rising population was beneficial. Godwin, Condorcet, and Price were spearheading a revolution in how people thought about population, resources, and well-being, with a mixture of mathematical analysis and Enlightenment optimism in the combustible decade of the French Revolution. However this body of theory is scarcely remembered today, "thanks to Malthus, who was to overpaint their portrait of society in very different colors before the revolutionary decade of the 1790s was out" (Mayhew 2014, 29).

Malthus's "overpainting" has held remarkable sway in intellectual, public, and public circles for centuries, and is still routinely cited in scientific papers, newspapers, popular books, college courses, and corporate media (especially by agricultural input industries). What Malthus actually said is important, so let us take a closer look.

Malthusian Theory

Reading Malthus is not straightforward. Even if we consider just *Population* and ignore his other works, there are contradictions between the six different editions he published. The most important changes occurred between the first (1798) and much longer second (1803) edition, in which he essentially reversed course on one of his key postulates (more about which in a moment). But it is those simple generalizations of the 1798 publication, known as the *First Essay*, that have played the key role in the history of our anxiety about food and agriculture. Therefore let us focus on this edition that brought him fame and encapsulated the perspective that would be termed "Malthusian," with attention only to the key changes in later editions.

Basic Postulates

In 1798 Malthus may have been an inexperienced first-time author, but he had a knack for persuasion and for critique. He opened with a rather patronizing portrait of Godwin and the other dreamers of perfectibility whose ideas had "warmed and delighted" him with the enchanting picture of society they painted. But he quickly zeroed in on Godwin's most improbable notions about sex, stressing the blunt realities of "the passion between the sexes." Malthus noted that humanity had made great progress in rising from "the savage state," but

> towards the extinction of the passion between the sexes, no progress whatever has hitherto been made. It appears to exist in as much force at present as it did two thousand or four thousand years ago.
>
> *(1798, 4)*

Then, since all animals must eat, Malthus arrived at the following basic "postulata":

> Population, when unchecked, increases in a geometrical ratio. Subsistence increases only in an arithmetical ratio. A slight acquaintance with numbers will show the immensity of the first power in comparison of the second.
>
> By that law of our nature which makes food necessary to the life of man, the effects of these two unequal powers must be kept equal. This implies a strong and constantly operating check on population from the difficulty of subsistence.
>
> *(Malthus 1798, 4–5)*

The "check on population" is the crux of Malthusian theory because it is the essential relationship between the "two unequal powers" of population and agriculture. The check took two different forms, Malthus reasoned. *Preventive checks* limit the numbers of babies born, chiefly through constraints on marriage. But since such checks cannot suppress population growth sufficiently, there must be *positive checks*. This is an odd name and Malthus was obscure in defining this as "the check that represses an increase which is already begun." But he was talking about mortality – anything that killed off people after they were born. Positive checks basically fall onto the "lowest orders of society." Positive checks are often assumed to refer to running out of food, but that is not what Malthus actually said; instead he stressed the social pathologies that were "ministers of depopulation." These "laws of nature" overrode culture, history, ecology, and the "human institutions" that Godwin and other Enlightenment writers emphasized.

We know from the first chapter that the relationships between population and food production have essentially gone in the opposite direction from what Malthus predicted. Clearly something is deeply wrong in the theory. To get at what the problem is let us first look more closely at the Malthusian demography, Malthusian agriculture, and the key relationship between them.

Malthusian Demography

Among the ironies of Robert Malthus is that while he immortalized the specter of exponential ("geometric") population growth, he never actually said this happens. He did point out what was obvious to anyone who passed junior high math: that population would increase exponentially if totally unchecked. But no human population has ever grown at more than a tiny fraction of an "unchecked" rate, because all human populations have preventive checks. Humans live in cultures and all cultures have multiple institutions that control sex, marriage, and childbearing. In fact, after holding up the odd specter of unchecked growth, Malthus recognized this explicitly:

> I think it will be allowed, that no state has hitherto existed (at least that we have any account of) where... no check whatever has existed to early marriages, among the lower classes, from a fear of not providing well for their families, or among the higher classes, from a fear of lowering their condition in life. Consequently in no state that we have yet known has the power of population been left to exert itself with perfect freedom.
>
> *(Malthus 1798, 6)*

Malthus knew little about preventive checks but assumed they were inherently insufficient – those randy Okewood peasants had sure been marrying young – which is why so much of his booklet concerns positive checks. Remarkably, he walked back this famous theory as soon as he learned a little about preventive checks. Soon after publishing the *First Essay*, a Cambridge friend invited him on a road trip to Scandinavia. For Malthus it would be part vacation from the "angry criticism ringing in his anonymous ears" (Dillard 2011, 122), but also part amateur ethnographic fieldwork as he could actually investigate the checks on population on which he had pontificated. In Scandinavia, he was taken aback to find a range of quite effective preventive checks on population growth. In Norway, he saw an intersection of government policies, church authority, and social conventions that ensured late marriage and few children per family. Godwin, despite his flaky ideas on sex and sleep, had been entirely correct on this.

Soon after returning, Malthus produced a greatly expanded and fundamentally changed essay. Published in 1803, the second edition of *Population* was, he said, a "new work" (Malthus 1803, V).[12] His trip to Scandinavia had changed his core views on population and food. No longer were "vice and misery" the only checks capable of keeping population down to the level of the food supply: now this also happened via "moral restraint," by which Malthus meant social conventions and "voluntary abstinence." As later writers would point out, this directly contradicts his core argument that "human nature is such that marked improvement in the level of living of the masses of humanity is biologically impossible" (Dillard 1967, 122). In fact, he now seemed to be apologizing for his first essay, which "was written on the spur of the occasion, and from the few materials which were within my reach in a country situation."

But Malthus's alarming image of unchecked growth has taken on a life of its own ever since. The assumption that population grows exponentially – rather than that it *would* grow exponentially if unchecked – is invoked repeatedly in discussions of resources and population. Here is Garret Hardin in the most cited social science article ever written:

> Population, as Malthus said, naturally tends to grow 'geometrically' … In a finite world this means that the per capita share of the world's goods must steadily decrease".
> *(1968, 1243)[13]*

Malthusian Agriculture

The reason that Malthus could never have conceived of agriculture as a runaway train is that he was positive that agriculture was basically inelastic. He saw the power of the soil as "original and indestructible,"[14] and believed that its improvement could only play a marginal role. In this key passage, Malthus summed up the possibilities for agricultural growth with a shrug:

> premiums might be given for turning up fresh land, and it possible encouragements held out to agriculture above manufactures, and to tillage above grazing. Every endeavour should be used to weaken and destroy all those institutions…which cause the labours of agriculture to be worse paid than the labours of trade and manufactures.
> *(Malthus 1798, 30)*

In other words, you can put more land under the plow. Malthus later makes vague mentions of production increases through changed practices – "When… all the fertile land is occupied, the yearly increase of food will depend upon the amelioration of the land already in possession" – but did not elaborate on how this might work except to note that the potential for "amelioration" would be "gradually diminishing." Throughout his career he was unwavering in his emphasis on how inelastic food production was. In 1830, in his "Summary view of the principle of population" (1970 [1830]), he was still stressing that despite "the prodigious power of increase in animals and vegetables, their actual increase is extremely slow" because of the shortage of fertile land. It was "arrogant and as absurd" to believe that "two ears of wheat should in future grow where only one had grown before" (Malthus 1803, 413).

This perspective on the ultimate inelasticity of agriculture was important at the time because it encapsulated the contrast between the optimistic Enlightenment writers and his dour theory of "nature." But it has proved to be even more important long after the Godwins and Condorcets were relegated to readings lists in history courses. It has evolved into the nearly ubiquitous assumption that the global agricultural system can only produce so much, and it is already producing it.

Ironically, Malthus was writing this during a time of particular growth in farm output, the causes of which were most definitely not his simple mechanism of more land being planted. English agricultural growth at the time is even called revolutionary, although historians disagree on dates for the revolution. Agricultural output in England doubled from 1750 to 1800; between 1801 and 1851 it tripled, and national production *per capita* doubled (Grigg 1980, 163). The amount of cultivated area rose by about a third in the 18th century (Grigg 1980, 177) before declining in the 19th century. Until the watershed in the 1830s when external inputs appeared in the form of fertilizer, the growth in agricultural production came mainly from the process of intensification (the subject of Chapter 7). Productivity per acre had been boosted by a wide range of practices and technologies: increasing labor inputs into tasks like manuring and weeding usually increased yields (Campbell 1983), as did adoption of new crops (such as turnips, clover, and potato), technologies (such as the seed drill), and new forms of animal husbandry (Grigg 1980, 179, Kerridge 1967).

Malthusian Checks

As persistent as his basic postulates about growth of population and agriculture have been, Malthus's even more abiding impact has been on how we think about the *relationship* between the two. Malthus's conviction on this relationship is often taken to be a simple truism: the imbalance between them is a fact of nature, and so must be mechanisms to check population. As summarized by one of his many followers:

> Wherever Providence sends meat He will send mouths. Wherever the people have room and food, they will marry and multiply their numbers, till they press against the limits of both, and begin a fierce struggle for existence, in which death is the punishment for defeat. Godwin and the whole French school are sadly wrong in attributing all inequality to human institutions; human nature is to blame.
>
> *(Bonar 1885, 20)*

But what actually happened when human numbers press against the limits of room and food was the crux of Malthusian theory. The core of the theory concerns the *indirect* ways in which nature checks population in the struggle for existence: although population tends to outgrow the food supply, it is not actually food shortage that normally checks population growth. Instead he described three levels of positive checks, of which famine was only "the last, the most dreadful resource of nature." Most people were killed off before that by something that obsessed Malthus: "vice." He wrote:

> The power of population is so superior to the power in the earth to produce subsistence for man, that premature death must in some shape or other visit the human race. The vices of mankind are active and able ministers of depopulation. They are the precursors in the great army of destruction; and often finish the dreadful work themselves.

It is only if vices "fail in this war of extermination" that things get really nasty and move to the second level of disease, in which

> sickly seasons, epidemics, pestilence, and plague, advance in terrific array, and sweep off their thousands and ten thousands.

Finally, and only if depopulation is still not "successful," then

> gigantic inevitable famine stalks in the rear, and with one mighty blow levels the population with the food of the world
>
> *(1798, 44).*

Malthus's enthusiasm for attributing a wide range of diverse phenomena to overpopulation, and to claim them to be natural checks on depopulation, has been among his most emulated habits of thought. This is despite the fact that the logic of these population-checking mechanisms disintegrates upon inspection. Consider that the "vices" that he cited as "able ministers of depopulation" included lack of "attention to children," "unwholesome trades," "drinking, gaming, and debauchery," and dirty houses. He even saw cities themselves as a vice, and extolled a vice-free world in which "crowds no longer collect together in great and pestilent cities for purposes of court intrigue, of commerce, and vicious gratifications." Later editions of the essay would expand the list of vices to include "all unwholesome occupations, severe labour and exposure to the seasons, extreme poverty, bad nursing of children, great towns, excesses of all kinds" (Malthus 1826). Waxing more prudish than logical, he added to the list of vices "promiscuous intercourse, unnatural passions, violations of the marriage bed, and improper arts to conceal the consequences of irregular connexions" (Malthus 1803, 11).[15]

The logic here, or lack thereof, is important. As historical geographer David Grigg points out, Malthus

> never makes clear the relationship between population growth, the positive checks and the means of subsistence…by the 'means of subsistence' he appears to mean the food supply, yet most of his positive checks were … in no way related to the food supply
>
> *(Grigg 1980, 13)*

I would be less gentle in assessing these crucial mechanisms: promiscuity, adultery, bad nursing, and the artful hiding of irregular connexions (whatever the hell that is) are obviously not nature's ways of alleviating crowding.

Malthus's belief that "living in towns" was a vice that lowered population was in a sense true, although it was hardly a natural mechanism as Malthus imagined. Late 19th century England was unique in Europe in how rapidly its population was moving to the city: by 1850 41% of the population in England and Wales would be urban, as compared to only 14% and 11% in France and Germany, respectively (Wood 2000, 37). Many of the people leaving the countryside had been dispossessed by Enclosure movements, and as they gravitated toward cities they had no choice but to work cheap and also buy cheap consumables, thus providing two key drivers of Britain's Industrial Revolution. Their lives as urban workers were often squalid indeed, but this was not because the city was a natural check on population but rather because they were poor and lacking in political resources to create healthier conditions. Friedrich Engels would famously show how living conditions had worsened with the spread of mills (Engels 1993[1845]).

And what about the second level: how is disease linked to overpopulation? Malthus was convinced that not just endemic disease but even plagues and epidemics could be partly chalked up to "crowded population and unwholesome and insufficient food" (Malthus 1798, 36). But infectious disease is not a normal result of food/population imbalance except in cases where hunger or malnutrition makes people more likely to catch the disease and less able to survive it (Grigg 1980). Malthus proposed that disease susceptibility came about as population outraced food and "a greater number would be crowded together in one house." It is unclear why people would start moving in together when they got hungry; the high-population density Kofyar from Chapter 1 lived in dispersed small-family compounds.

Even famine, the third and final positive check, while obviously linked to food supply, is "not necessarily a function of population growth; famines were a result of harvest failure due to bad weather or plant disease and the poor communications that made it difficult to transport grain to afflicted areas" (Grigg 1980, 13).

A final oddity is how little weight Malthus gave to armed conflict as a positive check. He mentions warfare several times in *Population*, but largely neglects it in his examination of the "active and able ministers of depopulation." He does refer to the "constant war that prevails among savages" (Malthus 1798, Chapter 3) although not to constant war between his country and France. But through the years, warfare has often featured prominently in accounts of population as being limited only by positive checks of "disease, famine, and fighting" (as William Vogt (1948, 226) put it, writing about India 20 years before Ehrlich and saying almost exactly the same thing).

In the end, it seems that Malthus, after lambasting Godwin for the "error of attributing all the vices of mankind to human institutions," himself attributes almost everything that goes wrong to population. And he does so with almost no viable causal mechanisms. This is perhaps the most profound and problematic legacy of Robert Malthus's, as countless writers in succeeding generations would not only point to population growth as an ominous and inexorable danger, but would attribute all manner of social ills to population even where there was no rational causal mechanism.

Backlash

Godwin's initial reaction may have been cordial, but *Population* was met with "an unprecedented eruption of fury" (James 1966, xv). "For thirty years it rained refutations" one biographer later wrote (Bonar 1885, 1). He was "the best abused man of the age...

who defended small-pox, slavery, and child-murder" (Bonar 1885, 1–2), a monster, a sycophant, a hypocrite. He was likened to a mischievous reptile, to menstrual pollution, to diarrhea of the intellect (Mayhew 2014, 88). "I have, in my life, detested many men," wrote William Cobbett in an 1819 open letter; "but never any one so much as you" (Mayhew 2014, 128).

Some Malthus followers have complained that he is misunderstood, or that the critics haven't actually read it: "there has probably never been anyone attacked and defended with so little regard for what he has written" (Wrigley 1986). *Population*, according to one Malthus biographer, "is a book which no one reads but all abuse" (Bonar 1885, 3). It is hardly true that all abused *Population*, but its detractors were legion, and from the beginning they raised objections concerning that are important for us to consider, especially as concerned religion and political economy.

Religion: What Kind of God?

Some of the most vociferous pushback to Malthus was based on religion. Many writers at the time assumed that the laws of human population growth, like other laws of nature, were controlled by God and could be inferred from the Bible. For instance, humans were made to live longer and breed more rapidly after the Great Flood in order to repopulate the Earth, after which lives were shortened and breeding proclivities were adjusted accordingly (Jarrold 1806). The idea that God would have muffed the population growth rates left many incredulous.[16]

But from the religious perspective, the real elephant in the room was that Malthus's God had created a world in which "vice and misery" were central to human ecology. How could God enjoin humans to "be fruitful and multiply" if multiplication caused rampant misery? (Malthus's discovery of "moral restraint" in the second edition made for a slightly rosier view of the world, but it is the dour view of the *First Essay* that has dominated thinking.) To reconcile this devastating design flaw in nature with a loving deity, Malthus opined that God had set up the imbalance between population and agriculture to get people's attention and force them to mental fight. This was His way of creating the "strong excitements" needed to get humans to exert themselves and to "form the reasoning faculty." Or, as one historian put it, "God put us all on short rations so that we could sharpen our wits" (Binion 1999, 568).[17] This God was oddly fixated on forcing humans to farm industriously, as he "ordained that population should increase much faster than food" in order to "urge man to further the gracious designs of Providence by the full cultivation of the earth."

Unanswered was the obvious question of why, if savage subsistence practices were so offensive to God that he relied on rampant misery to get people to avoid them, He had people practicing them in the first place. Malthus admitted the scheme was imperfect: "This general law…undoubtedly produces much partial evil, but a little reflection may, perhaps, satisfy us, that it produces a great overbalance of good." But this explanation only works if God is both vicious and inept: his population-agriculture imbalance tactic for bringing out the best in people was the paramount cause of all societal maladies. Malthus appears not to have believed in hell, regarding it as inconsistent with a loving God, and yet the same God would create a hell on Earth, featuring the inexorable immiseration of the poor because He wanted to have people thinking and plowing as much as possible.[18]

Political Economy: Who Is Looking Out for Whose Interests?

Another set of criticisms held that *Population* was politics masquerading as science. It is certainly true that, while presenting itself as a scientific study of the natural imbalance between agriculture and population, *Population* was explicitly a work of politics and economic policy. Malthus was clear that poverty and hunger were part of nature, with the poor complicit in their own plight, and from these truths he extrapolated broad principles (aid for the poor will only worsen their plight) and specific policy implications (England's welfare laws were counterproductive). The contrast to the prevailing Enlightenment conviction that social problems resulted purely from social institutions, which could be improved (even "perfected"), could not have been more stark.

Many saw *Population* as a "sinister attempt to excuse the massive inequities and injustices of the prevailing social order" (McCoy 1980, 260) – a "political bible of the rich" (Mayhew 2014, 87). Malthus was not just a philosopher who had innocently gotten it wrong, but a public relations agent for the Industrial Revolution elites who were amassing fortunes on the backs of the poor. The literary critic and philosopher William Hazlitt denounced him as "the overseer of a workhouse…disguised in the garb of philosophy," using false logic and garbled calculations (Mayhew 2014, 91).

This criticism came most forcefully from Marx and Engels some years later. Karl Marx was left spluttering with rage at the political subtext of *Population*, which claimed that it is "from the inevitable laws of nature" that even a perfectly conceived society would soon degenerate into "a society divided into a class of proprietors, and a class of labourers" (Malthus 1798, 64–65). Marx wrote scornfully that the working classes were right in believing Malthus to not be a "man of science…a shameless sycophant of the ruling classes" (Meek 1971).[19] It was "nothing more than a schoolboyish, superficial plagiary" that attracted attention only because it was so convenient for the elite (Marx 1967 [1867], chap. 25 note 6).[20]

It is true that the key ideas in *Population* had been published before, but had attracted less attention because they suited contemporary political interests less. It was, in other words, not a significant step forward in thinking about poverty so much as a repackaging perfectly timed to be convenient to early Industrial Revolution magnates. The new regime of factory production powered by disenfranchised laborers was born in England in the 1770s. Malthusian theory proved invaluable in shifting blame for hunger, poverty, and ill health onto human reproduction – a function it still fulfills today in some circles. In the case of early 19th century England, the political-economic impacts were substantial. We will see the role played by Malthusian theory (and by Malthus himself) in handling the Irish famine in the 1840s, but well before that his influence was unmistakable in changes in English welfare policy. The "New Poor Law," passed in 1834 (also the year of Malthus's death), widely acknowledged to have been shaped by Malthus's theories, restricted aid to harsh workhouses.[21] To Engels, the law and Malthus's theories behind it were an "open declaration of war" on the poor (Engels 1993[1845]).

But despite Marx's and Engels' bitter disagreements with Malthus, they did agree on one key point: reason. Recall that at the core of the Enlightenment intellectual project was the notion of reason, a direct challenge to the church and divine revelation. Malthus was a clergyman but he was not defending divine revelation. On the contrary, his theory was entirely materialistic, based on the supposed biological facts of demography and agriculture. What people thought about the situation was a result of these material conditions, not a driver;

God had supposedly created overpopulation to get people's attention and make them industrious. To Malthus it all stemmed from the material conditions of biology, and to Marx it stemmed from the material conditions of economies, but they agreed that human events were not under the control of reason.

A Case of Bad Timing? Malthus's Moment in History

Another challenge to Malthusian theory is one that not only specifies why he was wrong but also exonerates him. It is a critique that has been endorsed by several historians and economists. In this view, Malthus described the dynamics of a world that was disappearing as he wrote about it (Mayhew 2014, 133). In this view, the fundamental rules of population and food production were being rewritten by the Industrial Revolution. As argued by historian Edward Wrigley (2010, 1962), Malthus wrote his book in the twilight of the "organic economy" in which productivity was limited by the energy from the sun, as harnessed in the form of agrarian production, and augmented by wind and water power. The Industrial Revolution brought large-scale capture of fossil energy, particularly with coal-fired steam engines in textile factories. Therefore it was Malthus's fate "to frame an analysis of the relationship between population, economy and society during the last generation to which it was applicable" (Wrigley 1986, 4). Economist Paul Krugman agrees: "We only think Malthus got it wrong because the two centuries he was wrong about were the two centuries that followed the publication of his work," he writes; "The fact is that Malthus was right about *the whole of human history up until his own era*" (2008, italics original). So Malthus's theory flopped because the world was changing with the incorporation of energy from fossil fuels.

But is the energy theory true? Did Malthus explain the dynamics of agriculture and population and poverty that existed up until the time he wrote it? I am not convinced. The early decades of England's Industrial Revolution were actually powered almost entirely by water, a classic source of "organic economy" energy that was much cheaper than coal and steam engines. The Industrial Revolution was well under way when *Population* appeared in 1798, but that year there were only 84 steam engines powering British cotton mills as compared to around 1,000 water wheels. Wheel systems were even being enlarged and improved (Malm 2013, 27). Fossil fuel did not overtake water in British mills until the 1830s, and not because of any resource shortages but because steam power allowed factories to move to cities where owners had greater control over their laborers (Malm 2013, 36).

It is difficult to escape the harsh conclusion that Malthus's theory fit the pre-Industrial Revolution world as poorly as it fit what came after.

Proof: Malthus and Famine

We know that Malthus's theory, contrary to how it is often portrayed, wasn't really about famines: he expected actual starvation to only be nature's final resort for the rare cases when vice and disease failed in their job. But while Malthus's theory wasn't about famines, most famines have been about Malthus's theory. Every famine since 1798 has been ascribed by some observers to overpopulation, almost always with explicit references to Malthus. In this section we will look more closely at the most important of these, the Irish "Potato Famine" of 1845–1849, which was taken by many as indisputable proof of Malthusian principles. We will then look more briefly at major famines in India.

The Irish Great Famine

Ireland's Great Famine of 1845–1849 has long served as a textbook example of Malthusian principles in action. Ireland's population rose from around 4 million in 1780 to just over 8 million in 1845 (Connell 1950, Grigg 1980). Malthus died in 1834 so he never saw this famine, but he saw the preceding population buildup as confirming that population would grow as fast as the food supply allowed. He blamed the potato for lowering the age of marriage and boosting population, noting that "the cheapness of this nourishing root, and the small piece of ground which, under this kind of cultivation, will in average years produce the food for a family...[has] prompted them to follow their inclinations" and land themselves "in the most impoverished and miserable state" (Malthus 1826). He felt the Irish also confirmed his theory of positive checks operating mostly through indirect mechanisms, with death coming from "damp and wretched cabins" and poor clothing (Malthus 1826). In 1831 the potato crop failed and minor famine hit, providing Malthus with further validation of his theory.

Many contemporary observers also saw the Irish and their potatoes as confirming *Population*'s subtext of the poor lacking industry, morality, and worth. "Rural improver" Ninian Niven berated the Irishman for the "mania" with which he grew "his favorite root" and for refusing to adopt "a more rational and productive system of tillage" (Niven 1846, 23). Writers were still linking potato growing, overpopulation, and the disgraceful personality traits of the Irish a century later. Redfield Salaman's *History and Social Influence of the Potato* explains that

> The more the potato fulfilled the requirements of the household, the sooner was endeavour damped down and sloth and slovenliness exalted. As time went on, the sequence-poverty, potatoes; larger families, more potatoes, and greater poverty, became ever more firmly established, till nothing but revolution or catastrophe could break it.
>
> *(Salaman 1949, 343)*

"Only in Ireland," writes Eric Ross (1998, 39), "among the potato-eating regions of Europe, was the vicious circle posited that the potato made people lazy, while their laziness led them to depend solely on the potato."

The Great Famine was triggered by a plant disease called Late Blight, which could turn a potato field to a blackened ruin in 4 days (Turner 2005, 342).[22] It struck the eastern US in 1843 and Belgium in 1845, spreading quickly across Western Europe with significant losses to potato crops but no severe famines. But 1846 was a different story: potato yields recovered somewhat in Belgium and the Netherlands, but remained poor elsewhere, and crashed catastrophically in the Scottish Highlands and Ireland (Vanhaute, Paping, and Gráda 2007).

The severity of the famines varied across Europe, but nowhere suffered devastation approaching what happened in Ireland, where an estimated 88% of the 1846 potato crop was ruined; by horrendous coincidence the 1846 rye, wheat, and oat harvests were also disastrous. By 1847 the blight had abated but with no seed potato to plant, severe food scarcity continued until 1850. There were an estimated 1 million deaths between 1845 and 1850 and approximately a million more emigrated – out of a pre-blight population of 8.2 million. The actual cause of most deaths was recorded as disease such as typhoid fever, typhus, or dysentery (which spread like wildfire through over-crowded workhouses) (Mokyr and Ó Gráda 2002). But mortality from indirect causes rather than outright starvation seemed to fit Malthus's theory of the indirect nature of positive checks.

If Malthus's Dismal Theorem seemed to explain the cause of the disaster, his Utterly Dismal Theorem guided England's handling of the situation in its colony. Prime Minister John Russell viewed the crisis with "a Malthusian fear about the long-term effect of relief" (Prest 1972, 271). This view was shared by his choice to head the relief effort: treasury undersecretary Charles Trevelyan, who was not only a follower of Malthus but a former student in Malthus's classroom at the East India College, Haileybury. In a book he published in the middle of the famine, Trevelyan identified the real problem to be "surplus population" that remained despite "every practicable remedy." Still, a "deep and inveterate root of social evil remained, and this has been laid bare by a direct stroke of an all-wise and all-merciful Providence" (Trevelyan 1848, 201). A loving God was trimming the Irish herd.

Trevelyan put Malthusian principles into practice. While independent European countries hit by the blight imported food to make up for the shortfall, England offered scant aid to its starving colony. Relief policies were even designed to expropriate land from Irish cottagers: the poor relief act of 1847 denied aid to anyone owning more than a quarter acre of land, forcing tenants to relinquish land holdings (Ross 1998, 48).[23]

To ease any cognitive dissonance from crediting the handiwork of a merciful God with millions of peasants and their children starving, the Irish were often cast as deserving of divine wrath. Trevelyan wrote:

> The judgement of God sent the calamity to teach the Irish a lesson, that calamity must not be too much mitigated. ...he real evil with which we have to contend is not the physical evil of the Famine, but the moral evil of the selfish, perverse and turbulent character of the people.[24]

But while it is true that Ireland suffered a catastrophic famine after a sustained rise in population, Ireland had also suffered a crop failure and famine in 1740, long before the population surge. The 1740 famine was actually worse in relative demographic terms than the Great Famine (Ross 1998, 39–40). There had then been smaller famines in 1800, 1817, 1822, and 1831 (Ó Gráda 1998, 52), all when Ireland's population was not high by European standards (Grigg 1980, 138).

The population in Ireland in the 1840s unquestionably could have been supported with the agricultural technology available at the time. The real problem was poverty resulting largely from land ownership patterns: many of the 8 million Irish were scraping by as tenant farmers on small parcels rented from absentee landlords, and over one third of rural households were landless (Grigg 1980, 120–123).[25] The only way to feed a family on such plots that were often under a hectare in size was by growing potatoes, which offered up to three times the calories per acre as wheat (Grigg 1980, 125) and provided all major vitamins and nutrients except vitamin A and D, which could be provided by a small amount of dairy.[26] The potato is the true superfood (Nunn and Qian 2011, 599). It could also be fed to pigs which could bring desperately needed income. A potato crop could even be squeezed in between plantings of wheat, which was grown mainly for sale (Nunn and Qian 2011, 601). For the landless, potatoes were by far the most affordable food. Rather than being the Irishman's "lazy root" (Niven 1846), potatoes required approximately 2.5 times more labor input per acre cultivated than wheat, oats, or barley (Turner 1996). But they kept the peasants alive, and as many as half of the Irish peasantry lived virtually entirely on potatoes in the 1840s.

Intensive smallholder agriculture (Chapter 7) has often supported denser populations sustainably. But intensive smallholder agriculture was severely impeded here by tenant farmers lacking the land security needed to invest in land improvements. In fact, cottagers often found that when they did improve the land their rent went up (Regan 1983, 107). They also owed rent and taxes. The poorest cottagers, especially in the western provinces, were attempting to practice intensive agriculture, with potato and wheat yields comparable to anywhere in Europe (Grigg 1980, 127) and small-scale production of valuable cows and pigs, but the wheat was mainly to pay the rent and the pigs were mainly for occasional infusions of cash. Much of the wheat and pork left the island, often bound for England. While it is true that population was growing rapidly during the first half of the 19th century, food exports from the island were growing even faster. After 1784, when Britain passed a Corn Law subsidizing grain exports, Ireland's wheat exports to England rose steadily; by the 1830s, 406,000 tons of grain (principally wheat and oats) were being exported yearly, enough to feed 2 million people (Grigg 1980, 124). Livestock exports actually increased during the famine: in 1846 alone, at the height of the famine, Ireland exported an astonishing 730,000 cattle and pigs (Kinealy 2002, 105–111).

On the receiving end, Britain enjoyed an "extraordinary increase in the home supplies of corn" [i.e. grain] in the two decades before 1845, with increased food consumption and a surge in the number of horses fed on Irish oats (Anon 1854, 391). It is likely that in the 1820s Prof. Malthus, who blamed Irish food shortages on the poor having too many babies, and his student Charles Trevelyan, who would implement policies promoting Irish starvation, were both dining on Irish pork, beef, and wheat, and riding horses fed on Irish oats. As John Mitchel put it, "This million and a half, then, died of hunger in the midst of abundance, which their own hands created...Almighty God sent the potato-blight, but the English created the famine" (Mitchel 1905, 49).

Robert Malthus may have been Professor of Political Economy at the East India Company College, but Ireland can only be seen as a Malthusian disaster by ignoring the political economy.

Other Famines

Robert Malthus, his student Charles Trevelyan, and many pundits through the ages have looked at Irish food shortages and believed they saw the workings of important general principles of population and food. And in a sense they were just not the principles Malthus championed; it seems to be a general principle that whenever hunger rears its head, there are parties with vested interests in too-many-people explanations and many people are quickly persuaded. Of the many examples apart from Ireland, we will briefly consider one because of its odd parallels.

India's 1876–1878 famine was triggered by an unusually intense El Niño event that brought severe drought to most of southern India with summer monsoon precipitation dropping by as much as 75%. Such a climatic event obviously poses a major challenge for any government's ability to manage emergencies, and the British colonial government's failure was truly tragic, with an estimated 6–10 million Indians succumbing to starvation or related disease like dysentery. In rhetoric reminiscent of Ireland's Great Famine, the colonial viceroy, Lord Lytton, blamed Indians for having a population that had "a tendency to increase more rapidly than the food it raises from the soil" (Davis 2002, 32). The colonial finance minister insisted that "[E]very benevolent attempt made to mitigate the effects of famine and defective sanitation serves but to enhance the evils resulting from overpopulation." True to Malthusian dogma, a government report later asserted that

> 80% of the famine mortality were drawn from the poorest 20% of the population, and if such deaths were prevented this stratum of the population would still be unable to adopt prudential restraint. Thus, if the government spent more of its revenue on famine relief, an even larger proportion of the population would become penurious.
> *(Davis 2002, 32)*

Environmental historian Mike Davis (2002) debunks this self-serving account of a population-driven disaster. In the first place, the British colonial state (called "The Raj") had spread poverty for decades leading up to the 1870s. They had marginalized or crushed indigenous manufacturing institutions and extracted enormous wealth in the form of taxes to support British military adventures. Taxes on food producers were especially onerous as they were fixed to production averages rather than what individual farmers actually produced, ensuring that numerous farmers lost their land each year. The taxes also forced farmers to grow more cash crops and less nutritious food crops (including nitrogen-fixing legumes). The Raj seized control of commons that had formerly provided resources such as wood, dung, and water that were especially crucial to poor families.

Under British rule India had established a pattern of frequent famines even before 1876. But the failure of the monsoon for two years running in 1876–1877 created a dire situation that demanded an effective humanitarian response. Instead the response of the Raj was ineffective and vicious. Starving applicants for relief work were required to travel to distant dormitory camps for coolie labor on railroad and canal projects. Laborers were prohibited from seeking relief until "they had become indigent, destitute and capable of only a modicum of labour," and a deliberately cruel "distance test" forced able-bodied individuals to walk at least ten miles to get work. For those who were given relief work, rations were more meager than in Nazi concentration camps. The Raj did nothing to prevent grain speculation as the famine raged, insisting that the market needed to remain unfettered. It was "free market economics as a mask for colonial genocide," concludes Davis. As in Ireland before, "those with the power to relieve famine convinced themselves that overly heroic exertions against implacable natural laws, whether of market prices or population growth, were worse than no effort at all" (Davis 2002, 32).[27]

The last parallel with Ireland is the quantities of food exported from India as its peasants starved due to "food shortage." India exported a record 358,000 tons of wheat to UK in 1877–1878 (Davis 2002, 31–32).

Neo-Malthusianism

Malthus's belief in population growth as an irresistible force is still with us, as is his fondness for blaming population for all manner of problems, even with no credible causal link. Paul Ehrlich blamed everything "from rubbish to riots" on population (1969), and has gone on to blame population for global warming and other unconnected problems. Ecologist Paul Colinvaux flatly states that "All poverty is caused by the continued growth of population" (Colinvaux 1978, 222).

But while core elements of original Malthusianism live on, what has come to be more common and more influential are "neo-Malthusian" perspectives in which some key element of original theory has been adjusted or even reversed. The first neo-Malthusian was Malthus himself, who reversed his position on preventive checks between the first (1798) and second (1803) editions of *Population* as noted above. There is also a long history of neo-Malthusians who accept Malthus's view of population as an inexorable force and source of human misery but reverse his hostility toward contraception.[28] But the neo-Malthusianism central to our story concerns the importance of technology in agricultural growth. This is the sacred dogma underlying industrialized agriculture, and what I refer to as neo-Malthusianism is shorthand for what would properly be called Industrial neo-Malthusianism.

Malthus, despite his conviction that overpopulation was God's way of pushing humans to improve their farming, was decidedly cool on agricultural innovation. He saw food shortage as "so deeply seated that no human ingenuity can reach it" (Malthus 1798, 30). This perspective has changed little in some quarters since 1798. As Paul Ehrlich and the leaders of the 1970s environmental movement saw it, "since resources grow only arithmetically if at all, our exponential growth in population and in consumption levels is bound to bring us up against scarcity, shortages (even widespread famine) and the destruction of life on the planet" (Matthaei 1984, 83).

Neo-Malthusians replace this doctrine of fixed limits in agriculture with a belief in agricultural growth through development of technology. They retain Malthus's convictions on inexorable population growth, and even ramp up the demographic anxiety by citing the successes of modern medicine in keeping people alive (e.g., Borlaug 1988, 16), but they see agricultural science as a solution. This perspective gained momentum after World War II. "Modern science has the answer to Malthus," Orr and Lubbock insisted in their 1953 book *White Man's Dilemma: Food and the Future* (1953, 80). In his influential 1964 *Transforming Traditional Agriculture*, economist Theodore Schultz explained that peasant farmers could only boost production if "modern" technologies could be developed for them. "Malthus foiled again and again" tells us that salvation from disaster comes from the science of fertilizer and seeds (Trewavas 2002, 668). This reconfiguring of the Dismal Theorem has been invoked to justify every occasion on which agriculture is penetrated by a new external technology, even if the technology did not actually feed any more people – as we will see with the Green Revolution.

Green Revolution hero Norman Borlaug was the perfect embodiment of neo-Malthusianism. He repeatedly cited the inexorable power of population growth which he blamed for a dazzling range of social ills in the dubious manner of Malthus himself. But while Malthus had fretted over population growth causing sexual deviance and infidelity, Borlaug blamed it for loss of personal freedom and absence of world peace (Borlaug 1999[1970]). Population was "a monster," and it exasperated him that this was not appreciated by obstreperous college students with their love-ins (Borlaug et al. 1969). He was zealous in his belief in science as the only antidote, and his 1970 Nobel acceptance speech insisted that "we are dealing with two opposing forces, the scientific power of food production and the biologic power of human reproduction" (Borlaug 1970). That "scientific power" inevitably meant commercial technologies sold by private corporations, for which Borlaug was a persistent and combative proponent (Saha 2013, 307). He would appear in press conferences organized by the pesticide industry and promote proclamations on "High-Yield Farming" from the Hudson Institute, a think tank supported by the agricultural chemical industry (Sumberg,

Keeney, and Dempsey 2012). Late in life Borlaug was a militant proponent of the agricultural biotechnology industry and a disdainful critic of its detractors.

Borlaug's implacable conviction that agricultural technology was the way to avert starvation is remarkable given his own account of his formative first experience with hunger. On a trip to Minneapolis in 1933, the 19-year-old Borlaug happened upon a caravan of dairymen dumping milk in the streets, followed by hungry people desperately trying to scoop up the milk as they dodged baton-swinging cops. He claimed to have been profoundly affected by the scene and what it taught him: that "extreme hunger had more than just the stomach in its clutches; it strongly influenced the mind" (20th Century Time Machine 2016). This is an utterly perverse take-away for the budding neo-Malthusian. A more realistic lesson to be learned from witnessing one of the Depression-era milk strikes was that extreme hunger had absolutely nothing to do with population outpacing agriculture, and that starvation – Americans actually did starve to death during the Depression (Poppendieck 1985, xv) – often occurs alongside food surplus. Everyone knew that the milk was being dumped because *overproduction* had undercut milk prices so badly that dairies were going bankrupt (Wise 2019, 113). Elsewhere in the country, surplus oranges were being soaked in kerosene to prevent their consumption while communities in Appalachia were trying to stay alive on dandelions and wild greens (Poppendieck 1985, xv). Corn was so cheap that it was being burned for fuel, while cows, sheep, and horses were starving. Thousands stood in breadlines while the government sat on 160 million bushels of wheat it could not get rid of. The situation was hardly a secret; as one Congressman put it, "everyone knows...we have an abundance of food and yet there is widespread hunger" (Poppendieck 1985, 60–65). Breadlines, observed commentator James Crowther, were "knee-deep in wheat" (Poppendieck 1985, vx).

As we look in following chapters at key agricultural technologies, we will ask why they rose to dominance. The neo-Malthusian answer would always be the same: to keep up with population's food needs however we can. The assumption at the heart of neo-Malthusianism – that food production is forever in need of increase and that increase only comes from external technologies – flies in the face of such a large amount of research on intensive farmers, as we will see in the final chapter. But let us now turn our attention to the second form of agricultural growth – the industrialized agriculture that rationalized by neo-Malthusianism.

Notes

1 In college Malthus was advised against a career in the church because of his speech impediment, the result of a cleft palate. But Robert wrote his father of his wish for "a retired living in the country" where his speech would not be a problem (James 1979, 30). Interestingly, the first Malthus ancestor about whom much is known was his great-great-grandfather, also Robert Malthus, a clergyman in Middlesex. In 1660 his parishioners petitioned Oliver Cromwell to have him removed, complaining that he "hath not only a low voyce, but a very great impediment in his utterance, soe that your petitioners cannot receive any benefit by him" (McCleary 1953, 19). Our Robert was ordained a year after graduating, despite having taken no courses in theology (Pullen 1987, 131–132).

2 Rousseau also was a believer in the social and political benefits of population growth, writing that "All other things being equal, the government under which …the citizens increase and multiply the most, is infallibly the best government. That under which the people diminishes and wastes away is the worst" (Mayhew 2014, 25). He did visit once when Robert was an infant.

3 This is calculated by using the average earnings deflator.

4 However other British observers of agriculture were on the side of the peasants. In Chapter 4 we will meet Sir William Crookes, the late 19th century scientist who insisted that the British were "born wheat eaters" as compared to the more backward races.

5 Much has been written on the fundamental role Malthusian thinking has played in the eugenics movements that culminated with the Nazis; readers interested in this shameful but important history may begin with Eric Ross's *The Malthus Factor* (1998) and Allan Chase's *The Legacy of Malthus* (1977).

6 This cannot be blamed on a lack of demographic literature. The Enlightenment polymath Richard Price had published the results of determined efforts to identify Britain's population trends in his massive volume *Observations* in 1771 (Price 1771). Price concluded – and lamented – that British population was declining based on analysis of patterns across parish registers.

7 Godwin followed this much-discussed treatise by publishing a play, the title of which – more than a little ironic, given his flights of fancy – was *Things As They Are* (1794). This, of course, was precisely the catch-phrase with which Malthus would associate himself when he had dispatched Godwin.

8 Godwin surely appreciated the fact that his wife had become famous in the same way a few years before: Mary Wollstonecraft's anonymous *A Vindication of the Rights of Men* (1790) had shredded a recent book by conservative theorist Edmund Burke. Wollstonecraft had even skewered Godwin himself in print before they became close; Godwin had been magnanimous then too. After first meeting her in 1796, Godwin noted that although she "has frequently amused herself with deprecating me," he was "as prompt to do justice to an enemy as to a friend" (Sunstein 1975, 298).

9 Although not publicly revealed until publication of the second edition of *Population* in 1803, Malthus was known as the anonymous author in London's political/literary circles immediately. Publisher Joseph Johnson's house was a crossroads of the English intelligentsia.

10 Godwin's marriage to Mary Wollstonecraft provides a fascinating footnote to this era. Brilliant and unconventional, Mary was the first woman to carve out a career as a writer in Britain (Sunstein 1975). She was most famous (and controversial) for iconoclastic views on gender that would be called feminism when she was rediscovered her two centuries later. Wollstonecraft's first book, *Thoughts on the Education of Daughters* (1787), railed against the training of girls to play a decorative role in society. She expanded this theme in *A Vindication of the Rights of Woman* (1792), a founding text of modern feminism. Despite Godwin's critiques of the institution of marriage, the two married in 1797 after she became pregnant. Mary died soon after giving birth and so she never knew a daughter of whom she would have been proud. This daughter, under her married name of Mary Shelley, wrote one of the English language's most famous novels while still a teenager: *Frankenstein; or, The Modern Prometheus*. Godwin later published a controversial biography of Wollstonecraft (Godwin 1798). The book's unusually frank account of Mary's unconventional attitudes, suicide attempts, and love affairs was too much for contemporary mores, and she remained a marginal writer until her rediscovery in the 1960s.

11 In contrast to Godwin, who outlived his fame, Condorcet died in his prime, under suspicious circumstances, before *Population* was published. Although he had been a leader in the French Revolution, he had a severe falling-out with Robespierre, fled in disguise, and was later arrested and died in prison (Mayhew 2014, 40).

12 The 1803 edition was ponderously titled *An Essay on the Principle of Population, or, A View of Its Past and Present Effects on Human Happiness with an Inquiry into Our Prospects Respecting the Future Removal or Mitigation of the Evils Which It Occasions.*

13 In the years after World War II the warnings of exponential growth were often linked to improved medicine and antibiotics, as in 1950 when national science leader and futurologist Vannevar Bush argued that improving public health was creating the danger that population would "increase exponentially without limit, exhaust the resources of the earth, and leave a few miserable remnants crawling about in barbarism."

14 That phrase actually came from economist David Ricardo (1817), who agreed with Malthus on this key point (Foster 1999, 374).

15 Bafflingly, Malthus also designates these sexual acts as "preventive checks."

16 Writing in 1821, Piercy Ravenstone had merciless fun with Malthus's ratios by putting them into Biblical chronologies. Assuming Bishop Ussher's date of 4004 BC for the start of the world, he calculated that if Adam and Eve had just enough food for themselves, then the contemporary

world population had to be living on just enough food for 1,328 persons. Or if counted backward, then Adam and Eve would have had enough food for 6 million, which meant that Adam (blasphemously) didn't have to live by the sweat of his brow. But following the flood he dated to 2349 BC, if Noah's descendants had really doubled at the rate that Malthus cited – every 25 years – population would have reached 200 million in 6.5 centuries while food would only be enough for 162 million.

> Unless any country can be adduced in which men have been able to live without food, we are inevitably compelled to believe, that for the last 3500 years the geometrical and arithmetical ratios have jogged on quietly side by side.
>
> (Ravenstone 1821, 161–163)

17 This justification was cribbed from a 1786 book by welfare skeptic Joseph Townsend, in which he derided the poor who

> by their indolence and extravagance, by their drunkenness and vices…know little of the motives which stimulate the higher ranks to action – pride, honour, and ambition. In general it is only hunger which can spur and goad them on to labour…as the most natural motive to industry, it calls forth the most powerful exertions. Hunger will tame the fiercest animals, it will teach decency and civility, obedience and subjugation to the most brutish, the most obstinate, and the most perverse.
>
> (Townsend 1786, 15)

The same sentiment appears bluntly in *Population* in a passage deleted in later editions, noting that man is "inert, sluggish, and averse from labour," and would have never "emerged from the savage state" without food shortages (Malthus 1798, 114–115).

18 Rid of its toffish scorn for the poor, the theory of population growth > shortages > poverty > economic improvement has been repackaged several times, as in Richard Wilkinson's *Poverty and Progress: An Ecological Perspective on Economic Development* (1973). Wilkinson sees the animalistic tendency for population to outgrow resources as leading to poverty, which is crucial because humans "do not invent new methods of procurement because they are affluent, but because – and only when – they are poor" (Malm 2013, 22). Wilkinson explains the industrial revolution that was unfolding around Malthus as the result of just this process, with overpopulation forcing "substitution of mineral resources for landbased ones" (Wilkinson 1973, 101). This explanation is as flawed as its original Malthusian inspiration. The Industrial Revolution was famously driven by textile manufacturing in a late 18th century England where there was no shortage of cloth. In fact a primary cause of the new form of production becoming a "revolution" was not shortage but abundance – of cheap slave-grown cotton pouring out of the Americas from the 1790s on (Beckert 2014, 101–104). But most importantly, the Industrial Revolution was not driven by the switch to coal; as explored below (in "A Case of Bad Timing?"), factories were mostly powered by water until over a half-century into the revolution.

19 Many later scholars have arrived at the same conclusion; as population historian Emily Merchant has written recently, "Although Malthus is widely regarded as a scholar of population, the main purpose of his work was not to understand, predict, or control population growth, but rather to justify the existing social order…" (2015, 51).

20 In some ways, Malthus actually took well-known ideas and worsened them. The Malthusian theory of rent is an example. The Scottish writer James Anderson laid out the basic economic theory in 1777, but with a greater emphasis on the possibility of agricultural improvement; this, of course, was precisely the point on which Malthus had a blind spot.

21 These were the workhouses described luridly by Charles Dickens in *Oliver Twist* and *A Christmas Carol*.

22 Late Blight is caused by *Phytophthora infestans* mold, and the strain that rampaged in the 1840s was a uniquely destructive strain that had not been seen before or since.

23 Not everyone was as convinced as English policy-makers that the starving Irish would be better off without help. The Choctaw nation, although profoundly impoverished after their death march from Georgia to Oklahoma in 1831, scraped together a donation of $170. The gesture is still remembered and was commemorated in a plaque unveiled in County Cork in 2015.

24 The famine was commonly viewed in England as proof of the Dismal Theorem – the "promised land of principle of population" as Marx wrote disdainfully (1967 [1867], Chap 25, note 124).

Centuries later this interpretation was still endorsed by major social scientists such as Garrett Hardin (1993, 163) and economist Kenneth Boulding, who saw the potato as the equivalent of foreign aid, a technological improvement that allowed population to jump from 2 to 8 million by 1845, quadrupling the amount of misery on the unfortunate island (Boulding 1956).

25 Malthus felt it obvious that small parcels resulted directly from overpopulation but legislation enacted in 1793 awarded political power to landlords for the number of tenants, which incentivized breaking land into the smallest parcels possible (Regan 1983, 107).

26 Elsewhere in Europe, peasants had had various reactions to the potato after its spread in the 18th century; it became a staple in the Netherlands, as immortalized by Van Gogh's early masterpiece "The Potato Eaters," while Russian peasants staged "potato riots" to protest an edict forcing them to grow potatoes (Messer 1997, 108). Only in Ireland did peasants have no choice, given the meager holdings and the grinding poverty.

27 In a cruel twist of fate, Malthus's student Charles Trevelyan, who had shaped England's Draconian policies during the Irish famine, was the governor of Madras in 1877. Trevelyan also coined the term "feeble minded" in 1876 (McDonagh 2008, 304) – a major contribution to the eugenics movement which would later lead to involuntary sterilization of tens of thousands of Americans who were essentially guilty of nothing more than being born poor.

28 This position was endorsed by some of Malthus's contemporaries (Micklewright 1961), but it came into its own later in the 19th century with the formation of neo-Malthusian Leagues in Europe.

References

20th Century Time Machine. 2016. Norman Borlaug: The Man Who Saved the World From Hunger (online documentary). https://www.youtube.com/watch?v=699T-8aF7Yg.

Anon. 1854. "Corn Laws and Corn Trade." In *The Encyclopaedia Britannica, Or Dictionary of Arts, Sciences, and General Literature, 8th edition, Volume 7.* Edinburgh: Adam and Charles Black, 374–404.

Bashford, Alison, and Joyce E. Chaplin. 2016. *The New Worlds of Thomas Robert Malthus: Rereading the Principle of Population.* Princeton, NJ: Princeton Univ. Press.

Beckert, Sven. 2014. *Empire of Cotton: A Global History.* New York: Vintage.

Binion, Rudolph. 1999. ""More Men than Corn": Malthus versus the Enlightenment, 1798." *Eighteenth-Century Studies* 32 (4):564–569.

Bonar, James. 1885. *Malthus and His Work.* London: McMillan and Co.

Borlaug, Norman E. 1970. "Acceptance Speech." Nobel Prize, 10 December. Oslo. http://www.nobelprize.org/nobel_prizes/peace/laureates/1970/borlaug-acceptance.html.

Borlaug, Norman E. 1999[1970]. "The Green Revolution, peace, and humanity." In *Nobel Lectures in Peace 1951-1970,* edited by Frederick W. Haberman, pp. 445–480. Singapore: World Scientific Publishing.

Borlaug, Norman E. 1988. "Challenges for Global Food and Fiber Production." *Journal of the Royal Swedish Academy of Agriculture and Forestry Supplement* 21:15–55.

Borlaug, Norman E., Ignacio Navarez, Oddvar Aresvik, and R. Glenn Anderson. 1969. "A Green Revolution Yields a Golden Harvest." *Columbia Journal of World Business* 5:9–19.

Boulding, Kenneth. 1956. *The Image: Knowledge in Life and Society.* Ann Arbor: Univ. of Michigan Press.

Brundage, Anthony. 1978. *The Making of the New Poor Law.* New Brunswick, NJ: Rutgers Univ. Press.

Campbell, Bruce M. S. 1983. "Agricultural Progress in Medieval England: Some Evidence from Eastern Norfolk." *The Economic History Review* 36 (1):26–46. doi: 10.2307/2598896.

Chase, Allan. 1977. *The Legacy of Malthus: The Social Costs of the New Scientific Racism.* New York: Alfred A. Knopf.

Cobbett, William. 1834 [1984]. "Political Register, 1834." In *Cobbett on Ireland: A Warning to England,* edited by Denis Knight, 272. London: Lawrence and Wishart.

Colinvaux, Paul A. 1978. *Why Fierce Animals Are Rare: An Ecologist's Perspective.* Princeton, NJ: Princeton Univ. Press.

Condorcet, Nicolas 1795. *Sketch of an Historical View of the Progress of the Human Mind*. Philadelphia, PA: Lang & Ulick.

Connell, K.H. 1950. *The Population of Ireland 1750–1845*. Oxford: Clarendon Press.

Davis, Mike. 2002. *Late Victorian Holocausts: El Niño Famines and the Making of the Third World*. London and New York: Verso.

Dillard, Dudley. 1967. "Review of the Travel Diaries of Thomas Robert Malthus." Review of the Travel Diaries of Thomas Robert Malthus., Patricia James, Lord Robbins. *The Journal of Economic History* 27 (1):122–123.

Dillard, Dudley. 2011. "Review of The Travel Diaries of Thomas Robert Malthus, edited by Patricia James." *The Journal of Economic History* 27 (1):122–123. doi: 10.1017/S0022050700070972.

Ehrlich, Paul R. 1969. "Overcrowding and Us." *National Parks Magazine* 43:10–12.

Engels, Frederick. 1993[1845]. *Condition of the Working Class in England*. Oxford: Oxford Univ. Press.

Foster, John Bellamy. 1999. "Marx's Theory of Metabolic Rift: Classical Foundations for Environmental Sociology." *American Journal of Sociology* 105 (2):366–405.

Godwin, William. 1793. *An Enquiry Concerning Political Justice, and its Influence on General Virtue and Happiness*. London: GG and J Robinson. Online Library of Liberty edition.

Godwin, William. 1794. *Things as They Are, or The Adventures of Caleb Williams*. London: B. Crosby.

Godwin, William. 1798. *Memoirs of the Author of a Vindication of the Rights of Woman*. London: Joseph Johnson.

Godwin, William. 1820. *Of Population: An Inquiry Concerning the Power of Increase in the Numbers of Mankind, Being an Answer to Mr. Malthus' Essay on That Subject*. London: Longman, Hurst, Rees, Orme and Brown. Online Library of Liberty edition.

Grigg, David B. 1980. *Population Growth and Agrarian Change: An Historical Perspective*. Cambridge: Cambridge Univ. Press.

Groenewegen, Peter. 2003. "Condorcet and Equality of the Sexes: One of Many Fronts for a Great Fighter for Liberty of the Eighteenth Century." In *The Status of Women in Classical Economic Thought*, edited by Robert Dimand and Chris Nyland, 127–141. Cheltenham: Edward Elgar.

Hardin, Garrett. 1968. "The Tragedy of the Commons." *Science* 162 (3859):1243–1248. doi: 10.1126/science.162.3859.1243.

Hardin, Garrett. 1993. *Living within Limits: Ecology, Economics, and Population Taboos*. New York: Oxford Univ. Press.

James, Patricia. 1966. *The Travel Diaries of Thomas Robert Malthus*. New York: Cambridge Univ. Press.

James, Patricia. 1979. *Population Malthus: His Life and Times*. London: Routledge & Kegan Paul.

Jarrold, Thomas. 1806. *Dissertations on Man, Philosophical, Physiological, and Political, in Answer to Mr. Malthus's 'Essay on the Principle of Population'*. London: Cadell and Davis.

Kerridge, Eric. 1967. *The Agricultural Revolution*. London: George Allen & Unwin.

Kinealy, Christine. 2002. *The Great Irish Famine: Impact, Ideology and Rebellion*. New York: Palgrave.

Komlos, John. 2005. "On English Pygmies and Giants: The Physical Stature of English Youth in the Late-18th and Early-19th Centuries." *Research in Economic History* 25:149–168.

Krugman, Paul. 2008. Malthus was right! In *The Conscience of a Liberal*, 25 March. https://krugman.blogs.nytimes.com/2008/03/25/malthus-was-right/

Malden, Henry E., ed. 1900. *A History of Surrey*. London: Elliot Stock.

Malm, Andreas. 2013. "The Origins of Fossil Capital: From Water to Steam in the British Cotton Industry." *Historical Materialism* 21 (1):15–68.

Malthus, Thomas Robert. 1798. *An Essay on the Principle of Population As it Affects the Future Improvement of Society with Remarks on the Speculations of Mr. Godwin, M. Condorcet, and Other Writers*. London: J. Johnson. Electronic Scholarly Publishing Project edition. http://www.esp.org/books/malthus/population/malthus.pdf

Malthus, Thomas Robert. 1803. *An Essay on the Principle of Population, or, A View of Its Past and Present Effects on Human Happiness with an Inquiry into Our Prospects Respecting the Future Removal or Mitigation of the Evils Which it Occasions*. London: J. Johnson.

Malthus, Thomas Robert. 1826. *An Essay on the Principle of Population, or a View of its Past and Present Effects on Human Happiness; with an Inquiry into our Prospects Respecting the Future Removal or Mitigation of the Evils which it Occasions (6th edition of Population)*. London: John Murray.

Malthus, Thomas Robert. 1970 [1830]. *A Summary View of the Principle of Population*. Harmondworth: Penguin Books.

Marx, Karl. 1967 [1867]. *Capital: A Critique of Political Economy, Volume 1*. New York: Vintage.

Matthaei, Julie. 1984. "Rethinking Scarcity: Neoclassicism, NeoMalthusianism, and NeoMarxism." *Review of Radical Political Economics* 16 (2–3):81–94. doi: 10.1177/048661348401600204.

Mayhew, Robert J. 2014. *Malthus: The Life and Legacies of an Untimely Prophet*. Cambridge, MA: Harvard Univ. Press.

McCleary, G.F. 1953. *The Malthusian Population Theory*. London: Faber & Faber.

McCoy, Drew R. 1980. "Jefferson and Madison on Malthus: Population Growth in Jeffersonian Political Economy." *The Virginia Magazine of History and Biography* 88 (3):259–276.

McDonagh, Patrick. 2008. *Idiocy: A Cultural History*. Liverpool: Liverpool Univ. Press.

Meek, Ronald L. 1971. "Malthus Yesterday." In *Marx and Engels on the Population Bomb*, edited by Ronald L. Meek, 3–15. Berkeley, CA: Ramparts Press.

Merchant, Emily R. 2015. "Prediction and Control: Global Population, Population Science, and Population Politics in the Twentieth Century." PhD, History, Univ. of Michigan. https://deepblue.lib.umich.edu/handle/2027.42/113440

Messer, Ellen. 1997. "Three Centuries of Changing European Tastes Forthe Potato." In *Food Preferences and Taste: Continuity and Change*, edited by Helen M. Macbeth, 101. New York: Berghahn Books.

Micklewright, F. H. Amphlett. 1961. "The Rise and Decline of English Neo-Malthusianism." *Population Studies* 15 (1):32–51. doi: 10.2307/2172965.

Mitchel, John. 1905. *An Apology for the British Government in Ireland*. Dublin: O'Donoghue.

Mokyr, Joel, and Cormac Ó Gráda. 2002. "What Do People Die of during Famines: The Great Irish Famine in Comparative Perspective." *European Review of Economic History* 6 (3):339–363.

Niven, Ninian. 1846. *The Potato Epidemic, and Its Probable Consequences*. Dublin: James McGlashan.

Nunn, Nathan, and Nancy Qian. 2011. "The Potato's Contribution to Population and Urbanization: Evidence from A Historical Experiment." *The Quarterly Journal of Economics* 126 (2):593–650.

Ó Gráda, Cormac. 1998. "Was the Great Famine Just Like Modern Famines?" In *A World without Famine? Palgrave Development Studies Series*, edited by H. O'Neill and J. Toye, 51–71 London: Palgrave Macmillan.

Orr, J. B., and D. Lubbock. 1953. *The White Man's Dilemma: Food and the Future*. New York: British Book Centre, Inc.

Poppendieck, Janet. 1985. *Breadlines Knee-Deep in Wheat: Food Assistance in the Great Depression*: Rutgers Univ. Press.

Prest, John. 1972. *Lord John Russell*. London: MacMillan.

Price, Richard. 1771. *Observations on Reversionary Payments*. London: T. Cadell.

Pullen, John M. 2004. "Malthus, (Thomas) Robert (1766–1834)." In *Oxford Dictionary of National Biography (online edn, May 2008)*, edited by H.C.G. Matthew and Brian Harrison, 365–370. Oxford: Oxford Univ. Press.

Pullen, John M. 1986. "Correspondence between Malthus and His Parents." *History of Political Economy* 18 (1):133–154.

Pullen, John M. 1987. "Some New Information on the Rev. T. R. Malthus." *History of Political Economy* 19 (1):127–140.

Ravenstone, Piercy. 1821. *A Few Doubts as to the Correctness of Some Opinions Generally Entertained on the Subjects of Population and Political Economy*. London: John Andrews.

Regan, Colm. 1983. "Underdevelopment and Hazards in Historical Perspective: An Irish Case study." In *Interpretations of Calamity from the Viewpoint of Human Ecology*, edited by K. Hewitt, 98–120. Boston, MA: Allen & Unwin.

Ricardo, David. 1817. *On the Principles of Political Economy and Taxation*. London: John Murray.

Rosen, Frederick. 1970. "The Principle of Population as Political Theory: Godwin's of Population and the Malthusian Controversy." *Journal of the History of Ideas* 31 (1):33–48. doi: 10.2307/2708368.

Ross, Eric B. 1998. *The Malthus Factor: Population, Poverty, and Politics in Capitalist Development*. London: Zed Books.

Rousseau, Jean-Jacques. 1984 (1754). *A Discourse on Inequality*. Edited by Maurice Cranston. London, England: Penguin Books.

Saha, Madhumita. 2013. "Food for Soil, Food for People: Research on Food Crops, Fertilizers, and the Making of "Modern" Indian Agriculture." *Technology and Culture* 54 (2):289–316.

Salaman, Redcliffe N. 1949. *History and Social Influence of the Potato*: Cambridge Univ. Press.

Schultz, Theodore W. 1964. *Transforming Traditional Agriculture*. New Haven, CT: Yale Univ. Press.

Stanway, Rev. Oscar. 1940. The Story of Okewood Church (reprinted 2000). Surrey: Okewood Church.

Stapleton, B. 1986. "Malthus: The Origins of the Principle of Population?" In *Malthus and His Time*, edited by Michael Turner, 19–39. New York: St. Martin's Press.

Sumberg, James, Dennis Keeney, and Benedict Dempsey. 2012. "Public Agronomy: Norman Borlaug as 'Brand Hero' for the Green Revolution." *Journal of Development Studies* 48 (11):1587–1600.

Sunstein, Emily W. 1975. *A Different Face: The Life of Mary Wollstonecraft*: Little, Brown & Co.

Surrey Record Society. 1927. *The Parish Registers of Abinger, Wotton, and Oakwood Chapel, Co. Surrey*. London: Mitchell, Hughes & Clarke.

Townsend, Joseph. 1786. *A Dissertation on the Poor Laws by a Well-Wisher to Mankind*. London: Ridgways.

Trevelyan, C. E. 1848. *The Irish crisis*. London: Longman, Brown, Green & Longmans.

Trewavas, Antony. 2002. "Malthus Foiled Again and Again." *Nature* 418 (6898):668–670.

Turner, Michael. 1996. *After the Famine: Irish Agriculture, 1850–1914*. Cambridge, MA: Cambridge Univ. Press.

Turner, R. Steven. 2005. "After the Famine: Plant Pathology, Phytophthora Infestans, and the Late Blight of Potatoes, 1845–1960." *Historical Studies in the Physical and Biological Sciences* 35 (2):341–370. doi: 10.1525/hsps.2005.35.2.341.

Vanhaute, Eric, Richard Paping, and Cormac Ó Gráda. 2007. "The European Subsistence Crisis of 1845–1850: A Comparative Perspective." *Comparative Rural History of the North Sea Area*, January:15–40. doi: 10.1484/m.corn-eb.4.00017.

Vogt, William. 1948. *Road to Survival*. New York: William Sloane.

Wilkinson, Richard G. 1973. *Poverty and Progress: An Ecological Perspective on Economic Development*. New York: Praeger.

Wise, Timothy A. 2019. *Eating Tomorrow: Agribusiness, Family Farmers, and the Battle for the Future of Food*. New York: The New Press.

Wollstonecraft, Mary. 1787. *Thoughts on the Education of Daughters: With Reflections on Female Conduct, in the More Important Duties of Life*. London: Joseph Johnson.

Wollstonecraft, Mary. 1790. *A Vindication of the Rights of Men, in a Letter to the Right Honourable Edmund Burke*. London: Joseph Johnson.

Wollstonecraft, Mary. 1792. *A Vindication of the Rights of Woman with Strictures on Moral and Political Subjects*. London: Joseph Johnson.

Wood, Ellen M. 2000. "The Agrarian Origins of Capitalism." In *Hungry for Profit: The Agribusiness Threat to Farmers, Food, and the Environment*, edited by Fred Magdoff, John Bellamy Foster and Frederick H. Buttel, 23–42. New York: Monthly Review Press.

Wrigley, E.A. 1962. "The Supply of Raw Materials in the Industrial Revolution." *The Economic History Review*, 15 (1):1–16.

Wrigley, E.A. 1986. "Malthus's Model of a Pre-industrial Economy." In *Malthus and His Time*, edited by Michael Turner, 3–18. New York: St. Martin's Press.

Wrigley, E.A. 2010. *Energy and the English Industrial Revolution*. Cambridge: Cambridge Univ. Press.

3
INDUSTRIAL AGRICULTURE

Robert Malthus's theory of population and agriculture may have gotten the population part wrong and the agriculture part wrong, but he was right about the need to go back to first principles to build a theory from the ground up. Of course part of Malthus's problem was that he was ignorant of the other forms of agricultural growth – intensification and industrialization – so he could hardly have identified their first principles. In fact he couldn't have known anything about industrialization; he died in 1834 and 1840 was the year when we will see the birth pangs of industries for the external inputs that are the hallmark of this form of agricultural growth. Replacing resources developed on the farm with purchased inputs does not simply boost production (in fact sometimes it does not boost production at all); it fundamentally changes the nature of agriculture because the entities that develop, manufacture, provide, and promote the inputs all have their own interests. Industrial agriculture has not prevailed because it is inherently superior; it is stupendously wasteful, damaging to the environment and human health, surprisingly inefficient, and it is inexorably prone to overproduction. It exists, in a nutshell, because it is subsidized.

The question is *why*? If we are to get to first principles, we need to know who the beneficiaries are and how they benefit.

Cui Prodest?

Speculating on who, if anyone, had kidnapped Bunny in *The Big Lebowski*, The Dude struggled to recall an adage apparently from his college days. It's like Lenin said, "you look for the person who will benefit... and, uh... you know, you'll, uh... you know what I mean."

The actual quote was from V.I. Lenin's 1913 essay, *Cui prodest?*. Lenin's insights were of little value in figuring out what happened to Bunny, but they are invaluable in understanding agricultural industrialization. Lenin (1977 (1913)) wrote:

> There is a Latin tag, *cui prodest*? Meaning, "who stands to gain?" When it is not immediately apparent which political or social groups, forces or alignments advocate certain proposals, measures, etc., one should always ask: "Who stands to gain?"

DOI: 10.4324/9781003286257-3

This "who benefits?" perspective is key to understanding industrial agriculture because everyone claims to be working for the good of the farmer, or the hungry, or the environment. But there is a wide divide among who stands to gain as agriculture industrializes. As one writer observed between the wars, when agricultural industrialization was still in its early days, "Every happy turn of fate which brought fortune to the industrialist seemed to bring disaster to the farmer" (Burlingame 1939, 53). Industrialists are obviously beneficiaries but they are only part of power structure behind industrial agriculture. There are three beneficiaries that we will call science, industry, and the state. Of course the three are closely integrated: industry and the state employ many scientists and conduct science, and industry and the state have partial control over each other. But they are separable in their briefs: the state establishes and enforces laws and administers the nation, industry creates and sells goods and services for profit, and science endeavors to explain – and create technologies to manipulate – the world. All three sectors have reasons to promote agricultural industrialization.

Chapter 1 briefly introduced the three principles of industrial agriculture: appropriation, subsidy, and overproduction. Let us unpack these a bit and ask who benefits and why.

Appropriations

The Industrial Revolution brought a complete and rapid overhaul of production. In 1775 virtually all cloth in England was woven of flax and wool on handlooms by weavers; by 1800 home weaving had been eclipsed by several hundred factories where raw cotton, grown by people who had no choice, was converted into cloth by workers who had no skill.

The idea of a scaled-up production with routinized tasks and alienated laborers actually originated in agriculture: as early as the 17th century European states had established sugar colonies where slaves harvested and processed sugarcane in outdoor proto-factories (Mintz 1985). Yet agriculture would never undergo an Industrial Revolution.[1] What have been called "agricultural revolutions" in various times and places are a very different story, from the original "agricultural revolution" when Neolithic populations transitioned from hunting and gathering to agriculture-based villages to various claims by historians of agricultural revolutions in the 18th and 19th centuries in Europe.[2] But none of these changes brought the wholesale reformulation of production like in the Industrial Revolution.[3] The main reason for this was explained by Adam Smith in his 1776 *Wealth of Nations*:

> The spinner is almost always a distinct person from the weaver; but the ploughman, the harrower, the sower of the seed, and the reaper of the corn, are often the same. The occasions for those different sorts of labour returning with the different seasons of the year, it is impossible that one man should be constantly employed in any one of them.
> *(2008[1776])*[4]

Agriculture also is a unique form of production because of its close interaction with nature. In factories the land plays the passive role of providing space for the building, but cultivation takes place within the soil itself. Factory buildings control wind, temperature, light, air, and access, whereas agriculture takes place in the open (the Latin root *agri* refers to an open field) where complete control is never possible. Factory assembly lines are based on repetitive procedures that take worker decision-making out of production; the dynamic nature of weather, soil, plants, pests, work schedule and budget require farmers to make decisions continually.

Some of the elements of factorified production have persisted in various types of plantation agriculture in the wake of the early sugar plantations – major examples are tea, rubber, cotton, and oil palm. Other types of large-scale monocrop cultivation also showed some factorified elements: in the late 19th century the vast wheat farms of the Great Plains – managed mainly by steam-powered machines rather than workers or slaves – seemed to be the first "factory farms" by some historians (Fitzgerald 2003, 16). But there was still a huge gulf between all these operations and the actual industrial factory, in which nature was largely nullified and production was completely routinized and atomized into tasks performed by deskilled workers. The real industrialization of agriculture would take the form of integrating external industries, including true factories, into the farm operation and maneuvering the farmer into a position of dependence on those industries. Rather than a system-wide reconfiguration of production, industrialization followed a history of separate aspects of the farm being replaced by external inputs.

Karl Marx had a premonition that this would happen to agriculture, although during his lifetime industrial agriculture was only in its infancy. This is interesting because Marx misunderstood much about agriculture and about agrarian society. He was ignorant of the intricate choreography of social institutions for organizing the work of agriculture (as we will see with the Kofyar in Chapter 7); he famously declared agrarian society to be as unstructured as a sack of potatoes (Marx 1852). Perhaps this was because he was the ultimate city boy (Rostow 1955), and although he was a voracious reader, the scholarship on farms available at the time was limited and weak on the daily realities of farming. But Marx had some astute insights into how agriculture would be bent to suit capitalism's interests. Aside from farm machinery, which had been gradually developing for centuries, the one external input that made real inroads into agriculture during his lifetime was the early fertilizer industry. Marx was quick to recognize chemical fertilizer to be a more profound transformation than a simple boost to crop yields, and as was his wont, he looked to the big picture of how capitalism worked. He wrote that when capitalism met "the most naturally necessary and down-to-earth industry of all" – farming – it turned to science to create inputs which could displace agriculture's "natural conditions of production" and eventually become necessities. He envisioned machines, chemical fertilizer, and new kinds of seeds; of course he did not know that in the future science, paid by industry and subsidized by government, would develop non-replantable seeds that had to be purchased every year and crops that would require stupendous amounts of chemical fertilizer (Chapters 4 and 5). This "pulling-away of the natural ground from the foundations of every industry," he wrote in 1857, "is the tendency of capital" (Marx 1973[1857], 462).[5] However history would also show us that agriculture dependent on external inputs was hardly restricted to capitalist economies. In fact, soon after the Russian Revolution of 1917, Soviet planners began to promote key elements of US-style agricultural industrialization such as tractors and combines (Fitzgerald 1996).

An important book that followed up on Marx's point was *From Farming to Biotechnology: A Theory of Agro-Industrial Development* (Goodman, Sorj, and Wilkinson 1987). These sociologists show that Marx's "pulling-away" process has been very spasmodic. Unlike the complete revamping of production in the Industrial Revolution, there has been a "discontinuous but persistent" history of industry taking over separate elements of agricultural production – "broadcast sowing by the seed drill, the horse by the tractor, manure by synthetic chemicals" (Goodman, Sorj, and Wilkinson 1987, 2). Their term for agricultural processes being transformed into industrial activities and then re-incorporated into agriculture is *appropriationism*, and we can think of each separate "pulling away of natural grounds" as an *appropriation*. We can also think of appropriations as funnels, to remind us that what often appears to be a self-contained technology for increasing production is invariably a conduit for resources mobilized or created far from the farm (as we will see, this is always at government expense).[6]

Why America Created Industrial Agriculture

The development of agricultural appropriationist industries was led by the US. Other regions played roles, but the US strategy of building a nationally integrated set of agricultural input industries has been a hallmark of its economic growth. Industrial appropriations in agriculture are always underwritten by governments, and the primary reason for the US footing the bill for technology after technology was that it never was a colonial power. The obvious contrast is with Britain's colonial system, based on a global division of labor into a metropolitan industrial workshop and a peripheral agricultural hinterland (McMichael 2000, 128). Britain imported bulk agricultural goods – relying on coercion in its colonies and world markets for noncolonies – while Britain became the "workshop of the world," producing high-value finished products. She imported cotton to make textiles, jute to make sacks and rope, cacao to make chocolate, lumber to make furniture, and latex to make rubber – along with consumables like grain, vegetable oil, tea, coffee, and sugar for her industrial workers. Lacking colonies, the US turned to the integration of manufacturing with agriculture at the national level (McMichael 2000, 128–129). This began in the late 19th century and came into full flower in the 20th as waves of government subsidy underwrote agricultural industry after industry – not just the "big two" of fertilizer and hybrid seeds, but tractors, pesticides, GM crops, and digital agriculture. (A more thorough discussion would include other trajectories of agricultural industrialization; the USSR, for instance, was industrializing as quickly as the US in the 1920s (Fitzgerald 1996).)

The genius of this national integration form of agricultural development is that each agricultural input industry supports secondary and tertiary industries. The fertilizer industry supports factory builders, chemical companies, gas pipeline companies, trucking and shipping companies; the tractor industry supports steel producers, fuel companies, tire and rubber industries, and so on. The expense of running a modern industrial farm – a tractor alone can easily run $150,000 – requires credit, which supports the banking industry. Input industries also support research universities, where scientists develop appropriative technologies and applied economists study the technologies' benefits. Because so much of the economic activity that is funneled onto the farm is indirect, it is impossible to arrive at a precise estimate of the collective value of the enterprise, but the USDA reports that in direct costs alone (that is, excluding all the money circulating through secondary industries) American farmers these days spend $22 billion on fertilizer, $12 billion on fuel, $22.2 billion on seeds, $12.6 billion on tractors and other self-propelled farm machines, and $9.9 billion on interest.[7]

This array of economic players is vastly bigger than farming *per se*, and industrial farms exist to keep it afloat. "Farming," writes Richard Lewontin, "has changed from a productive process that originated most of its own inputs and converted them into outputs, to a process that passes materials and energy through from an external supplier to an external buyer," the farmers having little choice but to spend heavily on inputs (Lewontin 2000, 96).

For an example of how the farm has come to exist for the benefit of input industries, rather than the other way around, consider the corn seed Enogen. Released in 2011, this Syngenta product has been genetically modified to optimize its content of alpha-amylase for ethanol production (Goldenberg 2011). As of 2018, when nearly 40% of the US corn harvest was going to produce ethanol, Enogen corn was being used to produce over 2.5 billion gallons of ethanol to power vehicles including tractors (Syngenta Corp. 2018). Gone are the days of the tractor serving to help the farmer grow corn; the farmer and the corn now serve the tractor. And as is always the case in industrial agriculture, public funds were used to develop the technology. Key research leading to the Enogen was conducted by biologists at the University of Nebraska – a land grant university that supposedly exists to benefit the farmer and the public – with funding from the National Science Foundation (Rolfsmeier et al. 1998).

Each appropriation has its own story, and each has interacted with its moment of history. But although the appropriations have been mostly independent, they often have ways of promoting each other, as each new technology creates problems that provide openings for other new industries. The early fertilizer industry opened a wide niche for purchased external expertise in the form of soil analysis. Once breeding was professionalized as an external input by hybrid breeders, it redesigned the corn plant to suit mechanical pickers and to absorb more fertilizer. Borlaug's fertilizer-intensive wheat seeds provided the opening for irrigation and pesticide; the Green Revolution rice was designed for machine harvesting (Cullather 2010, 167). The pesticide-intensive cotton that Indian farmers adopted in the 1990s led to waves of resistant insects which opened a market for GM seeds, and as successive GM technologies lost effectiveness it opened up a succession of opportunities for new GM technologies (Stone 2011).

Whether the US could have or should have grown its agriculture along a different trajectory is a good question but not one we will tackle here. But we will tackle the question of *cui prodest*: who has benefited from the industrial agriculture pioneered in the US?

Industry Harvesting the State

> Agribusiness companies have such a powerful hold in the United States that they have convinced policy-makers and the general public – and even many farmers – that their interests are completely aligned with those of farmers. Nothing could be further from the truth, despite claims to the contrary by the self-proclaimed "farm lobby." Farmers want low costs and high prices. Agribusinesses want maximum production to maximize input sales and low farm prices to reduce the costs of processors' raw materials. Conveniently enough for agribusiness, maximum production tends to result in low farm prices.
>
> *(Wise 2019, 5)*

Marx saw the beginnings of this process and pointed the finger at capitalism, but there is more to it than that. Agricultural capital only winds up with profitable technologies through its interaction with the other spheres of government and science. Let us look at the interest bundles of these three spheres. We will look first at the subsidies industry enjoys, then at just why governments are wont to provide these subsidies, and finally at why scientists benefit from the system.

Perhaps because of our neo–Malthusian assumptions we think of agricultural technologies as inventions serving the public good, and we tend to think of the inventors and manufacturers and vendors as all deserving of profit. But the real force making these "wheels of industry" turn is the capture of value from the public purse. What appears almost like magic beans – *crops that produce their own insecticide! tractors that automatically apply the right amount of fertilizer!* – are actually congealed value that capital has harvested from the government. Agritechnological innovations always draw on prodigious amounts of scientific research and testing; production requires infrastructure, expertise, and sources of raw materials; purveyance requires promotion, sales, and distribution; use raises questions about side effects particularly on environment and health. In short, appropriations occur because they are made profitable by industries harvesting state resources. None of the major industrial technologies in modern farm production would have emerged without lavish and sustained state subsidy of each step in their development, dissemination, and use.

Of course, governments *should* subsidize technologies, practices, and even whole industries under some conditions, but just what those conditions should be is controversial. One reasonable view from many economists is that subsidies are desirable when their benefits to society outweigh the private gain by the subsidized parties (Jayne et al. 2018, 3). Chemical fertilizer is sometimes cited as an example, the claim being that society benefits from fertilizer's role in increasing production and farmers may find unsubsidized fertilizer too expensive (Jayne et al. 2018, 3). Other justifications for subsidies include environmental benefits and "social equity considerations" (Gautam 2015, 87). But we will see that state subsidies behind industrial agriculture have led to overproduction and environmental deterioration, while undermining other more sustainable forms of production that could also have been subsidized. But let us first understand the ways in which the state supports industrialization of agriculture by distinguishing between upstream and downstream subsidies.

Upstream Subsidies

Subsidies are considered upstream if they help a technology come into being, be produced, and be profitable. The most important such subsidy is paying for the scientific research and development costs for appropriative technologies. Such support is often claimed to be support for basic science, but what is basic science?

Francis Bacon held that science revealed the work of God and so "could only serve to make for a more humane society" (Busch 2000, 14). To Bacon the relationship between what we would today call basic science and applied science was obvious; any technologies arising from scientific research were also inherently good, able only to "bless the life of mankind" (Busch 2000, 14). The idealistic Baconian view of science still held sway in mid-20th century USA when modern industrial agriculture was beginning to assume its modern form. Outcomes of science were heralded as unmitigated goods for all by the founding head of the federal Office of Scientific Research and Development, Vannevar Bush (1945). In particular the development of crops was seen as unproblematic:

> Great advances in agriculture are also based upon scientific research. Plants which are more resistant to disease and are adapted to short growing season, the prevention

and cure of livestock diseases, the control of our insect enemies, better fertilizers, and improved agricultural practices, all stem from painstaking scientific research.

Therefore best policy was for government to provide the funds and let scientists determine the research priorities (Busch 2000, 46).

Today many scholars would see this as naive and argue that states produce knowledge to suit their own specific purposes, even as they allow scientists the illusion of autonomy (Mukerji 1989). That ideal of productivism – the absolute prioritizing of production increases – may have made perfect sense in 1863, but by the 1920s it made little sense as US farmers were being battered by overproduction and slumping grain prices. Meanwhile various branches of the US government were zealously promoting adoption of tractors (which both exacerbated overproduction and reduced demand by replacing draft animals) and also footing many of the bills for development of hybrid corn and chemical fertilizer industries (Chapters 4 and 5). As agricultural historians James Giesen and Mark Hersey conclude, US government policies had "married federal research with industrial agriculture" (Giesen and Hersey 2010, 273), funding "applied" research specifically to create technologies to industrialize agriculture at the expense of less industrial technologies. We will see that the US government was pouring resources into nitrogen fertilizer research when the country was awash in under-utilized animal manures, and that public breeding institutions were pouring resources into developing hybrid seeds when American farmers were going broke due to overproduction. Government funding paid for most of the science behind pesticides, GM crops, and factory farms (Boyd and Watts 1997).

The fixation on productivism would reverberate through the agricultural system, pushing the highly industrializable crop of corn to the forefront. Corn harvests have grown rapidly ever since, and today only 8% of the crop is being raised as food. The same fixation would reverberate through how we measured agricultural success: by the late 19th century the USDA had settled on the calorie as the metric to be maximized by research, with high-calorie diets deemed a route to national efficiency via "scientific eating" (Cullather 2010, 19). This caloric productivism would reverberate through the US impacts on world diets: as we see in Chapter 6, the scientists of the Green Revolution championed the spread of high-yielding wheat in Asia as a monumental success, despite it having led to overconsumption of grain and reduced consumption of pulses, dropping water tables, and rising use of pesticides.

Upstream subsidy also includes the establishment of legal rules of ownership to make appropriation technologies profitable. Thus in the case of genetic modification, the US Supreme Court ruled that an entire organism could be patented if a single gene had been modified in the lab, opening the door to patents on the use of naturally occurring genes (Sherkow and Greely 2015, Torrance 2010). The setting of rules to benefit agricultural input industries is not only a domestic practice. The WTO was formed in 1994, the same year that GM foods first appeared in the US market, and under strong US pressure the charter included requirements that all countries pass or accept laws offering strong patent-like protection on seeds and biomolecules.

Another upstream subsidy has been the promotion, encouragement, and even coercion of farmers to adopt appropriation technologies. We will see examples of this with academic land-grant university scientists actually being in the business of fertilizer sales, and hybrid seeds, which were aggressively promoted by public extension agents.

But since most of these forms of backing become invisible by the time appropriative technologies appear on the farm, we tend to attribute value to the technologies themselves rather than to the underlying arrangements that brought them forth.

Downstream Subsidies: Externalized Costs

While upstream subsidies made it possible for elements of agricultural production to be appropriated by external industry, downstream subsidies allow and encourage the industrial inputs to be bought and used even if they are economically inefficiency, environmentally and medically costly, and prone to overproduction. Laws and policies allowing industrial agriculture to externalize its costs are a subsidy, and a crucial one. The US (and other) governments can generally provide this subsidy with impunity, despite the harm to environment and public health, because of the distinctive nature of these costs of industrial agriculture: they are removed in time, space, and causal effect: they are *delayed*, *distant*, and *diffuse*.[8]

Delayed Costs

Much of the damage done by industrial agriculture occurs so long after the farming activity that they cannot be traced back to the cause. The long delay is one reason that many costs are never confidently identified.

The most dramatic examples of delayed costs concern pesticides. Insecticides were a central focus in Rachel Carson's influential book *Silent Spring* , published in 1962, when the vast majority of DDT in the US was being used on overproducing agricultural fields rather than on mosquitoes. The insecticide had been in use since 1945 and despite concerns that it had long-term impacts on public health, no convincing evidence was found until 2007. That year epidemiologist Barbara Cohn used blood samples from 1959 to 1967 to show that childhood exposure caused a staggering fivefold increase in adult cancer rates (Cohn et al. 2007). The cost was delayed in two senses: the disease struck decades after exposure, and it took 62 years for science to isolate this effect.[9] A growing body of evidence now suggests that pesticides can even have effects on subsequent generations through epigenetics (Collotta, Bertazzi, and Bollati 2013).

All appropriation technologies have delayed costs. Fertilizer runoff can contribute to nitrified water and algae blooms within a matter of weeks, but this is just the beginning of a long span of environmental impact. A major 2013 on the fate of fertilizer applied to agricultural fields in France showed that after 30 years, 8–12% of the fertilizer nitrogen had leaked into groundwater, while 12–15% of the nitrogen was still residing in the soil. The remaining fertilizer was expected to continue leaking toward the groundwater for at least another five decades (Sebilo et al. 2013).

The flip side of agricultural inputs' long-run costs is that many inputs appear to offer benefits in the short run. James McWilliams recounts how in 1903, with the boll weevil bedeviling cotton fields, exasperated editorialists in southern newspapers were calling for the abolition of the USDA. "With the bureau under the gun of public opinion, it was paramount to recognize that …many insecticides delivered their blows with lightning speed," making them imminently more politically and culturally valuable than the slower and more ambiguous non-chemical means (McWilliams 2008, 473). These were the bureaucratic realities that led the USDA to begin a long history of promoting insecticides, enjoying credit when sprays killed bugs, and blithely avoiding blame for environmental and human health costs that would not be known for decades.

Distant Costs

The externalizing of industrial agriculture's costs is also eased by its environmental, economic, and public health impacts occurring far from the sites of production and use. The ocean "dead zones" noted above are an example. Dead zones result from algae blooms that consume oceanic oxygen and starve out aquatic life, the principal cause being fertilizer runoff from distant farms. The Gulf of Mexico dead zone, which grows to over 5,000 square miles each summer (Manuel 2014), is fed by farms spread out over more than a million square miles, with many of the biggest contributors of fertilizer runoff being over 1,000 miles to the north. The amount of midwestern fertilizer runoff is greatly increased by over 20 million hectares of subsurface drainage pipes (Dinnes et al. 2002, 154) that act as a pollution zipline to streams and rivers (J. Hanschu, pers comm).

Fertilizer runoff is only one of many long-distance costs of industrial agriculture. Animal production facilities produce several hundred million pounds of toxic pollutants, much of which goes into waterways and wreak havoc on the environment thousands of miles away (Hamilton 2016).

Diffuse Costs

Most of the worst external costs of industrial agriculture are causally diffuse: the impacts of any specific use of the agricultural technology are mingled with other causes. The impacts can be causally diffuse in two different ways. First is that the impacts of "nonpoint source" pollution result from many small contributions. This is very different than "point source" problems like foodborne disease outbreaks that trace back to specific facilities or pollution that emanates from a specific factory; just as the Gulf of Mexico dead zone is caused by runoff from thousands of individual farms, the spread of antibiotic-resistant bacteria is furthered by thousands of swine factory farms (Li et al. 2017). Nonpoint source pollution is known to economists as a particularly elusive problem in the world of external costs (Griffin and Bromley 1982).

But even if there were some way to compile an account of which farms had contributed how much fertilizer runoff, it would be difficult to blame the farms because of the second type of diffuse causality: agricultural inputs are not the sole causes of these costs. Factors other than fertilizer runoff contribute to algae blooms, and hypoxic zones may even occur without any fertilizer runoff. Similarly, pork factory farms spread antibiotic-resistant bacterial diseases, but bacteria also develop antibiotic resistance even without factory farms. This sort of causality reminds us of the debates surrounding lung disease and smoking: for years the tobacco industry argued that lung diseases could not be definitively tied to smoking, as some people who never smoke contract lung cancer and emphysema and some chain smokers did not. Eventually the evidence of direct causality became indisputable: cigarettes turned lungs black and dysfunctional and sharply raised the chances of lung and heart disease. But in contrast, the heaviest costs of industrial agriculture are never so causally direct, and millions of farmers apply fertilizers and spray pesticides simply to grow their crops, inadvertently contributing to a range of environmental and health problems.

Can We Measure these External Costs of Industrial Agriculture? That industrial agriculture externalizes its costs is no secret and scholars have tried to quantify those costs in what are called valuation studies. While it is helpful to spotlight that the external costs really are very large numbers, these studies necessarily leave much out and so produce greatly underestimated numbers. For instance Tegtmeier and Duffy estimated the external costs of agriculture in the US to be between $5.7 and $16.9 billion per year, although this tally only includes "selected" costs (2004, 4) and they stress that research is needed on other costs not included. There are whole categories of environmental and public health costs that are not just difficult to measure, but completely unknown. For example, it is entirely unknown how the spraying of several billion gallons of pesticide since the end of World War II has affected the microbiome of the world's soil; if we have little idea what sort of damage is being done, we obviously can't measure it. Estimates of external costs also leave out types of costs that are impossible to put a dollar figure on – such as the human misery caused by farmers being pushed out by industrial farm concentration or the cruelty inflicted on billions of factory farmed animals.

But the global warming problem probably poses the greatest challenge of all to measuring external costs of industrial agriculture. Industrial agriculture is a major producer of greenhouse gasses and thus a major contributor to global warming. The chemical fertilizer that is at the heart of industrial agriculture is the dominant cause of greenhouse gas production (Chapter 4). This is obviously not only a devastating external cost but also the perfect case of a cost that is delayed, distant, *and* diffuse. Estimates vary, but some realistic figures put agriculture's contribution to greenhouse has production as high as 25%.

Can We Keep Industrial Agriculture from Externalizing these Costs? With downstream effects being delayed, distant, and diffuse, forcing input producers and users to internalize costs would be extremely hard even if governments wanted to do so. But if they wanted to, governments do have tools that could be used to force some costs to be internalized, even if all have major weaknesses. First is regulation: either law or policy can require avoidance or specified ways of using specific technologies, as DDT was banned for normal agricultural use in 1972. But countries vary in their willingness to regulate technologies even when they are known to be toxic, and the DDT ban was out of character for the US, instituted by the newly created Environmental Protection Agency which was not yet heavily influenced by industry. (The ban was protested furiously by chemical companies and Green Revolution hero Norman Borlaug (1971).) The EPA soon lost enthusiasm for banning agricultural chemicals, and the US has become an international outlier in allowing toxic pesticides. (Paraquat, for example, which is strongly linked to Parkinson's disease and banned in much of the world even including China, is allowed in the US (Hakim 2016).)

Second are Pigovian taxes. Named for economist Arthur Pigou, who developed the concept of externalities, these taxes penalize the manufacture, purchase, or use of technologies with negative externalities. The carbon tax instituted by British Columbia in 2008 is a Pigovian tax. Pigovian taxes have many ardent supporters but also skeptics; even the British Columbia tax, which by all appearances has significantly lowered fossil fuel use without damaging local economies (Porter 2016), is dismissed by some (Dudley 2018). The potential for Pigovian taxes to lead to internalization of industrial agriculture's costs is debated (Lusk 2016) but I suspect it is low. Carbon taxes would probably raise the cost of fertilizer by too small of an amount to stimulate development of less fertilizer-intensive seeds, and the added cost of fuel for farm machinery would be trivial compared to the farmers' sunk costs in the machines.[10]

Third is regulation by tort law – essentially controlling others' actions and acquiring reparations through lawsuits (Cane 2002, 305). Regulation by tort has potential to force the internalizing of some costs, or at least to punish externalizing of some costs, especially where the harm from industrial agriculture is readily demonstrable. Input industries are worried enough about regulation by tort to exert intensive pressure on lawmakers to provide protection. Every state in the US has some form of "right to farm" law, defined by the Congressional Research Service as a law that "denies nuisance suits against farmers who use accepted and standard farming practices, even if these practices harm or bother adjacent property owners or the general public...agricultural nuisances may include noise, odors, visual clutter and dangerous structures." Missouri revised its state statutes in 2013 to protect agribusinesses from lawsuit; for instance, if a lawsuit is found to be "frivolous," the defendant may recover all of their legal costs from the plaintiff. In 2014 it actually amended the state constitution "to ensure that the right of Missouri citizens to engage in agricultural production and ranching practices shall not be infringed" – a hopelessly vague law obviously designed to further insulate industrial agriculture from internalizing costs.

But beyond the specific limitations of these remedies is the larger fact that they depend on governments wanting to curb the cost-externalizing nature of industrial agriculture. On the contrary, governments have a suite of reasons to promote industrial agriculture, and as we have stressed, it is only because of government enthusiasm that we have the industrial agriculture we have. Let us consider why.

State Interests

> whoever could make two ears of corn, or two blades of grass, to grow upon a spot of ground where only one grew before, would deserve better of mankind, and do more essential service to his country, than the whole race of politicians put together.
>
> *(Swift 1950[1726])*

Jonathan Swift's intrepid traveler Lemuel Gulliver was discussing the art of government with the King of Brobdingnag when the King praised agricultural technology developers over government officials. In the early 18th century, it made perfect sense for Swift and his wise fictional king to valorize any attempt to boost plant growth. It was also understandable when, in 1863, the newly formed US Department of Agriculture adopted the same philosophy and even the same phrase: its first annual report proclaimed that "it should be the aim of every young farmer...to make two blades of grass grow where but one grew before" (Harding 1947). Of course Jonathan Swift could never have imagined a time when over seven ears of corn grew where one had before and politicians were paying farmers not to grow more ears.[11] But more surprising yet would be the extent to which those extra ears were growing *because* of the support from government officials.

When we ask the "who" question – *cui prodest?* – it is not surprising to find that the main beneficiaries of agricultural industrialization are input corporations. Appropriationist industries prosper because of subsidy and failed regulation, and as we will see, the industries only come into being in the first place with government financing. But why do governments – particularly the US government – pay for the spread of agricultural technologies that make us sick, poison our environment, and overproduce?

There are several answers to this. Let us consider some basic functions of the US federal government. It functions as an administrative entity (that is supposed to run things), a social entity (promoting certain types of traits and behaviors in its citizens), and an economic entity (especially facilitating the production of goods and services, including food). Also consider that government is staffed and run by individuals managing their own careers, whether it is getting elected or seeking rewards for doing their job. Let us see how agricultural industrialization is attractive to government entities and people in each of these capacities.

Administration: Expanding Bureaucracy and Power

The administrative priorities of governments tend to favor promotion of certain types of agriculture. Anthropologist James Scott shows that the state benefits from ordering, standardizing, and simplifying agricultural production because of its need to tax, to regulate, to build appropriate infrastructure, and to prevent rebellion. It needs to be able to recognize, to count, to measure, and in general to *know* (Scott 1998). Governments have no good entry points for control and monitoring of smallholder intensive farmers who produce with local resources, but external inputs can provide a range of avenues for control and monitoring. Consider mechanization. US tractor adoption surged in the 1920s in large part because of the growth of the new specialty of agricultural engineering, a field staffed by experts at government-supported land-grant colleges whose real knowledge lay not in how to farm but in how to analyze and "modernize" farming methods (Fitzgerald 2003, 22, Giesen and Hersey 2010). The more mechanized agriculture became, the more central was the engineers' role of analyzing and advising, even as many farmers were driven out of business by overproduction and low market prices in the 1920s. By 1921 a major study showed that tractor adoption was hurting farmers more than helping, and by 1922 over 1 million farmers per year were leaving the countryside (Fitzgerald 2003, 22, 99). That the countryside was shedding its smaller and more self-sufficient farms in favor of larger more mechanized "clients" was a boon to agricultural engineers, especially since they escaped blame for the worsening problems of surplus. In 1927, when the Iowa State College's Dean of Agriculture admitted that the ongoing agricultural depression was partly due to mechanization, other agricultural scientists skewered him. The American Society of Agricultural Engineers dismissed his claim that shifting from horsepower to tractor power would only force farmers to pay "more for gasoline and less for corn." And "in a rare moment of honesty about the social implications of industrializing agriculture," the organization acknowledged that its goal was to replace farmers with factory workers making labor-saving equipment (Giesen and Hersey 2010, 287–288).

Agricultural engineering was a flagrant case of bureaucratic expansion at the expense of farmers and the public but it was hardly the only example of this connected to mechanization. Tractor adoption also allowed for the expansion and increased importance for extension services, which positioned themselves as the logical hub to coordinate local farmers, bankers, and merchants (Daniel 1985).

In some cases the spread of industrial inputs even paid for the expansion of the bureaucracy. In 1874, Georgia established its own department of agriculture to expand its regulatory powers and monitor the fertilizers entering the state each year. State chemists inspected and labeled every bag of fertilizer entering the state and the fees from fertilizer manufacturers for this service funded the new department. State chemists were soon inspecting close to

50,000 tons of fertilizer annually, and profits from inspection fees allowed the department to expand into the regulation of other commodities, agricultural research, and geological surveys. Other southern states followed Georgia's lead, creating their own profit-making regulatory schemes (Johnson 2016, 43–44).

Governments in the Global South have also found that supporting agricultural industrialization can provide attractive opportunities to extend control. In the Philippines, the input-intensive Green Revolution rice allowed President Marcos to set up a coordinating council to direct the supply of seed, chemicals, loans, and machinery – "enabling the government to control prices and supply at every step of cultivation" (Cullather 2010, 171). Within a few years he had also set up a network of rural cooperatives that promoted input-intensive practices while monitoring peasant activities. Whether in the US or developing countries, agricultural industrialization helps make agriculture "legible." What states often claim to be a modernizing or even a "civilizing" process is really more a way to "make the countryside, its products, and its inhabitants more readily identifiable and accessible to the center" (Scott 1998, 184). Large, regularly shaped farms producing uniform products are highly legible, especially when they have enormous operating budgets involving loans and government payouts. Small and non-factorified farms are devilishly opaque, especially when they generate and use many of their own resources internally. Fertilizer from farm animals, seeds grown on the farm, and the farmers' own labor are nearly impossible to measure, monitor, control, or tax.[12]

Social: Promoting "Good" Farmers

Government political and economic aims often have implications for what types of values and economic orientations its citizens have, and governments have various ways to promote what they define as "good" people and marginalize those deemed "bad." Farming is both highly variable and important to national economy, security, and self-image, and governments in many times and places have taken a particularly keen interest in defining such qualities in farmers.

Marxist governments have held strong – but often contradictory – views of what were good and bad farmers. Russian revolutionaries scorned peasant farmers in general because they wanted their own land and were supposedly uninterested in revolution. Bolshevik writer Maxim Gorky accused the peasants of "animal-like individualism" and a total lack of social consciousness, and Lenin liked to quote Marx on the "idiocy of rural life" (Becker 1996, 28). But in China, Mao headed a Marxist revolution propelled by peasant farmers, who were lionized as long as they were not deemed "kulaks" – prosperous land-owners – in which case they risked being beheaded (Becker 1996, 30–34).

The US has held contradictory ideals about farmers as well. Thomas Jefferson admired "yeoman" farmers not for turning a profit but producing "a simple abundance" (Appleby 1982, 834). Yet the early US government encouraged profitable commercial farming to take control of Indian lands. By the early 20th century, with the rise of Taylorization, assembly-line production, and the "industrial ideal" in agriculture (Fitzgerald 2003), the yeoman farmer had been recast as backward, ignorant, and an inefficient drag on national progress. In 1907, the federal government threw its support behind the Country Life Movement, a campaign to remake yeomen or replace them with farmers who conformed to the industrial ideal. By 1926, one popular writer would note with satisfaction that the "national spasm for standardization, modernization, and efficiency... is driving the old-time, bucolic, turkey-in-the-straw style of farmer from the... countryside" and replacing him with "a business man, a capitalist, an executive... a cog in a machine well-oiled with efficiency" (Danbom 1979, 136). Country Life bureaucrats, including leaders at the USDA, believed they were working for the good of the larger society, but as historian David Danbom writes,

> their virtue was never as clear as they pretended. Certainly, the bureaucracy did not represent the interests of most farmers, and many of its activities were manipulative of and detrimental to those farmers. In short, the activities of the bureaucracy were aimed at aiding one segment of society and expressing its values without regard to the consequences for another segment.
>
> *(1979, 141)*

As the 20th century unfolded and the US developed its national integration model of agricultural development, government ideals became increasingly inseparable from ideals of input corporations. Government and corporate marketing images reliably depict the farmer deploying an input technology. Images from US publications in the 1950s were particularly wont to depict the large futuristic "push-button farm" run by a single man; these make a fascinating comparison with contemporary posters from Communist China depicting work parties of happy men and women using simple technology (Stone 2022, Figure 2).

In the US, governments at various levels have often been partial to industrialized farmers for their political leanings and activities. The more industrialized a farm operation, the more the farmer was tied to government subsidy; nonindustrialized farmers, on the other hand, have a history as pesky populists, joining with labor movements and making trouble for corporations. When production of various crops began to surge out of control in the 1960s (Chapters 4 and 5), and a "plague of cheap corn" squeezed out many of the smaller farmers, it helped achieve the dream shared by government and input industries: fewer restive farmers, great input sales, and cheaper raw materials (Pollan 2006, 50).

Economics

For all of its flaws, industrial agriculture can be very good for business...certain businesses anyway. In 1976, in order to produce goods worth $14.5 billion, US farmers purchased $60 billion of goods and services (Barlett 1987, Cochrane 1979, 160). By 2019, the US Department of Agriculture calculated that US farmers were spending $368.4 billion running their farms, excluding dwelling costs (Economic Research Service 2018). (Interestingly, $14.5 billion of that was directly subsidized by the federal government: government handouts were as much as actual farm production in 1976 (Congressional Research Service 2018, Figure 15).) This flood of money cascades through other businesses that provide raw materials, build factories, and transport and sell goods, which means that the actual amount of business generated by industrial agriculture is much greater than these figures. The money also cascades through universities like one where I work, where labs thrive on government funding often justified as research needed to feed the world. The profits for so many industries inevitably translate into political power and the ability to induce the government to continue its upstream and downstream subsidies to agricultural inputs.

Industrial agriculture also makes for "cheap food," which generally pleases consumers and which generally benefits those in political power. "Whether or not greater productivity would aid the farmer," writes Daniel Danbom, "it would aid those who carried and processed the product... it did lower food prices, dampen worker discontent" (1979, 40). But "cheap food" remains in quotes because, as several other writers have pointed out forcefully, the food is not really cheap: we all pay for it indirectly through our tax dollars (which go to subsidizing industrial agriculture), through our degrading environment, and our health.

The state also competes on the international economic stage, which leads it to back industrial agriculture. We will see that the US government poured money, expertise, and resources into building a nitrogen fertilizer industry not to produce more food – of which there was plenty – but to catch up with Germany's more advanced industry.

Careers

Since governments have institutional interests in industrializing agriculture, the individuals who staff the offices of government act to promote those institutional interests. But these individuals have their own career interests as well, and we can parse out the individuals' interests and find that in many ways government career advancement tends to align with the interests of agricultural industrialization. The first of these ways is seen in the process called regulatory capture, particularly important because it helps explain why industrial agriculture is allowed to keep externalizing its costs.

Regulatory Capture

Outside of industrial farming systems, farming is subjected to minimal government regulatory control. Even when laws require or prohibit small nonindustrial farm practices, they are rarely enforced. For instance, many tropical countries routinely ignore their own laws banning slash and burn cultivation (Schecter and Wright 2015). But the creation and use of industrial inputs brings a wide range of environmental interactions that governments may be interested in regulating, and industrial agriculture has from its beginnings been an outstanding case of *regulatory capture* – the process of parties most affected by regulatory laws and policies influencing those laws and policies for their own benefit (Dal Bo 2006, 203).

Through much of the 20th century, thinking on regulation policies hinged on the assumption that decisions would be made by benevolent planners. So for instance when situations lent themselves to monopoly control – like power grids – government allowed but regulated monopolistic corporations mainly to protect the public from exploitation (Dal Bo 2006, 204–205). In retrospect this was a naive view, and a more realistic perspective was proposed by economist George Stigler's path-breaking 1971 article pointing out that "as a rule, regulation is acquired by the industry and is designed and operated primarily for its benefit" (Stigler 1971, 3).[13] Stigler pointed out that monied industries provide support for politicians to be elected, and the electorate is poor at checking regulatory abuses because regulatory policies tend to be poor campaign issues.[14] Of course such "captured" regulation reduces competition and raises consumer costs (or prevents potential consumer benefits), but for the politician this poses only an abstract political cost that is more than compensated by the favored industry's ability to make campaign contributions and mobilize voters (Peltzman 1976, Nestle 2007, 102-107).

Regulatory capture is particularly acute in industrial agriculture because of the long shadow cast by Malthusian beliefs. Input industries routinely direct attention to the threat of overpopulation and away from the long history of agricultural overproduction. In the US, regulatory capture in industrial agriculture is also promoted by a quirk in the presidential elections process: Iowa, the most "agricultural" state in the country (as measured by percentage of the state's gross domestic product coming from the farm sector), holds the crucial first primary election (technically a caucus). This always attracts enormous press attention, and candidates invariably talk up policies that benefit the state's industrial farm sector and carefully avoid any positions in favor of regulating agriculture.

An interesting twist on regulatory capture is when industry seeks and obtains *more* regulation when it would be advantageous. An example comes from the early days of agricultural biotechnology, when government regulation of the genetically modified seeds being developed by Monsanto was up for grabs. In 1986 Monsanto executives called on Vice President George Bush, asking that the federal government would classify GM foods to be regulated but also to all be safe, to reassure a potentially skeptical public about the new technology. The White House complied, reported the *New York Times*, "working behind the scenes to help Monsanto – long a political power with deep connections in Washington – get the regulations that it wanted" (Eichenwald 2001). This outcome would be repeated, again and again, through three administrations:

> What Monsanto wished for from Washington, Monsanto – and, by extension, the biotechnology industry – got. If the company's strategy demanded regulations, rules favored by the industry were adopted. And when the company abruptly decided that it needed to throw off the regulations and speed its foods to market, the White House quickly ushered through an unusually generous policy of self-policing.
>
> *(Eichenwald 2001)*

Regulatory capture is also promoted by the revolving door between careers in government regulatory agencies and in the industries being regulated. It is no surprise that government officials are often knowledgeable about industries they regulate and that industry leaders are often knowledgeable about government regulatory apparatuses. There is therefore a natural basis for individuals from one side to be hired by the other, and it can be rewarding to one's career to cross the divide. The beneficiary in such movement is almost always the industry side, as this is one key process by which has "married federal research with industrial agriculture" (Giesen and Hersey 2010, 273).

Consider the case of Michael Taylor, who has "made an art of the role-swapping dance between the food industry and the agencies that regulate it" (Philpott 2009). Taylor began his career as executive assistant to the FDA commissioner, then was soon hired away by a law/lobbying firm representing Monsanto where he built their food and drug law practice. In 1991 he returned to the federal government, first back to the FDA as Deputy Commissioner for Policy and then as Administrator of the Food Safety and Inspection Service (FSIS) at the USDA. Then back to the corporate sector as Vice President for Public Policy at Monsanto, then back to the FDA (Nestle 2007, 101). In 1988, when he was in between postings at the FDA, Taylor published an influential article in a toxicology journal that helped persuade the government to allow low-level carcinogens in foods. At the FDA in 1992 he ignored several of the agency's top scientists and he ruled that GM foods would be treated as "generally recognized as safe." Then at FSIS he was influential in the release of unlabeled GM foods in the US.

Monsanto is in some ways unique in the world of input corporations in that it develops and sells seeds, pesticides, GM traits, and data – four major classes of industrial inputs – and perhaps not surprisingly, no company has had more revolving door executives. Aside from Taylor, Monsanto has enjoyed having one of its directors serve as US commerce secretary and US trade representative and another director serve as EPA administrator; its director of UK government affairs serve as assistant to the president for intergovernmental affairs; its chief legal strategist serve as White House chief of staff; its VP of Public Affairs serve as assistant administrator of the EPA Office of Prevention, Pesticides and Toxic Substances; its Senior VP of Clinical Affairs (for its former pharmaceutical division) serve as acting FDA commissioner; and its VP of public and government affairs serve in Congress (Luoma 2000, 58).

But major boosts for industrial agriculture have also come from careers entirely within government. The individual most instrumental in throwing government resources behind chemical-intensive insect control was the ambitious entomologist Leland O. Howard, head of the Federal Bureau of Entomology from 1894 to 1927. Howard epitomized the "government entrepreneur," powerfully mediating among agriculture, industry, and science to grow the prestige, influence, and funding for his bureaucracy (McWilliams 2008, 470). Howard took office at a time when the weight of evidence was firmly against chemicals being effective for insect control, and his first major project was a search for biological controls of the gypsy moth. But this search failed, and he concluded that painstaking, time-consuming searches for often elusive biological control agents were a poor career strategy, especially when the Progressive Era mentality called for rapid outcomes by scientists (McWilliams 2008, 476). Pushing the Bureau of Entomology toward an increasingly pesticide-oriented helped vault him into the ranks of the "hero-scientists" of the era (McWilliams 2008, 470). Howard helped guide American farmers into the early stages of the modern pesticide regime.

Farmers

> Whether or not greater productivity would aid the farmer, it would aid those who carried and processed the product, those who sold the means to raise it, and those who lent the funds necessary to obtain those means. National businessmen, moreover, were always in favor of high agricultural productivity, and though it might not aid the farmer it did lower food prices, dampen worker discontent, and result in a general "quickening of the wheels of industry.
>
> *(Danbom 1979, 40)*

Might not aid the farmer??

If industrial agriculture basically benefits input industries that milk the state, the obvious question is how farmers could possibly not benefit. Don't farmers voluntarily adopt the external inputs? Input industries will certainly tell you so; websites and press releases from Mosaic Fertilizer, Pioneer Hybrid, and Monsanto all insist they exist only to help the farmer.

Actually farmers do not always voluntarily adopt external input technologies. Mao forced Chinese peasants to use large dysfunctional tractors (Becker 1996), Julius Nyerere forced Tanzanian farmers to use government seeds and fertilizers (Scott 1998), and cotton companies in Burkina Faso obliged farmers to use genetically modified seeds (Dowd-Uribe 2014). Even in the US, farmers have been given subsidy payments in the form of fertilizer and have been cornered into buying tractors to qualify for loans (Fitzgerald 2003, 100).

But it is true that most of the time, farmers adopt technologies without a gun to their head; they are simply making a decision. And yet farmer decision-making is anything but simple. Farmers can and repeatedly do adopt external inputs that are not in the overall interests of the community of farmers and sometimes not in their own individual interests. And it has nothing to do with being fools; it has to do with the peculiar features of figuring out how to farm.

Why Do Farmers Adopt Input Technologies Anyway?

Hybrid corn, one of the most transformative technologies in agricultural history (Chapter 5), is a famous case of technology adoption. Hybrid seeds debuted in Iowa corn country in 1928. They were billed as raising yields, although they had to be purchased anew every year, unlike conventional corn which produced its own seed. Farmers mostly ignored or only dabbled with the hybrids until the late 1930s, to the consternation of the breeders at the Agricultural Experiment Station who has developed them (Rogers 2003, 55). To understand the farmers' apparently irrational behavior, the Station hired sociologists Bryce Ryan and Neal Gross to survey farmers in two communities. Their 1943 article "The Diffusion of Hybrid Seed Corn in Two Iowa Communities" (1943) is still read as an early classic in the study of the diffusion of innovations (Rogers 2003).

The sociologists analyzed both how farmers observed crops and observed each other. Farmers supposedly make decisions about technologies and practices based on their own experiments and observations, and yet hybrid seeds did not catch on until a "social snowball" (Rogers 2003, 35) began to roll, with farmers being increasingly influenced by the combined actions of others. Adoption, it turned out, was partly a social process. Later researchers would come to see agricultural decision-making as driven by the twin processes of *environmental learning* and *social learning*.[15]

Environmental learning occurs when farmers base decisions on observations of "payoff" information. They may observe their own or neighbors' farms, but it is the empirical results they are using as a guide, not the neighbors themselves. They are looking at farming activities as experiments and assessing such factors as relative advantage, compatibility with existing resources, difficulty of use, and "trialability" – how well can it be experimented with (Rogers 2003, 15–16). But that criterion of "trialability" turns out to be a real problem; it's true that farmers are always experimenting, but working farms are very flawed laboratories.[16] Farmers cannot set up the controlled conditions of professional test plots in research facilities. Farmers also often confront complex and difficult to observe phenomena that would be hard to manage even if they could run controlled experiments. Moreover farmers can rarely acquire payoff information on more than a few of the production methods they might use, which makes the criterion of "relative advantage" hard to gauge. Farmers *always* need guidance from sources other than observation.

This is why farmers always rely to some extent on *social learning* – observing and basing decisions on what other people do. Social learning hinges on *who* is doing the farming more than on empirical observation of their results. We often pick our models on social criteria that have little to do with how well the technology works. Terms for emulation (like the verb "to ape") have negative connotations, but emulation is an indispensable practice in our species. We begin social learning as children, emulating our parents because they are our parents, not because of empirical indicators that they are good at what they do.

There are two key criteria by which we pick models to emulate, whether it is for agricultural adoptions or other endeavors. One is *prestige*: we tend to copy admired individuals, even when we don't know how well the technology is working for them. Agricultural input sellers have known this all along and they have a history of trying to persuade high-prestige farmers to try their technologies, sometimes giving them products for free. This is manipulation of social learning; if farmers were actually basing their decisions purely on environmental learning, it shouldn't matter who was using the new technology. The second key criterion for social emulation has to do with *conformity* – deciding to adopt because of the number of others who are adopting. This is sometimes called "conformist bias" (Henrich and Boyd 1998) or "herd behavior" (Stone 2007, Stone, Flachs, and Diepenbrock 2014), but the term "social snowball" is apt because every time a person joins a crowd it enlarges the crowd and makes it more likely that others will join. Granovetter explains this dynamic as a matter of thresholds for joining, defined as the proportion of the group one would have to see join before he would do so (1978, 1422). Consider a crowd of people, each with their own threshold for joining a riot. Someone with a threshold of zero could start trouble on their own, causing others with low thresholds to join, in turn activating those with moderate thresholds, the growing crowd eventually bringing in even those with the highest thresholds. Think of it this way: if the whole herd runs away, you will run away too, and not because you have conducted your own empirical assessment of the situation but because everyone else is running. Of course herd behavior may be adaptive: there may be wisdom in crowds. But crowds strongly affect decisions whether those decisions are wise or not.[17]

Some writers see environmental and social learning as largely explaining innovation adoptions in agriculture (Henrich 2001, McElreath 2004), but restricting ourselves to these two processes whisks from view a crucial third force in farmer decision-making. Both environmental and social learning are based on vested interests internal to the farming community; but there are many off-farm parties with their own interests in how farming is conducted. Farmers are often targeted for advice, information, instruction, marketing, and orders from colonial officers, consultants, agricultural engineers, farmer field schools, environmental activists, marketers, measurement-minded bureaucrats, regulatory authorities, book authors, non-governmental organizations (NGOs), social movements, and organic schemes. Decisions being shaped by such off-farm sources are the third process of *didactic learning* (Stone 2016). "Didacts" with vested interests were right there in Ryan and Gross's Iowa cornfields: seed salesmen were the leading source of early information on hybrid seed, and state extension agents promoted hybrid corn and disseminated favorable test plot results (Ryan and Gross 1943, 16). Agricultural didacts' methods and agendas vary, but they comprise a conceptually coherent category, distinct from environmental and social learning because they introduce off-farm interests.

The most obvious form of agricultural didactics is product marketing, on which agricultural input industries have long been lavish spenders. Input industries may like to salute the astuteness of farmers when they are adopting their products, but their zealous efforts at marketing reveal just how malleable they know farmers can be. But persuasion comes in many other forms as well, and whether the aim is to sell products, make farming practices legible, achieve public recognition, or please funders, didacts' interests are never fully aligned with the farmers'. How could they be, given that the farmers themselves have varied interests? For instance, extension agents in developing countries often prioritize large-scale and wealthy farmers with whom recommended technologies and practices are most likely to make a large splash (Brush 2004, Stone 2016, 12). Agricultural didacts always insist that they are just helping farmers, whether it is an input seller pointing to sales or extension projects in developing countries claiming to have "empowered" farmers (Mosse 2005), but they rarely work for the farmer and they always pursue the goals for which their employer rewards them.

None of the three forms of agricultural learning ensure that farmers adopt technologies and practices that will serve their own interests, and all three have within them the possibility of leading farmers astray. Environmental learning can never provide all of the information the farmer needs; social learning can capture the wisdom of other farmers but it can lead to herd behavior; didactic learning can provide useful information and products but it also pushes the farmer in directions that benefit external interests. The takeaway is crucial to this book: the idea that farmers only buy inputs that are in their interests is a fiction. An excellent, if tragic, example comes from my long-term research in India.

The Harsh Example of Indian Cotton Farmers

Cotton farmers in southern India provide a striking illustration of farmers adopting technologies that are not in their own interests because of the peculiarities of agricultural decision-making. My students and I have studied cotton farmers in Warangal District, Telangana state, over the last 20 years (Stone 2007, Flachs 2019, inter alia). As late as the 1970s cotton was mostly a minor cash crop that offered very low yields. But in the 1970s government breeders developed hybrid cottons that appeared on the market in the 1980s. The hybrids were created with New World cottons that were vulnerable to Indian crop pests, and so farmers adopted insecticides along with the new seeds. For many the package was profitable at first, but by the late 1990s cotton pests showed resistance to all major insecticides (Kranthi et al. 2002). Many cotton farmers found themselves in a triple bind as they simultaneously faced an agronomic problem (serious pest attacks), an economic problem (rising debts), and a knowledge problem (environmental, social, and didactic learning all floundered to solve the problem). The more they sprayed their fields the deeper they fell into debt and the more the insects became resistant, leaving them constantly desperate for the new insecticides that slowly appeared in the local shops. Pesticide producers insisted they were giving farmers what they wanted, and the farmers were voluntarily buying their products; yet no farmer wanted a technology regime that would lead them onto such an unsustainable treadmill (Stone and Flachs 2014). These pesticide problems were compounded by seed problems. As hybrids spread in the 1990s the number of commercial brands proliferated at a furious pace. The seed market eventually offered over 1,000 hybrid cotton seed brands, with some quickly disappearing and being replaced by new brands (Stone 2007). Effective environmental learning became nearly impossible and social and didactic learning began to run wild, with farmers adopting whatever seed seemed popular in their village and being heavily influenced by advertising and shopkeeper recommendations (Figure 3.1). Input companies claimed that farmers were adopting seeds that provided "consistent benefits" (Stone 2007, 67), but there was nothing consistent about the cotton production; most farmers were planting whole fields with seeds they had never used before and about which they knew nothing except that they were popular (Stone 2007, Stone, Flachs, and Diepenbrock 2014). By the late 1990s farmer suicide rates had climbed to alarming numbers.

FIGURE 3.1   Faced with a breakdown of environmental learning due to rapidly changing and opaque technologies, a cotton farmer in Telangana, India, decides which seed to plant by asking a shopkeeper which seed is popular this season (Flachs 2019, Stone 2007, Stone, Flachs, and Diepenbrock 2014). Photo by G. Stone.

During the early 2000s genetically modified *Bt* cotton seeds were widely adopted (following a "social snowball" pattern very similar to hybrid corn in Iowa) (Stone 2011). Monsanto and like-minded proponents of GM crops proclaimed that the adoption showed indisputable benefits to the farmers, but a major retrospective analysis showed that the benefits were "modest and largely ephemeral," and that a few years after the snowball adoption Indian cotton farmers were spending much *more* on insecticides than before the *Bt* seeds were released (Kranthi and Stone 2020, 194-195).

A takeaway from this research is that while environmental learning is a crucial component in successful farming, it has important limitations. There is nothing "wrong" with the Warangal farmers; they are doing the best they can in a horrible information environment. But they certainly give the lie to the assumption that adoption indicates external inputs are in the farmer's interests.

Overproduction

Farms have become specialized, open-air factories whose levels of production can be increased spectacularly provided that large quantities of energy derived from outside the farm can be transmuted on the farm into an increased flow of agricultural products. Modern industrial economies…are embarrassed by agricultural overproduction.
(Wrigley 1988)

Agricultural overproduction may seem a jarring idea to readers today who still read about the world's hungry, and according to Malthus it is physically impossible. But if he were alive today, Malthus would not see the world permanently contorted by shortages as he imagined, but instead a world perennially contorting itself to manage industrial agriculture's overproduction.

Yet we tend to continually underestimate the problem of agricultural overproduction, and there are understandable reasons for this. In the first place we constantly hear that we are running short on food – even in the US where overproduction has been the most intractable. Accounts of agricultural overproduction strike us as odd and probably fleeting, even a good problem to have.[18] It is not, and not just because it reflects so much public money wasted on overproduction and storage. To appreciate what a severe problem overproduction is we need to recall Malthus's insistence that we consider the *indirect* effects of agricultural imbalances. Overproduction is an inherent feature of industrial agriculture with indirect effects that are deep and costly and diverse.

But what is "overproduction"? If it just means any production of food above immediate consumption demands, then even intensive systems sometimes overproduce. A crop may do better than expected; food stores may turn out to be more than what was needed for lean periods. Smallholders can usually put surplus to good use; they engage in "social production" in which agricultural goods are produced to be used as gifts or in rituals. But as long as agricultural production is a local affair, there are built-in checks on production (Chapter 7). But as external input industries come to dominate agriculture, there are no good checks to regulate production; there is no optimal amount of seed, fertilizer, or other products to be manufactured and sold, but rather the more the better.

Input industries also tend to stimulate each other and promote each other's growth. We will see that the rapid growth in the US chemical fertilizer industry in the 1950s pushed breeders to create fertilizer-intensive corn, which provided an ever-expanding market for fertilizer and pesticide. Industry profits were plowed into political influence to capture regulation and ensure policies to protect farmers from their own overproduction. The billions flowing from US farms to input corporations supports hundreds of corporations, tens of thousands of careers, and millions of shareholders, all of whom benefit from selling as many inputs as possible. These indirect benefits of input sales are the most important single factor making overproduction endemic to industrial agriculture.

Less obvious is the phenomenal amount of money and resources that flow indirectly to industrial agriculture through funding for science. Whatever problems overproduction causes, we can at least understand why input corporations maximize sales: it is their business. Not so basic scientists. Yet scientists of various stripes carefully duck the crucial question of "why raise production?" In unpacking the history of hybrid corn in the US, Deborah Fitzgerald was struck by how public breeders simply assumed that more corn was a good thing; their job was to benefit farmers, but while "it did not require a Ph.D. in economics to realize that higher yields were likely to lower prices…breeders, for the most part, were silent on this issue" (Fitzgerald 1990, 70–71). The reason the breeders would be silent on this issue is that they were rewarded for breeding higher-yielding seeds more than for helping farmers (Chapter 5). Again we see the essential feature of industrial agriculture that it is driven by off-farm entities with off-farm interests.

The process of developing higher-yielding technologies is a self-amplifying process. Once new inputs become established, a process is unleashed that causes farmers to keep buying new technology and overproducing. This was explained in agricultural economist Willard Cochrane's theory of the *technology treadmill* (Cochrane 1958). This classic theory points out that agricultural technologies are taken up by early adopters who reap initial profits. As more farmers adopt the new technology, overall production rises and prices drop, putting farmers under pressure to produce even more. Then other farmers are pressured to adopt the new technology in hopes of higher yields. The so-called "laggards" – especially those with smaller operations – can't afford the greater outlay, and are less able to recover the higher production costs at the lower output prices. This squeezes non-adopting farmers out of farming, leaving them to be "cannibalized" by selling or leasing to larger farmers who need to expand to capitalize on the technologies they are buying (Ramey 2010, 382).

This is why every turn of the technological treadmill leads to fewer farmers on larger farms, spending more and more money on inputs, growing more and more crops, and needing to be subsidized by more and more government payments to protect them from the economic consequences of their overproduction (Figure 3.2).

Overproduction treadmills squeezed out a staggering number of smaller American farmers in the decades following World War II (Cochrane 1979, 138–139), despite government payouts. The USDA had been paying farmers to idle land since the 1930s (see Chapter 5); it also established price support programs, stored commodities, and bought up large amounts of surplus grain. As one measure of how much overage the government supported, it is estimated that if left to the laws of supply and demand, farm prices would have dropped a further 40% in the 1950s and 1960s (Cochrane 1979, 139). The US farm economy had reached "a chronic state of surplus" (Cochrane 1979, 139), and in 1960 Nobel laureate economist Theodore Schultz would write of the "vast" farm surpluses:

> Not so long ago when CCC stocks were still small and still had some connection with supply and demand contingencies, it was the "ever normal granary." Now, however, the prophecy of G. F. Warren has been fulfilled: "a granary easy to fill but impossible to empty"! The more farm surplus we dispose of the larger the remaining surplus becomes! Thus we have invented still another tread mill.
>
> *(1960, 1019–1020)*

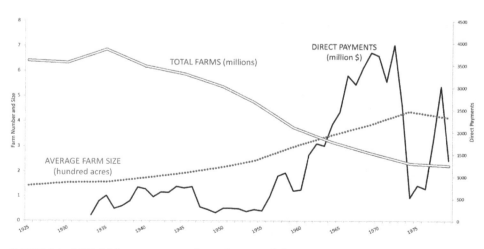

FIGURE 3.2 Mid-20th century trends on farms and direct government payments. The modern high-input system of agriculture that gelled in the US in the decades following World War II had treadmill effects that, coupled with government policies favoring large farms, led to the dramatic pattern of farm consolidation. Farmers also became increasingly reliant on government payments (which reached $46 billion in 2020). Data are from the USDA Economic Research Service.

In a sense, then, input companies and their farmer customers conspire to overproduce. But still we have to consider: "over" what?

"Over" What?

Overproduction is a slippery concept. To Ehrlich, the Delhi street population was "over" his personal discomfort limit; to Malthus, population was perpetually "over" the level allowing members of society to live virtuous lives. So when we say that a key feature of industrial agriculture is overproduction, we have to ask, over what exactly?

One meaning of overproduction is that the individual farmer is producing too much of one product as opposed to other products. This meaning hinges less on overall supply than with how farmers manage their operations. It was in this sense that the plight of the impoverished Southern farmers after the Civil War was attributed to "overproduction" of cotton (DeCanio 1973). As described by John Hicks (1961, 48),

> When prices went down, the farmer... saw no way out except to rent more land and raise more cotton. By attempting to farm too much he of course cut down the effectiveness of his work and got a smaller return per acre. He found, moreover, that his expenditures for seed, fertilizers, and supplies had increased as much as the returns from his crop, and his debt at the store might be even more than it had been the year before...[so] he sought the next year to raise more bales of cotton.

Cotton growing was not yet industrialized, but still agribusiness interests benefited from farmers' spiral of debt and cotton production, as did merchants who kept farmers on the treadmill by offering loans only for cotton production (Ransom and Sutch 1972). From the productivist mindset the arrival of the voracious boll weevil in the 1910s was a disaster, but some communities felt themselves rescued by the bug that broke the cycle and forced a more balanced agriculture. The southern Alabama town of Enterprise even erected a monument to the boll weevil.

Another definition of overproduction used in government policies is anything beyond requirements for domestic use or export sale, or that which cannot "find a commercial home" (Cochrane 1979, 140). By this definition agricultural output is overproduced when it is wasted due to lack of demand or sold at a loss. By this measure the US farm economy during its wild surge in grain production from the mid-1950s to the mid-1960s (Chapter 4) was overproducing by an estimated 7%. But this is a very narrow concept of overage; even a tiny profit constitutes a "commercial home." But more importantly, with its myopic focus on the farmer's profits this definition misses indirect societal impacts. And as supply of any agricultural commodity mushrooms under industrial agriculture, the value of the commodity drops and low-value uses abound, many of which have undesirable effects on economy, environment, and health. It is these indirect costs that are an important measure of overproduction. In short, industrial agriculture "overproduces" because its ever-rising output consistently tends to come to no good. Overproduction imposes costs on the taxpayer, on farmers in both the producing country and the "aid receiving" countries, on public health, and on maladaptive uses.

The economic costs of managing unneeded farm products – ultimately borne by the taxpayer – are the most obvious and persistent harm. That 7% figure for the 1950s–1960s excess may not sound huge, but by 1965 the government costs for procurement and storage alone were up to $10.9 billion per year (Cochrane 1979, 140). By 2020 the cost to the US government for "acreage reduction" programs (which pay farmers to stop growing so much) and other direct payments topped $46 billion.

The US government's long-time policy of reducing surplus by procuring and dumping excess grain on developing nations has had perverse effects on farmers in those countries, and despite the US glibly referring to this as "aid," it has rarely fed anyone who would not have eaten otherwise. (We return to a famous case of food aid in Chapter 6 on the Green Revolution and see how US surplus dumping was more of a cause than a solution to India's supposed food woes.)

The public health costs of industrial agriculture's output are the most troubling of industrial agriculture's indirect impacts. Industrial agriculture has always longed for people to eat more. This applies not just to agribusiness but to the government agricultural establishment; as early as 1915, the agriculturist in charge of the USDA's Office of Farm Management said that "One even hears the remark that there is no such thing as overproduction; the trouble is underconsumption" (Spillman 1915). But it was the swelling grain harvests in the decades following World War II that led the US food industry to raise the practices of getting us to eat more into a high art.[19]

But arguably the most perverse cost of overproduction is that surplus is plowed back into further overproduction. Since 2010, the top use of American corn has been for fuel – mostly to the highly inefficient production of ethanol to help run cars, trucks, and *tractors*. As noted, Syngenta has even developed a genetically modified corn for ethanol production. The company markets the corn as "meeting the growing demand for American ethanol" although the whole corn ethanol industry arose to absorb corn overproduction.

This has been an exploration of the underlying logic of industrial agriculture. However maladaptive it is, this logic is real, comprising the three key pieces that fit together. Agriculture has never undergone a complete reorganization as did textiles (and then other factory commodities), but separate components of farm production have been "appropriated" and converted to off-farm industrial activities. Although presented as benefiting farmers and consumers, appropriative technologies have a remarkable history of appearing when overproduction is a problem and their adoption is largely powered by involuntary treadmill effects. But they are lucrative for the companies selling the products and services, largely because of the deep and varied government subsidy for each new technology. The government has institutional interests in industrializing agriculture, and individuals in government have career reasons as well. Appropriations reconfigure the interests driving the agricultural system in ways that make it highly prone to overproduction – "over" mainly because of the indirect harms caused by the surplus.

With this account of the general process of agricultural industrialization, we now turn to our case studies of the core technologies in industrial agriculture: fertilizer and seeds.

Notes

1 The early sugarcane proto-factories routinized many parts of production. The sugarcane was insistent in its scheduling demands, needing to be cut precisely when ripe and then ground as soon as it was cut. This led to the "synthesis of field and factory" as sugar plantations quickly became both cultivation and processing facilities (Mintz 1985, 47), all well before the Industrial Revolution.

2 For England, some see one protracted agricultural revolution stretching across the 17th and 18th centuries (Foster 1999); some see it in the late 18th and early 19th centuries (Allen 1999, 209); some identify a revolution in the mid-19th century (Foster 1999, 373) or one stretching across most of the 19th century (Thompson 1968).

3 Although various people, for various reasons, have yearned for an agricultural revolution. Marx and Engels, although critical of the effects of the Industrial Revolution, called for the merging of "agriculture with manufacturing industries" (Marx and Engels 1848). At the other end of the political spectrum, the Rockefeller Foundation has explicitly sought an "industrial revolution in agriculture, whereby agricultural personnel are taken off the land and put to work in factories to make farm machinery" (Cullather 2010, 242). Early 20th century industrial theorists became enthralled with the idea that agriculture could be Taylorized and the farm turned into a factory (Fitzgerald 2003, chapter 3).

4 There have been "factory farms" since the 1940s, producing animal products through confinement. These are generally considered to be agriculture, but I am using the term in its etymological sense, meaning growing things in fields.

5 Karl Kautsky, the philosopher who emerged as the dean of Marxian scholarship after Engels' death in 1895, provided the best-known Marxist dive into agriculture in *The Agrarian Question* (1988[1899]). But Kautsky's grasp of the makeup of agrarian society wasn't much better than Marx's, and he concluded dourly that "agriculture is not a social activity, and is not therefore amenable to social organization." He felt the way capitalism exploited smallholders was by dividing the countryside into rich peasants and the poor peasants who worked for them as laborers.

6 Seeing these technologies as having their own power, and turning a blind eye to the actual source of their power, is technology fetishism. Fetish is an interesting concept. In everyday language the term usually refers to an unusual object of sexual desire, but in social scholarship it has a larger meaning. This meaning arose from the process of European traders' early encounters with West Africans, as the Europeans struggled to make sense of the Africans attributing power and value to objects ranging from anthropomorphic statues to elephant bones (Graeber 2005, 416). Any object believed to have self-contained or magical powers to affect the world was termed a fetish (Harvey 2003, 3). Marx turned this term for how Africans misinterpreted power back on Westerners, writing that commodities in capitalist society are fetishes because they are seen as containing powers that actually reside in the people who deal with the commodities. Marx pointed to religion, where "products of the human brain appear as autonomous figures endowed with a life of their own, appear as autonomous figures enove and shape the world inheres not in the holy water or sacred book but in the individuals who bless the water or interpret the book (Marx 1967 [1867]).

We fetishize technologies of agricultural industrialization in similar ways, our case studies being good examples. We will see that hybrid corn and Green Revolution grains are credited with nearly magic power – the mysterious "hybrid vigor" in the corn and "built-in productivity" in the wheat and rice. Yet we will see that corn hybrids are not inherently more productive than earlier forms of corn; they are just able to capture the labor of public breeders to find the few superior seeds. And Green Revolution grains were not inherently more productive, just responsive to chemical fertilizers subsidized by governments.

7 These figures are from USDA NASS Quickstats, and are based on 2017, the last year of the agricultural census.

8 British agriculture specialist Jules Pretty and colleagues (2001, 265) provide a valuable, but slightly different, analysis of externalized costs. They point out that the types of externalities in the industrial agriculture have four features: (1) their costs are often neglected; (2) they often occur with a time lag; (3) they often damage groups whose interests are not represented; and (4) the identity of the producer of the externality is not always known.

9 The same team that linked childhood DDT exposure to adult breast cancer also found that daughters whose mothers had high levels of DDT while pregnant were more likely to develop breast cancer (Cohn et al. 2015). Another study found that boys whose pregnant mothers had high levels of DDT were also more likely to develop testicular cancer (Cohn, Cirillo, and Christianson 2010).

10 There is the possibility of tort (lawsuit) remedies. As I write this, controversies are raging around the lawsuits against Monsanto by plaintiffs who blamed their cancers on Roundup herbicide. When negative externalities such as disease can be clearly linked to a product, tort remedies may offer some relief although it may take many years for this to materialize (as the tortured history

of tobacco lawsuits shows). But tort relief will always be hampered by the delayed, distant, and diffuse nature of agricultural externalities.

11 The USDA yearbook tables give production figures back to 1866. Between 1866 and 2018 the US corn yield rose from 24.3 to 176.4 bushels/acre, so 7.3 bushels were growing where one bushel had grown.

12 I say "next to impossible" because with the GM crop revolution we have arrived at the point where some farmers can indeed be dragged into court for using seeds they grew themselves.

13 Industries benefit from both loosening regulation on themselves and tightening it on competitors. The railroad industry, for instance, achieved stringent regulations to strangle competition from truckers in inter-city transport of farm goods in the 1930s. State-level regulations won by the railroads to protect themselves were brazen, including strict payload limits on trucks serving (and therefore competing with) two or more railroad stations, but not on trucks serving only one station (and so not competing with it) (Stigler 1971, 8).

14 Stigler did not actually use the term "regulatory capture" but the dynamics he described are now generally known by that term.

15 However Ryan and Gross themselves did not use those terms.

16 On agricultural experimentation, see Stone (2016), Sumberg and Okali (1997), Richards (1986), Haverkort and Millar (1992).

17 Another aspect of social learning is that decisions are sometimes influenced not just by what others are doing but by what others will think of one's decision. The image one wishes to project may affect their inclination to go organic, or buy a high-end tractor, or keep particularly tidy fields.

18 For instance, in his Nobel lecture, Norman Borlaug said:

> Some critics have said that the green revolution has created more problems than it has solved… [t]his I cannot accept, for I believe it is far better for mankind to be struggling with new problems caused by abundance rather than with the old problem of famine.
>
> (Borlaug 1999[1970])

But as we will see, there was no widespread famine in India leading up to the Green Revolution.

19 Michael Pollan (2006) traces the effects of corn overproduction through the US diet, and Marion Nestle (2007) shows how the process of regulatory capture has played out in food and nutrition.

References

Allen, Robert C. 1999. "Tracking the Agricultural Revolution in England." *The Economic History Review* 52 (2):209–235. doi: 10.1111/1468-0289.00123.

Appleby, Joyce. 1982. "Commercial Farming and the "Agrarian Myth" in the Early Republic." *The Journal of American History* 68 (4):833–849. doi: 10.2307/1900771.

Barlett, Peggy F. 1987. "Industrial Agriculture in Evolutionary Perspective." *Cultural Anthropology* 2 (1):137–154.

Becker, Jasper. 1996. *Hungry Ghosts: Mao's Secret Famine.* New York: The Free Press.

Borlaug, Norman E. 1999[1970]. "The Green Revolution, peace, and humanity." In *Nobel Lectures in Peace 1951-1970*, edited by Frederick W. Haberman, pp. 445–480. Singapore: World Scientific Publishing.

Borlaug, Norman E. 1971. "DDT, the First Domino." *New York Times*, 21 Nov, 13.

Boyd, William and Michael Watts. 1997. "Agro-industrial Just-in-time: The Chicken Industry and Postwar American Capitalism." In *Globalising Food: Agrarian Questions and Global Restructuring*, edited by David Goodman and Michael Watts, 192–224. London: Routledge.

Brush, Stephen B. 2004. *Farmers' Bounty: Locating Crop Diversity in the Contemporary World.* New Haven, CT: Yale Univ. Press.

Burlingame, Roger. 1939. "Rainbow Over the Farm." *Harpers* Dec:50–59.

Busch, Lawrence. 2000. *The Eclipse of Morality: Science, State and Market.* New York: Aldine.

Bush, Vannevar. 1945. *Science the Endless Frontier.* Washington, DC: US Govn Printing Office. https://www.nsf.gov/about/history/nsf50/vbush1945.jsp

Cane, Peter. 2002. "Tort Law as Regulation." *Common Law World Review* 31:305–331.

Carson, Rachel. 1962. *Silent Spring*. Boston, MA: Houghton Mifflin.

Cochrane, Willard W. 1958. *Farm Prices, Myth and Reality*. Minneapolis: Univ. of Minnesota Press.

Cochrane, Willard W. 1979. *The Development of American Agriculture: A Historical Analysis*. Minneapolis: Univ. of Minnesota Press.

Cochrane, Willard W., and Mary Ellen Ryan. 1976. *American Farm Policy: 1948–1973*. Univ. of Minnesota Press.

Cohn, Barbara A., Piera M. Cirillo, and Roberta E. Christianson. 2010. "Prenatal DDT Exposure and Testicular Cancer: A Nested Case-Control Study." *Archives of Environmental & Occupational Health* 65 (3):127–134. doi: 10.1080/19338241003730887.

Cohn, Barbara A., Michele La Merrill, Nickilou Y. Krigbaum, Gregory Yeh, June-Soo Park, Lauren Zimmermann, and Piera M. Cirillo. 2015. "DDT Exposure in Utero and Breast Cancer." *The Journal of Clinical Endocrinology & Metabolism* 0 (0):jc.2015-1841. doi:10.1210/jc.2015-1841.

Cohn, Barbara A., Mary S. Wolff, Piera M. Cirillo, and Robert I. Sholtz. 2007. "DDT and Breast Cancer in Young Women: New Data on the Significance of Age at Exposure." *Environmental Health Perspectives* 15 (10):1406–1414.

Collotta, M., P.A. Bertazzi, and V. Bollati. 2013. "Epigenetics and Pesticides." *Toxicology* 307:35–41. doi: 10.1016/j.tox.2013.01.017.

Congressional Research Service. 2018. *U.S. Farm Income Outlook for 2018, updated December 11, 2018*. Washington, DC. https://crsreports.congress.gov/product/pdf/R/R45117.

Cullather, Nick. 2010. *The Hungry World: America's Cold War Battle against Poverty in Asia*. Cambridge, MA: Harvard Univ. Press.

Dal Bo, Ernesto. 2006. "Regulatory Capture: A Review." *Oxford Review of Economic Policy* 22 (2):203–225. https://academic.oup.com/oxrep/issue.

Danbom, David B. 1979. *The Resisted Revolution: Urban America and the Industrialization of Agriculture 1900–1930*. Ames: Iowa State University.

Daniel, Pete. 1985. *Breaking the Land: The Transformation of Cotton, Tobacco, and Rice Cultures since 1880*. Urbana and Chicago: Univ. of Illinois Press.

DeCanio, Stephen. 1973. "Cotton "Overproduction" in Late Nineteenth-Century Southern Agriculture." *The Journal of Economic History* 33 (3):608–633. doi: 10.2307/2117116.

Dinnes, Dana L., Douglas L. Karlen, Dan B. Jaynes, Thomas C. Kaspar, Jerry L. Hatfield, Thomas S. Colvin, and Cynthia A. Cambardella. 2002. "Nitrogen Management Strategies to Reduce Nitrate Leaching in Tile-Drained Midwestern Soils." *Agronomy Journal* 94 (1):153–171. doi: 10.2134/agronj2002.1530.

Dowd-Uribe, Brian. 2014. "Engineering Yields and Inequality? How Institutions and Agro-ecology Shape Bt Cotton Outcomes in Burkina Faso." *Geoforum* 53:161–171.

Dudley, Brier. 2018. "Look to B.C. for Evidence Carbon Tax Doesn't Work." *Seattle Times*, 25 January. https://www.seattletimes.com/opinion/look-to-b-c-for-evidence-carbon-tax-doesnt-work/.

Economic Research Service. 2018. "Farm Income and Wealth Statistics: Production Expenses." https://data.ers.usda.gov/reports.aspx?ID=17834.

Eichenwald, Kurt 2001. "Biotechnology Food: From the Lab to a Debacle." *New York Times*, 25 Jan. https://www.nytimes.com/2001/01/25/business/redesigning-nature-hard-lessons-learned-biotechnology-food-lab-debacle.html.

Fitzgerald, Deborah. 1990. *The Business of Breeding: Hybrid Corn in Illinois 1890–1940*. Ithaca, NY: Cornell Univ. Press.

Fitzgerald, Deborah. 1996. "Blinded by Technology: American Agriculture in the Soviet Union, 1928–1932." *Agricultural History* 70 (3):459–486.

Fitzgerald, Deborah. 2003. *Every Farm a Factory: The Industrial Ideal in American Agriculture*. New Haven, CT and London: Yale Univ. Press.

Flachs, Andrew. 2019. *Cultivating Knowledge: Biotechnology, Sustainability, and the Human Cost of Cotton Capitalism in India*. Tucson: Univ. of Arizona Press.

Foster, John Bellamy. 1999. "Marx's Theory of Metabolic Rift: Classical Foundations for Environmental Sociology." *American Journal of Sociology* 105 (2):366–405.

Gautam, M. 2015. "Agricultural Subsidies: Resurging Interest in a Perennial Debate." *Indian Journal of Agricultural Economics* 70 (1):83–105.

Giesen, James C., and Mark Hersey. 2010. "The New Environmental Politics and its Antecedents: Lessons from the Early Twentieth Century South." *The Historian* 72 (2) Summer:271–298.

Goldenberg, Suzanne. 2011. "GM Corn being Developed for Fuel Instead of Food." *The Guardian*, 15 Aug. https://www.theguardian.com/environment/2011/aug/15/gm-corn-development-food-fuel.

Goodman, David, Bernardo Sorj, and John Wilkinson. 1987. *From Farming to Biotechnology: A Theory of Agro-Industrial Development*. Oxford: Basil Blackwell.

Graeber, David. 2005. "Fetishism as Social Creativity: Or, Fetishes Are Gods in the Process of Construction." *Anthropological Theory* 5 (4):407–438. doi: 10.1177/1463499605059230.

Granovetter, Mark. 1978. "Threshold Models of Collective Behavior." *American Journal of Sociology* 83 (6):1420–1443.

Griffin, Ronald C., and Daniel W. Bromley. 1982. "Agricultural Runoff as a Nonpoint Externality; A Theoretical Development." *American Journal of Agricultural Economics* 64:547–552.

Hakim, Danny. 2016. "This Pesticide Is Prohibited in Britain. Why Is It Still Being Exported?" *New York Times*, 20 Dec. http://mobile.nytimes.com/2016/12/20/business/paraquat-weed-killer-pesticide.html.

Hamilton, Hayden. 2016. How Corporate Agribusinesses Are Fouling Our Waters. *TribTalk* 18 July. https://www.tribtalk.org/2016/07/18/how-corporate-agribusinesses-are-fouling-our-waters/

Harding, T. Swann. 1947. *Two Blades of Grass*. Norman: Univ. of Oklahoma Press.

Harvey, David. 2003. "The Fetish of Technology: Causes and Consequences." *Macalester International* 13:Article 7.

Haverkort, Bertus, and David Millar. 1992. "Farmers' Experiments and Cosmovision." *ILEIA Newsletter* www.metafro.be/leisa/1992/8-1-26.pdf.

Henrich, Joe, and Robert Boyd. 1998. "The Evolution of Conformist Transmission and the Emergence of Between-Group Differences." *Evolution and Human Behavior* 19 (4):215–241. doi: 10.1016/S1090-5138(98)00018-X.

Henrich, Joseph. 2001. "Cultural Transmission and the Diffusion of Innovations: Adoption Dynamics Indicate That Biased Cultural Transmission Is the Predominate Force in Behavioral Change." *American Anthropologist* 103 (4):992–1013.

Hicks, John. 1961. *The Populist Revolt*. Lincoln: Univ. of Nebraska Press.

Jayne, Thomas S., Nicole M. Mason, William J. Burke, and Joshua Ariga. 2018. "Review: Taking Stock of Africa's Second-generation Agricultural Input Subsidy Programs." *Food Policy* 75:1–14. doi: 10.1016/j.foodpol.2018.01.003.

Johnson, Timothy. 2016. "Growth Industry: The Political Economy of Fertilizer in America, 1865–1947." PhD, History, Univ. of Georgia.

Kautsky, Karl. 1988[1899]. *The Agrarian Question*. Translated by Pete Burgess. London: Zwan Publications.

Kloppenburg, Jack Ralph, Jr. 2004. *First the Seed: The Political Economy of Plant Biotechnology, 1492–2000, 2nd edition*. Madison: Univ. Wisconsin Press.

Kranthi, K.R., D.R. Jadhav, S. Kranthi, R.R. Wanjari, S.S. Ali, and D.A. Russell. 2002. "Insecticide Resistance in Five Major Insect Pests of Cotton in India." *Crop Protection* 21 (6):449–460. doi 10.1016/S0261-2194(01)00131-4.

Kranthi, K.R., and Glenn Davis Stone. 2020. "Long-Term Impacts of Bt Cotton in India." *Nature: Plants* 6 (March):188–196. doi 10.1038/s41477-020-0615-5.

Lenin, V.I. 1977 (1913). "Who Stands to Gain?" *Pravda* 84 (in Lenin Collected Works, Vol. 16, pp. 53–54. Progress Publishers, Moscow.).

Lewontin, Richard C. 2000. "The Maturing of Capitalist Agriculture: Farmer as Proletarian." In *Hungry for Profit: The Agribusiness Threat to Farmers, Food, and the Environment*, edited by Fred Magdoff, John Bellamy Foster and Frederick H. Buttel, 93–106. New York: Monthly Review Press.

Li, Jun, Nansong Jiang, Yuebin Ke, Andrea T. Feßler, Yang Wang, Stefan Schwarz, and Congming Wu. 2017. "Characterization of Pig-associated Methicillin-resistant Staphylococcus aureus." *Veterinary Microbiology* 201:183–187. doi: 10.1016/j.vetmic.2017.01.017.

Luoma, Jon R. 2000. "Pandora's Pantry." *Mother Jones* Jan–Feb:53–59.

Lusk, Jayson L. 2016. "Lunch with Pigou: Externalities and the "Hidden" Cost of Food." *Agricultural and Resource Economics Review* 42 (3):419–435. doi: 10.1017/S1068280500004913.

Malm, Andreas. 2013. "The Origins of Fossil Capital: From Water to Steam in the British Cotton Industry." *Historical Materialism* 21 (1):15–68.

Manuel, John. 2014. "Nutrient Pollution: A Persistent Threat to Waterways." *Environmental Health Perspectives* 122:A304–A309. doi: 10.1289/ehp.122-A304.

Marx, Karl. 1852. "The Eighteenth Brumaire of Louis Bonaparte." http://www.marxists.org/archive/marx/works/1852/18th-brumaire/.

Marx, Karl. 1973[1857]. *Grundrisse (Outlines of the Critique of Political Economy).* New York: Vintage Books.

Marx, Karl. 1967 [1867]. *Capital: A Critique of Political Economy, Volume 1.* New York: Vintage.

Marx, Karl, and Frederick Engels. 1848. "Manifesto of the Communist Party." http://www.marxists.org/archive/marx/works/download/pdf/Manifesto.pdf.

McElreath, Richard. 2004. "Social Learning and the Maintenance of Cultural Variation: An Evolutionary Model and Data from East Africa." *American Anthropologist* 106:308–321.

McMichael, Philip. 2000. "Global Food Politics." In *Hungry for Profit: The Agribusiness Threat to Farmers, Food, and the Environment*, edited by Fred Magdoff, John Bellamy Foster and Frederick H. Buttel, 125–143. New York: Monthly Review Press.

McWilliams, James E. 2008. "'The Horizon Opened up Very Greatly': Leland O. Howard and the Transition to Chemical Insecticides in the United States, 1894–1927." *Agricultural History* 82 (4):468–495.

Mintz, Sidney W. 1985. *Sweetness and Power: The Place of Sugar in Modern History.* New York: Penguin Books.

Mosse, David. 2005. *Cultivating Development: An Ethnography of Aid Policy and Practice.* London: Pluto Press.

Mukerji, Chandra. 1989. *A Fragile Power: Scientists and the State.* Princeton, NJ: Princeton Univ. Press.

Nestle, Marion. 2007. *Food Politics: How the Food Industry Influences Nutrition and Health, revised and expanded edition.* Berkeley: Univ. of California Press.

Peltzman, S. 1976. "Toward a More General Theory of Regulation." *Journal of Law and Economics* 19:211–248.

Philpott, Tom. 2009. "Monsanto's Man Taylor Returns to FDA in Food-Czar Role. *Grist Magazine*, 9 July, https://grist.org/article/2009-07-08-monsanto-fda-taylor/.

Pollan, Michael. 2006. *The Omnivore's Dilemma: A Natural History of Four Meals.* New York: Penguin.

Porter, Eduardo. 2016. "Does a Carbon Tax Work? Ask British Columbia." *New York Times*, 1 March. https://www.nytimes.com/2016/03/02/business/does-a-carbon-tax-work-ask-british-columbia.html.

Pretty, Jules, Craig Brett, David Gee, Rachel Hine, Chris Mason, James Morison, Matthew Rayment, Gert van der Bijl, and Thomas Dobbs. 2001. "Policy Challenges and Priorities for Internalizing the Externalities of Modern Agriculture." *Journal of Environmental Planning and Management* 44 (2):263–283.

Ramey, Elizabeth A. 2010. "Seeds of Change: Hybrid Corn, Monopoly, and the Hunt for Superprofits." *Review of Radical Political Economics* 42 (3):381–386. doi: 10.1177/0486613410378005.

Ransom, Roger, and Richard Sutch. 1972. "Debt Peonage in the Cotton South after the Civil War." *Journal of Economic History* 32:641–669.

Richards, Paul. 1986. *Coping with Hunger: Hazard and Experiment in an African Rice Farming System.* London: Allen and Unwin.

Rogers, Everett M. 2003. *Diffusion of Innovations, 5th edition.* New York: Free Press.

Rolfsmeier, Michael, Cynthia Haseltine, Elisabetta Bini, Amy Clark, and Paul Blum. 1998. "Molecular Characterization of the α-Glucosidase Gene (malA) from the Hyperthermophilic Archaeon Sulfolobus solfataricus." *Journal of Bacteriology* 180 (5):1287.

Rostow, W.W. 1955. "Marx Was A City Boy, or, Why Communism May Fail." *Harper's Magazine*, 1955 Feb 01, 25–30. https://harpers.org/archive/1955/02/marx-was-a-city-boy/.

Ryan, Bryce, and Neal C. Gross. 1943. "The Diffusion of Hybrid Seed Corn in Two Iowa Communities." *Rural Sociology* 8:15–24.

Schecter, Kate, and Edd Wright. 2015. "Indonesia's Burning Problem: Putting a Stop to Slash and Burn." *Foreign Affairs* 11 Nov. https://www.foreignaffairs.com/articles/2015-11-11/indonesias-burning-problem.

Schultz, Theodore W. 1960. "Value of U.S. Farm Surpluses to Underdeveloped Countries." *Journal of Farm Economics* 42 (5):1019–1030. doi: 10.2307/1235653.

Scott, James C. 1998. *Seeing Like a State: How Certain Schemes to Improve the Human Condition Have Failed.* New Haven, CT: Yale Univ. Press.

Sebilo, Mathieu, Bernhard Mayer, Bernard Nicolardot, Gilles Pinay, Andre Mariotti. 2013. "Long-term Fate of Nitrate Fertilizer in Agricultural Soils." *Proceedings of the National Academy of Sciences of the United States of America* 110 (45):18185–18189.

Sherkow, Jacob S., and Henry T. Greely. 2015. "The History of Patenting Genetic Material." *Annual Review of Genetics* 49:161–82.

Smith, Adam. 2008[1776]. *An Inquiry into the Nature and Causes of the Wealth of Nations.* London: Oxford Univ. Press.

Spillman, W. J. 1915. "The Efficiency Movement in Its Relation to Agriculture." *The Annals of the American Academy of Political and Social Science* 59:65–76.

Stigler, George J. 1971. "The Theory of Economic Regulation." *The Bell Journal of Economics and Management Science* 2 (1):3–21. doi: 10.2307/3003160.

Stone, Glenn Davis. 2007. "Agricultural Deskilling and the Spread of Genetically Modified Cotton in Warangal." *Current Anthropology* 48:67–103.

Stone, Glenn Davis. 2011. "Field versus Farm in Warangal: Bt Cotton, Higher Yields, and Larger Questions." *World Development* 39 (3):387–398. doi: 10.1016/j.worlddev.2010.09.008.

Stone, Glenn Davis. 2016. "Towards a General Theory of Agricultural Knowledge Production: Environmental, Social and Didactic Learning." *Culture, Agriculture, Food and Environment* 38 (1):5–17. doi:10.1111/cuag.12061.

Stone, Glenn Davis. 2022. "Surveillance Agriculture and Peasant Autonomy." *Journal of Agrarian Change* 2022:1–24. doi:10.1111/joac.12470.

Stone, Glenn Davis, and Andrew Flachs. 2014. "The Problem with the Farmer's Voice." *Agriculture and Human Values* 31 (4):649–653. doi: 10.1007/s10460-014-9535-1.

Stone, Glenn Davis, Andrew Flachs, and Christine Diepenbrock. 2014. "Rhythms of the Herd: Long term Dynamics in Seed Choice by Indian Farmers." *Technology in Society* 36:26–38. doi: 10.1016/j.techsoc.2013.10.003.

Sumberg, J., and C. Okali. 1997. *Farmers' Experiments: Creating Local Knowledge.* Boulder, CO: Lynne Rienner.

Swift, Jonathan. 1950[1726]. *Gulliver's Travels: Travels into Several Remote Nations of the World.* New York: Harper.

Syngenta Corp. 2018. Syngenta Reports Enogen® Premiums-to-date Paid to Corn Growers Will Top $100 Million in 2018. http://www.syngenta-us.com/newsroom/news_release_detail.aspx?id=206352

Tegtmeier, Erin M, and Michael Duffy. 2004. "External Costs of Agricultural Production in the United States." *International Journal of Agricultural Sustainability* 2 (1):1–20.

Thompson, F.M.L. 1968. "The Second Agricultural Revolution, 1815–1880." *The Economic History Review* 21 (1):62–77. doi: 10.2307/2592204.

Torrance, Andrew W. 2010. "Gene Concepts, Gene Talk, and Gene Patents." *Minnesota Journal of Law, Science & Technology* 11 (1):157–191.

Wise, Timothy A. 2019. *Eating Tomorrow: Agribusiness, Family Farmers, and the Battle for the Future of Food.* New York: The New Press.

Wrigley, E.A. 1988. *Continuity, Chance and Change: The Character of the Industrial Revolution in England.* Cambridge: Cambridge Univ. Press.

4

FERTILIZER AND THE "NATURAL GROUNDS"

We have shown how agricultural industrialization is a process of appropriations, made profitable to input industries because of government subsidy. No appropriation has played as fundamental role in industrializing agriculture as fertilizer – that is, the chemical stuff that is manufactured rather than obtained from plants or animals.[1] Fertilizer was the first major industrial input; it is the biggest input in terms of energy (Pimentel 1980); and it has also opened the door to the most other appropriations.

We are interested here in fertilizer in general but also in one element in particular: N (nitrogen). One reason is that N is of paramount importance in crop growth because it is the main limiting factor in most crops under most circumstances. Another reason is that N can be synthesized in a factory. Most other nutrients cannot be synthesized or substituted, so we are stuck with what the earth provides. N is also important because some common forms of it are highly explosive. This has led the history of fertilizer to be entangled with the history of warfare, and without this entanglement our agriculture would look vastly different than it does.

Ammonia – the basic compound produced in nitrogen synthesis – is the world's second largest chemical product (behind sulfuric acid), and 85% of it goes to fertilizer (Petrowiki 2018). N does play a major role in feeding the planet today, but it is misleading to conclude that we need the fertilizer simply because we have so many hungry mouths to feed; it's more that we have so many hungry overproduced crops to feed. Fertilizer has carved out its outsize role in our agriculture by pushing out (and preventing development of) more sustainable methods. The main reason that we use and waste such vast quantities of the stuff is that it has been made artificially cheap: fertilizer has had a rich history of raking in profits underwritten by governments paying for research, building infrastructure to manufacture and distribute it, subsidizing the market price, and lobbying farmers to buy it. Governments have likewise gone out of their way to absolve the industry of responsibility for the costs of fertilizer use. Fertilizer pioneered the model of industry sponging state subsidy, and also gave us our first examples of input producers being able to externalize their costs to environment and public health with impunity.

DOI: 10.4324/9781003286257-4

Fertilizer has also played a formative role in how we even think about agriculture: it was the lever that first pried open the door to the industrial mindset that permeates input-intensive agriculture. Fertilizer was the original funnel that opened the door to other funnels – irrigation, chemicals, and transgenics. Fertilizer also brought us our first examples of the aims and conduct of "basic science" being appropriated by commercial agricultural interests.

But it is hard to look critically at fertilizer because of the public relations the stuff enjoys.

Fertilizer enjoys a halo that has been carefully cultivated by vested interests connected to it. Even in the 19th century, when the fertilizer industry was relatively tiny, programs and faculty lines in land grant universities were tied to fertilizer promotion and sales (which worked wonders for turning professors into boosters). By the turn of the century the industry propaganda and lobbying arm, the National Fertilizer Association (NFA), was running its own demonstration farms, hiring agronomists to praise fertilizer, and savaging fertilizer's critics. In many ways, writes historian Timothy Johnson, NFA propaganda anticipated the "merchants of doubt" later employed by tobacco and fuel corporations to undermine federal regulation with dubious scientific studies (2016a, 109).

Industry strategies for wooing the public have been quite inventive. If you had attended a fertilizer sales convention in Atlanta in 1917 you could have heard blatant racism used as a marketing device, with speakers warning that "once flourishing communities" had "passed into the hands of negroes," because white landowners had not applied enough fertilizer. In 1918 you could have read that buying fertilizer was the best way for farmers to aid the war effort. If you were in a 4-H club in the 1930s you may have watched an NFA movie and received a coloring book about fertilizers (Johnson 2016a, 107, 226). If you read comic books in the early 1950s you may have read about Prosper Plenty, a talking bag of fertilizer who assures startled children that he is their friend (Figure 4.1).

But fertilizer rhetoric has mainly centered on claims that it is needed to feed the world and fend off Malthusian collapse. In the early 20th century, NFA letterhead said "Fertilizer Feeds the Plants that Feed the World"; today we are told that without it 2 billion of the world's

FIGURE 4.1   Images from the National Fertilizer Association's 1951 comic (Ater and NFA 1951). Malcolm Ater Collection, Univ. of Nebraska-Lincoln and West Virginia Univ.

people could not survive (Charles 2005, xiv). Philanthropist Bill Gates admits to being "obsessed" with the stuff (Fitzsimmons 2016). Criticize fertilizer and you will be charged with standing in the way of the feeding of Africa (Borlaug and Dowswell 1995, 123).

But the truth is that fertilizer is filthy, dangerous, and expensive stuff; that it is spectacularly wasteful; that it makes our bodies and environment sick; that it is the most important single cause of our chronic overproduction; and that it has only risen to its exalted position today by commandeering more government subsidy than any other agricultural input. Consider:

Fertilizer Is Hazardous to Make and Move

Production of ammonium nitrate, the explosive form of nitrogen, has a horrible history of deadly accidents. Fertilizer plants exploded in Oppau, Germany, in 1921 (585 killed), Kent, UK, in 1916 (115 killed), New Jersey in 1924 (18 killed, 40 buildings destroyed), Tessenderlo, Belgium, in 1942 (189 killed, 900 injured), Roseburg, Oregon, in 1959 (14 killed, 125 injured), Iowa in 1994 (4 killed), Shaanxi, China, in 1998 (22 killed, 56 injured), Toulouse, France, in 2001 (31 killed, 2442 injured), and West, Texas, in 2013 (15 killed, 260 injured, and over 150 buildings destroyed).

The worst industrial accident in US history was the 1947 explosion of a cargo ship loaded with ammonium nitrate fertilizer in Texas City, Texas, killing 581 people. Three months later, a cargo ship laden with ammonium nitrate blew up in Brest, France, killing 29. In a three-month period in 2004, trucks hauling ammonium–nitrate exploded in Spain and Romania, killing 20, and a train carrying ammonium nitrate near the China/North Korea border exploded, killing 162. Ammonium nitrate fertilizer detonated in 2015 in the port of Tianjin, China, killing 173, and in 2020 in Beirut, killing 178 and leaving 300,000 homeless.

Fertilizer Is Filthy to Make

Fertilizer factories are serious polluters of both water and air. In 2012 a chemical fertilizer factory in Changzhi, China leaked 39 tons of potentially carcinogenic aniline into the water supply for over a million people (Wong 2013). In 2016 a 45-foot-wide sinkhole formed under a wastepile in a Florida fertilizer plant, sending 200 million gallons of radioactive water into an underground aquifer (Philpott 2016). Polluted air within fertilizer factories leaves workers with lung cancer (Stayner et al. 2012; Yiin et al. 2016), emphysema (Block et al. 1988), and leukemia (Yiin et al. 2016). The plants have serious impacts on the atmosphere as well. Even the most efficient plants release two tons of heat-trapping CO_2 for every ton of ammonia produced (LeCompte 2013). A single fertilizer plant may generate as much atmospheric CO_2 as 432,000 cars driven for an entire year (Wendle 2015). Fertilizer factories spew out 100 times the amount of the potent greenhouse gas methane as previously thought (Zhou et al. 2019). In the US today most factories use natural gas, so the environmental costs of fracking are partly due to our fertilizer addiction (Meng 2017).

Fertilizer Is Ridiculously Wasteful

Most applied fertilizer is lost to the environment as it washes off into streams, leaches through the soil into the water table, and volatilizes into the air (Good and Beatty 2011, UNEP 2007, 13). Less than half is taken up by crops (Tilman et al. 2002, 673) and even less actually gets into our food: of the 100 million metric tons of factory-produced nitrogen, only 17% actually ended up in the human diet (Erisman et al. 2008, UNEP 2007). The proportion of waste is getting worse, not better; the nitrogen use efficiency of cereals – i.e., how much actually goes into the plants – dropped from around 80% in 1960 to around 30% in 2000 (Erisman et al. 2008, 637).

Fertilizer Destroys Soil Fertility

Most soils have plant nutrients locked up in stone particles and other forms not accessible to the plants. The key to using these nutrients are beneficial microbes that extract mineral nutrients from rock fragments and help to break down organic matter. Synthetic fertilizers interrupt these interactions and kill beneficial microbes so the crop becomes chemical-dependent (Montgomery 2017). The fertilizer that does remain in the soil has almost no staying power or positive cumulative effects. Compare this fertility-destroying process to the staying power of manure: a famous English study in which dung was applied to a field for 20 years (1852–1872) and then stopped found higher soil fertility than non-dunged control plots even 100 years later (Stoll 2002, 151).[2]

Fertilizer Is Dirty to Use

That fertilizer washing into bodies of water is the most widespread contaminant in the world (Bhatnagar and Sillanpää 2011). It feeds outbreaks of pernicious pfiesteria plankton, causing fish kills, and algae blooms that kill aquatic life in dead zones (Zhang, Chen, and Vitousek 2013). An unprecedented 33 mile[2] toxic bloom described as "smelly guacamole" in Florida's largest freshwater lake was declared a state of emergency in 2016 (Beyond Pesticides 2016); a 2011 Lake Erie toxic algal bloom that was over three times larger than any previously observed bloom. By 2050, an estimated 59% of all nitrogen fertilizer will be applied in developing regions located upstream of the type of marine ecosystems most vulnerable to phytoplankton blooms (Beman, Arrigo, and Matson 2005).

Even more troubling are effects on the atmosphere. Nitrogen fertilizer produces even more greenhouse gas when applied than when it is made. Fertilizer in soil feeds microbes that belch out nitrous oxide (N_2O), a notorious greenhouse gas. Standard estimates that overall agriculture contributes 10–15% of global greenhouse gas (Burney, Davis, and Lobell 2010) underestimate the problem; a recent major study in the US corn belt found that previous estimates of N_2O emissions should be doubled (Turner et al. 2015). Fertilizer is also a major contributor to acid rain, the scourge that killed trees and fish and dissolved parts of statues on the National Mall in the 1970s and the 1980s (Tennesen 2010). But rather than sulfur emissions from power plants, the main driver of acid rain today is the gasses released from fertilizer use.

Fertilizer Makes Us Sick

Fertilizer runoff percolates directly into groundwater and drinking water; as many as 20% of wells in the midwestern US are contaminated (Nolan et al. 1997).[3] Concentrated nitrates in drinking water cause "blue-baby syndrome" in infants (UNEP 2007); some towns in the US receive regular alerts to keep babies from consuming tap water to avoid nitrate poisoning. There are also indirect effects such as toxins released by fertilizer-induced algae blooms which damage skin, stomach, and liver (Manuel 2014, A305).[4] Processes for pulling nitrates out of water supplies are too expensive for the towns and rural communities that suffer most from groundwater nitrate poisoning (Gerlock 2015).[5]

Research also now links fertilizers to long-term alterations in the endocrine, nervous, and immune systems, colorectal and thyroid disease, birth defects (Ward et al. 2018) and to alterations in gene expression (Guillette and Edwards 2005, Sumners 2016). But we are alarmingly ignorant of long-term effects of low doses of fertilizer on our health.[6]

A rogues' gallery of toxins also hitchhikes along in fertilizers. This is primarily a problem in the US, where regulations are relatively lax; for instance, permitted levels of heavy metal are eight times that of Canada and most European nations (Foster and Magdoff 2000). National laws such as the Clean Water Act, EPA policies, and state regulations all fail to keep fertilizers from containing mercury, arsenic, cadmium, lead, and even carcinogenic, endocrine-disrupting dioxins, which then find their way into plant, animal, and seafoods (Waliser 2003, 62–69). (The health risk posed by the low levels of dioxins in foods is poorly known. In 2000 the US Environmental Protection Agency has estimated the lifetime cancer risk from dioxin to be ten times greater than previous estimates (APHIS 2000).)

We did not wind up so dependent on such a toxic and wasteful mode of agriculture because growing populations pushed scientists to help farmers make more food. The story is more one of chemists claiming they could deliver perfect crop nutrition while they invested in fertilizer factories; of government supporting a fertilizer industry instead of the nonchemical means many agriculturalists advocated; of the US pushing fertilizer-intensive farming into the developing world, where today some countries spend more than 15% of their GDP on fertilizer subsidies (Huang, Gulati, and Gregory 2017, 2). And most of all it is a story of fertilizer makers and users in most of the world being allowed to avoid paying for fertilizer's costs like those detailed above. The story begins at an important moment in history around 1840.

An Important Moment in History

Throughout most of the human career in agriculture, fertility management has been a local affair, involving animals, floodwater deposits, and other solutions. The emergence of fertilizing with external materials was the first major appropriation in agriculture and it began early: the watershed was in 1840, when the core elements of industrial agriculture – productivist farming based on subsidized, external, factory-produced inputs promoted by self-interested science – gelled for the first time.

That year brought changes on two fronts. First, at a time when interest in soil fertility was at an all-time peak, a whole new paradigm in the science of soil fertility appeared. Second was the start of trade in off-farm fertilizer which would evolve from bird guano to mined nitrates to chemical fertilizer from factories. An outgrowth of these developments was a fundamental change in thinking on agriculture, as external inputs and services came to be thought of as scientific and as progress. Together these changes had sweeping and transformative effects on what was to come.

There were reasons these changes came when they did. In the early 1800s soil fertility in major parts of both Europe and the US was being rapidly depleted. In Europe the reasons were closely linked to the Industrial Revolution, which had taken hold in England in the late 1700s and was helping to generate the poverty that Malthus misidentified as the result of overpopulation. England had Europe's highest rural-to-urban migration, as peasants who had been squeezed off their land by Enclosure acts moved to join the urban workforce. As the mills cranked up in the cities, the English and Welsh countryside was increasingly given over to commercial agriculture (Wood 2000) with profound effects on the circulation of nutrients, as rural fertility flowed into cities in what later scholars would call the "metabolic rift."

Parts of the US were also suffering from soil degradation, particularly in the south where growing nutrient-hungry tobacco and corn had taken a severe toll. Then the new textile mills of the Industrial Revolution brought an era of ravenous demand for raw cotton. With its favorable climate, its vast lands being expropriated from its Indian inhabitants, and its enslaved laborers, the US South was perfectly positioned to capitalize on this demand; by 1820 cotton was accounting for 32% of all US exports. Cotton cultivation devastated southern soils in the early 19th century as settlers, with slaves in tow, "drifted from South Carolina to Central Texas in search of fresh soil, leaving a trail of eroded and exhausted 'old fields' in their wake" (Johnson 2016a, 34). An 1818 article described farmed out lands being abandoned and grown over with "vast and gloomy thickets" (Garnett 1818, 55–57). That year ex-president James Madison delivered a famous speech in which he pleaded with his fellow planters "to make the thieves restore as much as possible of the stolen fertility" in order to "rescue ... our farms from their present degraded condition."

But while we are used to problems like soil exhaustion being joined at the hip with "overpopulation," the problems that Madison bemoaned resulted more from *under*population created by appropriation of Indian lands in the south. Planters romped through freshly depopulated lands in a grotesque parody of the sustainable shifting cultivation described in Chapter 7. As one Georgia cotton grower put it, "We appear to have but one rule – that is, to make as much cotton as we can, and wear out as much land as we can" (Beckert 2014, 103). Under these conditions it was profitable to farm until yields crashed, sell the land cheaply, and move on rather than restore the "stolen fertility."

Thus in both Europe and the US, the Industrial Revolution had led farmers into uncharted territory of soil depletion, and interest in fertility solutions became increasingly urgent. But restoring fertility was easier said than done, and early 19th century farmers lacked knowledge and tradition for managing degraded soils. Some agriculturalists championed marl (Stoll 2002, 150); some advocated manure, leading to "manure rushes" (Barles and Lestel 2007, 797); a bonemeal craze in 1830s Europe led to the ghoulish practice of exhuming bones from Napoleonic battlefields (Foster and Magdoff 2000, 44).[7]

But the 1830s also saw the beginnings of trade in even more distantly sourced fertilizers, as a remarkable chapter of "guano imperialism" began, providing an odd but crucial prelude to the rise of industrial fertilizer.

It Starts with Guano

Bird shit is called *guano*.[8] Peru would become the center of the commercial guano trade because of an unusual convergence of natural factors off its northwest coast: trade winds bring up nutrient-rich waters, which support plankton, which feeds fish, which feed birds that nest on coral islands, where the exceedingly dry climate allows vast piles of white dung to accumulate. Early chroniclers compared the guano islands to snow-covered mountains (Cushman 2013, 7).

Guano's value as fertilizer was long known in the Andes. Among the Incas, guano fertilizer was valued so highly that killing birds or even disturbing them during breeding season were capital offenses (Cushman 2013, 8, Leigh 2004, 78). There was small-scale trade in guano from these islands by the 1820s but the real trafficking began around 1840; by 1858, over 300,000 tons was arriving each year in Britain (Clark and Foster 2009). Trade to the US was smaller but still lively: by 1849 yearly imports had risen to 20,000 tons. Peruvian elites profited handsomely from it; from 1840 to 1880 guano accounted for three quarters of national income (Mathew 1970).

Guano was not industrial in the sense of being produced in factories, but it certainly was an external input and it played a key role in the birth of industrial agriculture. On one hand, it established in a practical way the dependence on off-farm resources, and it did so just as science was forwarding a paradigm of soil fertility that promoted externally produced fertilizers (as we will see). Guano was organic and the "scientific" fertilizers were mineral, but the two developments worked in tandem to kick open the door of external-input agriculture.

The guano business also gave us our first view of how external inputs are able to harvest subsidy.

Starting Subsidy

The guano trade marked the first time that distantly sourced inputs were incorporated into farming on a large scale, and it brought a set of novel problems. Getting guano to farmers required someone having access to the deposits, mining equipment, laborers, crewed ships, protection in transit, and distribution channels. A firm operating in a free market would have to work out each of these steps and build their cost into the price of the guano, but governments, inspired by many of the factors that historically have propelled governments to subsidize industrial agriculture (Chapter 3), stepped in to subsidize each of these steps.

In Britain, guano traders were given military support. The royal navy was sent to protect private merchant ships carrying guano and to seek out new sources (Cordle 2007, 121–129). Envious of the windfall profits being made by British merchants, American industrialists connived to capture some of the same government-sponsored wealth. Their influence had reached the highest levels of government by 1850, when President Millard Fillmore used his State of the Union speech to insist that

> Peruvian guano has become so desirable an article to the agricultural interest of the United States that it is the duty of the Government to employ all the means properly in its power for the purpose of causing that article to be imported into the country at a reasonable price.
>
> *(Skaggs 1994, 17)*

In 1856 the US congress passed the Guano Islands Act which provided state backing for Americans to claim possession of uninhabited islands containing bird feces. Such islands could be annexed as US territory simply by notifying the State Department (Burnett 2005, 783). The Act empowered the president to use the military to protect islands so claimed, putting the taxpayer-supported military at the service of commercial fertilizer interests. There soon erupted a period of "guano island mania" (Wines 1985) – or "guano imperialism" (Foster and Magdoff 2000, 45), and guano extraction boomed in the 1850s and 1860s.

Some of the islands claimed under the Guano Islands Act found their way into history books. One was Midway atoll, the scene of the 1942 Battle of Midway which some believe to be the most decisive naval battle in history. Probably the oddest use of the law was by Ernest Hemingway's brother Leicester. In 1964 Leicester declared his raft, which was anchored off the coast of Jamaica, to be the micro-nation of New Atlantis. Citing bird droppings on the deck, Hemingway invoked the Guano Islands Act and claimed the raft to be under US sovereignty. Hemingway's actual intent was to promote marine research and protect the fishing around Jamaica, but his claim was recognized by neither the US nor Jamaica, and New Atlantis was destroyed by a tropical storm two years later.

A particularly vile form of subsidy concerned labor. Guano was mined mostly by hand and it was dirty and dangerous work. Miners had to live and work in excrement, on sweltering rat-infested islands far from family and amenities. In the 1840s much of the work was done by African slaves. When Peru banned slavery in 1854, mining firms quickly turned to new sources of labor, much of which was forced. A major source was China, where many workers were duped by promises of better lives in the New World while others were "simply kidnapped, chained together in the holds of ships that were little different from African slavers" (Skaggs 1994, 162). The so-called "yellow trade" brought over 100,000 Chinese to Peru (Melillo 2012), many of whom committed suicide (Cushman 2013,55, Mathew 1970). Years later a visitor noted that each island had a Chinese graveyard "where garments, detached bones, and twisted corpses of poor coolies" were exposed (Cushman 2003, 72). On the island the mining companies had complete control over miners' lives and routinely forced them to work long hours and load up to four tons per day (Mathew 1977, 44), go without wages when injured, pay wildly inflated prices at the company store, and be locked in stocks for insubordination. In many cases workers were not even transported home after completing their contracts (Burnett 2005).

None of the governments involved – Peruvian, American, or European – regulated the abuse of guano laborers. Some governments even *supplied* labor, as when the Maryland state penitentiary struck a deal with an American importer to supply prisoners to the island mines (Wines 1985, 67). Permitting and abetting the use of involuntary and abused workers is a subsidy: producing agricultural inputs that skirt labor costs is a shameful externalized cost.

When the US government did intervene in guano island issues, it was to protect mining company supervisors rather than workers. Navassa Island near Haiti, claimed under the Guano Islands Act, was the scene of an 1889 uprising by African-American workers in which five supervisors were killed. After the uprising there were no charges against the mining company or any supervisors, but dozens of workers were tried and convicted of felonies, with three sentenced to death. After the conditions of work on the island were revealed, an appalled president Benjamin Harrison commuted the sentences to life in prison. This rule-proving exception is the closest the US ever came to regulating labor conditions in fertilizer mines.

Lasting Effects: The Metabolic Rift

The manure that farmers have traditionally used and the guano being shipped after 1840 were composed of animal droppings and their nutrient content was similar, but the political economy of the two substances could hardly have been more different. Guano was called the first "artificial manure" (Page 2016, 386) as it was produced outside of the agricultural system. It was the first such external input sold on a large scale, and the telling feature of industrial agriculture was on unmistakable display: the profitability of the fertilizer was the result not of the technology itself, but of corporate actors seizing on state subsidies including military, legislative and economic support as well as the failure to regulate work conditions.

The era of guano imperialism is more than an odd story from the 19th century: it led to a reconceptualization of agriculture as running on external resources. Except for scattered exceptions,[9] the production cycle of the mixed farm was a closed circuit and, as historian F.M. Thompson notes, "this was its whole beauty and symmetry" (1968, 64). But the guano trade

> marked in a spectacular way expansion of the geographic reach of these farms and smoothed the way for the purchase of other inputs. Together, these practices gradually displaced the old system of farm self-sufficiency and waste recycling and opened the way for the eventual triumph of input-intensive farming practices based on one-way patterns of production, consumption, and waste.
>
> *(Cushman 2013, 52)*

By revolutionizing the flow of nutrients, guano "thumped a shock wave through the ecology that unifies producers and consumers," introducing for the first time "a one-way transfer of material from some point of extraction or production to the farm where it went into the crops, and from there to consumers" (Stoll 2002, 190). Nothing came back. The lingering effects on how farmers and society thought about agriculture were crucial. As historian Steven Stoll writes,

> Something important was happening. The purchase of this substance, not fashioned on the farm but imported from far away, became (in the minds of some) an emblem of progressive farming. Guano stands as the first chemical input, for although it came from an island and not a laboratory, although no one manufactured it, it filled the same niche and arrived in the same way that synthetic chemicals would soon arrive: in a bag from a supply company.
>
> *(2002, 189)*

Although Marx did not specify guano as a factor, it is precisely this change that he described in this way:

> an irreparable rift in the interdependent process of the social metabolism, a metabolism prescribed by the natural laws of life itself. The result of this is a squandering of the vitality of the soil, which is carried by trade far beyond the bounds of a single country.
>
> *(Marx 1981 [1883])*

This was "the metabolic rift" noted above (Foster 1999).

Politics, Science, and Soil

Scientific research played little role in the guano trade, although some chemists had conducted analyses of the stuff; it was just a readily transportable powder, high in several key agricultural nutrients, and rendered artificially cheap by government subsidy and coerced labor. But even as guano was used by farmers in England and the US, it was increasingly apparent that there was a serious gap in general knowledge on agricultural soil fertility. What worked on your neighbor's farm might not work on yours; or what worked at first on your farm might let you down after a few years. The basic mechanisms involved in crop growth had long baffled observers; Virgil's Georgics lamented the ignorance on the subject in the first century AD, and the state of knowledge was not much better in the early 19th century. James Madison (the ex-president mentioned above) was renowned for his agricultural knowledge, but in his 1818 address he struggled to make sense of the conflicting theories of soil fertility. Some advocated use of "pulverized earth" (promoted in England by Jethro Tull), some recommended "putrified animal and vegetable matter," and some preferred gypsum (often effective but no one knows why). As the problem of soil degradation in the early 19th century worsened, abundant publications for farmers, academic journals, and books offered wildly contradictory theories of soil fertility (Rossiter 1975, 8–9).[10]

The most fundamental disagreements concerned the life-giving power of *humus* (L., "earth"), the dark upper later of soil in which crops rooted. Many writers attributed the power to some version of *vitalism* – the premise that all living organisms were animated by a life force that was acquired by other living organisms. Various scientists over the years had tried to specify what this life force was or how it worked. Seventeenth and 18th century scientists envisioned a *spiritus rector* (L., guiding spirit), or *spiritus mundi* (L., world spirit), or *vis vitalis* (L., vital force) (Merchant 2010, 119, van der Ploeg, Bohm, and Kirkham 1999, 1057). Late 17th century writers proposed something called *nitre* or "spirit of the air," a mysterious substance that was somehow different from the four basic elements of life.[11] Nitre supposedly existed in the air and could also take material form in manure – not bad as a rough draft of the idea of nitrogen, which was discovered a century later (Leigh 2004, 96). Some opined that the key ingredients in humus were actually oils or bituminous substances, while others proposed the life force as a set of (wildly inaccurate) chemical reactions (Brock 1997, 146–147, Manlay, Feller, and Swift 2007). In short, the early 19th century science on ameliorating degraded soils was confused, contradictory, and largely ineffective.

But change was on the way. Although the key year was 1840, seeds for it were planted by several events in the mid-1830s. This was, appropriately enough, the same time that the theorist of inelastic agriculture left the scene: Robert Malthus died on a trip to Bath in 1834. Around the same time, two wealthy European landowners independently began to turn their estates into agricultural research stations. The young English aristocrat John Lawes inherited a Hertfordshire estate named Rothamsted, and having dropped out of Oxford, he began a lifelong program of agricultural experiments there. Overseen by Lawes, and for decades managed by chemist Joseph Gilbert, Rothamsted became the world's first open-air agricultural laboratory (and it continues as an agricultural research center today). Meanwhile the French chemist Jean-Baptiste Boussingault, who had married an asphalt heiress, began agricultural experiments at their estate in Alsace.

Meanwhile in Germany, the University of Giessen chemist Justus von Liebig took on the problem of agricultural fertility as a laboratory problem. Liebig is an intriguing character: a hot-headed workaholic described by biographers as cunning, irascible, and devious (Brock 1997, viii, Munday 1990, 7) who would rise to a level of fame and wealth few scientists ever achieve and have a transformative effect on both agriculture and food science. His work on agricultural chemistry, the result of an 1837 commission from the British Association for the Advancement of Science, led to his 1840 book *Chemistry and Its Application to Agriculture and Physiology.* Although its key ideas had been published by another German scientist in the 1820s (van der Ploeg, Bohm, and Kirkham 1999), it was this book that transformed thinking about agriculture, as it appeared at time of high anxiety about depleted soils and offered a highly confident and scientific paradigm for solving the problem (Brock 1997, 150, Rossiter 1975, 20). Let us look at Liebig's actual message to see how it could lead to such transformative changes.

Liebig and Reductionism: *Cui Prodest?*

Chemistry and Its Application waded straight into the long-running debate on the role of humus in soil fertility, attacking the belief that humus was key to plant growth and scorning the notion of any vital force. Instead, Liebig presented what came to be called the Mineral Theory in which soil fertility was broken down into a small set of specific, identifiable, chemical elements. These elements could be present as soil minerals (as he correctly thought phosphorus was), or could be absorbed from the air (as he incorrectly thought nitrogen was), but they could be just as easily supplied by the farmer; the source of the elements was irrelevant. Neither humus nor animal manures offered any synergistic or cumulative benefit: they simply supplied the inorganic elements that soil lacked (Rossiter 1975, 25). Soil nutrition therefore was a matter of chemistry rather than biology; any plant's mineral content could be determined in the laboratory and the chemist could prescribe what was needed by identifying element(s) that were constraining yield (the "Law of the Minimum"). As proof, Liebig grew plants in his lab on a diet of inorganic compounds.

Chemistry and Its Application established Liebig as an international public figure, his name synonymous with agricultural chemistry (Brock 1997, 145, Rossiter 1975, 26). But, in retrospect, he had gotten everything wrong, even including the fundamentals on the most important element in plant growth. He insisted that plants absorb nitrogen freely from the air and not from the soil (as Boussingault's field experiments had shown). The 1843 edition of *Chemistry and Its Application* doubled down on his misguided theory, insisting that it was a waste of time for farmers to augment crops' nitrogen levels (Brock 1997, 166). Lawes and Gilbert too published empirical results showing how adding nitrogen clearly boosted yields, particularly in the form of barnyard manure, whereas Liebig's recommended minerals didn't help. In 1855, an enraged Liebig published *Principles of Agricultural Chemistry, with Special Reference to the Late Researches in England* in which he disputed these findings and accused Lawes of just trying to boost sales of his own patented fertilizer over Liebig's own artificial manures.

Ironically, Liebig's chemical-reductionistic paradigm became a victim of its own success by launching the field of agricultural chemistry which brought a growing number of experiments that undermined his claims. Even the Law of the Minimum was shown to be a gross oversimplification, as crop yield could be boosted by adjusting various factors other than the supposedly limiting factor. Liebig had to eventually introduce a "Law of Compensating Factors" to account for this, but he could not explain the mechanism of "compensation" and all he really accomplished was to cancel his own law (Cohen 1998, 241). Later research would uncover the crucial role of trace elements, organic and structural properties of soil, and micronutrients and microbiotics that Liebig has dismissed (Loneragan 1997, 165).

But more important than the blown specifics of crop nutrition was Liebig's impact on basic conceptualizations of agriculture. A famous critique of this influence came from Sir

Albert Howard, an English botanist/agronomist who went to India in 1905 to teach Western agricultural methods and came back 20 years later to teach the West about what he had
learned there.[12] His classic 1940 book *An Agricultural Testament* – known as the founding text
of modern organic farming, although he does not use that term – lambasted not just Liebig's
reductionistic perspective but the vested interests it served. Howard wrote:

> The factories engaged during the Great War in the fixation of atmospheric nitrogen for
> the manufacture of explosives had to find other markets, the use of nitrogenous fertiliz-
> ers in agriculture increased, until to-day the majority of farmers and market gardeners
> base their manurial programme on the cheapest forms of nitrogen (N), phosphorus (P),
> and potassium (K) on the market. What may be conveniently described as the NPK
> mentality dominates farming alike in the experimental stations and the country-side.
> *Vested interests, entrenched in time of national emergency, have gained a stranglehold.*
>
> *(Howard 1940:chap. 1, italics added)*

So it wasn't just how agriculture was conceived; *it was how vested interests had taken hold.* A few
years later Howard pointed out that the external fertilizer industry benefited not only those
in the industry but the Ministry of Agriculture, the experiment stations, the agricultural
colleges, and the agricultural press. "All urge upon the farmer and the gardener the use of
more and more chemicals almost as a moral duty" (Howard 1946, 7).

Howard's charge that the reductionist paradigm benefited researchers and scientific institutions at the expense of the farmer was true, but it was true well before the "Great War."
The first beneficiary of the mineral paradigm was the profession of chemistry, as it rede-
fined agricultural progress as requiring laboratory services that only chemists could provide
(Rossiter 1975, 30–38). Liebig's book promoted a vision of farm fields fertilized by chemical
solutions comparable to medicines with chemists being the doctors "diagnosing any soil's
mineral needs" (Brock 1997, 121, 145). A whole new day of "rational agriculture," as Liebig
put it, was dawning (Rossiter 1975, 45), as he successfully pushed German governments to
fund agricultural chemical laboratories and teaching positions (Finlay 1991, 156).

Chemistry labs also profited handsomely off of the farmers themselves as a craze for soil
chemical analysis erupted in 1844. Laboratories advertised assays for $2–5 (Rossiter 1975,
46) – a considerable sum to many farmers at the time. Prestigious universities including Yale
were quick to capitalize, taking one of the first steps down a path that would eventually lead
to many academic science departments operating essentially as for-profit entities (although
retaining their legal classification as non-profit and evading taxes).[13] The soil analysis craze
had waned by the late 1840s. One problem had been that it was well suited to hucksters,
as analyses were difficult to monitor and evaluate. But even reputable academic labs struggled to provide valuable analyses for the farmer; the equipment and terminology provided
a veneer of scientific rigor (Uekötter 2014, 76), but the theoretical understanding of crop
chemistry was actually far too simplistic to allow for useful advice.[14]

However even as the soil analysis fad shrunk, agricultural chemistry continued to do well
in many universities. In Germany, agricultural chemistry emerged as a distinct academic
discipline (Brock 1997, 169). Agricultural experiment stations began to proliferate, usually
directed by chemists (Uekötter 2014). In France, professorships in agriculture were replaced
by professorships in agricultural chemistry – which is how Liebig's nemesis Boussingault lost
his position (Brock 2008, 370).

But the professional and economic interests of academic chemists would prove to be minor compared to the interests of the fertilizer industry that was ushered in by Liebig's reductionism. Liebig himself was adamant that the practical implication of his theory was that on-farm fertility sources such as humus and manure – which were hard to sell as commodities –should be replaced by chemicals from factories. As he wrote, "The entire action and benefit of stable manures may be produced by use of mineral manures…[from] chemical manufactories" (Stoll 2002, 152). Here we have the first agricultural appropriation: farm-generated sources of fertility being replaced by off-farm industry, animal rearing and compost making and manure spreading being replaced by tendering cash for products created in factories.

A door was opening through which fortunes would clearly flow. At first, Liebig held himself personally above the commercial fertilizer business. After an agricultural tour of England in 1842, he wrote to British Prime Minister Robert Peel that English soils were in a state of exhaustion, but that he knew of sources of the needed nutrient (viz., phosphates, in natural deposits in this case rather than factory-produced). He went on:

> As this material must acquire great value I was led to consider that I might draw from my discovery the advantage for myself…. [But] as a man of science and not of Commerce I have thought it therefore preferable to communicate my discovery to her Majesty's government.
>
> *(Brock 1997, 121)*

But others were jumping in to capitalize on the surging interest in artificial manures, including John Lawes, whose agricultural research at Rothamsted had continued apace. Lawes' and Liebig's research methods clashed, with Lawes relying on the field experimentation and Liebig on the laboratory, and the prickly Liebig considered Lawes an enemy and charlatan. However they had reached the same conclusions on a few key questions and found themselves in a bitter patent battle over rights to one method of fertilizer manufacture: dissolving bones in sulfuric acid to make nutrients more water-soluble and thus more available to plants. While Liebig had found this in his lab, Lawes had seen its effectiveness on his fields and had patented it, and was eagerly trying to start his own fertilizer business. Ignoring his aristocratic mother (who felt a gentleman should not be selling "manures"), Lawes canceled his planned honeymoon on the continent and instead went boating on the Thames in winter, with disgruntled bride in tow, looking for a site for a fertilizer factory (Dyke 1993, 15). When his "superphosphate manures" joined guano on the market in 1843, British farmers suddenly faced a watershed moment in the early history of external inputs. Powered by his capital and marketing skills, Lawes' farm-tested products quickly gained a following (Brock 1997, 120–122).

By 1844 Liebig had shed his inhibitions about commerce and leapt into the fertilizer business, partnering with Liverpool alkali manufacturer James Muspratt. And as the academic chemist became a producer of agricultural inputs, the conceptual and financial boundary between basic scientific research and individual profiteering dissolved. Also blurred were lines between scientific theories and products, as Liebig's theory of nitrogen absorption from the air led him to produce manures light on that crucial element (Brock 1997, 124) – certainly one reason that his fertilizers flopped. But Liebig was slow to admit this, and for years stubbornly insisted his theories were correct, although the benefits of his "patent manures" were so far from its advertised claims that today he would be prosecuted for deception (Brock 1997, 123, Finlay 1991, 156).

Liebig and Muspratt produced their ineffective fertilizers until 1848 before closing shop and stopping their financial losses. Liebig would return to fertilizer investing in 1857, by which time there were dozens of fertilizer factories in Britain and the Germanies – mostly run by his students. By 1863, a British farming magazine would note that "there is a manure manufactory in almost every town," and no other branch of industry offered "a surer investment for capital" (Anonymous 1863, 270–271).

The events of the 1840s also laid bare the inherent conflict between the aims of basic science and inputs industries that would become a recurrent theme in agricultural science revolutions. Consider that the whole point of science is *disclosure*. In his classic analysis of the norms of science, Robert Merton (1942) pointed out that science does not and should not aim to generate intellectual property for scientists, but rather to reward them for adding to common knowledge through publication. Liebig was a publicly supported basic scientist, but when he turned his theories of plant nutrition into fertilizer products, he was adamant that the ingredients remain secret. When his partner's son revealed a fertilizer recipe, a livid Liebig accused him of "criminal indiscretion" (Brock 1997, 124). Of course even a state-supported scientist has the right to moonlight as an entrepreneur, but here we had a chemist who had achieved international fame as a leader in figuring out agricultural soil fertility, militantly blocking disclosure of the contents of one of the world's first commercially produced fertilizers in hopes of lining his own pockets. This was not illegal or grounds for firing. Indeed that is the point; the nature of agricultural science is, and has been from its 19th century beginnings, that external interests erode and taint the aims of basic science while usually carefully avoiding the level of fraud. (This compromised nature would mushroom in the era of biotechnology, as basic scientists at public universities became pitchmen for genetically modified crops while the industry patted them on the backs for wearing the "big white hats" of objective science (Lipton 2015).)

What was really dawning in the mid-19th century was a newly profitable agriculture and a crescendo of rising influence and size of chemical research institutions. But it was not clear just how rational Liebig's "new day of rational agriculture" really was. Results of fertilizing were highly uneven, leading many agricultural chemists to regret that Liebig and others had been so "naively optimistic" (Rossiter 1975, 109). The truth was that chemical analysis and fertilizer "prescriptions" didn't work particularly well; they were oblivious to micronutrients, soil structure, microbiological activity, and other factors now known to be important in crop growth. But Liebig had simultaneously laid the foundation for the artificial fertilizer industry and set up his academic discipline of chemistry with "a hegemonic grasp" on fertilizer (Uekötter 2014, 69).[15] By the early 20th century, there was increasing disillusionment with agricultural chemistry and calls to replace Liebig's static view of plant nutrition with a more dynamic theory, but the fertilizer industry was growing into a multibillion dollar enterprise able to exert considerable influence on science and policy relating to crop nutrition. The commercial aspects of fertilizer research show us what we see again and again in the history of science in agriculture: institutional and financial interests strongly influencing the results, interpretations, and disclosures of supposedly basic science. "Science and business interests make for an uneasy mix," notes environmental historian Frank Uekötter (2014, 71), "and the fertilizer business was no exception."

One of the scientists to denounce the corrupting influence of fertilizer commerce was Heinrich Himmler, who quit his job at a fertilizer company near Munich in 1922 because of pressure to produce "cooked reports...which were to show that a specific amount of [fertilizer] was best for farming, which I naturally declined to do." When leading Nazis are able to question your scientific ethics from a higher moral plane, it is perhaps time to take stock.

Fertilizer and the Origins of Externalized Costs

We say that the 1840s fertilizer industry marked the beginning of industrialized agriculture not just because it opened the door to external inputs but because it shows all of the key processes of agricultural industrialization outlined in Chapter 3. First, recall that the economic logic of industrial agriculture is the state providing both upstream and downstream subsidy. Upstream subsidy was certainly important in the form of government sponsorship of fertilizer research in Europe and the US. The classic downstream subsidy of allowing input industries to externalize costs of production and use of their wares also appeared in the early fertilizer trade. Lawes' first factory opened in 1843 in the east London site he selected on his unromantic honeymoon, his second in 1857 (Dyke 1993, 15–19). This and other superphosphate factories spewed toxic fumes that ruined pastures, defoliated parks (Thompson 2000, 1028), and even killed people near the plants (Dyke 1993, 21). A 1907 report, by the medical officer for the London district where the Lawes' factories were multiplying, wrote:

> In the mile length of Rotherhithe Street there are no less than nine factories for the fabrication of patent manure, that is to say, nine sources of foetid gases. The process gives out a stench which has occasioned headache, nausea, vomiting, cough, &c. Many complaints have been made by the inhabitants.
>
> *(Brock 1997, 163)*

State regulation of these environmental and health effects was largely ineffective. England had no statutory reaction to the plants' pollution until the 1863 Alkali Act, which mandated installation of equipment to clean flue gases, but this "led to the discharge of more strongly polluted liquid effluents" (Thompson 2000, 1029). This was followed by the relatively toothless 1876 River Pollution Act. By the early 20th century, there are much more graphic accounts of the costs of fertilizer production on the local environment and public health, including the workers: in shifts often lasting over 12 hours, they worked with sulfuric acid which dissolved their clothes and burned their flesh. The workers were mostly European immigrants who had no ability to protest conditions, and to strike was to take your life into your hands. (Ida Tarbell reported on a strike against two New Jersey fertilizer plants in which 18 workers were shot, mostly in the back (Tarbell 1915).) In the US South it was usually Blacks who put up with jobs that were "among the most dangerous and degrading positions in the America's industrial economy" (Johnson 2016a, 89).

Even before its hypercharged expansion after the two world wars, and indeed from its origins in the 1840s, the fertilizer industry had ample clout to protect the invaluable subsidy of government inaction.

The Strange Seventh Edition

Liebig had published six editions of *Chemistry and Its Application* between 1840 and 1846 and then stopped. But as research in the field that he had largely founded continued to shine a harsh light on his work, and as his methods of chemical soil analysis were increasingly side-lined by findings by his hated experimental field researchers, his reputation suffered, and he had become a subject of ridicule by the 1850s (Finlay 1991, 157). The famous chemist now produced a seventh and final edition – much changed and quite strange. Appearing in German in 1862, this edition atoned for some of his past aggressions, the normally bombastic scientist expressing contrition and admitting to scientific errors and his own "blindness." He now even acknowledged the value of the experimental research by his nemesis John Lawes.

Was this the self-correcting nature of science in action? I don't think so, and neither does historian and Liebig scholar Mark Finlay, who writes that "It is only slightly cynical to point out another possible concern – that by restoring his name and credibility, Liebig was able to make large profits in his business ventures of the 1860s" (1991, 156). (Liebig would go on to make a fortune in the food extracts business.)

But another surprise in the seventh edition would help to undermine the very industrial agriculture he had helped launch. Liebig now added crucial material on the movement of nutrients on the landscape (essentially, the "town-country metabolism" described in Chapter 7). Early editions of *Chemistry and Its Application* had complained about nitrogen being lost by crops being sent to the city, but the whole idea was dropped in the third (1843) edition. Then in 1859 he had taken the topic up with zeal in a book *Letters on Modern Agriculture* (1859), offering a heated denunciation of *robbau* – "robbery agriculture" – whereby nutrients flowed from country to town without being replenished. The worst in this regard was British "high farming," which

> deprives all countries of the conditions of their fertility. It has raked up the battle-fields…and now annually destroys the food for a future generation of three millions and a half of people. Like a vampire it hangs on the breast of Europe and even the world, sucking its lifeblood without any real necessity or permanent gain for itself.
>
> *(Marald 2002, 74)*

Liebig added that the British were tall and healthy because they had robbed the rest of Europe of nutrients that would have nurtured soils and allowed others to reach the same physical stature as the British. These barbs about the height of the British remind us of the earlier discussion of diet and stature in Malthus's Okewood flock; the real disparity in height had been within the British themselves, among whom the elites towered over the poor.[16] It is then interesting to note that imported fertilizers were overwhelmingly bound for fields of elite farmers. Guano was used by only a quarter of English farms between 1840 and 1879 – "mainly large, prosperous landowners who loudly trumpeted their accomplishments to demonstrate their dedication to the new religion of progress" (Cushman 2013, 51). So Liebig was partly right – the consumers of imported agricultural fertility were tall – although *most* Britons were not.

In contrast to his disdain for agriculture in America and Europe, Liebig deeply admired Japanese agriculture which represented the "perfect circulation of the forces of nature." In Japan, manure and nightsoil from towns

> is sent every night and morning in its natural form into the country around, to return again after a time in the shape of beans or turnips…[t]housands of boats may be seen

early each morning laden with high heaps of buckets full of the precious stuff, which they carry from the canals in the cities to the country.

(Liebig 1863, 395)

Liebig's hopes for making a major impact with the new edition were dashed when the British agricultural establishment did not appreciate the denunciation of their high farming. Rather than promptly putting out a translation, Liebig's British publisher destroyed its only copy (Foster 2002). When they did publish an English translation, it had been abridged, renamed *The Natural Laws of Husbandry*, and stripped of its critical introduction.

But one London scholar was able to read the original German edition, and it set his mind racing. In 1866 Karl Marx wrote to Engels that he "had to plough through [Liebig's] new agricultural chemistry in Germany…which is more important for this matter than all of the economists put together" (quoted in Foster 2002). Marx added an enthusiastic discussion of Liebig's analysis of the destructiveness of modern agriculture to Volume 1 of *Capital* (1967 [1867], 638). But where Liebig had not seriously engaged the question of who was at fault in modern agriculture, Marx did, laying the blame squarely at the feet of capitalism and its metabolic rift, which

> prevents the return to the soil of its constituent elements consumed by man in the form of food and clothing… All progress in capitalist agriculture is a progress in the art, not only of robbing the worker, but of robbing the soil; all progress in increasing the fertility of the soil for a given time is a progress towards ruining the more long-lasting sources of that fertility.
>
> *(Marx 1967 [1867])*

Marxist scholars have hailed Liebig for his attacks on *robbau* that inspired Karl Marx's famous analysis of capitalist agriculture (Foster 1999, 2002, 376). Liebig indeed had condemned wealthy England for appropriating Europe's soil nutrients, a critique that fit perfectly with Marx's view of capitalism as a system in which those in power leverage their economic advantage to extract wealth. Yet capitalist agriculture would evolve quite differently than what Marx imagined. The crux of agricultural industrialization, as we have seen, is not in robbing value from the soil, but in maneuvering the farmer into buying inputs such as fertilizers. And no single individual has played a more pivotal role in leading us down this path than Marx's muse, Justus von Liebig!

The US Government Thumb on the Scale

Europe and its cast of characters like Liebig and Lawes pioneered the fertilizer industry, but it would be the US that would subsidize it into the dominant element in industrial agriculture by the 1960s. But it was long before then that the government would commit itself to promoting chemical agriculture over less industrial forms.

When the US government first involved itself in agriculture, no input industries were established and so the focus was on the farmers rather than corporate products. In 1862 President Abraham Lincoln established the Department of Agriculture (USDA) with an original mission of mainly disseminating agricultural information and seeds. The same year Congress passed the Morrill Act which established land grant universities (or colleges) in every state. It did this by granting federal land to be sold to finance colleges devoted to "agriculture and the mechanic arts" – a major departure from the established colleges that focused on educating elites. Then the 1887 Hatch Act provided federal funds for state agricultural experiment stations – a term that may conjure an image of shack in a corn field, but stations quickly grew into large multi-million research centers.

Stations were not originally intended to research and develop industrial inputs, but some took a keen interest in industrial fertilizer from the beginning.[17] One role taken on by early stations was chemical analysis of fertilizers to expose fraudulent claims by manufacturers and salesmen (Porter 1979, 84). This was a service to the farmer, but it served other interests as well, notably the chemists who were positioning themselves as the ones who "alone could protect the public from dealers of fraudulent goods" and so who merited state support and power (Marcus 1987, 48). During the 1880s most states appointed state chemists to analyze fertilizers and attach tags specifying nutrient content. Fertilizer manufacturers disliked these interventions, but the safeguards the chemists provided helped the industry grow. And grow it did: between 1869 and 1889 the number of US fertilizer plants jumped from 126 to 390 (Marcus 1987, 50).

But the consumer protection function morphed inexorably into outright support for the industry, and in the US South, where states were slow to support their land grant schools and experiment stations, state scientists actually had become commercial fertilizer sellers. Alabama's land grant school at Auburn, established in 1883, was charged with fertilizer testing and it funded itself by selling fertilizer. The state agriculture department was responsible for regulating the fertilizers but also for "promoting their extension and use" which greatly boosted fertilizer use (Giesen and Hersey 2010, 275).

The scientific staffs at land grant schools, experiment stations, and the USDA were not of one mind, and many scientists advocated for nonindustrial paths to agricultural growth. Even decades after experiment stations developed policies that put them in bed with fertilizer manufacturers, some state-supported scientists were still urging farmers to use manure, and an irate agronomist at one experiment station published a book accusing the fertilizer industry of bilking farmers out of millions (Hopkins 1910). But by the 1880s the linkage with commercial fertilizer interests ran deep, and state departments of agriculture and the land grant schools were actively promoting commercial fertilizers. New state departments of agriculture were funded by taxes and inspection fees on fertilizers, which created a strong incentive to promote fertilizer use. Where there had been some tension and conflicting aims between the chemists working for the government and for industry – especially since one job of government chemists was investigation of fertilizer manufacturers' claims – by the late 1880s "commercial and state chemists had reached a truce, and their connections grew closer over the ensuing years" (Giesen and Hersey 2010, 275).

Remarkably, there was no agreement that the stream of government-backed fertilizers was even a boon to agriculture. In fact, editors of farm journals in the 1870s–1880s deplored the heavy use of commercial fertilizers. When in 1887 the governor of North Carolina cited "strong and stimulating fertilizers" as the cure for worn out lands, the editor of *The Progressive Farmer* called the recommendation "A fallacious theory, a theory which has cost the farmers of North Carolina millions and millions of dollars since the War and well nigh bankrupted everyone who has relied on it" (Taylor 1953, 313).

The Fertilizer Industry versus Black Farmers

George Washington Carver, known to history as a champion of Southern Black farmers and advocate of the peanut, was an important agricultural/environmental thinker apart from his promotion of one crop. He came to the poorly funded Tuskegee Agricultural Experiment Station in Alabama in 1896 and did much of his most important work in the early years of the 20th century. This was just when the "industrial ideal" was ascendant in US agricultural thinking (Fitzgerald 2003), and it is interesting to follow Carver's changing convictions on agriculture and the role of fertilizer.

Carver initially assumed that "scientific agriculture seemed to promise salvation," and that he could best help Southern Black smallholders by facilitating access to "up-to-date methods and machinery" (Hines 1979, 71–72). The most pressing problem for these farmers was soil degradation from cotton growing, and so Carver began to experiment with chemical fertilizer, which, in good Liebig reductionist fashion, he saw as containing the nitrogen, potash, and phosphoric acid that the soil needed (Carver 1899, 4). But as his experiments showed that the quantities of fertilizer needed were unaffordable by most Black smallholders (Carver 1899, 5), he began experiments with local resources – intensification rather than industrialization. The experiment station's remarkable 1905 bulletin, "How to Build Up Worn Out Soils," reveals how quickly his thinking moved away from input-intensive farming and toward his aim to "keep every operation within reach of the poorest tenant farmer occupying the poorest possible soil" (Carver 1905, 5). He reported on experiments on worn out soils, using green manuring with nitrogen-fixing legumes and resources from the "natural fertilizer factory" of local forests and swamps (Giesen and Hersey 2010, 282). Within a few years, the thin grey soils "began to look dark, rich, and mellow" (Carver 1905, 7). Over the next few years Carver evolved into a campaigner against chemical fertilizers, which he came to see as a "quick chemical fix" that impoverished soils in the long run, and a waste of the school's money (Giesen and Hersey 2010, 283).

Carver's evolving philosophy of farm and food was strikingly similar to positions and attitudes that have become popular and influential in recent years. His ideas parallel contemporary concerns for the health effects of the industrial diet as exemplified by Michael Pollan, in particular that heavy use of chemical fertilizers made foods both less nutritious and more toxic. Carver supported the local foodways and shortened food chains that have brought today's boom in farmers' markets. But while Carver's views may resonate well with influential thinking on agriculture today, at the time he found himself increasingly out of step with the modernist and productivist thinking fashionable in the early 20th century. Carver was explicitly concerned with the farmer's productivity *and* well-being in an era that was increasingly focused on "efficiency" and cheaper food to power the industrial economy. While discussions of agriculture predictably claimed to be out to help the farmer, by the early 1920s, "many agricultural reformers sympathetic to the plight of the nation's farmers had, like Carver, begun to question whether modernity as defined in efficiency and productivity actually redounded to the farmers' benefit at all" (Giesen and Hersey 2010, 286).

But by the 1920s, research at agricultural colleges and experiment stations had grown into a big business and was largely funded by big business – or by the USDA which was serving the interests of agribusiness. Moreover, write Giesen and Hersey (2010, 286–287), "industrial interests like commercial fertilizer manufacturers and implement manufacturers had by and large overcome earlier conflicts with the land grant schools, and, in fact, had begun working with them" – work that primarily consisted of product research and development of agribusiness products on the public dime.

Racism and Chemistry at the *fin de siècle*

The rhetoric surrounding the rise of state-subsidized fertilizer in the 19th century was not particularly neo-Malthusian; there was little of the discussion about impending starvation that would characterize later agricultural appropriations. In the US, the primary recipients of the fertilizers were not even food producers, but rather cotton and tobacco planters in the South. But neo-Malthusian anxieties were injected jarringly into agricultural thinking in 1898 by a famous speech to the British Association by Sir William Crookes. Later described as "the most unusual presidential address ever given by a nineteenth-century man of science" (Brock 2008, 375), the speech featuring an urgent appeal for a radical shift in agriculture (Smil 2001, 58) and a "clarion call to chemists" on the importance of nitrogen fertilizer (Leigh 2004, 15, Nelson 1990, 193). But the speech's place in history books is an oddly sanitized version of this moment in the history of industrial agriculture.

Crookes himself was an interesting character: an accomplished chemist (trained by a Liebig disciple), a popular writer, inventor, and investigator of (and unflappable believer in) séances and spiritualists. The occasion of his speech was his election to the presidency of the prestigious Scientific Society after being knighted by Queen Victoria. The historic context of the speech is important. Britain was wallowing in an agricultural depression caused by changes in world trade patterns: transport and refrigeration technologies had advanced to where agricultural products from afar – like American grain and Australian meat – could be imported profitably. Falling prices undercut British farmers and arable land was being abandoned, with rural population moving to cities.

Although Britain's agricultural problems were hardly Malthusian – farmers were *abandoning farmland* – Crookes appeared before the large Bristol crowd in a feverishly Malthusian frame of mind. He told the crowd that

> England and all civilized nations stand in deadly peril of not having enough to eat. As mouths multiply, food resources dwindle. Land is a limited quantity, and the land that will grow wheat is absolutely dependent on difficult and capricious natural phenomena…our wheat-producing soil is totally unequal to the strain put upon it.
>
> *(Crookes 1898)*

It was specifically *wheat* that Crookes was alarmed about, for reasons that are often scrubbed from accounts of the event (e.g., Smil 2000, 58–59). Appealing directly to "the imperialistic and eugenist assumptions of his audience" (Brock 2008, 377), Crookes explained that

> We are wheat-eaters. Other races, vastly superior to us in numbers, but differing widely in material and intellectual progress, are eaters of Indian corn, rice, millet, and other grains; but none of these grains have the food values, the concentrated health sustaining power of wheat, and it is on this account that the accumulated experience of civilized mankind has set wheat apart as the fit and proper food for the development of muscle and brains.

(Winston Churchill would later echo Crookes' grain chauvinism, writing that "yellow men, brown men and black men" had not "learned to demand and become able to afford a diet superior to rice" (Belasco 2006, 34).) But the civilized wheat-eaters could be starved out by a bad turn in weather or a "hostile combination of European nations" turning against them. At the time Britain was importing a whopping 75% of its wheat, and Crookes calculated that it would take a full quarter of England's land area to achieve wheat self-sufficiency (Crookes 1898, 439).

But Crookes saw a way out: "It is the chemist who must come to the rescue." The key would be nitrogen, the fixation of which was a great discovery "awaiting the ingenuity of chemists"; otherwise, "the great Caucasian race will cease to be foremost in the world, and will be squeezed out of existence."

Actually industrial methods for fixing nitrogen already existed; they were just too energy-intensive to be profitable to industry (Nelson 1990, 194–195) and thus to ease Crookes' worries about Caucasian foodstuffs. But the speech greatly stimulated interest in nitrogen fixation, both among scientists and the public, and was reprinted and discussed widely. The following issue of *Punch* magazine featured a chemist's bakery shop of future with saltpeter scones, nitrogen bread, nitrate buns, and "chemical wedding cakes made to order" (Punch 1898).

Given our focus on the vested interests behind agriculture, it is worth noting that Crookes' motivation was not only to keep the wheat sandwiches coming for the great Caucasian race. His speech was a self-serving paean to the importance of his profession of chemistry. It also epitomized the neo-Malthusian logic that agricultural growth came only by scientific technologies produced in factories. The technology in this case was fertilizer and William Crookes was in the fertilizer business. Since 1871 he had been a director of Native Guano Company (which actually trafficked in sewage fertilizer, not guano) and he had his own firm, Crookes and Company, which produced fertilizer from animal refuse. In short, he had an abiding financial interest in research on new forms of fertilizer.[18]

At the end of the day, then, the speech that is cited as a key moment in humanity's technological battle against overpopulation was something quite different. It was the appropriation of a scientific address for a Caucasian to warn Caucasians of the rise of darker peoples with different diets, for a chemist to claim that chemists were needed as saviors, and for a fertilizer executive to hail fertilizers – all delivered in a rabidly neo-Malthusian package at a time when the country's farmers were actually abandoning farmland. But with its intoxicating mix of "imperial arrogance, apocalyptic visions, and technological faith," it "caught a monster wave in the surging Zeitgeist" of its time (Charles 2005, Loc 1144). Among the many leaders who were influenced by it was the head of Karlsruhe University, who echoed it in a speech the next year. In the audience for that speech was a young chemist named Fritz Haber.

Inventing Fertilizer

By the time of Crookes "clarion call," the world had hundreds of fertilizer factories, but the scale of fertilizer production was tiny compared to what was to come, and the factories were mainly applying acid to bones to produce phosphate fertilizers. According to standard accounts of agricultural history, Crookes' call was answered in Germany in 1909, when Franz Haber worked out a method of fixing nitrogen and Carl Bosch developed a means of upscaling the process to the factory level. The Haber-Bosch process has been hailed as the most important invention of the century, essential to the feeding of almost half the planet (Smil 2001).

Nitrogen is an odd element with two natures. Its inert form is the most common single element in the air, but it exists there in N_2 molecules: two atoms tied closely by a nearly unbreakable triple bond, unavailable for most chemical interactions and unable to nourish leaves or roots. "Fixing" nitrogen means to break apart the N_2 molecules and lure them into reactive compounds like ammonia (NH_3). Ammonia can then be packaged into various forms including ammonium sulfate, ammonium phosphate, urea…or ammonium nitrate and nitric acid, its explosive forms. "Plant foods and cannon foods come from the same ammonia spigot" (Chemical & Engineering News 1950, 3104).

Breaking the bonds in N_2 molecules takes enormous levels of energy, and nature has only a few ways to do it. Lightning can do it; so can some species of bacteria that enter into a complicated biological bargain with certain plants (like legumes) that provide sugars in exchange for the fixed nitrogen. Industry had three ways of fixing nitrogen before Haber came along. The most important was the creation of ammonia sulfate as a by-product of processing coal into coke. Coal processors sold by-product nitrogen to fertilizer companies to avoid the cost of disposing of it, so it was priced at whatever the market would bear. By-product nitrogen was not surpassed by synthesized nitrogen until well into the 1930s.

Nitrogen could also be synthesized by the arc and cyanamide methods, but both were hampered by their enormous electricity requirements. In the arc method, air was blown through an extremely hot magnetic field to create something like a miniature lightning bolt. The few arc factories built in the early 1900s turned out to be unprofitable. The cyanamide process involved fusing nitrogen with calcium and carbon to produce cyanamide, from which ammonia could be coaxed by steaming. Cyanamide fertilizer factories were being built from the 1890s until well after the Haber-Bosch process was developed. So Haber did not invent industrial nitrogen fixation, but he did develop a cheaper and more productive way of doing it, and his process would eventually open the floodgates of excessive fertilizer usage.

Haber and Bosch

Fritz Haber is an intriguing character in the history of agriculture, a man whose life combined the heights of wealth and fame with remarkable tragedy. He was brilliant and charismatic but also so tightly wound as to need yearly time-outs at a sanatorium to recover his nerves (Charles 2005).

Haber had risen to full professor of chemistry at Karlsruhe University by age 37, in a career only slightly slowed by his being a Jewish convert to Christianity. He began experiments on nitrogen fixation in 1904 and in 1908 signed a contract with BASF, Germany's largest chemical company, putting him on the BASF payroll. This doubled his university salary and left his lab supported as much by private capital as by the state. In return, BASF got all of Haber's research results and controlled his right to publish details of his work (Charles 2005, Loc 1258–1259). Haber would also earn 10% of net profits from any commercial products based on his work.

Haber began to experiment with increasingly higher pressures, eventually so high that his team had to design special valves to contain the gases. The breakthrough came in March

1909: with the gases compressed to 200 atmospheres, synthesized ammonia came dripping out. Haber ran through the chemistry department to drag his colleagues to see the miracle; they were amazed. He then informed BASF of the experiment; they were not. The company's research director saw no commercial potential for Haber's method because of the outlandish pressures it required. The BASF chairman came to Haber's lab, accompanied by the research director and the young chemist Carl Bosch. The research director remained unimpressed, pointing out that they had equipment that would explode at seven atmospheres (Charles 2005, Loc 1285–1306).

Bosch said, "I think it can work."

In retrospect, all would agree that the developments of 1909 in Haber's lab were historic, but there are different ways of reckoning its significance. The work was obviously momentous for the careers Haber and Bosch, both of whom would be rewarded with Nobel prizes. The work would also play a key role in the history of warfare: BASF opened its first ammonia factory in Oppau in 1913, and within a year it was producing munitions for the newly started war. But most important to our interest in the drivers of agricultural change is that this was a striking early example of the academic science being appropriated by industry – with the support of the state. The remarkable arrangement with BASF transformed Prof. Haber into an entrepreneur working for a private corporation while remaining a full time civil servant in a state-supported university. While experimental research on nitrogen synthesis is an admirable activity for a public academician to contribute to general knowledge, Haber's ceding of publication rights in exchange for corporate funding eliminates any pretense of serving the master of scientific knowledge. That the arrangement was not only approved by, but arranged by, the university administration was unusual for the time, but such practices would become routine in later phases of agricultural technology development. The appropriation of interests and merging of roles went into overdrive as nitrogen fertilizer production began:

> Trade organizations maintained academic journals, funded research projects, and happily supplied scientists and advisors with fertilizer for field trials, blurring the line between academic and commercial interests. Settling conflicts, ensuring quality, and weeding out bad products were all pointed toward a synergy of academic and industrial interests.
>
> *(Uekötter 2014, 72)*

Among the effects of this industrialization of research agendas was the promotion of overproduction:

> The dubious effects of commercial sponsorship were less obvious. Fertilizer manufacturers had no interest in research on over-fertilization or on the side effects of intensive fertilizer use. Consequently, these issues were generally neglected until problems became impossible to ignore.
>
> *(Uekötter 2014, 72)*

Thus neo-Malthusian histories cite nitrogen synthesis as the key to feeding the planet, but the forces behind it had little to do with food shortages and everything to do with the financial interests of individuals and institutions of science and of industrial capital.

And of the state: World War I started soon after BASF's Oppau plant came online, and it was quickly converted to ammonium nitrate production for the military. "Here," writes Vaclav Smil, "is clearly one of the origins of a phenomenon that marked so much of Germany's, and the world's, subsequent history: the rise of a military-industrial complex" (2001, 103).

While "military-industrial complex" may be a phrase associated with 1960s-era political activism, it was popularized not by long-haired radicals but by a bald ex-military Republican president. "We must guard against the acquisition of unwarranted influence, whether sought or unsought, by the military-industrial complex," said US President Dwight Eisenhower in his 1961 farewell address; "[t]he potential for the disastrous rise of misplaced power exists and will persist." The original draft of the speech used the term "military-industrial-scientific complex," which better captures what was happening, but his science advisor persuaded him to drop the "scientific" (Brinkley 2001).[19] Haber was the early personification of this nexus of interests: he was a public academic scientist, employed by the chemical industry to develop technologies for them, who assumed a leadership role in the war effort. Royalties he received on every kilogram of ammonia left him a very wealthy man (Charles 2005, Loc 2353).

Scientists outside of Germany "marveled at the German marriage of science and warfare, and rushed to imitate it" (Charles 2005, Loc 2380). In the US, the crash program to develop nitrogen synthesis did not yield a single bomb during the war (below), but it did forge enduring links and merging of interests between universities and the military.[20]

An Afterword on Fritz Haber

Haber's life following nitrogen synthesis mixed triumph and tragedy. He moved to Berlin in 1911 as founding director of a major research institute, where he continued to be a leading figure in German science and friend of Albert Einstein. During World War I his institute developed poison gasses and he played a key leadership role in organizing gas warfare, earning for himself the title of Father of Gas Warfare. He was awarded the Nobel Prize in Chemistry in 1918.

But tragedy stalked Fritz Haber in the latter years of his life and after his death. Tragedies often come in threes, and so it was with Haber. The first occurred in 1915 just at a moment of triumph. By then Haber had become a leader in Germany's wartime science and directed deployment of gas at the second Battle of Ypres. When he came home soon after the battle, his wife Clara stole away with his service revolver and shot herself through the heart. It is likely that Haber's recent role in inaugurating gas warfare, which he must have seen as a triumph, was a cause of Clara's suicide.

The second occurred in 1933, when the Nazis took power in Germany and promptly targeted Jewish scientists. Haber hoped that that as a converted Christian and a war hero he would be safe, but he was not: he was attacked and fled the country, dying soon after in Switzerland.

The third tragedy unfolded after his death. During the war, scientists working under Haber had developed a hydrogen cyanide insecticide to kill insects in flour mills, but because of its lack of detectable odor, it caused several accidental deaths. After the war ended, scientists reformulated the insecticide to be safer by adding foul smelling compounds. It was named *Zyklon A* (Cyclone A). In 1920 the scientists moved to a nearby institute where they continued work on the gas with funding secured by Haber. There they reformulated the gas again, adding a cautionary eye irritant and naming it *Zyklon B*. So while Haber did not actually invent *Zyklon B*, he was instrumental in development of the gas that killed his sister's children in concentration camps, after Nazi scientists reformulated it to remove the odorous additives.

Creating an Industry

The Old Testament trope of beating of swords into plowshares[21] is generally used as a metaphor for any "tactical to practical" conversions of military technology to peacetime use. But the metaphor is agricultural and influences of military technology on agriculture have been especially consequential. This is particularly true of nitrogen. A well-known watershed in the industrialization of American agriculture was when World War II nitrogen factories were redirected toward farmlands (Pollan 2006, 41), but actually the government had put agriculture on the road toward chemical fertilizers decades before. Ironically most leading agriculturalists in the early 20th Century were advocating the increased and improved use of on-farm resources rather than purchased inputs.[22] Soil scientist F. King's *Farmers of Forty Centuries* popularized conservation practices based on Asian farming; agronomist William Esten showed how farmers could manage fertility with organic material and avoid commercial fertilizer; agronomist Cyril Hopkins's *Soil Fertility and Permanent Agriculture* urged crop rotation instead of chemical fertilizers. George Washington Carver, as we have seen, pushed for soil restoration using local natural resources. And virtually all agriculturalists championed increased use of manure, as did Asst. Secretary of Agriculture Carl Vrooman in *Stop Tremendous Manure Waste*. Even when agronomists recommended purchased fertilizers, many urged "home mixing" whereby farmers would cooperatively buy nutrients wholesale and then adjust the mixes to local conditions, cutting out the "middle man" of the fertilizer company.

The young fertilizer industry lashed out at such obstructions to profits. When the Illinois Farmers Institute militated for on-farm sources of fertility in 1915, the National Fertilizer Association defended its right "to organize and support a propaganda for the judicious use of commercial plant foods, including nitrogen" (Bowker 1915, 8). A fertilizer periodical urged experts touting manure and home mixing be countered with ridicule, "used sparingly for the good of agricultural progress." Some agronomists who advocated alternatives to commercial fertilizers even found their jobs being threatened (Johnson 2016a, 111–115).

But the early century fertilizer industry need not have been so anxious; the winds would soon begin to blow its way.

War and Muscle Shoals

During and after World War I, the US government embarked on a course of action that built a chemical fertilizer industry at the same time that it undermined the manure system. This began with the 1916 National Defense Act, prompted by the ongoing "European War" and conflicts with Mexico following incursions by the revolutionary Pancho Villa; the act put the federal government in the business of producing nitrates for both bombs and fertilizer and allocated $20 million to build factories. Development of the country's nitrogen-fixing capacity took on more urgency the next year when the US entered the war, and President Woodrow Wilson began a search for a production site far from the coast (to prevent attack) and near to supplies of limestone and coke, rail, and a waterway. A spot on the Tennessee River near a cluster of towns known as Muscle Shoals, Alabama, fit the bill. Muscle Shoals is better known for its role in the history of music than agriculture; the list of artists who have recorded at FAME Studios reads like a who's who of rhythm & blues and jazz. But it once was the subject of headlines and national debate spanning five presidencies, and the Muscle Shoals affair showcases how deeply input industries can get their snouts into public coffers.

The Muscle Shoals community actually played a role in the National Defense Act being enacted in the first place. The American Cyanamid Corporation had identified the town as a lucrative spot for a factory, well located to sell to the southern cotton planters who were the main customers for chemical fertilizers. Company officials persuaded Alabama senator Oscar Underwood to introduce into Congress a document they had prepared, peppered with neo-Malthusian warnings about how "without fixed nitrogen the earth would soon become an inhospitable waste." Underwood did not mention that the country's main fertilizer users were actually cotton farmers. After Wilson chose Muscle Shoals as the production site, the War Department hired none other than American Cyanamid to build cyanamide and Haber-Bosch plants there, neither of which were finished when the Armistice was signed in November 1918.

After the war, a House committee investigating war expenditures issued a scathing report on the $116 million that had been squandered on nitrate plants instead of other essentials that would have actually helped win the war (US House of Representatives 1920). It further condemned the whole Muscle Shoals program as an American Cyanamid scheme to get the government to erect expensive nitrate plants which it could then take over. By 1921 Congress began debate on the Wadsworth-Kahn Bill which would establish a government-owned company to operate the Muscle Shoals plant for the benefit of the military and farmers.

Fertilizer manufacturers frantically lobbied to keep their government subsidies while making sure the government did not take any of their market. Some supporters of the bill claimed it would help farmers; others were scornful including Rep. Madden of Illinois who said

> The proposal to do something for the farmer, is a subterfuge. You are throwing sand into the farmer's eyes in order that you may be able to put your hands up to the elbows into the treasury of the United States.
>
> *(Hubbard 1961, 21)*

The bill failed, and in March 1921 the Harding administration invited proposals for liquidating the entire Muscle Shoals holdings. Industrial hero Henry Ford stepped forward with an offer to buy the two nitrate plants for $5 million and take a 100-year lease on two government hydroelectric dams; he would produce fertilizer and other industrial goods (like parts for his company's autos) and use the electric power to develop the area into an industrial empire. A national debate on Ford's plan erupted, with his supporters claiming it would be a godsend for the farmer and critics seeing it as a brazen use of unenforceable promises about fertilizer to appropriate the region's electric power. Ford embarked on a speaking tour to promote his plan, bringing legendary inventor Thomas Edison in tow. Ford touted his vision of economic development, the well-ordered agrarian life, and the elimination of war – which he blamed on the international "Jewish menace" (Hubbard 1961, 35–37).

He insisted that his real aim was to help the farmer, whose problems he also blamed on the Jews – although his proposal did not actually obligate him to produce *any* fertilizer.

Thus the story fits the theme running through each phase of agricultural industrialization: it was an attempt to use agricultural technology and claims about agricultural growth to capture public wealth. Ford was offering $5 million for resources the government had spent $100 million to build and which were worth $12 million in scrap alone (Hubbard 1961, 46). It almost worked: the proposal was approved in Congress in 1924, but questions about control of hydroelectric power remained, and he finally withdrew the offer.

The Muscle Shoals debate dragged on until Franklin Roosevelt's election in 1932. Roosevelt soon established what he called "the widest experiment ever conducted by a government": the Tennessee Valley Authority, a government-owned corporation that would provide for economic development for Tennessee and neighboring states. The TVA also put the federal government into the fertilizer business on a large scale, providing an enormous boost to the rapidly growing industry. There is more to be said about the TVA, but first let us turn our attention to why there was a growing fertilizer industry to boost in the first place. Throughout much of the time that the Muscle Shoals controversy had dragged on, another branch of the US government had been underwriting the development of this industry and undermining less industrial methods of fertilizing.

The Lab Hidden in Plain Sight

While the struggle over fertilizer production at Muscle Shoals was the stuff of headlines and national debate, key policies of government support for a particular agricultural future were being devised behind the scenes. At the Fixed Nitrogen Research Laboratory, an agency created to repurpose leftover World War I explosives and related technologies, federal bureaucrats and scientists quietly made decisions that would enable the creation of a domestic fixed-nitrogen industry and point the country toward a future in which its farms were increasingly fed by chemicals (Johnson 2016b, 212). By 1920 the lab had grown to a staff of 108 housed in several buildings at American University (Lamb 1920), where it was "hidden in plain sight."

The FNRL did not start out to build a private industry; it was supposed to be investigating potential uses of leftover bombs and nitrogen-fixing infrastructure. In this capacity it actually came close to literally beating swords into plowshares, as when it used the barrel of a large naval gun as a high-pressure tank for synthesizing fertilizer (Lind 1926). It also considered giving out decaying explosives to be used as fertilizer until the lab found them to be of little value. It soon turned its attention to research and evaluation of the commercial potential for the cyanamide, arc, and Haber processes (Lamb 1920), guided by the aim to "subsidize chemical companies, not farmers." Its priority was not producing more or better food (of which there was no shortage), but "furthering the nitrogen fixation industry of America" and competing with Germany's more advanced industry (Johnson 2016b, 221–222). The FNRL's public funds and scientific expertise supported a gusher of upstream subsidy, developing prototype technologies to be used in private fertilizer factories. The FNRL also developed and manufactured catalysts for private fertilizer companies at no cost and shared patented and declassified military technologies with fertilizer companies, sometimes even providing them with cash incentives. It even built a model ammonia plant in Muscle Shoals, providing design details to chemical companies.

The US's first commercial Haber-Bosch plant opened in Syracuse in 1921, built by an offshoot of General Chemical (which had learned how to make the plant on the government's dime) (Nelson 1990, 226). By the time it was absorbed into other agencies in 1926, the FNRL had distributed enormous public largesse to, and granted federal endorsement of, chemical-input agriculture (Johnson 2016b, 224–226). By 1932, 11 plants were running with technologies developed by the FNRL, when the depression brought construction to a halt (Nelson 1990, 323–325).

Plowshares for Whom?

The FNRL's motivations for paving the way for commercial fertilizer were mixed, but it was no neo-Malthusian struggle: there was too much food around and farmers were suffering through an agricultural depression. State support for chemical agriculture was driven in part from forms of idealism that were prominent in early 20th century US. Farmers were widely believed to need external "scientific management," and helping the fertilizer industry was the way to make this happen. Many in government saw it as "enlightened bureaucracy" to serve the public by serving American business and many FNRL scientists thought that fertilizer would help "forge a path into a brave new world of abundant food and fiber" (Johnson 2016b, 221–224). But behind the idealism were worries about international economic competition. With a new nitrogen age dawning, many countries were drawn into a "nitrogen rush," competing to develop self-sufficiency and export dominance (Stocking and Watkins 1946). With Germany, Great Britain, France, Norway, and the US in the lead, world synthetic N production rose by 190% between 1924 and 1929 (Markham 1958, 98).

Brave or not, US agriculture did begin moving into a new world. Nitrogen factories proliferated and the price of ammonium nitrate plummeted from 20 cents/lb in 1920 to 5 cents/lb in 1932 (Markham 1958, 100). Nitrogen fertilizer use would rise *much* more after the 1950s, but its rise in industry's early years was still impressive, doubling between 1920 and the eve of World War II in 1941. Industry leaders proclaimed the rising fertilizer use a boon to the farmer and credited nitrogen with feeding the country (Brand 1945, 107), and a history of the fertilizer industry explained that "ammonia synthesis offered mankind the first real hope that the world's bread crops could meet food needs" (Nelson 1990, 230).

The triumphant narrative was fanciful. The rising use of N and other fertilizers raised yields inconsistently before World War II: between 1920 and 1941 corn and wheat yields only rose 4% and 24%, respectively. Farmers were just starting to buy more external inputs – a similar pattern to what we will see with the Green Revolution. And farmers did not necessarily adopt fertilizers simply because of economic benefits. Farmers had long struggled with decisions on fertilizer, and were known to often pick fertilizers on their smell, texture, advertising, and packaging. The "fertilizer craze" in the South following the Civil War was based in large part on misrepresented or fraudulent products (Nelson 1990, 47). Some states had passed laws to try – not always successfully – to protect farmers from adulterated fertilizers that were sometimes sold at up to 30 times the value of their nutrient content (Markham 1958, 23, 231).[23]

Information for farmers attempting to remedy their lack of knowledge was being skewed by the National Fertilizer Association. The NFA was actively subverting scientific challenges to chemical fertilizers and even constructing its own "shadow USDA" to "perform and propagate flattering agricultural research and information" (Johnson 2016b, 177–178). But more often than not, government agencies advocated and subsidized fertilizers.

Government policies also encouraged farmers to think of fertilizers as an entitlement. Following the National Defense Act, with its provisions for development of nitrate production, Congress allocated $10 million to import nitrate fertilizers to be given to farmers at cost. The policy had scant effect on wartime food production but "created a widespread belief that a fertilizer subsidy was due to American farmers" (Johnson 2016b, 218).

By the 1930s the USDA's Bureau of Chemistry (into which the FNRL had been absorbed) was moving ahead with fertilizer development and embracing the philosophy that "Every farm is a chemical factory" (Johnson 2016a, 155). The federal government even doled fertilizers out, as in 1935 when the Agricultural Adjustment Administration began to make commodity payments to farmers in the form of fertilizers. But it was the Tennessee Valley Authority that was responsible for the most extensive and sustained government effort to transform the American farm into a funnel for chemical fertilizer.

The TVA

Chapter 3 explored the different processes in farmer decision-making, and how persuasion by external sources, or didactic learning, may play on a large role. Soil fertility management can be particularly tricky, and farmers may be susceptible to persuasion on what to apply to their soil (as we saw with the 19th century soil analysis craze). From its beginnings in 1933, the Tennessee Valley Authority not only produced chemical fertilizer but promoted it so aggressively that it has been called the "public research and development branch of the American fertilizer industry" (Johnson 2016a, 214). By 1944 the TVA's test-demonstration program was running 32,000 farms that were basically advertisements for fertilizer.

Between 1936 and 1945, the TVA distributed an average of 1 million tons of fertilizer each year. (In 1942 this was non-nitrogenous fertilizer since the N was going for munitions.) The TVA gave out free fertilizer to farmer co-operatives (Chemical & Engineering News 1950, 3106) and to individual farmers who agreed to allow neighboring farmers to inspect their fields. (These fertilizer giveaways were biased. The rhetoric of helping the farmer notwithstanding, Black and poor white farmers "were left to wither while well-connected white farmers accumulated benefits" (Selznick 1949).) The fertilizer industry, although hostile to the government give-aways, benefited enormously in the long run by the government strategies for fertilizer penetration. TVA's fertilizer program would also play a central role in the internationalizing of fertilizer-intensive agriculture after World War II. Today, according to one estimate, as much as 75% of the fertilizer used worldwide may be traced to research by TVA staff (IFDC 2008).

All during a Time of Gluts

Clearly the inter-war years were a crucial time when the US government sponsored a particular trajectory of agro-technological development that would prove impossible to escape. When Theodore Schultz bemoaned the national "granary easy to fill but impossible to empty" (1960, 1019–1020), he was talking about post-World War II surpluses, but it was between the wars that agricultural surpluses reached emergency proportions.

Overproduction problems grew throughout the 1920s, as both crop exports and domestic demand dropped and adoption of tractors led to declining numbers of grain-eating horses and mules. As crop prices sank, the federal government began to grapple with how to protect farmers from the costs of overproduction. It considered buying up and reselling most of the wheat, corn, and cotton needed for domestic consumption, but instead formed a Federal Farm Board in 1929 which failed to control overproduction (Bowers, Rasmussen, and Baker 1984, 2–3). By the end of the decade, almost 50,000 farmers had gone bankrupt (Stam and Dixon 2004), and some officials had begun to ponder paying farmers to stop growing.

The 1920s, then, was a remarkable but telling decade: cash-strapped farmers were going broke and the country was staggering under the weight of agricultural overproduction, at the same time the government was aggressively developing industrial fertilizer resources that private companies could sell to farmers to boost production.[24] This was the same time that the government was pushing tractor adoption (Fitzgerald 2003) and, as we will see, lavishing resources on developing hybrid seeds for private companies to sell.

Wartime Munition and Nutrition

The US government had several motivations for subsidizing an inter-war chemical fertilizer industry, but for the most part they were not military. But government thinking about nitrogen began to change in 1940 with Hitler invading Poland, Japan expanding its war with China, and storm clouds threatening the US. The US began expanding its nitrogen-fixing capacity that year in anticipation of entering the war, building a nitrogen plant using a variant of the Haber-Bosch process in Morgantown WV in 1941. Following Japan's attack on Pearl Harbor in December 1941, the US embarked on an extraordinary campaign of nitrogen plant construction. By 1945, national production capacity had skyrocketed from its 1940 level of 390,000 to 1.2 million short tons (Markham 1958, 106), over 95% of which came from government plants.

By 1943 nitrogen production was high enough that ammonia was being diverted to use as fertilizer (Nelson 1990, 327), not only for food production but to keep suburban lawns green. Wartime ads for Vigoro, a mixed nitrogenous fertilizer, showed a smiling pipe-smoking dad maintaining the "velvety lawn" just the way their soldier son remembers it.

Thus, even in the thick of World War II, government-produced nitrogen was spilling over onto farms and suburban lawns. Anyone looking down the road ahead could see a world awash in fixed nitrogen, with enticing possibilities for profit. At its 1942 meeting, the American Society of Agronomy heard from its president that after the war there would be "at least twice as much nitrogen as we have ever used at a price much less then we have ever paid" (Kloppenburg 2004, 118). A 1944 government analysis was certain that nitrogen production capacity developed under inflated wartime conditions "will greatly exceed normal peacetime demands" (Johnson 1946, 1526).

The federal government, characteristically, was investing resources in making such overproduction profitable; the USDA busied itself in research on industrial uses of fertilizer-intensive crops such as making automotive antifreeze from corn in 1942 (Belasco 2006). Decades before ethanol fuel production became the top use of corn, the US government was already hard at work using surplus corn, grown with surplus fertilizer, to run vehicles – during the world war, yet.

Postwar Fertilizer and Modern Agriculture

While the foundation of the fertilizer industry had been laid before World War II, it was in the years after the war that the modern form of high-input chronically overproducing industrial agriculture took shape. No input is as important as nitrogen fertilizer, and few questions are as central to understanding agriculture as what happened with nitrogen after the war.

When World War II concluded in September 1945, the US owned wartime industrial plants worth over $15 billion (Wilson 2016, 196), including 12 nitrogen plants. President Franklin Roosevelt was intent on selling off these wartime industrial assets quickly to boost the economy. The War Assets Administration was created to dispose of the wartime facilities, and its handling of the selloff was an astonishing windfall for big business, indeed called "the greatest scandal arising out of the war" (Wilson 2016, 255). Six of factories the government had built at a cost of $142 million were sold to chemical companies for $50 million (Chemical & Engineering News 1950, 3106–3107). As after the previous war, the federal government was primed to give generous aid to fertilizer companies, but now it would be on an even grander scale.

Yet despite the size of the war-fattened nitrogen industry, there were critical shortages worldwide including in the US (Martin 1959, 380, New York Times 1947). Nitrogen prices in the US agricultural heartland climbed to a peak in 1949 (although postwar inflation was partly to blame) (Finke 1973, 37) before beginning a steady decline last through 1969; by then the fertilizer industry had quadrupled in size and American agriculture had been transformed.

The war itself had done much to chemicalize American agriculture, as farmers had scrambled to meet unprecedented food production goals and many who had not used chemical fertilizers before had taken advantage of government fertilizer (New York Times 1947). The fertilizer industry used its marketing muscle to help usher in an era of widespread fertilizer use. Government officials were also pushing chemicalization, as in February 1945 when Secretary of Agriculture Claude Wickard urged farmers – with a bizarre level of specificity – to use 328% more fertilizer than the prewar level (Christian Science Monitor 1945).

With the war over and demand for fertilizer going unmet, the federal government found new ways to promote the industry. These included price supports – farm prices jumped in 1946–1948 largely due to government price guarantees (Cochrane 1993, 124) and special tax incentives and low-interest loans for construction of nitrogen plants. One of the government's motivations was to boost capacity for the Korean War (1950–1953), but agricultural industrialization remained important as well. We can see, then, that we aren't so much "eating the leftovers from World War II," as Vandana Shiva puts it, as we are "reaping the harvest of generous federal subsidies" for the fertilizer industry since the 1920s (Johnson 2016a, 232).

Throughout the 1950s and 1960s, the fertilizer industry grew fat as the pattern continued. By the mid-1950s, fertilizer shortages were giving way to surplus, and an alarmed *Chemical Week* reported that the operating plants had a production capacity of 3.5 million short tons of anhydrous ammonia, with at least 15 companies planning expansions of a "whopping 4.35 million tons" in the next year (Chemical Week 1955, 75). Some of the ammonia could be exported, and some was used in industry – including in the manufacture of nylon hose, plastics, and refrigerants – but most went to fertilizer. Prospects for boosting exports and industrial use were limited, but the sky seemed to be the limit in agriculture, where "more hustling may boost demand for ammonia- based commercial fertilizers" (Chemical Week 1955, 75).[25]

The hustling to absorb more nitrogen in agriculture had already begun, and would soon bear fruit – or, more accurately, lock in the maladaptive regime of high-input, overproducing chemical agriculture that dominates the land today.

The Politics of Crowding

Despite the US government's history of promoting fertilizer, by the end of World War II most US farmers were still using only modest amounts. The main exception was farmers in the Southeast, where commodity crops like cotton had degraded soils and where land grant universities and agricultural experiment stations had supported themselves by selling fertilizers. Most crops were not well adapted to nutrient-dense fertilizers – even corn, the crop that would lead the postwar industrialization of US agriculture. By the end of World War II, most US corn farmers had adopted hybrid seeds (Chapter 5), but these corn hybrids responded poorly to fertilizers, developing weak stalks and becoming sickly (Steele 1978, 32). But corn would now lead the way toward fertilizer-intensive farming: the plant itself was about to be redesigned, transforming agriculture in the process.

It is amusing to hear agricultural companies today claim to be trying to develop crops that use less fertilizer (e.g., Gilbert 2016), because the top postwar breeding goal was making corn use *more* fertilizer. With subsidized nitrogen plants going up and fertilizer prices dropping, breeders embarked on a program of breeding corn to absorb large amounts of nitrogen fertilizer.

Breeders have various ways to adapt a crop to higher doses of fertilizer. They could breed plants that absorb more fertilizer and produce more product (as Green Revolution breeders did with wheat and rice). But postwar corn breeders took a different approach that would have major consequences for industrial agriculture: they bred corn for tolerance to high plant densities – that is, to grow in crowded fields.

Ironically, corn had previously been so productive partly because of its wide spacing. The plant has an extensive root network allowing it to draw nutrients from a large area. Wide spacing also makes corn amenable to intercropping; the Mesoamerican intercropped trio of corn, beans, and squash was a remarkably productive combination. The diverse plant communities growing in many peasant corn fields may horrify "scientific agronomists," writes Arturo Warman (2003 [1988]), but these assemblages serve the same function as crop rotation and fallow elsewhere.

But corn is also a highly adaptable plant, able to be the star in an intercropped swidden field on a peasant farm in Latin America and also in an input-intensive industrial field in the US Midwest. Most of the work of creating nitrogen-intensive corn was done by public breeders developing seeds that private companies could multiply and sell (Steele 1978, 32–33). By the 1950s, corn plants were being bred to survive being packed closer together in rows and in rows moved closer together, with increased applications of fertilizer and irrigation. By 1955 the first of the new hybrids appeared on the market; after 1965 they were the norm. The new model of corn cultivation was called the "high profit trio idea": use the new hybrids, plant them thicker, and fertilize heavier (Steele 1978, 33). The made-over corn plants are commonly saluted as "high yielding," which is misleading as most of the higher productivity comes from crowding rather than yield per plant (Tokatlidis and Koutroubas 2004). By 1980, average corn seeding rates would be twice as high as they had been in 1955.

At the same time that corn fields were becoming more crowded in space they were becoming more crowded in time: fertility management by crop rotation and manuring was increasingly replaced by continual cultivation of chemically fertilized corn (Steele 1978, 33). By the early 1960s, the new crowding in space and time was absorbing much of the flood of nitrogen. Figure 4.2 shows the steady increase in fertilizer use starting with the 1943 release of military ammonia and lasting through the 1950s, followed by the dramatic surge after crowded corn became the norm around 1960. Other crops have partly caught up with corn as a fertilizer hog, but over half of the fertilizer used in the US still goes onto this one crop (Stuart and Matthew 2018, 3).

Recall Malthus's insistence that the crowding of humans had wide-ranging indirect negative effects on society. Although the theory didn't work very well for humans, it turns out to fit crop crowding well, as the effects of high densities rippled through the ecology of the field and beyond. Crowded seeds need more water and the high concentrations of plants, fertilizer, and moisture were a haven for weeds, insects, and diseases. Therefore this was the time in which the spigot opened for intensive use of pesticides – including herbicides, insecticides, and fungicides (Rottstock et al. 2014, Yarwood 1970). An enthusiastic history of the US fertilizer industry explains that US farmers in the 1950s were not only learning the benefits of "large amounts of chemical nitrogen," but were also "doing a better job of controlling plant pests" (Nelson 1990, 323) – but they *had* to devote new kinds of attention to controlling plant pests because plant pests were booming as they never had before. Conveniently, wartime research had provided a wealth of new chemicals (including DDT and 2,4-D) and pesticide manufacture soared after the Korean War broke out in 1950 (Chemical Week 1955, 76).

The crowding of crops that began in the 1960s has only continued to climb. The 500 in^2 of real estate that a typical pre-war corn plant had to call its own had dropped to under 200 in^2 by the 1980s (Duvick 2005, 86). Seeding rates in some cases are approaching 150 K/ha (Gullickson 2016). If you look closely at a corn field today, you can find plants that are literally growing on top of each other.

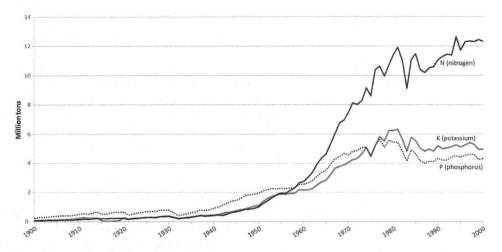

FIGURE 4.2 Fertilizer use in the US.
Source: US Departments of the Census and of Agriculture.

Farmers continue to be presented with a procession of "improved" corn seeds and are urged by seed companies to apply ever-higher amounts of fertilizer (Stuart and Matthew 2018, 8). Farmers are not getting wealthier but the people pushing corn crowding are. When Forbes magazine recently surveyed the richest person in each US state, the winner in Iowa was corn breeder Harry Stine, who was saluted as developing "seeds bred to thrive when they are densely planted, dramatically increasing harvests."

I describe this as the birth of "modern industrial agriculture" because while some chemical fertilizers, pesticides, and irrigation had been around for decades, the model of densely crowded fields of heavily fertilized, watered, and sprayed crops only emerged in the late 1950s and early 1960s. Meanwhile more sustainable organic forms of fertilizing declined dramatically in the US, and in much of the world later in the 1960s as the Green Revolution pushed chemical fertilizers throughout much of Asia (Chapter 6). The world went from getting about 50% of its nitrogen from biological fixation in the 1950s to only 20% by the mid-1990s (Crews and Peoples 2004, 280, Smil 2001). Global N use climbed from 11 million tons/year in 1960 to 86 million tons/year in 2000 (Crews and Peoples 2004, 280). Population growth was not driving that 620% jump in N use: during those years world population rose 102% and world agricultural output rose 146%. The postwar years brought us the birth of modern industrial agriculture in terms of both dependence on chemical inputs and the modern regime of overproduction, as US agriculture entered its modern predicament with a national granary impossible to empty.

Losing the Battle of Overproduction

The densely planted, heavily fertilized corn fields in the US Midwest were intended to increase yields and they did. Figure 4.3 shows that yields began to grow at an unprecedented rate in the mid-1950s. In the 15 years after 1954, corn yields rose from 39 to 86 bushels.

But corn yields were clearly growing much faster than corn *production*. The reason is that the number of acres planted to corn had been dropping for years, and they would

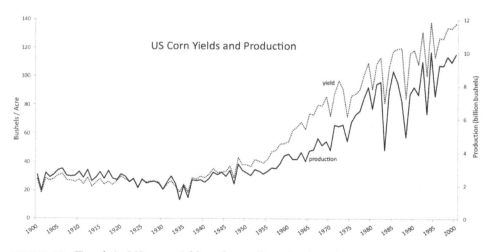

FIGURE 4.3 Trends in US corn yields and overall production. Data are from the USDA.

drop even more beginning in the mid-1950s due to increased payments for setasides. The point, we might conclude, was to sell fertilizer more than to produce corn. In fact it is clear that actual corn production did not begin to really surge until the mid-1960s (more on which in Chapter 5). But the fertilizer industry had begun to congratulate itself on its neo-Malthusian triumph over hunger well before that. The National Fertilizer Association's 1951 comic depicted Prosper Plenty – the animated bag of fertilizer in Figure 4.1– leading the way into a well-fed future as the Grim Reaper beats a hasty retreat.

Prosper Plenty and other industry media were playing off of a convenient surge of post-war Malthusian alarms. William Vogt's *Road to Survival* and Fairfield Osborn's *Our Plundered Planet*, both published in 1948, had issued dire warnings of overpopulation in the developing world. Vogt had channeled Malthus's Utterly Dismal Theorem (and presaged Ehrlich) in warning that we should not "ship food to keep alive ten million Indians and Chinese this year, so that fifty million may die five years hence" (Vogt 1948, 281–282).[26] But neither the wave of Malthusian anxiety nor the view of agricultural chemicals as a solution fit the realities of agriculture. Prosper Plenty and his magic chemicals were gushing onto the farm fields of a country that had been fighting a losing fight against runaway grain agriculture for decades. Stocks of feed grains had reached record levels before the Agricultural Adjustment Act of 1933 began to slow production. The setasides established by this act coupled with droughts in 1934 and 1936 brought stocks down briefly, but they soon roared back with the grain surplus reaching a new peak of 23.1 million tons by 1941. The surplus dipped during the war but surged again soon afterward. By 1949 the government was trying to figure out how to give away millions of dollars worth of food (Washington Post 1949), but the surplus still hit a new peak of 30.5 million tons by 1950, and kept growing.

By 1954, with the federal government paying $700,000 a day just to store grain surpluses, Agriculture Secretary Ezra Benson pushed to end the price supports (Graves 1954) but was outgunned by farm state legislators who managed to keep the price supports in place.[27] Finally in 1954 Congress passed Public Law 480 (PL 480), establishing a program for disposing of agricultural surplus in Asia. By 1958 this program was shipping over $6 billion worth of farm products, the largest shipments going to India. But despite PL 480 – actually in part because of PL 480 – grain stockpiles kept growing, and by 1959 storage costs topped $2.7 million per day (Cullather 2010, 142). Animal feedlots began to spread in the 1950s, absorbing stupendous amounts of the corn. But the country was drinking from a firehose; even with exports and livestock absorbing surplus, stocks climbed to record after record, reaching 85 million tons by 1961 (ERS 1963, 1). This was the background to the lament by Theodore Schultz, noted above: farm surpluses had become completely unconnected to supply and demand, and the more farm surplus we dispose of the larger the remaining surplus becomes (Schultz 1960, 1019–1020). And that was written in 1960 – the year that nitrogen-fueled yields took off!

The subsidy of overproduction was well known – LIFE magazine fumed that the

> government program of farm support has mounted to such staggering heights it takes $1,000 a minute of taxpayers' money just to maintain the surplus crops…[y]et with all the support of the farmer's prices and the complex attempts to restrict his production, farm income has long been on the decline.
>
> *(Ritter 1960, 91)*

In the 1960 presidential campaign, both John Kennedy and Richard Nixon advocated controls to lower production and price supports. Once elected, Kennedy pushed through an emergency program that idled 65 million acres – a remarkable figure considering that only 288 million acres were harvested that year (Cochrane and Ryan 1976, 298). There was still too much, but the government kept buying up grains at supported prices, and farm income boomed by a billion dollars (Hurt 2002, 128). When he signed an extension of the program in 1963, Kennedy claimed credit for having lowered the stocks by 860 million bushels (out of a 3 billion bushel surplus) and saved taxpayers over $800,000 a day (Kennedy 1963).

These interventions did manage to keep corn production flat in the early 1960s, but with fertilizer usage and yields climbing rapidly, it would be impossible to keep production down for long.

Collateral Damage: Nutrient Metabolisms

The hyperfertilized grain production of the 1950s created havoc not just by how much was produced, but by where it was produced. Before the advent of cheap fertilizer and crowded corn, American farms commonly practiced mixed crop and livestock production. The synergies of the combination are well known: the crops fed the livestock, the livestock fertilized the crops, and the farmer also grew legumes (like alfalfa) which both fertilized crops and fed animals. The chemical nitrogen diet decreased the value of both legumes and animal manure, making specialized grain production more profitable (Foster and Magdoff 2000). Factory farming of livestock, which had started (with government funding) on a relatively small scale in the 1930s, rapidly grew into the dominant means of raising both poultry and cattle in the 1950s; hogs would follow in the 1970s (Boyd and Watts 1997).

The new regime of producing meat and dairy products concentrated livestock in facilities and concentrated facilities in geographic regions, as producers favored areas with lax environmental laws, impoverished populations, and low threat of union activity. Beef feedlots concentrated in the southern Great Plains, poultry in Arkansas and on the Delmarva Peninsula, and hog production in parts of the Midwest and in North Carolina (Foster and Magdoff 2000), where the manure that had been fertilizer became a severe pollutant.

In this way, overproduction cascades inexorably through the system. Overproduction of fertilizer beyond what crops can absorb leads to redesign of crops and overproduction of grain beyond what the country can absorb. This leads to redesign of animal production practices and to overproduction of manure.

Even today, the surge in fertilizer use is explained in neo-Malthusian terms – the result of population growth (Erisman et al. 2008, 638). But it seems that the increase in nitrogen use during the 1950s and 1960s, the culmination of long years of state subsidy of the fertilizer industry, brought us the perfect anti-Malthusian moment. In contrast to farm output being fixed except for land expansion, the 1950s marked the confluence of state-supported technological regimes and unstoppable overproduction. It is referred to as "efficient," but it is efficient only because they have garnered extraordinary government support over other forms of agricultural growth. And its disastrous effects on environment and public health are not only severe but worsening. As this book was going to press, a major study in the Proceedings of the National Academy of Sciences (Liu, et al. 2022) reported that since 1980, cropland ammonia emissions had increased by a harrowing 128%, with no end in sight.

Notes

1 Guano, discussed below, is a special case. It is produced by birds rather than in a factory, but in other important senses it is an industrial input.

2 Fertilizer can also affect soils far away from where they are applied, as ammonia gasses drift hundreds of kilometers and cause soil to acidify where they come to rest.

3 "The worst-kept secret," says the director of the University of Iowa's Center for Health Effects of Environmental Contamination, "is how vulnerable private wells are to agricultural runoff" (Newman and McGroarty 2019). Farmers themselves help keep the problem secret: many refuse to have their well water tested because finding nitrates in their water would lower their property values.

4 Fertilizer runoff is not the only cause of the high nitrate concentrations, but it is often the primary cause (Agrawal, Lunkad, and Malkhed 1999) — and the most inexcusable because it is washing wastefully off of overproducing fields.

5 India, pushed into fertilizer-intensive agriculture by the Green Revolution but hard pressed to afford nitrate removal, "has already endangered the safety of potable groundwater for future generations in both rural and urban areas" (Agrawal, Lunkad, and Malkhed 1999, 67).

6 Making it even harder to study is that chemicals often have very different effects in various combinations that they do not have alone. For instance, nitrate fertilizer mixed with pesticides causes endocrine, immune, and behavior changes in animal models that it does not cause by itself (Porter, Jaeger, and Carlson 1999).

7 But no one knew why the bonemeal sometimes helped and sometimes did not, and the active ingredient was debated inconclusively for years (Rossiter 1975, 40).

8 The word comes from the Andean language of Quechua, in which *huanu* referred to any bird droppings used as fertilizer.

9 One exception to complete self-sufficiency on European farms was the purchase of seeds for specialty crops. For instance, by the 18th century Kent was known for producing turnip seed, and Holland for clover seed (Thompson 1968, 64).

10 In the early/mid-19th century there were dozens of local agricultural journals (Merchant 2010, 213) as well as a procession of books including de Saussure's *Chemical Research on Vegetation* in 1804, Thaer's *Principles of Rational Agriculture* in 1809, Davy's *Agricultural Chemistry* in 1813, Grisenthwaite's *A New Theory of Agriculture, in Which the Nature of Soils, Crops and Manures Is Explained* in 1819, Low's *Elements of Practical Agriculture* in 1838, Sprengel's *Science of Cultivation and Soil Amelioration*.

11 This nitre was different from the solid of the same name that had long been used in gunpowder (Leigh 2004, 71).

12 His 1931 book *The Waste Products of Agriculture* promoted humus-based strategies for maintaining soil fertility. See Michael Pollan's *Omnivore's Dilemma* (2006) for further exploration of the contrast between Sir Albert Howard and Justus von Liebig.

13 Chemist John Norton was offered a professorship in agricultural chemistry lab at Yale, which he ran as a commercial enterprise and "fought like a missionary with a cause to spread the gospel of soil analysis" (Rossiter 1975, 103–114).

14 By 1852, soil analysis and the science behind it were largely discredited, and the prevailing sentiment was that farmers knew as much as soil analysts (Rossiter 1975, 133).

15 It took years for its role as self-interested referee on fertilizer chemistry to erode, but in the end it was "far too limited in its cognitive abilities to define patterns of best use with scientific authority" (Uekötter 2014, 69).

16 Heights of the British poor were actually declining in the 1840s as the elites grew taller (Komlos 2005).

17 Examples are the Connecticut state agricultural experiment station (founded before the Hatch Act) which focused on fertilizer studies and the North Carolina Experiment Station (established in 1877) which started out as a fertilizer testing lab.

18 For an actual example of how a nation can have food imports disrupted by hostile powers and yet still feed itself without new scientific technology, we need look no further than Britain itself. Just a few years before World War II in the mid-1930s, Britain was importing 87% of its wheat, 92% of its fats, 51% of its meat, 69% of its cheese, and 77% of its fruit. As the Axis powers moved to cut off its imports, Britain swung quickly and effectively toward food self-sufficiency, with its tilled

acreage leaping from 5.2 to 8.2 million acres between 1939 and 1944 (Lamer 1957, 509). Food imports were cut in half (Collingham 2012, Chap. 5). This was not a triumph of innovation and new external inputs; the surge in production came about by generous incentives to British farmers who applied more work and more manure on more cultivated area (Collingham 2012, Chap. 5, Lamer 1957, 509–516). They were incentivized to intensify and they did. Italy too ran into the sort of precarity Crookes had feared. By 1925, Mussolini's fascist state was so squeezed by League of Nations sanctions that it was forced to launch its own "Battle for Wheat" which raised wheat production by 40% within the decade (Collingham 2012).

19 Another draft of the speech used the term "military-industrial-congressional complex."

20 German nitrogen synthesis had other indirect effects as well. Consider how history may have unfolded had it not been developed in Haber's Karlsruhe lab in 1909. Haber's nitrogen probably prolonged the war by three years. Daniel Charles (2005, Loc 2450–2457) speculates that if Germany had been forced to surrender in 1915,

> Lenin might never have made it back to Russia from exile in Switzerland. The Bolshevik revolution might never have happened, or it might have taken a milder course. Germany, too, would have been much less likely to descend into economic chaos and political bloodletting. In the absence of Fritz Haber, in other words, we might never have heard the names Hitler and Stalin.

21 And he shall judge among the nations, and shall rebuke many people: and they shall beat their swords into plowshares, and their spears into pruninghooks: nation shall not lift up sword against nation, neither shall they learn war any more (Isiah 2:4; repeated in Micah 4:3).

22 This was true even though in the South some institutions had to resort to selling fertilizer for operating income, as noted above.

23 In 1915 the agronomist and chemist Cyril Hopkins wrote:

> *Through lack of fundamental knowledge*, the general farmer of the east has been led to depend on mixed commercial fertilizers, and ten million acres once classed as improved farm land, but now agriculturally abandoned, represent the sign for Illinois farmers to look upon before adopting the fertilizer system now so extensively advertised in the Middle West.
> (quoted in Bowker 1915; italics in original)

24 It is worth considering the behavior of companies on the receiving end of the government largesse. There was a remarkable record of industry bullying, with the NFA undermining farmer co-ops that sought to buy chemicals directly (instead of from fertilizer dealers). The NFA also intensively lobbied county agents of the new Extension Service and threatened agents who showed farmers how to cut fertilizer costs (Johnson 2016a, 183–184).

The industry also has a history of concentration, cartels, and price fixing. Those in the nitrogen industry of the 1920s knew that overproduction of their product was going to be a problem, with much of the world already awash in agricultural surplus, many new fertilizer plants being planned, and world population not expected to grow fast enough to the additional calories that would be produced by the fertilizer (Speyer 1928, Page 2016, 390). By 1926, international ammonia producers were colluding to limit production, and an international cartel formed in the early 1930s.

Meanwhile the US producers colluded brazenly enough to prompt one of the largest antitrust investigations in US history. The Federal Trade Commission found evidence of price fixing, price discrimination against farmer cooperatives, improperly influencing government officials, and predatory lending practices. Allied Chemical and DuPont were indicted in 1939 for arranging to suppress production, fix prices on all forms of nitrogen fertilizer (Martin 1959, 376–377). Many companies pled no contest, but the National Fertilizer Association was convicted at trial. Cartels would become a permanent feature of the fertilizer industry, with today's leading companies operating "not as direct competitors, but through cooperation, quietly agreeing on prices for their products…[and taking] advantage of market shocks by hiking prices en masse" (Fernholz 2016). Such market manipulation even played an important role in exacerbating the food crisis of 2007–2008 (Gnutzmann and Spiewanowski 2014).

25 Globally, output of ammonia synthesis tripled during the 1950s, nearly one third of it from US sources. Worldwide, fertilizer production boomed from 9.7 million nutrient tons in 1946–1947 to 46.3 million tons in 1965–1966 (Johnston and Cownie 1969, 571).

26 Vogt had also included in his book a section entitled "Too Many Americans," and President Truman urged Americans to go meatless on Tuesdays.
27 The flood of grain led to other surpluses, notably dairy foods. The military did its part to reduce some of these surpluses, doubling milk rations for the soldiers in Korea and thus reducing the amount of butter the government had to buy. Officials claimed this would save taxpayers money but only because the cost of cold storage for butter was even more than the subsidized payments for the milk (Washington Post 1954).

References

Agrawal, G.D., S.K. Lunkad, and T. Malkhed. 1999. "Diffuse Agricultural Nitrate Pollution of Groundwaters in India." *Water Science and Technology* 39 (3):67–75. doi: 10.1016/S0273-1223(99)00033-5.

Anonymous. 1863. "Artificial Manures." *British Farming Magazine* 44:270–271.

APHIS. 2000. Dioxins in the Food Chain: Background. *USDA APHIS website* https://www.aphis.usda.gov/animal_health/emergingissues/downloads/dioxins.pdf

Ater, Malcolm W., and National Fertilizer Association. 1951. *The Conquest of Hunger: Featuring Prosper Plenty and His Magic Chemicals*. Washington, DC: Commercial Comics for the National Fertilizer Association.

Barles, Sabine, and Laurence Lestel. 2007. "The Nitrogen Question." *Journal of Urban History* 33 (5):794–812. doi: 10.1177/0096144207301421.

Beckert, Sven. 2014. *Empire of Cotton: A Global History*. New York: Vintage.

Belasco, Warren. 2006. *Meals to Come: A History of the Future of Food*. Berkeley: Univ. of California Press.

Beman, J. Michael, Kevin R. Arrigo, and Pamela A. Matson. 2005. "Agricultural Runoff Fuels Large Phytoplankton Blooms in Vulnerable Areas of the Ocean." *Nature* 434 (7030):211–214. http://www.nature.com/nature/journal/v434/n7030/suppinfo/nature03370_S1.html.

Beyond Pesticides. 2016. Toxic Algae Bloom in Florida's Largest Lake Tied to Chemical-Intensive Agriculture. *Beyond Pesticides*. 15 July. https://beyondpesticides.org/dailynewsblog/2016/07/toxic-algae-bloom-floridas-largest-lake-tied-chemical-intensive-agriculture/

Bhatnagar, Amit, and Mika Sillanpää. 2011. "A Review of Emerging Adsorbents for Nitrate Removal from Water." *Chemical Engineering Journal* 168 (2):493–504. doi: 10.1016/j.cej.2011.01.103.

Borlaug, Norman E., and C. Dowswell. 1995. "Mobilising Science and Technology to Get Agriculture Moving in Africa." *Development Policy Review* 13 (2):115–129.

Bowers, Douglas E., Wayne D. Rasmussen, and Gladys L. Baker. 1984. *History of Agricultural Price-Support and Adjustment Programs, 1933–1984. Economic Research Service, Agriculture Information Bulletin Number 485*. Washington, DC: USDA.

Bowker, W.H. 1915. "The Relation of the Fertilizer Industry to the Agricultural and Industrial Development of the Country." Address to the 22nd Annual Convention of the National Fertilizer Assn, Hot Springs VA, July 13.

Boyd, William, and Michael Watts. 1997. "Agro-industrial Just-in-time: The Chicken Industry and Postwar American Capitalism." In *Globalising Food: Agrarian Questions and Global Restructuring*, edited by David Goodman and Michael Watts, 192–224. London: Routledge.

Brand, Charles J. 1945. "Some Fertilizer History Connected with World War I." *Agricultural History* 19 (2):104–113.

Brinkley, Douglas. 2001. "Eisenhower's Farewell." *American Heritage* 56 (6) https://www.americanheritage.com/eisenhowers-farewell

Brock, William H. 1997. *Justus von Liebig: The Chemical Gatekeeper*. Cambridge: Cambridge Univ. Press.

Brock, William H. 2008. *William Crookes (1832–1919) and the Commercialization of Science*. Aldershot and Burlington: Ashgate.

Burnett, Christina Duffy. 2005. "The Edges of Empire and the Limits of Sovereignty: American Guano Islands." *American Quarterly* 57 (3):779–803.

Burney, Jennifer A., Steven J. Davis, and David B. Lobell. 2010. "Greenhouse Gas Mitigation by Agricultural Intensification." *PNAS* 107 (26):12052–12057.

Carver, Georgw W. 1899. *Fertilizer Experiments on Cotton (Tuskegee Institute Experiment Station, Bulletin 3.* Tuskegee, AL: Tuskegee Inst.

Carver, George W. 1905. *How to Build Up Worn Out Soils (Tuskegee Institute Experiment Station, Bulletin 6.* Tuskegee, AL: Tuskegee Inst.

Charles, Daniel. 2005. *Master Mind: The Rise and Fall of Fritz Haber, the Nobel Laureate Who Launched the Age of Chemical Warfare.* New York: HarperCollins.

Chemical & Engineering News. 1950. "A C&EN Staff Report." *Chemical & Engineering News Archive* 28 (37):3104–3109. doi: 10.1021/cen-v028n037.p3104.

Chemical Week. 1955. "Too Much, Too Soon?" *Chemical Week* 76 (5 Feb):75–76.

Christian Science Monitor. 1945. "Wickard Sees Need for More Fertilizer Use." *Christian Science Monitor*, 23 Feb, 15.

Clark, Brett, and John Bellamy Foster. 2009. "Ecological Imperialism and the Global Metabolic Rift." *International Journal of Comparative Sociology* 50 (3–4):311–334. doi: 10.1177/0020715209105144.

Cochrane, Willard W. 1993. *The Development of American Agriculture: A Historical Analysis, 2nd ed.* Minneapolis: Univ. of Minnesota.

Cochrane, Willard W., and Mary Ellen Ryan. 1976. *American Farm Policy: 1948–1973*: Univ. of Minnesota Press.

Cohen, Joel E. 1998. "How Many People Can the Earth Support?" *New York Review of Books* 8 Oct. https://www.nybooks.com/articles/1998/10/08/how-many-people-can-the-earth-support/

Collingham, Lizzie. 2012. *Taste of War: World War II and the Battle for Food.* New York: Penguin.

Cordle, Celia. 2007. "The Guano Voyages." *Rural History* 18 (1):119–133. doi: 10.1017/S0956793306002044.

Crews, T.E., and M.B. Peoples. 2004. "Legume versus Fertilizer Sources of Nitrogen: Ecological Tradeoffs and Human Needs." *Agriculture, Ecosystems and Environment* 102:279–297.

Crookes, Sir William. 1898. "Inaugural Address." *Nature* 58 (1506):418–448.

Cullather, Nick. 2010. *The Hungry World: America's Cold War Battle against Poverty in Asia.* Cambridge, MA: Harvard Univ. Press.

Cushman, Gregory T. 2003. "The Lords of Guano: Science and the Management of Peru's Marine Environment, 1800–1973." PhD, History, Univ. of Texas.

Cushman, Gregory T. 2013. *Guano and the Opening of the Pacific World: A Global Ecological History.* New York: Cambridge Univ. Press.

Duvick, Donald N. 2005. "The Contribution of Breeding to Yield Advances in maize (Zea mays L.)." *Advances in Agronomy* 86:83–145.

Dyke, G. V. 1993. *John Lawes of Rothamsted: Pioneer of Science, Farming and Industry.* Harpenden, Herts, UK: Hoos Press.

Erisman, Jan Willem, Mark A. Sutton, James Galloway, Zbigniew Klimont, and Wilfried Winiwarter. 2008. "How a Century of Ammonia Synthesis Changed the World." *Nature Geoscience* 1 (10):636–639. doi: 10.1038/ngeo325

ERS. 1963. An Economic Appraisal of the 1961 Feed Grain Program. In *Agricultural Economic Report 38*: USDA Economic Research Service.

Fernholz, Tim. 2016. A Global Corporate Conspiracy Helped Catalyze a Food Crisis and Drove 44 Million into Poverty. *Quartz* 23 September. https://qz.com/787943/a-literal-global-conspiracy-doubled-world-food-prices-and-drove-44-million-into-poverty/

Finke, Jeffrey. 1973. "Nitrogen Fertilizer: Price Levels and Sales in Illinois, 1945–1971." *Illinois Agricultural Economics* 13 (1):34–40. doi: 10.2307/1349001.

Finlay, Mark R. 1991. "The Rehabilitation of an Agricultural Chemist." *Ambix* 38:155–169.

Fitzgerald, Deborah. 2003. *Every Farm a Factory: The Industrial Ideal in American Agriculture.* New Haven, CT and London: Yale Univ. Press.

Fitzsimmons, Alex. 2016. "Will Humans Run Out of Fertilizer?" *The Atlantic* 14 December. https://www.theatlantic.com/technology/archive/2016/12/will-humans-run-out-of-fertilizer/510557/

Foster, John Bellamy. 1999. "Marx's Theory of Metabolic Rift: Classical Foundations for Environmental Sociology." *American Journal of Sociology* 105 (2):366–405.

Foster, John Bellamy. 2002. "Marx's Ecology in Historical Perspective." *International Socialism Journal* 96. http://pubs.socialistreviewindex.org.uk/isj96/foster.htm

Foster, John Bellamy, and Fred Magdoff. 2000. "Liebig, Marx, and the Depletion of Soil Fertility: Relevance for Today's Agriculture." In *Hungry for Profit: The Agribusiness Threat to Farmers, Food, and the Environment*, edited by Fred Magdoff, John Bellamy Foster and Frederick H. Buttel, 43–60. New York: Monthly Review Press.

Garnett, James M. 1818. "Defects in Agriculture." *Memoirs of the Society of Virginia for Promoting Agriculture*. Richmond, VA: Shepherd & Pollard.

Gerlock, Grant. 2015. Nitrates a Costly, Persistent Problem for Small Towns. *Iowa Public Radio* 25 November. http://www.iowapublicradio.org/post/nitrates-costly-persistent-problem-small-towns#stream/0

Giesen, James C., and Mark Hersey. 2010. "The New Environmental Politics and its Antecedents: Lessons from the Early Twentieth Century South." *The Historian* 72 (2) Summer: 271–298.

Gilbert, Natasha. 2016. "The Race to Create Super-crops (alt. title "Frugal Farming")." *Nature* 533:308–310. doi:10.1038/533308a.

Gnutzmann, Hinnerk, and Piotr Spiewanowski. 2014. "Did the Fertilizer Cartel Cause the Food Crisis?" *SSRN*. 6 December. doi: 10.2139/ssrn.2534753

Good, Allen G., and Perrin H. Beatty. 2011. "Fertilizing Nature: A Tragedy of Excess in the Commons." *PLoS Biol* 9 (8):e1001124. doi: 10.1371/journal.pbio.1001124.

Goodman, David, Bernardo Sorj, and John Wilkinson. 1987. *From Farming to Biotechnology: A Theory of Agro-industrial Development*. Oxford: Basil Blackwell.

Graves, Aubrey. 1954. "Farm Price Support Debate Gets Hotter." *The Washington Post and Times Herald*, 6 Aug.

Guillette, Jr Louis J., and Thea M. Edwards. 2005. "Is Nitrate an Ecologically Relevant Endocrine Disruptor in Vertebrates?" *Integrative and Comparative Biology* 45 (1):19–27. doi: 10.1093/icb/45.1.19.

Gullickson, Gil. 2016. Harry Stine's Accidental Discovery May Revolutionize Farming. *Successful Farming* 2 August. http://www.agriculture.com/crops/corn/harry-stine-s-accidental-discovery-may-revolutionize-farming.

Hines, Linda O. 1979. "George W. Carver and the Tuskegee Agricultural Experiment Station." *Agricultural History* 53 (1):71–83.

Hopkins, Cyril G. 1910. *Soil Fertility and Permanent Agriculture*. Boston: Ginn & Co.

Howard, Albert. 1940. *An Agricultural Testament*. New York and London: Oxford Univ. Press.

Howard, Albert. 1946. *The War in the Soil*. Emmaus, PA.: Rodale Press.

Huang, Jikun, Ashok Gulati, and Ian Gregory, eds. 2017. *Fertilizer Subsidies—Which Way Forward?* Muscle Shoals: International Fertilizer Development Center.

Hubbard, Preston J. 1961. *Origins of the TVA: The Muscle Shoals controversy, 1920–1932*. Nashville: Vanderbilt Univ. Press.

Hurt, R. Douglas. 2002. *Problems of Plenty: The American Farmer in the Twentieth Century*. Chicago: Ivan Dee.

IFDC. 2008. TVA Fertilizer Technology Used Worldwide – But Few New Products since 1970s In *AAAS EurekAlert* 25 Sugust. https://www.eurekalert.org/pub_releases/2008-08/i-tft082508.php

Johnson, Bertrand L. 1946. "Nitrogen Compounds." In *Minerals Yearbook 1944*, edited by E. W. Pehrson and C.E. Needham, 1525–1531. Washington, DC: US Government Printing Office.

Johnson, Timothy. 2016a. "Growth Industry: The Political Economy of Fertilizer in America, 1865–1947." PhD, History, Univ. of Georgia.

Johnson, Timothy. 2016b. "Nitrogen Nation: The Legacy of World War I and the Politics of Chemical Agriculture in the United States, 1916–1933." *Agricultural History* 90 (2):209–229. doi: 10.3098/ah.2016.090.2.209.

Johnston, Bruce F., and John Cownie. 1969. "The Seed-Fertilizer Revolution and Labor Force Absorption." *The American Economic Review* 59 (4):569–582.

Kennedy, John F. 1963. Remarks upon Signing the Feed Grain Bill. 20 May. https://www.presidency.ucsb.edu/documents/remarks-upon-signing-the-feed-grain-bill

Kloppenburg, Jack Ralph, Jr. 2004. *First the Seed: The Political Economy of Plant Biotechnology, 1492–2000, 2nd edition.* Madison: Univ. of Wisconsin Press.

Lamb, Arthur B. 1920. "The Fixed Nitrogen Research Laboratory." *Chemical & Metallurgical Engineering* 22 (21):977–979.

Lamer, Mirko. 1957. *The World Fertilizer Economy.* Stanford, CA: Stanford Univ. Press.

LeCompte, Celeste. 2013. Fertilizer Plants Spring Up to Take Advantage of U.S.'s Cheap Natural Gas. *Scientific American*, 25 August. https://www.scientificamerican.com/article/fertilizer-plants-grow-thanks-to-cheap-natural-gas/

Leigh, G. J. 2004. *The World's Greatest Fix: A History of Nitrogen and Agriculture.* Oxford: Oxford Univ. Press.

Liebig, Justus von. 1859. *Letters on Modern Agriculture.* London: Walton & Maberly.

Liebig, Justus von. 1863. *The Natural Laws of Husbandry (Excerpt from 7th edition of Chemistry and its Application).* London: Walton & Maberly.

Lind, S. C. 1926. "The Fixed Nitrogen Research Laboratory." *Scientific Monthly* 22.

Lipton, Eric. 2015. "Emails Reveal Academic Ties in a Food War: Industry Swaps Grants for Lobbying Clout." *New York Times*, 5 Sept. http://www.nytimes.com/2015/09/06/us/food-industry-enlisted-academics-in-gmo-lobbying-war-emails-show.html.

Liu, Lei, et al. 2022. "Exploring global changes in agricultural ammonia emissions and their contribution to nitrogen deposition since 1980." *Proceedings of the National Academy of Sciences* 119(14):e2121998119. doi: 10.1073/pnas.2121998119

Loneragan, Jack F. 1997. "Plant Nutrition in the 20th and Perspectives for the 21st Century." *Plant and Soil* 196 (2):163–174. doi: 10.1023/a:1004208621263.

Manlay, Raphael J., Christian Feller, and M.J. Swift. 2007. "Historical Evolution of Soil Organic Matter Concepts and Their Relationships with the Fertility and Sustainability of Cropping Systems." *Agriculture Ecosystems & Environment* 119:217–233.

Manuel, John. 2014. "Nutrient Pollution: A Persistent Threat to Waterways." *Environmental Health Perspectives* 122:A304–A309. doi: 10.1289/ehp.122-A304.

Marald, Erland. 2002. "Everything Circulates: Agricultural Chemistry and Recycling Theories in the Second Half of the Nineteenth Century." *Environment and History* 8 (1):65–84.

Marcus, Alan. 1987. "Setting the Standard: Fertilizers, State Chemists, and Early National Commercial Regulation, 1880–1887." *Agricultural History* 61:47–73.

Markham, Jesse W. 1958. *The Fertilizer Industry: Study of an Imperfect Market.* Nashville: Vanderbilt Univ. Press.

Martin, William H. 1959. "Public Policy and Increased Competition in the Synthetic Ammonia Industry." *The Quarterly Journal of Economics* 73 (3):373–392. doi: 10.2307/1880610.

Marx, Karl. 1967 [1867]. *Capital Volume 1: A Critique of Political Economy.* New York: Vintage.

Marx, Karl. 1981 [1883]. *Capital Volume III: The Process of Capitalist Production as a Whole.* New York: Vintage.

Mathew, W.M. 1970. "Peru and the British Guano Market, 1840–1870." *The Economic History Review* 23 (1):112–128.

Mathew, W.M. 1977. "A Primitive Export Sector: Guano Production in Mid–Nineteenth-Century Peru." *Journal of Latin American Studies* 9 (1):35–57.

Melillo, Edward D. 2012. "The First Green Revolution: Debt Peonage and the Making of the Nitrogen Fertilizer Trade, 1840–1930." *The American Historical Review* 117 (4):1028–1060. doi: 10.1093/ahr/117.4.1028.

Meng, Qingmin. 2017. "The Impacts of Fracking on the Environment: A Total Environmental Study Paradigm." *Science of the Total Environment* 580:953–957. doi: 10.1016/j.scitotenv.2016.12.045.

Merchant, Carolyn. 2010. *Ecological Revolutions: Nature, Gender & Science in New England 2nd ed.* Chapel Hill: Univ. of North Carolina Press.

Merton, Robert K. 1942. "Science and Technology in a Democratic Order." *Journal of Legal and Political Science* 1:115–126.

Montgomery, David R. 2017. *Growing a Revolution: Bringing Our Soil Back to Life.* New York and London: W. W. Norton & Company.

Munday, Pat. 1990. "Social Climbing through Chemistry: Justus Liebig's Rise from the Niederer Mittelstand to the Bildungsbürgertum." *Ambix* 37 (1):3–19. doi: 10.1179/amb.1990.37.1.3.

Nelson, Lewis B. 1990. *History of the U.S. Fertilizer Industry*. Muscle Shoals, AL: Tenn Valley Authority.

New York Times. 1947. "Fertilizer Supply Short of Demand." *New York Times*, 23 Feb, 12.

Newman, Jesse, and Patrick McGroarty. 2019. Farms, More Productive Than Ever, Are Poisoning Drinking Water in Rural America. In *Wall Street Journal* 18 January. https://www.wsj.com/articles/farms-more-productive-than-ever-are-poisoning-drinking-water-in-rural-america-11547826031

Nolan, Bernard T., Barbara C. Ruddy, Kerie J. Hitt, and Dennis R. Helsel. 1997. "Risk of Nitrate in Groundwaters of the United States A National Perspective." *Environmental Science & Technology* 31 (8):2229–2236. doi: 10.1021/es960818d.

Osborn, Fairfield. 1948. *Our Plundered Planet*. Boston, MA: Little, Brown and Company.

Page, Arnaud. 2016. ""The Greatest Victory Which the Chemist Has Won in the Fight (…) against Nature": Nitrogenous Fertilizers in Great Britain and the British Empire, 1910s–1950s." *History of Science* 54 (4):383–398. doi: 10.1177/0073275316681801.

Petrowiki. 2018. "Gas as Fertilizer Feedstock." Petrowiki blog, accessed 19 Oct. https://petrowiki.org/Gas_as_fertilizer_feedstock.

Philpott, Tom. 2016. "A Massive Sinkhole Just Dumped Radioactive Waste Into Florida Water." *Mother Jones*, 21 Sept. http://www.motherjones.com/environment/2016/09/sinkhole-florida-radioactive-water-fertilizer.

Pimentel, David editor. 1980. *Handbook of Energy Utilization in Agriculture*. Boca Raton, FL: CRC Press.

Pollan, Michael. 2006. *The Omnivore's Dilemma: A Natural History of Four Meals*. New York: Penguin.

Porter, Jane M. 1979. "Experiment Stations in the South, 1877–1940." *Agricultural History* 53 (1):84–101.

Porter, W.P., J.W. Jaeger, and I.H. Carlson. 1999. "Endocrine, Immune, and Behavioral Effects of Aldicarb (carbamate), Atrazine (triazine) and Nitrate (fertilizer) Mixtures at Groundwater Concentrations." *Toxicol Ind Health* 15 (1–2):133–50.

Punch. 1898. "The Baker's Shop of the Near Future." *Punch*, 133.

Ritter, Norman. 1960. "Battle of the Farm." *Life*, 91–98.

Rossiter, Margaret W. 1975. *The Emergence of Agricultural Science: Justus Liebig and the Americans, 1840–1880*. New Haven, CT and London: Yale Univ. Press.

Rottstock, Tanja, Jasmin Joshi, Volker Kummer, and Markus Fischer. 2014. "Higher Plant Diversity Promotes Higher Diversity of Fungal Pathogens, While it Decreases Pathogen Infection Per Plant." *Ecology* 95 (7):1907–1917.

Schultz, Theodore W. 1960. "Value of U.S. Farm Surpluses to Underdeveloped Countries." *Journal of Farm Economics* 42 (5):1019–1030. doi: 10.2307/1235653.

Selznick, Philip. 1949. *TVA and the Grass Roots: A Study in the Sociology of Formal Organization*. Berkeley: Univ. of California Press.

Skaggs, Jimmy. 1994. *The Great Guano Rush: Entrepreneurs and American Overseas Expansion*. New York: St. Martin's Griffin.

Smil, Vaclav. 2000. *Feeding the World: A Challenge for the Twenty-first Century*. Cambridge, MA: MIT Press.

Smil, Vaclav. 2001. *Enriching the Earth: Fritz Haber, Carl Bosch, and the Transformation of World Food Production*. Cambridge, MA: The MIT Press.

Speyer, F. C. O. 1928. *Some Nitrogen Problems*. London: Vaccher and Sons.

Stam, Jerome M., and Bruce L. Dixon. 2004. Farmer Bankruptcies and Farm Exits in the United States, 1899–2002. US Department of Agriculture.

Steele, Leon. 1978. "The Hybrid Corn Industry in the United States." In *Maize Breeding and Genetics*, edited by David B. Walden, 29–40. New York: John Wiley.

Stocking, George W., and Myron Watkins. 1946. *Cartels in Action*. New York: 20th Century Fund.

Stoll, Steven. 2002. *Larding the Lean Earth: Soil and Society in Nineteenth-Century America*. New York: Hill & Wang.

Stuart, Diana, and Houser Matthew. 2018. "Producing Compliant Polluters: Seed Companies and Nitrogen Fertilizer Application in U.S. Corn Agriculture." *Rural Sociology.* doi:10.1111/ruso.12212.

Sumners, Christina. 2016. Agricultural Compounds in Drinking Water Linked to Birth Defects. *Vital Record* 21 April. https://vitalrecord.tamhsc.edu/agricultural-compounds-drinking-water-linked-birth-defects/

Tarbell, Ida M. 1915. "Sticking to the Old Ways: The Golden Rule in Business." *American Magazine*, June pp. 36–39, 93–99.

Taylor, Rosser H. 1953. "Fertilizers and Farming in the Southeast, 1840–1950: Part 1, 1840–1900." *The North Carolina Historical Review* 30 (3):305–328.

Tennesen, Michael. 2010. Sour Showers: Acid Rain Returns--This Time It Is Caused by Nitrogen Emissions. *Scientific American* 21 June. https://www.scientificamerican.com/article/acid-rain-caused-by-nitrogen-emissions/

Thompson, F.M.L. 1968. "The Second Agricultural Revolution, 1815–1880." *The Economic History Review* 21 (1):62–77. doi: 10.2307/2592204.

Thompson, F.M.L. 2000. "Agricultural Chemical and Fertiliser Industries." In *The Agrarian History of England and Wales, Vol 7, 1850–1914, Part II*, edited by E.J.T. Collins, 1019–1044. Cambridge: Cambridge Univ. Press.

Tilman, David, Kenneth G. Cassman, Pamela A. Matson, Rosamond Naylor, and Stephen Polasky. 2002. "Agricultural Sustainability and Intensive Production Practices." *Nature* 418:671–677.

Tokatlidis, I.S., and S.D. Koutroubas. 2004. "A Review of Maize Hybrids' Dependence on High Plant Populations and its Implications for Crop Yield Stability." *Field Crops Research* 88 (2–3): 103–114. doi: 10.1016/j.fcr.2003.11.013.

Turner, Peter A., Timothy J. Griffis, Xuhui Lee, John M. Baker, Rodney T. Venterea, and Jeffrey D. Wood. 2015. "Indirect Nitrous Oxide Emissions from Streams within the US Corn Belt Scale with Stream Order." *Proceedings of the National Academy of Sciences* 112 (32):9839–9843. doi: 10.1073/pnas.1503598112.

Uekötter, Frank. 2014. "Why Panaceas Work: Recasting Science, Knowledge, and Fertilizer Interests in German Agriculture." *Agricultural History* 88 (1):68–86. doi: 10.3098/ah.2014.88.1.68.

UNEP. 2007. *Reactive Nitrogen in the Environment: Too Much or Too Little of a Good Thing.* Falmouth, MA: The Woods Hole Research Center.

US House of Representatives. 1920. Report 998: War Expenditures-Ordnance.

van der Ploeg, R.R., W. Bohm, and M.B. Kirkham. 1999. "On the Origin of the Theory of Mineral Nutrition of Plants and the Law of the Minimum." *Soil Science Society of America Journal* 63:1055–1062.

Vogt, William. 1948. *Road to Survival.* New York: William Sloane.

Waliser, Shawn. 2003. "Another Tragedy of the Commons: Placing Cost Where It Belongs by Banning Hazardous Substances in Fertilizer through State Legislation." *Journal of Environmental Law and Litigation* 18 (1):51–128.

Ward, Mary H., Rena R. Jones, Jean D. Brender, Theo M. de Kok, Peter J. Weyer, Bernard T. Nolan, Cristina M. Villanueva, and Simone G. van Breda. 2018. "Drinking Water Nitrate and Human Health: An Updated Review." *International Journal of Environmental Research and Public Health* 15 (7):1557. doi: 10.3390/ijerph15071557.

Warman, Arturo. 2003 [1988]. *Corn and Capitalism: How a Botanical Bastard Grew to Global Dominance.* Chapel Hill: Univ. of North Carolina Press.

Washington Post. 1949. "Way Cleared to Give Surplus Food Away." *The Washington Post*, 19 Oct.

Washington Post. 1954. "Army Doubles GI Milk Ration To Help Ease Farm Surplus." *The Washington Post and Times Herald*, 8 Oct.

Wendle, Abby. 2015. "More Fertilizer Plants Come Online and Bring Their Baggage: CO_2." *Harvest Public Media* 11 Dec. http://www.harvestpublicmedia.org/post/more-fertilizer-plants-come-online-and-bring-their-baggage-co2.

Wilson, Mark R. 2016. *Destructive Creation: American Business and the Winning of World War II.* Philadelphia: Univ. of Pennsylvania Press.

Wines, R. A. 1985. *Fertilizer in America: From Waste Recycling to Resource Exploitation.* Philadelphia, PA: Temple Univ. Press.

Wong, Edward. 2013. "Spill in China Underlies Environmental Concerns." *New York Times*, 2 March. https://www.nytimes.com/2013/03/03/world/asia/spill-in-china-lays-bare-environmental-concerns.html

Wood, Ellen M. 2000. "The Agrarian Origins of Capitalism." In *Hungry for Profit: The Agribusiness Threat to Farmers, Food, and the Environment*, edited by Fred Magdoff, John Bellamy Foster and Frederick H. Buttel, 23–42. New York: Monthly Review Press.

Yarwood, C.E. 1970. "Man-Made Plant Diseases." *Science* 168:218–220.

Zhang, Fusuo, Xinping Chen, and Peter Vitousek. 2013. "Chinese Agriculture: An Experiment for the World." *Nature* 497 (7447):33–35. doi: 10.1038/497033a.

Zhou, Xiaochi, Fletcher H. Passow, Joseph Rudek, Joseph C. von Fisher, Steven P. Hamburg, and John D. Albertson. 2019. "Estimation of Methane Emissions from the U.S. Ammonia Fertilizer Industry Using a Mobile Sensing Approach." *Elementa: Science of the Anthropocene* 7. doi: 10.1525/elementa.358.

5

HEROES OF THE HARVEST

Chemical fertilizer may have a halo, but the halo for seeds – not seeds that farmers themselves have been producing for millennia, but seeds from breeders – is even brighter. After all, fertilizer is a chemical compound from a factory, while seeds are the very stuff of life. Crop breeders occupy a noble niche in the world of food and agriculture – the "Heroes of the Harvest" according to the USDA (Wilson 2015). Some become famous, like Luther Burbank, some rich, like Henry Wallace, and some legendary, like Norman Borlaug. The goals and motivations of crop breeders are generally assumed to be simple and humanitarian: they do what they do to "meet societal needs" and seek "harmony between agriculture and the environment" (Brummer et al. 2011, 561). But most importantly, they work on the front lines of that neo-Malthusian struggle between "the scientific power of food production and the biologic power of human reproduction," as Borlaug put it in Oslo (1970). "Fortunately," wrote a corn breeder in 1951, "modern science has provided us with many new tools to aid in increasing food supply to keep pace with population growth…one of these new tools is genetics, the science of heredity" (Jenkins 1951, 84).

All of this is said to be especially true of the game-changing breeding technology of hybrid corn. "Little did Malthus know," we learn from a US government *Yearbook of Agriculture*, "that corn, specifically hybrid corn, would delay for almost two centuries the impact of his dire predictions" (Harpstead 1975, 213). Or to quote a distinguished National Academy of Science breeder,

> Around the turn of the twentieth century, farmers in the United States began to look harder than before for ways to increase maize yields. Urban populations were increasing rapidly [and] as new lands were no longer available for exploitation, increased production needed to come from higher yields. The use of plant breeding to produce new and/or improved, higher-yielding varieties of maize looked like a promising option. Those farmers and scientists who selected new breeding varieties rose to the challenge.
>
> *(Duvick 2001, 69)*

DOI: 10.4324/9781003286257-5

The upswing in US corn yields we saw in Figure 4.3 is often attributed to the adoption of hybrid corn in the 1930–1940s (although we know it actually had more to do with fertilizer). Hybrid crops have been compared in importance to nuclear power (Kloppenburg 2004, 91), heralded by TIME magazine as one of the greatest achievements in the last previous 1,000 years (Holmes 1992), credited with keeping the world fed, paying for the development of the atomic bomb, and checking the spread of Communism (Kloppenburg 2004, 6).

Crop breeding even seems to have the remarkable power to help but not to harm. It "does indeed generate substantial benefits and is remarkably free of unfavourable side-effects," says a famous textbook on the subject; "plant breeding, *per se*, is a wholly benign technology, any enhancement of it must be welcomed as being in the public good, no matter who does it" (Simmonds 1979, 38).

However when we take a critical look at the history of crop breeding, the agreeable vision of contributing to the "public good" fades into a story of clashing interests and seeds being developed to bestow those "substantial benefits" on some (especially seed companies) and "unfavourable side-effects" on others (especially farmers). Crop breeders hardly show up to work every day with nothing but societal benefits on their mind; like other applied scientists, they work on problems for which their employers reward them, and the interests of their employers may diverge sharply from the interests of consumers and some farmers (Busch et al. 1991, 52).[1] Consider that during the 20th century professional breeders have substantially lowered the levels of protein, iron, and zinc in wheat (Busch et al. 1991, 115–118, Garvin, Welch, and Finley 2006, Shewry, Pellny, and Lovegrove 2016), reduced nutrients in vegetable by as much as 38% (Davis, Epp, and Riordan 2004), reduced the nitrogen-fixing capability of African cowpeas (Makoi, Chimphango, and Dakora 2009), and bred hard tasteless and low-nutrition tomatoes (Estabrook 2011). They have used genetically modified traits to raise the nicotine content in tobacco (Leary 1994), create cotton that is dependent on pesticides that lose effectiveness and leave farmers on technological treadmills (Stone 2011, Stone and Flachs 2017), and develop crops that lead farmers to spray herbicides that probably cause cancer and definitely ruin neighbors' fields (Egan, Kathryn, and David 2014). Even breeders in nonprofit institutes have created potatoes that require smallholder farmers to take credit to pay for chemicals and labor (van der Ploeg 1993, 220).

But most importantly, breeders created hybrid crops – specifically hybrid corn, which revolutionized agriculture in ways that many breeders themselves knew to be problematic. Concerns about who would benefit from the invention led to an intense struggle among public sector breeders in the early 20th century. After the "rediscovery of Mendel" (described below) the rapidly growing breeding establishment split into camps of "selection breeders" and Mendelians, and their disagreements ran deep. They differed in what they considered accomplishment and measured success, in how they interacted with the farmers who were supposed to be their clients, and in how they served agricultural capital. Many Selectionists thought hybrid corn was the utterly wrong direction to take given the interests of the farmers that were supposed to be their constituency.

The Selectionists had a point: we will see that hybrid corn turned out to help seed companies profit from government subsidy more than help farmers profit from their crop. Hybrid corn arrived on the market during a grain glut, relied on government breeding to develop marketable products and on government promotion to induce farmers to adopt, choked off most improvement of non-hybrids so farmers could not switch back, and helped to increase farmer dependence. Hybrid technology itself didn't even raise yields very much, although when it was re-bred to facilitate chemical-intensive farming it played a key role in disastrous overproduction. Hybrid corn turns out to be a very poor fit for the neo-Malthusian story told above, but an example par excellence of the principles of agricultural industrialization laid out in Chapter 3. Let us explore how this all came about.

Farmer Breeding

Crop breeding refers to intentional manipulation of successive generations of crop plants, which humans have been doing for a very long time. The practice of choosing plants with desirable characteristics as the seed stock for the next planting is called *population improvement* or *mass selection* because the seeds chosen for replanting are mixed together into a population that is constantly being improved according to someone's criteria.[2] The practice is conceptually simple and over time can be remarkably effective in shaping plants to human purposes.

Mass selection can improve a crop while retaining diversity within the population of plants. Each field full of plants contains raw material for future improvement and for adaptation to threats like disease or pests (unlike the genetically narrow hybrid crops). Importantly, when farmers practice mass selection they normally do it on the location where the seeds will be cultivated. Each field has its own combination of soil type, microbes, local climate, and drainage, and farmers often adapt their seeds to the fields where they are being grown. (In contrast, professionally improved varieties have to be adapted to more standardized conditions, particularly with hybrids, as we will see; this is why professionally bred seeds have played a key role in the change from adapting the seed to the field to adapting the field to the seed with chemicals.)

Mass selection also has its disadvantages. In outcrossing species – meaning that seed-bearing female part of the plant is normally pollinated by another plant of the same species – the breeder has little control over the male parent. This is one reason that mass selection can reduce, but generally not eliminate, undesirable traits. Mass selection also focuses on the qualities of the plant itself rather than the qualities of its offspring – which is not always the same. Mass selection as practiced by farmers was often a bit genetically sloppy as the crop was subject to influx of traits out of the farmers' control (Kloppenburg 2004, 95); breeders at formal facilities were in a better position to control this. Farmers also crossed different varieties to make their own "varietal hybrids." (Any crosses of different seed types could be called "hybrids," but the term hybrid would soon take on an important different meaning as we discuss below.)

Pro-Farmer Professional Breeding

Throughout the first half of the 19th century the US government's main contribution to farmers was, rather oddly, through the Patent Office. With Congressional funding, the office sent out over 1 million free packets of seeds to farmers in the 1840s (Kloppenburg 2004, 55–56). (These were the first packages to be handled by the US Post Office, which had heretofore transmitted only letters.) It was then up to farmers themselves to conduct their own growing and breeding experiments to adapt and improve the crops. This they did with much success, creating famous improved cultivars, such as Red Fyfe wheat, Grimm alfalfa, and Rough Purple Chili potato, based on seeds originating in Poland, Germany, and Panama. The results of these experiments moved among farmers, who continued to improve and adapt seeds to local conditions by mass selection. This system of seed management was aligned with the interests of the farmers themselves, and by 1860, a host of crops was well established and crucial in regional agricultural economies (Kloppenburg 2004, 57).

Then came 1862, a watershed year for the US government's support for the farmer – or so it seemed – with the establishment of the US Department of Agriculture (USDA). The aims of the USDA, as laid out by its first commissioner (who was actually named Isaac Newton), appeared to align reasonably well with the interests of the individual farmer: the agency would publish useful agricultural information, introduce new plants and animals, answer farmer inquiries, and analyze soils, crops, and manures (Cochrane 1993, 96). The land grant universities (LGUs) were established the same year with the mission "to teach such branches of learning as are related to agriculture and the mechanic arts," also seemingly aligned with farmer interests.

And yet farmers were not at all in agreement on welcoming these developments. The lobbying that led to the USDA was not by farmers but by agricultural societies and journals; many farmers were wary of the government's role morphing from the simple provision of seeds to a full-blown bureaucracy. The objections boiled down to vested interests, with many farmers believing that "parasitic politicians would take every opportunity to live off the fruit of [their] labor" (Danbom 1979, 17). And as for the LGUs, many farmers felt – understandably – that whatever the professors had to teach on the "mechanic arts," they wouldn't be able to tell farmers how to farm. Meanwhile the funding for these schools came from the public purse and from selling off *land*, the primary resource of agriculture. The agrarian South had been especially cool on the idea of LGUs when it was first proposed in 1857, and the Morrill Act only passed after the Confederate states left Congress. However beneficial it was on the surface, the system of LGUs was in some ways a transfer of resources from the practice of agriculture to the science of agriculture, from farmers to professors, and from local ways of learning to institutionalized professional science. The Act refers to benefiting "agriculture" but nowhere mentions farmers, and in retrospect the skeptical farmers seem to have had a prescient understanding that a struggle was starting for control of the country's largest production system.

The scientists' view of their role smacked of self-interest, writes agricultural historian Alan Marcus:

> Only scientific principles could improve farming and only scientists could deduce them. Farmers might utilize these principles, but they could not produce them. Scientists preached, and farmers applied what scientists preached, a situation that demanded that agriculturists know what scientists were preaching. Farmers needed to rely upon scientists for their well-being; rather than an autonomous group, *farmers were a dependent caste.*
>
> *(1986, 28–29, emphasis added)*

Marcus, who has studied the public agricultural institutions in depth, finds that throughout the 1870s and 1880s American farmers "persistently voiced dissatisfaction, even disgust, with the condition of American agricultural colleges" (1986, 22). Farm organizations sent delegations to scrutinize the schools and demanded school officials appear for questioning. "Rarely were college faculties exonerated," and the colleges were generally declared to be farces (Marcus 1986, 23). The farmers couldn't know what the future held for seed breed-ing, but they had no trouble discerning that these institutions and their scientific staffs did not necessarily have their backs. American farmers engaged in a decades-long struggle to push public sector scientists "to test seed, fertilizer, and soil samples and to answer the practical questions they had regarding farming operations" instead of the "abstract and ap-parently impractical pursuits of 'research'" (Kloppenburg 2004, 76) – a struggle they would decisively lose in the 20th century.

Farmer resistance notwithstanding, the LGU system was expanded to the former Confederate states by a second Morrill Act in 1890, and public agricultural science (and especially breeding) was boosted by the establishment of agricultural experiment stations (AESs) in each state. By the late 19th century, the public sector of American crop breeding had taken shape, anchored by the LGUs, AESs, and the USDA.

Farmer skepticism notwithstanding, for a time the interests of the public breeders were not so out of whack with interests of farmers. Until the first decades of the 20th century, public breeders and farmers alike, and often in collaboration, were using mass selection to improve crops in many directions. Their roles were complementary; the farmers could be as competent at selection as the scientists, and since there were far more of them they produced a wealth of varieties (Kloppenburg 2004, 68). They were also the ones who could see how seeds fared under actual growing conditions. They were "the linchpin of corn improvement efforts," their knowledge of the corn plants and of their own fields being powerful tools in shaping their own economic stability (Fitzgerald 1993, 334). Meanwhile the breeders had the resources to experiment more systematically and without fear of crop failure. What they could also do much better than the farmers was the trick of backcrossing, by which specific traits could be moved between varieties by several generations of crosses. By the 1890s public breeders were producing and distributing a stream of new varieties, often working directly with farmers and with cooperatives that helped to multiply seed (Kloppenburg 2004, 80).

Note that these public breeders were not working to develop "appropriationist" tech-nologies that would turn farmers into obligate customers. For instance the USDA's tobacco breeding program of the early 1900s, which it touted as a model of plant "improvement," strove for varieties that would give the farmer a higher yield *without* increased input costs (Varno 2011, 74–75). In this most important sense, they were not promoting agricultural industrialization.

Years later, after the worlds of agricultural discourse had become obsessed with yield increases and blinded to the perennial problems with grain overproduction, breeders would paint the early 20th century as a dark time for American farmers because yields were climb-ing slowly. Breeder David Duvick writes that "[d]isappointingly, the use of 'improved varieties' did not produce substantial increases in yield…[a]verage maize yields in the mid-western Corn Belt state of Iowa, for example, were essentially unchanged during the first three decades of the twentieth century." The problem was that "selection methods were not very powerful, as judged by modern standards" (Duvick 2001, 69). Corn breeding had also taken an early-century turn toward agritainment that militated against yield growth: corn shows were wildly popular events at which growers competed with their own farm-bred ears of corn for substantial prizes. But as the contest criteria emphasized cosmetic qualities like kernel uniformity and ear shape which had nothing to do with yield, corn shows actu-ally depressed corn yields (Stone 2018, 679–680). After 1910 scientists began to recognize the problems caused by the shows, but by then the corn show priorities were "well estab-lished among farmers, extension agents, and even many academics" and difficult to dislodge. Into the teens, American corn breeding had the feeling of being at an impasse (Kloppenburg 2004, 97, Simmonds 1979, 152).

And yet the early decades of the 20th century are known as the "golden age of American agriculture" (Wood 1986, 142)! The number of people profitably employed on farms reached an all-time peak, which many saw as a virtue in this time before government lead-ers would decide there were too many farmers and agricultural engineers would contend that the fewer farmers and the more factory workers, the better (Giesen and Hersey 2010, 288–290). Farm acreage and output were on the rise, but with food demands keeping pace and farmers not yet having the high costs of industrial inputs, they prospered (Lake 1989, 91–93). From 1900 to 1920, the value of American farms (including land, livestock, tools, and machines) jumped from 20 to 75 billion (US Census Bureau 1950); between 1910 and 1920 farm income jumped from $5.8 billion to $12.6 billion. Farmers believed that the years 1910–1914 brought "a natural and just equilibrium" that most subsequent agricultural policies would seek to restore (Lake 1989, 93).[3] But with the seemingly unstoppable growth of agricultural input industries, this was not to be. And crop breeding was about to become one of those input industries.

Taking Over Seeds I: Breeders Get Scientific

The "rediscovery of Mendel," which would eventually lead to profound changes in how and for whom crop breeding was conducted, was an odd chapter in the history of science, but the fact that Mendel even needed to be discovered in the first place is even odder. Gregor Mendel was not the obscure monk puttering around in an abbey garden as he is often depicted; he was a well-trained young scientist who had studied in Vienna under top scientists. His botany professor had been a major proponent of research on variation within species and this gave Mendel his direction. His meticulous pea experiments were carried out between 1856 and 1863 and in 1865 he gave two separate presentations to the Natural History Society of Brunn (as the Czech city of Brno was then known), which generated lively discussion and notices in the local press (Moore 2001). He published his work in 1866 in the *Proceedings of Natural History Society of Brunn*, and while it is true that this was a minor scientific journal, his 48-page article was a masterful piece that was not shy in calling atten-tion to its own importance, noting that it concerned a question "the importance of which cannot be over-estimated in connection with the history of the evolution of organic form" (Mayr 1982, 711). Mendel described the basic principles of heredity using the term "ele-ments," which corresponded fairly well to what we now call genes (Mayr 1982, 616). He did not have a clear understanding of what we would now call alleles, he had a muddled view of the concepts of hybrid and species, and he did not make the crucial conceptual distinc-tion between genotype and phenotype. But he did find that each hereditary character was represented in the plant's fertilized egg by hereditary elements from both male and female parent; that variant genes are dominant or recessive; and that genes are inherited separately. The journal was distributed to over 100 institutions and Mendel sent copies to several top scientists. The article was even cited in following years by other scientists. But those who cited it were treating it as a study in hybridization; remarkably, the fundamental nature of his theory of heredity flashed over the collective head of contemporary science.[4]

Scientific neglect of this corpus of theory − the foundations of the field of genetics − ended abruptly in 1900 when three European botanists all published articles containing rules of heredity they believed they had discovered independently. These rules provided the core to a powerful theory of biological change centered on the concept of segregating characters: each parent contributes one genetic unit (gene) to offspring, the genes segregating independently of each other. The next few years were a time of extraordinary excitement and ferment among those concerned with this aspect of biology. Rather than focusing on whole organisms or composite properties (such as "yield" in crops), Mendelism was essentially the study of − and the *manipulation* of − hereditary units (Mayr 1982, 736). Of course the physical basis for heredity was not yet known and the term *gene* then referred to units of heredity and not physical structures. By the late 1920s it was clear that DNA was the molecule responsible for inheritance, but the molecular structure allowing the magic of self-replication was not deciphered until 1953 (Watson and Crick 1953) and no physical genes within the molecule were identified until 1969. But breeders could clearly see inheritance patterns in genes in their test plots, and the new paradigm of heredity began to transform the world of crop breeding in the early years of the century.

But transformed ***how***? First and foremost Mendelism was expected to raise the status of inheritance research in the world of science. To English biologist William Bateson, who would later provide the name "genetics" for the emerging field, biologists would soon be able to determine the exact constituents of the organisms they studied, much as chemists were learning to analyze materials. Others saw precise prediction replacing "crude empiricism" and "groping around in the dark" (Harwood 2015, 348). The implications for plant breeding were enormous: Mendelism would give the breeder more power to control and understand. In 1902 Bateson wrote that the plant breeder would "be able to do what he wants to do instead of merely what happens to turn up." Previous methods of varietal crossing had produced "a hopeless entanglement of contradictory results"; now the "period of confusion" would end (Bateson 1902) and hybrids could be planned "rationally" and scientifically.

These claims sound quite similar to claims in the next century when plant genetic modification came along and biotechnologists pointed to Mendelian breeding as the haphazard and uncontrolled system that needed to be replaced. But just as Mendelian breeding was much less sloppy than the biotechnologists claimed, 19th century breeding was much less sloppy than Mendelians claimed. Many 19th century breeders in the US and Europe were creating "planned" crosses in the 19th century, "rationally" selecting particular parents whose traits they wished to combine (Harwood 2015, 349). Moreover, while it is true that pre-Mendelian breeders often made unplanned crosses to create diversity and hope for the best, this is not that different than what Mendelian hybrid breeding ended up doing − as we will see.

But despite the excitement that spread rapidly among some breeders, many in the breeding community saw that the Mendelian approach was not true to their mission at all. Selection breeding had been making improvements in corn, and it was improving with the development of better selection techniques and statistical models (Hogg 2000, 153–155). Yields may not have been rising by much, but that is only one goal in breeding and it was not the goal breeders had been prioritizing. The farm sector was doing well, there was plenty of corn around, and it is hard to see how selection breeding was a problem. Mendelian breeding would eventually vanquish selection breeding, but its victory, Deborah

Fitzgerald writes, "had to do less with its intrinsic superiorities than its appeal to the first generation of geneticists – and to seed producers who knew a profitable innovation when they saw one" (Fitzgerald 1990, 23). Mendelian breeding brought with it a breaking apart of the shared interests between breeders and farmers that had prevailed for several decades before the early 1900s.

Types of Science

One key point of divergence between farmers' and Mendelian breeders' interests concerned the rise of research that required trained breeders with bureaucratic infrastructures. This gap appeared at the dawn of Mendelian corn breeding. In a pivotal article in 1906, Edward Murray East laid out a baroque breeding system with painfully detailed rotation charts that "only the most compulsively progressive farmers" would have a chance of following (Fitzgerald 1990, 33). Just as chemists a few decades before had bent agriculture into something requiring chemists, Mendelian breeders were busily bending agriculture into something requiring Mendelian breeders.

Mendelism swept through the public breeding establishment in part because of the way it affected scientists' careers. The change had to do with how public breeders prioritized applied science versus basic science. Some leaders of the public agricultural science establishment, such as A.C. True of the Office of Experiment Stations in Washington, advocated for what was then termed "original" (basic) research. But station directors had good reasons for promoting "teleological" (applied) research: their jobs depended on showing politically appointed state boards results of economic value to the state (Porter 1979, 86). Station scientists, writes historian Jane Porter, were caught in the middle:

> On the one hand, they had been taught that career advancement – their hopes of one day being on the faculty of a prestigious university – lay in publishing papers based on pure research. On the other hand, the annual renewal of their appointments to the experiment station staff, their bread and butter, lay in producing solutions to the problems of farmers. The second objective usually took precedence.
>
> *(Porter 1979, 86)*

The selectionist breeder's activities as applied scientist, such as backcrossing useful traits into farmer varieties and testing varietal crosses, surely benefited farmers. It is unknown how many breeder varieties were adopted during the pre-Mendelian era, but it is clear from the institutions' publications that scientists were tackling many issues of clear relevance to their constituent farmers. Most reports concerned experimental results on such topics as plant spacing, fertilizing, chemical and nutritional properties of grains, and optimal planting times. They also reported on the properties and performance of lines they had bred, some of which were released to farmers. They were much less focused on basic science, and anyway theoretical insights are rare when comparing grain outputs of local varieties of corn. Public breeders also had "consular" duties including classes for farmers and lectures at farmer meetings, which helped fund the stations.[5] These activities could benefit local farmers but the staff were often seen as second-class citizens in the world of science, and experiment stations – especially in the South – struggled to attract top scientists (Porter 1979, 87).

Mendelian breeding, however, was conducive to scientific advancement, including empirical findings (e.g., which specific traits were dominant and which recessive) and general theoretical advances (such as findings on basic principles of heredity) (Kimmelman 1983, 167). Mendelian breeders could claim that their findings on evolutionary processes would rebound to the farmers' benefit, but the goal clearly was scientific publication, and it was scientific publication that boomed rather than the flow of improved cultivars for farmers. In 1913 the American Breeders Association refashioned itself as the American Genetic Association and replaced its American Breeder's Magazine with the more scientific *Journal of Heredity* as its official publication (Varno 2011, 113); its other publication, the *Proceedings*, doubled the amount published during the teens (Kimmelman 1983, 166). As publication-oriented Mendelians moved into positions of authority, professional yardsticks such as criteria for hiring and promotion adjusted to value scientific publication over the practical accomplishments of population improvement.

Not only did Mendelism's experimental nature generate copious material for scientific publication, but Mendelian concepts gave breeders valuable assets in the jostle among scientific disciplines for status and authority. Biology, points out biology historian Garland Allen, had long been dominated by concerns of descriptive natural history and taxonomy. Even after being revolutionized in the mid-late 19th century by Darwin's theory of evolution by natural selection, it still remained a poor cousin among scientific disciplines because Darwin's theory was seen as "non-experimental, nontestable, and ultimately, speculative" (Allen 2000, 1082). However Mendelian experiments generated quantitative results, and findings could be expressed in rigorous concepts: "factors" or "genes" were to geneticists what atoms were to chemists and physicists – fundamental, basically unchangeable, non-historical units (Allen 2000, 1083). Much as Liebig had championed a scientific paradigm to benefit his intellectual tribe, breeders turned to Mendelism to climb the ladder of scientific status.

Competition for intellectual status is the reality of the world of professional knowledge production; it is self-serving but hardly sinister. But the rise of Mendelian crop breeding was responsible for developments in agricultural science that were chilling indeed. We have seen that Mendelian breeding moved quickly to shrink the farmers' role and expand the breeder's role in crop improvement. At stake was the basic definition of "improvement" and the control over reproduction of seeds. For the breeders the organisms in question were plants (and livestock), but these shifts in control by external "science" had a direct parallel in the control of humans. Edward Murray East, arguably the most important and influential of the breeders promoting Mendelism, and Charles B. Davenport, a leading writer on Mendelian principles in poultry breeding, quickly emerged as leaders of the American eugenics movement. In 1906, the same year that East published "The improvement of corn in Connecticut," Davenport published the book *Inheritance in Poultry* and both men were obsessed with the application of breeding principles to the "improvement" of humans (Davenport 1911). In 1910 Davenport founded the Eugenics Record Office, which quickly emerged as the world's leading eugenics research institution. East would go on to write numerous eugenics tracts, including the notorious *Mankind at the Crossroads* which announced that since the facts of population growth and agriculture showed that "the Malthusian prediction" had arrived, the Mendelian genetics that ruled "the inheritance of the denizens of the garden and the inmates of the stable" should be applied to people (1923, vi–viii). But there was a crucial difference: a corn plant's genes could be kept out of the next generation simply by not planting its seeds, whereas humans had to be sterilized (or institutionalized). At the core of American eugenics was the audacious conceit that not only did society (and the "race") benefit from sterilizing certain categories of people, but so did the sterilized (who were "freed" from the danger of producing more people like themselves).[6]

Mendelism as a Power Grab

We cannot say with certainty how much Mendelian breeding revolutionized agricultural growth (more on this below), but it certainly was revolutionary in how it separated the interests of the breeders from farmers and consumers. When breeders were using the tried and true methods of mass selection, varietal crosses and backcrossing, it made perfect sense to talk about an "improved seed"; improvement was defined as development of varieties adapted to farmers' localities and growing conditions situations. But Mendelism brought a rethinking of the role and goals of public breeders, and the breeding community quickly found itself in a major philosophical and practical struggle over what "improvement" meant. The struggle would last throughout the 19-teens. Bateson and others could paint Mendelian breeding as a straightforward case of progress, with certainty replacing confusion, but there was much more at stake. Mendelism took hold of the public breeding establishment because it furthered "the economic, social, and professional interests" of the breeders (Fitzgerald 1990, 28), concentrating expertise "in the hands of researchers as opposed to farmers" (Hogg 2000, 153–154).

The farmers who were suspicious of the expanding public breeding institutions in the 19th century felt that the institutions, while proclaiming to serve agriculture, actually represented a power grab. The extent to which that is true in the 19th century is open to debate, but as Mendelism allowed public breeders to claim resources and authority in agriculture in the early 20th century, the farmers would seem to have been proven right. Then within a few years of the arrival of Mendelism in the world of breeding, the new approach would spawn one of the most important technologies in the history of agriculture. This would raise external control of crops to a new level. It is also the case *par excellence* of the march of industrial agriculture: a new technology proclaimed a boon to farmers' harvests actually turns out to be a new way for agricultural capital to harvest government subsidy for inputs that farmers are obliged to buy. The technology is hybrid corn.

Hybrid Corn

Corn led the march to agricultural industrialization in part because of the plant's unusual set of features. First, *Zea mays* has the potential to be unusually productive because it is a "C4 plant," meaning that it is one of the rare plant species that use a more efficient biochemical mechanism to process sunlight than the rest of the plant kingdom.[7] Corn also lends itself well to professional breeding efforts; unlike wheat, for instance, it is a large plant with prominent features, easy to handle and analyze; and its genetic traits segregate. As a bonus, each plant produces large numbers of seeds.

Even more important was corn's method of reproduction. Like most crops and all grains, the corn plant is monoecious, meaning that it has both male and female flowers on each plant.[8] But it is unique among cereal crops in having its male and female flowers on separate organs – the male tassel and the female ear. This gives the breeder an unusual level of control over fertilization. So does corn's reproductive strategy of outcrossing, meaning that each plant's male tassels pollinate the female silks on different corn plants. Most major crops, including wheat, rice, soybean, potato, and cotton, are "selfers" that normally self-pollinate; there are only a few other outcrossing crops including sugarcane, sunflower, and sweet potato. No other crop is so naturally well suited to the hybridization trick we examine in this section.

To facilitate outcrossing, corn pollen is very light to allow it to float on the wind, and it can travel over a mile. Varieties developed and propagated by wind pollination are called open-pollinated varieties or OPVs. Corn plants rarely self-pollinate or inbreed on their own, but breeders have experimented with forced inbreeding of corn for a long time. (Pollen is taken from a tassel and put on the silks emanating from the ear, then the tassels are covered up so they cannot pollinate any other plants.) Breeders generally found that the offspring of inbred corn tended to be unhealthy and stunted. Writing in 1898 – on the eve of the arrival of Mendelian breeding – an Illinois corn breeder wrote that "The effects of inbreeding appear both pronounced and disastrous, the second generation from inbred seed being less than two-thirds normal size and nearly barren" (quoted in Fitzgerald 1990, 18). This phenomenon was known as inbreeding depression.[9]

Inbreeding depression made corn inbreds mostly useless to 19th century breeders but not to Mendelians, with their focus on isolating and manipulating units of heredity. Edward Murray East was an early leader in corn inbred experiments; another of the new Mendelians to experiment with corn inbreds was George Shull, a plant physiologist working under Charles Davenport (the eugenicist we met before).[10] Based on a multi-year study of corn inbreeding, Shull published a 1908 paper that was crucial to the future of breeding. In "The Composition of a Field of Maize" Shull wrote that the corn field should be thought of as a set of "elementary species" or "biotypes" that could be revealed by creating inbred lines by repeated self-pollination (1908, 299). The inbred biotypes themselves were not very productive, but they could be productively crossed.

That the progeny of diverse parents could sometimes outperform either parent was already known; Charles Darwin himself had written about this possibility (1876). The phenomenon was called hybrid vigor, although Shull would coin the more obscure term *heterosis* for it. What was path breaking was Shull's announcement that corn breeders had been going at it all wrong in evaluating lines on their productivity in the field; they should be isolating and evaluating inbred lines on the quality of their offspring when crossed with other inbred lines (Shull 1908, 299). Since Shull did not actually understand the underlying genetic mechanisms – he admitted that he could not explain inbreeding depression or the vigor of hybrids – he said there was no way to predict which crosses of inbred lines would be fruitful. So, he suggested, the way forward was to seek out the crosses that are "only at the highest quality in the first generation, thus making it necessary to go back each year to the original combination, instead of selecting from among the hybrid offspring the stock for continued breeding" (Shull 1908, 300). Shull had not made his own inbred crosses yet, but this paper established the theoretical basis for hybrid corn. It also pointed to two key aspects of the future of hybrid crop breeding: a *lot* of experimental seeking would be needed, and the winners would only be good for *one season* (Figure 5.1).

The next year Shull reported his own initial attempt at hybridizing inbreds (1909). He had taken the first two inbred lines that had reached a stable homozygous state and crossed them, producing what modern breeders would call the F1 (or first hybrid) generation of seeds.

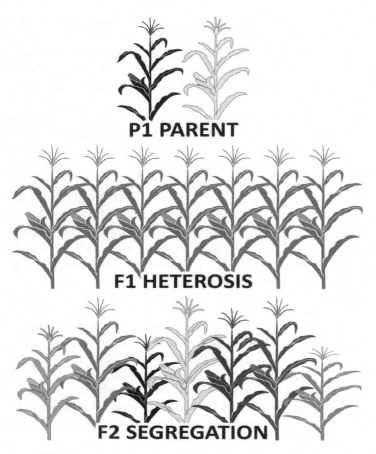

FIGURE 5.1 Two inbred parent lines produce a genetically uniform F1 hybrid generation that could be sold commercially if it exhibits heterosis (although most F1 crosses do not). However if the farmer replants F1 seeds the next year, the traits will segregate and the field will contain diverse plants, most of which are less productive than the F1 parents. (This schematic simplifies the breeding process by leaving out the production step in the "double-cross" method.)

The next season he had grown out the F1 seeds and found them to be more productive than the parent seeds – not surprising since the parents had not been bred to be productive but simply to have a pure set of traits. But the F1 seeds also "yielded a little more grain" than the OPVs from which the inbreds had been made. "To be sure," Shull admitted, "the difference is not great enough to seem of any particular significance in itself," but there were a lot of inbred biotypes to try and some would surely produce higher-yielding offspring. Corn breeding should be creating pure lines and looking for productive offspring (Shull 1909, 55–56).

Because of the 1908–1909 articles Shull is often called the inventor of hybrid corn. But his sometime-collaborator and sometime-rival Edward Murray East probably deserves just as much credit for the invention, and also for recognizing the implications for how it would change the economics of breeding. Since the wonders of heterosis were only good for one planting – because of the convenient segregation of traits in F2 generations (Figure 5.1) – farmers would have to buy new seeds every year instead of producing their own as before. With this Mendelian trick, breeders had managed to "pull away the natural grounds from the foundation" of farming, just as Marx had predicted. Since the breeder could keep the parental lines and give out only the non-replantable hybrid crosses, this was the appropriationist technology par excellence. East wrote with delight that "for the first time in agricultural history, a seedsman is enabled to gain the full benefit from a desirable origination of his own" (1919, 224). Note that the point of crop breeding had shifted to **breeders finally gaining the full profit from their handiwork**. And who had been keeping breeders from getting full profit up till then? The farmers with their unfortunate habit of replanting their own seeds. And the breeders were mainly public scientists, paid by public funds to work in institutions created to benefit farmers![11]

This new economic logic would eventually bring dramatic change to the world of breeding, but little happened after Shull's 1909 article. Leaders of the seed corn industry, which was tiny (since most farmers saved seed), were unimpressed with Shull's method (Crabb 1947, 108). Hybrids could outperform their sickly inbred parents, but they would have to be significantly better than OPVs for farmers to buy them, and the search for such hybrids would take a lot of time and resources. And even if such super-seeds were found, there was a fatal flaw in Shull's method: the production of marketable quantities of hybrid seeds was limited by the supply of those inbred parent seeds that were notoriously unproductive. Eugene Funk, whose Funk Farms was the nation's largest seed-corn producer, decided that the method had no commercial potential (Crabb 1947, 108); others who experimented with the method gave it up. Well into the 19-teens, there was no consensus on the direction corn breeding should take.

Donald F. Jones was a young breeder working at the Connecticut AES under Edward Murray East. His experiments there led to a 1918 article describing a "double-cross" method by which inbreds were crossed and their offspring crossed again. This meant that hybrid seeds could serve as the parents of the marketable hybrids, which solved Shull's production problem. But the double-cross had another important economic implications, which East and Jones recognized immediately: the technique was far too sophisticated and capital-intensive for any but the largest agricultural interests to pursue (Varno 2011, 114).

But finding those productive offspring would be a huge undertaking. Although heterosis is often said to produce inherently more productive offspring, this is misleading; the crosses are just more variable, exhibiting new combinations of traits. Crosses could be *less* vigorous even than the sickly parents (called "negative heterosis") and there was no way to predict whether two inbreds would produce a winner.[12] Early Mendelians' boast that they could replace the throw-it-at-the-wall-and-see-what-sticks approach to crossing varieties with scientifically "planned" crosses was false; "the only way breeders could find hybrids which were high yielding was simply to examine all of the possible combinations which could be constructed from the available inbred lines…[which] was, of course, nothing less than trial and error of a very laborious kind" (Harwood 2015, 358). "Given only 100 inbred lines," asks Kloppenburg, "there are 11,765,675 possible double-cross combinations…[h]ow could all those crosses be made?" (2004, 103). Superior combinations were rare, and to be of economic value, the offspring had to not only outperform farmers' corn, but beat it enough to warrant the expense of buying seeds. Even writers in full-throated praise of hybrid seed admitted that "hybrid vigor" was vanishingly rare. "One major seed company annually tests approximately fifteen hundred different combinations of inbred lines," notes a classic 1958 article on the economics of hybrids; "[o]f these, at most three or four prove to be successful" (Griliches 1958, 426). It was like searching for needles in haystacks (Figure 5.2).

Finding needles in the haystack required time, expertise, and a lot of land. Even double-cross inventor Donald Jones stressed that inbreeding and crossing were of little use unless practiced on a large scale. Funk Brothers was the first private seed company to take up hybrid breeding with the double-cross method. In 1921, breeders flocked to the Funks' research fields in Illinois to see the new hybrid breeding in operation. They were struck by the scale of operation: Funk Brothers owned 22,000 acres of prime farmland. But that was the sort of scale needed to let breeders wade through the unpredictable results of inbred crosses (Crabb 1947).

But a lineup of state and federal agencies was about to offer up the time, expertise, and land without which hybrids had little to offer, allowing a private hybrid seed industry to be launched on a sea of public funding. This would happen at the same time that public funding was laying the foundation for the synthetic fertilizer industry, and its effects on farm-generated seed would be as profound as those efforts were on farm-generated fertilizer.

The Manhattan Project for Corn

In *First the Seed*, Jack Kloppenburg writes that the "miracle" of hybrid corn

> was the product of political machination, a solid decade of intensive research effort, and the application of human and financial resources that, as breeder Norman Simmonds

FIGURE 5.2 Mid-century advertisement by Henry A. Wallace's seed company, Pioneer Hybrid, stressing the experimental research needed to produce a marketable hybrid seed. But Pioneer was launched with plants from public breeding and in reality the man in the white shirt usually would have been a publicly funded breeder, essentially working for seed companies because of Wallace's influence.

(1979, 153) writes, "must have been enormous by any ordinary plant breeding standards." It also entailed the abandonment of the potentially productive well of population improvement. Two decades before the Manhattan Project, the agricultural sector had already witnessed the birth of "big science." Indeed, the development of hybrid corn can usefully be understood as agriculture's Manhattan Project.

(2004, 104)

Like the wartime Manhattan project, this would be funded by public money; however the beneficiary would not be the public, but rather private seed corporations. The story of how this happened revolves around Henry A. Wallace, the farmer/intellectual who edited the influential magazine *Wallace's Farmer*. Wallace had experimented with Shull's single-cross method with an eye toward going into the seed business, but he found (as others had) that it was uneconomical for large-scale production. But when the double-cross method arrived in 1918, Wallace reconsidered. He began a new round of experiments, now using inbred parent lines from USDA breeder Frank Richey who was working intensively with hybrids. Wallace concluded that the double-cross method could be the basis of a lucrative commercial enterprise if some way could be found to bring research costs down. The USDA seemed unlikely invest heavily in this line of research: the Cereal Investigations department was headed by C.P. Hartley, a devoted selectionist breeder who was hostile to hybrid corn research. But conveniently, in 1920 Wallace's father, Henry C. Wallace, was appointed Secretary of Agriculture. Seizing the chance to maneuver government breeders into hybrids, son urged father to put Richey in charge of cereal investigations in 1922 (Hogg 2000, 158).

Actually Richey's experiments had left him with reservations about the economics of hybrid breeding; that year he wrote that he was unsure of the "practical possibilities of this method as a means of obtaining larger yields of corn" (Hogg 2000, 160, Richey 1922, 13). But he was well aware of why he had been promoted, and kept his reservations to himself and threw the weight of the agriculture department behind corn improvement "only through investigations based on inbreds." In 1925 the Purnell Act provided funding to launch "an unprecedented venture in directed scientific investigation," with allotments rising to $60,000/year for each state agricultural experiment station (Kunze 1988, 139). As most of these funds went to inbred hybrid breeding, Richey began to isolate and bypass departments that maintained selectionist experiments. Still, by 1935, public agencies had only developed hybrids that yielded 10–15% more than open-pollinated counterparts at best (Hogg 2000, 158) – decidedly underwhelming considering the Herculean effort involved and also that selectionist breeding would have also raised yields at a lower cost.

Central to the "Manhattan Project" for corn was the routine and free transfer of germplasm and breeding lines from the public sector to private companies. The leading beneficiary of this policy was Henry A. Wallace himself. In 1920, he had produced a hybrid called Copper Cross from inbred parents supplied by the Connecticut AES and the USDA. Copper Cross first appeared at the 1921 Iowa Corn Yield Test – an annual event started the year before at Wallace's urging as an alternative to the popular Corn Shows that stressed cosmetic attributes. Wallace's hybrid was outyielded by local OPVs that year and again in 1922 and 1923, but triumphed in 1924 – or so Wallace said, although the records show it actually came in second to a USDA hybrid (Iowa Corn and Small Grain Growers' Association 1924). The seed was sold that year by the Iowa Seed Company, described in the catalog (in text supplied by Wallace himself) as "An Astonishing Product [that] Produces Astonishing Results." In 1926 Wallace co-founded the Pioneer Hi-Bred Corn Company.[13]

The services of expert personnel from the public breeding sector were another important form of subsidy, even before Richey took the helm. It is true that the Funk Brothers were running their own hybrid breeding program, but the USDA had established a field research station right on Eugene Funk's farm in 1918. To run it they hired the Funks' top breeder, J.R. Holbert, making him a federal employee and covering his salary – although his relationship with the company was essentially unchanged and "it was nearly impossible to distinguish between Holbert's company research and his federal research" (Fitzgerald 1990, 151). This arrangement and the fiction that Holbert was simply looking after public sector tests was a workaround necessitated by the official USDA policy of not collaborating with any corporations. It lasted for 20 years, during which time Funks was one of the country's top purveyors of hybrid corn, after which Holbert officially returned to Funks as vice president for research.[14]

The New Division of Labor

In the world of industrial agriculture, hybrid corn companies are saluted for their service to farmers since the 1930s. Some even see these companies as having performed a great service to the public breeding establishment. Shull himself cited Wallace's company as "absolutely essential to the success which has come to hybrid corn" (Shull 1946, 548) and in his history of hybrid corn, Richard Crabb writes that the brilliant work of the early hybrid breeders would have come to naught had not private enterprise stepped in by "raising up a new industry to convert the fruits of their research into something farmers could use" (Crabb 1947, 265). But actually the modern hybrid seed industry emerged from intense struggles against farmers and public breeders, struggles it won by carving out an impenetrable niche for itself between the farmer and the public breeder.

Recall that before the advent of Mendelian breeding, public breeders worked with farmers directly or ran experiments aimed at directly informing farmer practices. Their results were provided free of charge; after all, public breeding had been launched to benefit agriculture, which at the time meant farmers rather than input industries. The ethos of contributing directly to farmers suffered during the struggles over the direction of breeding in the teens and 20s, but it maintained a toehold even as hybrid seeds came to prominence. Administrators at many AESs and LGUs assumed that farmers would produce their own hybrid seed and that the role of public breeding institutions was to support them (Kloppenburg 2004, 106). By the mid-1920s, experiment stations were offering courses in hybrid production to farmers and providing inbred parent lines and instructions for making their own double crosses (Ziegenhorn 2000, 139). Many farmers were producing hybrid seed for themselves and for their neighbors in the 1930s; in 1939, Wisconsin alone had 436 farmers engaged in the new enterprise (Kloppenburg 2004, 106, Steele 1978). Public breeding institutions also released finished hybrids to farmers, along with information on each hybrid's pedigree.

But this would not last: corporations generally loathe competition, and in the 1930s seed companies loathed competing with farmer breeders as well as public breeders. The seed industry went into overdrive after the mid-1930s in their efforts to marginalize farmer breeders. The major seed companies leveraged their privileged access to public germplasm to outcompete farmer breeders. They also campaigned against breeding by farmers, who they claimed lacked the "natural ability and intuition to make good plant breeders" and who consequently risked discrediting hybrid breeding (Fitzgerald 1990, 203).

But seed corporations' real coup was to shut off the flow of breeding lines and hybrids from the public breeding establishment to farmers. This began in the 1930s, as the hybrid seed industry was growing rapidly, with dozens of companies appearing on the scene and big three of Pioneer, Funk, and DeKalb pressuring the government to stop competing with private enterprise. The states that were home to those companies ended hybrid releases first, and by 1970 the shutdown of public hybrids was virtually complete. This accomplished much more for the seed corporations than simply eliminating competition; it was an ingenious way to put those former competitors in the public breeding world to work for the seed industry. This was because public breeders are mandated to prioritize practical application, and with seed companies alone producing the marketable hybrids, public breeders had to fit their research activities to the goals of those companies. To control commoditized seed, writes Kloppenburg, is "thus to control upstream state-subsidized research" (2004, 128). By relegating public breeders to "basic" science which had to further the "applied" commercial uses of seed companies, the industry ensured that the value of the public breeding establishment could be captured then and in the future. Henceforth, new knowledge produced by agricultural science would increasingly reach the farmer not as a public good but as commodities developed by public breeders and then sold by private enterprises.

But this new division of labor was not the only way that the seed industry diverted the mission of public science to capture wealth from it. It also managed to turn the system of agricultural knowledge production into a system for knowledge suppression.

Science and Secrets

Ask a dozen scientists what science is and you may get a dozen different definitions, but all would at least agree that science is a system for producing knowledge. Public breeders being cornered into producing knowledge primarily for seed company profits may have been contrary to the spirit of the public institutions' mandate, but at least they were producing scientific knowledge of a sort. However from the perspective of the growing seed industry, public breeders were only causing problems by disclosing information on the seeds to farmers. Crucial to the success of hybrid corn was a monopoly on information that hid the underlying identities of seeds from farmers; profits from hybrid corn essentially depended on a system of trade secrecy that limited competition. Secrecy not only prevented farmers and other companies from making the same crosses, it allowed a company to sell the same cross under different names (Ziegenhorn 2000, 136–137). This was a lucrative practice but it also eroded farmers' environmental learning and was even illegal, banned by the 1940 Federal Seed Act. However, in a glaring example of regulatory capture (Chapter 3), the law was largely ignored (Kloppenburg 2004, 107).

One industry trick for obscuring the identity of a hybrid seed was to simply take a public line and slap a proprietary designation on it, thereby obscuring its parentage. Companies would also hide a hybrid's pedigree by treating it as a trade secret. Public breeders complained bitterly about both practices but could do little. USDA breeder Merle Jenkins wrote in the 1936 *Yearbook of Agriculture*:

> Among the private corn breeders and producers of hybrid corn, a tendency seems to be developing to regard the information they have on their lines and the pedigrees of

their hybrids as trade secrets which they are reluctant to divulge... It would seem to be an extremely shortsighted policy, and one that probably will have to be modified in the future when the purchaser of hybrid seed corn demands full information on the nature of the seed he is buying.

(Jenkins 1936, 107)

But Jenkins' boss was Henry A. Wallace, who had led the charge for hybrid corn and who also led the charge for secrecy in breeding. Wallace's Pioneer hybrids were being sold without pedigree information as early as 1931[15]. Most seed companies even kept pedigree information secret from their agents. The sole exception was the legendary breeder Lester Pfister, whose Pfister Seeds listed full pedigree information on all its seeds. Pfister insisted that

if we have the right by law to know what goes into a 35-cent can of fly spray, we also have the right to know what inbreds and inbred crosses have gone into the production of the hybrid seed corn...on which we stake the greater part of our farm income.

(Fitzgerald 1990, 199–200)

Pfister's company prospered but no other companies followed his lead, and he was widely known as "Crazy Lester."

What Was the Point of Hybrid Corn?

Just what was the point of a state-supported "Manhattan Project" to develop hybrid corn and undermine farmer breeding so that private companies could sell seeds of secret parentage to farmers? It is an uncomfortable question in agricultural history. Unsurprisingly, seed companies push the neo-Malthusian answer; Wallace's Pioneer company still insists that "Few other scientific developments have had greater impact on increasing food supplies available to the world's population than the development of hybrid corn" (Pioneer 2019). But let us consider the food supply situation in the US at the time hybrid corn was rolled out.

We know that the government subsidy for the fertilizer industry in the 1920s coincided with a growing predicament of agricultural overproduction. With fields bursting with grain, traction animals being supplanted by tractors, and exports dropping, farmers were struggling to sell their crops at a profit and many were going broke. Throughout the late 1920s the federal government floundered in its attempts to prop up farm prices. Farmers' continuing productivity only worsened the problem, but they were in effect trapped. Historian David Danbom points out that

despite the overproduction of major farm products and the rural realization that overproduction was the principal cause of the agricultural depression, production remained high in the twenties. The farmer recognized that his own productivity was his worst enemy, but since there was no way to limit the output of the agricultural sector as a whole he was reluctant to gamble on limiting his own output.

(1979, 132)

By the early 1930s, with farm production unabated and the Depression in full swing, overproduction had become a crisis, and farmer frustration boiled over on many fronts. The national farmer strikes demanded by the militant National Farmers Holiday Association did not materialize, but local strikes did. In the Milk Strikes of 1933, thousands of gallons of milk were dumped and creameries were dynamited. (The neo-Malthusian Green Revolution hero Norman Borlaug recounts having witnessed a violent strike in Minnesota. The lesson he claims to have learned was the "hunger affects the mind" (20th Century Time Machine 2016). We explore Borlaug's impact on agricultural economies in Chapter 6, but suffice it to say that he might have learned that mindless pursuit of production can do as much harm as good.) Many farmers lost their farms but some held on due to civil disobedience by other farmers. One innovative tactic was for neighbors to descend on a farm foreclosure auction and turn it into a "penny auctions," in which farmers bid pennies on house, land, and equipment and intimidated legitimate bidders into silence. The new "owners" would then lease the farm back to the original owner for pennies.

Franklin Roosevelt became president in January of 1933 and the Secretary of Agriculture who inherited this mess was none other than Henry A. Wallace. Stressing that "the agricultural emergency calls for prompt and drastic action" (Culver and Hyde 2000, 115–126), Wallace promptly pushed through the Agricultural Adjustment Act (AAA). The act pulled the two big levers governments had to balance production and consumption. The first of these levers was to buy up the surplus, and price support programs quickly became an important part of Roosevelt's New Deal. The second lever was to pay farmers not to farm. Such programs are technically called acreage reduction programs, although US farmers usually call them "setasides" (and sometimes refer to taking acreage reduction payments as "raising setasides" in a bit of wry humor). "Farming the government" may be a core part of modern industrial agriculture (Manning 2004, 95), but few policies are so fundamentally perverse as the government paying farmers not to farm. Yet the AAA put the government in the business of paying to keep food cheap and protect farmers from being run over by the runaway train of industrial agriculture. The program was explicitly intended to be temporary, yet it has been followed by a procession of other programs that either directly or indirectly paid farmers to reduce production. The original program and its successors have failed in most of their objectives and liberals and conservatives alike oppose them in principle. Yet the payments remain.

Even more perverse yet is paying farmers to plow under crops already growing in their fields, which was also a significant part of the Wallace's program to cut oversupply. Setasides did bring production down a bit in the 1930s, and fortunately – at least from the perspective of supply – a drought struck wheat country. The drought saved the government from paying farmers to plow under their growing wheat, but cotton country had no such "luck" and the government paid out over $100 million in precious Depression-era dollars for farmers to plow under 10 million acres of cotton. But the most intractable surpluses were in corn and pork. To tackle the pork problem the government paid farmers to slaughter 6 million young pigs to keep them from reaching full size (Culver and Hyde 2000, 123–124). But by 1933, in some places a corn crop had negative value: in South Dakota, for instance, grain elevators were *charging* farmers three cents per bushel to take corn off their hands. Setasides helped to bring corn production down from its Depression-era peak of 2.6 mb (million bushels) in 1932 to 1.1 mb in 1934, but it soon began to climb again, topping 2.8 mb in 1942 (NASS 2016, 29).

This was therefore a watershed in the history of agricultural industrialization in which the US government was paying to mitigate the effects of overproduction at the same time it was paying public breeders to develop seeds for private companies to sell with claims of increased yields. The neo-Malthusian claim that breeders were trying to meet the challenge of growing populations is exactly backward. Deborah Fitzgerald asks why breeders even thought it was necessary to boost yields:

> It is true that disease, especially in the midwestern states, affected yield somewhat adversely, but this problem was being attacked by the traditional method of educating farmers in selection techniques...with considerable success. In any case, despite losses from disease, there was no chronic shortage of seed corn during this period...It did not require a Ph.D. in economics to realize that higher yields were likely to lower prices, but breeders, for the most part, were silent on this issue.
>
> *(Fitzgerald 1990, 70–71)*

But not everyone was as silent as the breeders. Congressman Miles Allgood said that the overproduction problem was bad enough that research was needed to propagate crop diseases. The proposal was not entirely tongue-in-cheek; as the former Alabama Commissioner of Agriculture, he had seen suppression of the boll weevil cause overproduction to the point of disastrous oversupply and realized that the boll weevil had been the "best friend the cotton farmer ever had" (Kloppenburg 2004, 296). Many farmers were overtly hostile to what government-supported science was bringing to their door. Wallace was well aware of the problem and in 1934 he wrote:

> it may seem that the farmer has a quarrel with science; for science increases his productivity, and this tends to increase the burden of the surplus... They ask why the Government agencies help farmers to grow two blades of grass where one grew before, and simultaneously urge them to cut down their production. They declare it is almost criminally negligent for a Government to promote an increase of production, without facing the results of that increase. These ideas lead to something of a revolt against science, and to demands for a halt in technical progress until consumption catches up with production.
>
> *(1934, 25)*

But the man who had done more than any other individual to build the hybrid corn breeding industry was not about to second-guess that technology. "It is undeniable that science creates problems," he wrote, what we need "is not less science in production, but more science in distribution" (Wallace 1934, 25). Wallace sold his holdings in Pioneer when he joined Roosevelt's cabinet (Weber 2018, 384) but was still active in the running of the seed company and even had the company build an experiment station outside of Washington DC that he could visit on weekends (Culver and Hyde 2000, 148). And from the time he accepted the appointment as Secretary of Agriculture he put the full weight of the Federal government behind an advocacy of hybrid corn (Sutch 2008). The most charitable explanation for Wallace's continued boosterism for hybrid corn at the same time he was overseeing a lavish program to lower production is that he imagined a future time when yield boosts from hybrid corn would benefit the nation. But as economist Richard Sutch points out, "the glaring conflict of interest between Wallace's financial interest in the Pioneer Hi-Bred Company and the use of the government agency he controlled to advertise and advocate his product" was outrageous (Sutch 2008).

The hybrid revolution was the greatest paradox of Henry Wallace's life. As his biographers write,

> Even as he was teaching Iowa farmers how to produce more corn, Wallace was in Washington wrestling with the problem of overproduction. And as he was bringing scientific advancement to the farm, he was setting in motion forces that would drive ever more farmers off the land. He recognized the paradox. But he could never resolve it.
>
> *(Culver and Hyde 2000, 149–150)*

But while Wallace may have never resolved the paradox of overproduction and farm technology, he never hesitated in choosing a side. And of course, American farmers did choose to buy hybrid seed, a fact that industrial agriculture enthusiasts cite as obvious confirmation of the benefits to those farmers. But was it?

Adopting Hybrid Corn?

The 1930s brought American farmers the miracle of hybrid corn, billed as boosting their production if they would buy seeds instead of making their own. But the country was already mired in grain surpluses, farmers were short on cash and going bankrupt, and it turns out that the hybrids did not actually boost production very much. And yet hybrid adoption climbed from 0.4% of US corn acreage in 1933 to 90% in 1945 to over 96% in 1960. For a book analyzing the interests driving agriculture, the question of why they adopted hybrids is crucial.

We explored the theories of technology adoption in Chapter 3, starting with Ryan and Gross's seminal 1943 finding that hybrid corn did not spread until a "social snowball" developed. Ryan and Gross were oddly uninterested in the actual agronomic and economic advantage of hybrids, simply accepting the breeders' insistence that the seeds were "sturdier" and that adoption was a "good (economic) farm practice" (1943, 15–16). But in the 1950s innovation adoption research was being taken over largely by economists (Ruttan 1996) who replaced the social questions with a fixation on economic advantages. Again hybrid corn was the leading case: in an influential 1957 study that is still taught in graduate programs (Sutch 2008), Zvi Griliches attributed hybrid corn adoption to a 15–20% yield boost (1957, 1960). He showed that state-specific adoption curves differed because seed companies had rolled out seeds adapted to the most profitable areas first (Griliches 1960, 275). He saw the speed of adoption as a function of the size of the yield advantage, slowed only by farmers' "imperfect knowledge" and the time it took them to realize what was in their best interests. So adoption was earliest and fastest in Wallace's home state of Iowa, where hybrids were sold first, and later and slower in the southern states (Figure 5.3). Later agricultural statistics seemed to confirm the hybrids' superiority: US corn yields, which had been generally flat until the mid-1930s, began their long climb (Figure 4.3) after hybrids spread, topping 175 bu/acre today.

But those agronomic benefits that the sociologists took for granted and the economists thought were a near-perfect explanation for adoption were greatly exaggerated. Economist Richard Sutch shows that in the early years of adoption, hybrids offered little or no economic advantage – even in Iowa. Griliches' claimed 15–20% yield advantage was based on unpublished marketing data and actually pertained to seeds developed later (Sutch 2011, 204);

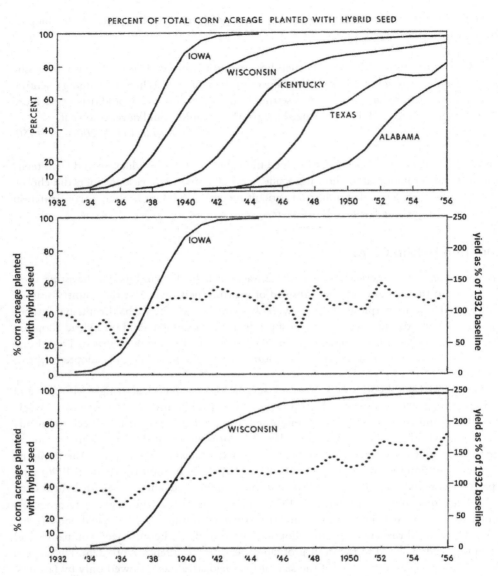

PERCENT OF TOTAL CORN ACREAGE PLANTED WITH HYBRID SEED

FIGURE 5.3 Top: adoption of hybrid corn in five states from Griliches (1957). In the two lower graphs, adoption rates for the early-adopting states are compared to corn yield trends for those states (expressed as percentage of the state yield in the baseline year of 1932). Yield data are from the USDA.

records of the Iowa Corn Yield Tests show that hybrids' yield advantage was not enough to cover the cost of buying seed instead of producing it on farm.[16] Wallace's Copper Cross cost a whopping $52 per bushel when first marketed in 1924; it was aimed at wealthy early adopters and the price was intentionally inflated "to convince farmers they were buying something special" (Sutch 2011, 212). That price became nonsensical when the Great Depression hit and the market price of a bushel of corn plummeted from as much as $.85 in the 1920s to $.31 in 1932 (Griliches 1957) to below zero by 1933. The price of a bushel of hybrid seed dropped to $6, but the yield advantage was not even close to being big enough to cover the cost of seed.

The hybrid superiority narrative completely falls apart when we consider that while corn yields were trending upward during the years of hybrid adoption, yields of *non-hybrid* crops were rising even faster. Major changes were taking place throughout agriculture, including a doubling of the use of commercial fertilizer; a fourfold increase in mechanical harvesters and tractors between 1935 and 1955 (Bogue 1983); and the spread of pesticides throughout the Corn Belt.[17] Indeed the same seed salesmen who pushed hybrid seeds also pushed these other industrial inputs. This bundle of technological changes brought yield increases in **most** major crops in the US after the 1930s. Table 5.1 provides a snapshot of yield growth in major US crops in the 20th century. Note that claims of "miracle seeds" notwithstanding, during the 1930–1960 period when hybrid seeds were being adopted, corn yield growth was in *last place behind the non-hybrid crops*. Corn yields did not start to climb sharply until the 1960s, and the cause was the advent of hyper-fertilized close-planting described in Chapter 4.

It is also interesting to revisit Griliches' state patterns that supposedly showed hybrid corn adoption to be explained by raised yields. Figure 5.3 breaks out the state-specific trends in corn yields and hybrid adoption; it shows that in most states the period when adoption surged to 80–90% there was hardly any increase in the rate of yield growth at all.

Jean-Pierre Berlan and Richard Lewontin once concluded that the economists' eagerness to attribute the march of hybrid corn to some innate superiority was really just putting "a final ideological touch to this fairy tale of science and technology" (1986, 46) and they had a point. We clearly need another explanation of why hybrids took over American cornfields in the 1930s, so let us return to the processes of environmental, social, and didactic learning that drive farmers' technology adoption (Chapter 3). Environmental learning hardly explains adoption as Griliches claimed, but it did play some role; some farmers would have seen larger-than-average yield advantages and some could absorb the added seed cost. Hybrid sellers also benefited from a timely midwestern drought in 1936 which revealed that some hybrids

TABLE 5.1 To compare corn to crops with very different weights, the figures show percentage change in yield from the base year of 1900. Soybean data do not start until 1924 so the soybean series uses that base year. Data are from the USDA.

	Corn (%)	Potatoes (%)	Tobacco (%)	Cotton (%)	Wheat (%)	Rice (%)	Soybean (%)
1900	**100**	100	100	100	100	100	
1910	**99**	108	104	90	112	137	
1920	**106**	129	99	96	111	147	
1930	**73**	126	99	81	116	171	118
1940	**103**	154	132	130	125	188	147
1950	**136**	294	162	138	135	194	197
1960	**195**	356	217	229	214	280	214
1970	**258**	440	270	225	254	378	243
1980	**324**	510	247	207	275	361	241
1990	**422**	563	283	325	324	453	310
2000	**487**	733	286	324	344	514	346

had good drought tolerance, leading some to adopt hybrids despite their "commercial unattractiveness in normal years" (Sutch 2011, 197). Hybrids' yield advantage grew throughout the 1930s because the resources being poured into developing hybrids brought OPV breeding to an almost complete stop. In 1924, 99% of the entries in the Iowa Corn Yield test were OPV's; by 1938 less than 6% were OPV's (Robinson and Knott 1963, 72). Hybrid corn yields were growing more slowly than other major non-hybrid crops; the only thing they were outpacing were OPV corn yields because OPV breeding had been crushed. So by the late 1930s, environmental learning would have been pointing farmers to adopt hybrids and scramble along on Cochrane's technology treadmill because of the demise of OPV's.

Social learning also played a role in the technology's spread. The s-curves are now understood to result mainly from social snowball effects (Henrich 2001) rather than Griliches' notion of some farmers being slow to understand their situation (1957, 516). The adoption curves are too steep to be explained by personal experimentation catching up with farmers, and as Ryan and Gross noted, "once the wave of adoption swelled, hybrid practically 'took the field' in the space of four years" (1943, 17–18).

But the real key to hybrid adoption in the 1930s was didactic learning, especially what Richard Sutch calls "a sustained propaganda campaign conducted by the USDA at the direction of the Secretary of Agriculture, Henry Agard Wallace" (Sutch 2011, 203–204) (Figure 5.4). The seed industry had been pressuring the USDA to stop advocating seed self-sufficiency even before hybrids came along, insisting that "[t]here is no reason why the business of legitimate seedsmen should be interfered with and farmers and gardeners urged to produce their own" (Fitzgerald 1993, 337). But with hybrids the stakes were much higher, and by 1933 the industry didn't have to convince the USDA to support its interests, as it had infiltrated the USDA at the top. We have seen how Wallace managed to turn the USDA's research priorities to hybrids; he also pulled all available levers of persuasion to promote the seeds, even devoting the entire 1936 *Yearbook of Agriculture* to "a single subject – the creative development of new forms of life through plant and animal breeding" (Wallace 1936).

Didactic learning was also important at the state level, where extension agents promoted hybrids and disseminated favorable test plot results (Ryan and Gross 1943, 16), and at the level of the farm, where seed salesmen came with well-honed pitches for desperate farmers in the Depression. Salesmen also passed out free seed to farmers willing to tell neighbors about the product and gave various inducements to lower the costs and risks of adoption (Sutch 2011, 217).[18] Marketing even helps to explain the spatial patterning in hybrid corn adoption that Griliches attributed the development of locally adapted hybrids. As Griliches himself writes, almost 90% of seed in the midwestern Corn Belt is "sold by individual salesmen who call on each farmer," whereas

> almost all of the seed in the South is sold through stores where the farmer must come and get it…[t]he small size of the corn acreage per farm, the relative isolation of the small farm, and the large proportion of corn on noncommercial farms make the type of marketing used in the Corn Belt prohibitively expensive in the South.
>
> *(1957, 510)*

"Remarkably Free of Unfavourable Side-Effects"

Crop breeding's most heralded accomplishment of the last century turns out to have not been inherently superior for farmers or consumers but highly profitable to seed companies.

FIGURE 5.4 Henry A. Wallace (center) with Mexican Minister of Agriculture Gomez and a farmer during his 1940 trip to observe peasant agriculture in Mexico. The trip by the US Vice President-elect is sometimes cited as the original impetus for what became the Green Revolution (Chapter 6). Henry A. Wallace Collection MsC0177, Special Collections & Archives, the University of Iowa Libraries.

It was made so by the public institutions being maneuvered into doing most of the research for a research-intensive technology, into suppressing information about that research, and into aggressively promoting adoption of the new seeds before they even offered an economic advantage. Let us then return to the claim that crop breeding is "remarkably free of unfavourable side-effects" and ask what unfavorable side-effects have been brought to us entirely or partly by hybrid crop breeding. There are several worth pausing a moment to consider.

Promoting Further Industrialization and the Big at the Expense of the Small

The development and spread of hybrid seed left most farmers obligated to buy the seeds they had formerly created. The switch did not bring an overall rise in crop yields but it did bring a new expense that would only mushroom through time. US farmers spent about $500 million on purchased seeds in 1960, at the dawn of highly input-intensive modern agriculture; by 1997 they were spending $6.7 billion (Fernandez-Cornejo 2004, 7).

But the issue has not only been purchase of seed, but what kind of seed. At the level of seed biology, there is nothing inherently input-intensive about hybrids other than the hybrid itself: farmers have to buy seeds each year, but hybrid seeds could be bred to thrive without other inputs such as irrigation, chemical fertilizer, or pesticide. But they aren't. Hybrid breeding established the principle of public breeders creating crops for the benefit of input companies, and the domination of public breeding priorities by the interests of agri-capital has only grown. We have seen how mid-century breeders worked overtime to create hybrid corn and other grains to be fertilizer, irrigation, and pesticide sponges.

Farmers differ enormously. A new seed that benefits one group of farmers will not benefit another, and indeed may lead to economic harm to some (as we saw with Cochrane's technology treadmill). A dominant theme that we see in the history of crop breeding is "improvement" being defined as breeding seeds that will benefit larger and better-capitalized farmers (an issue we will see in the Green Revolution as well). This has often led to breeders prioritizing seeds for high-external-input farms – instead of, say, breeding for stressed or low-input conditions.

These breeding priorities have contributed to a general pattern of public agricultural research transferring wealth from smaller to larger farmers and contributing significantly to increasing farm size in the middle of the last century (Busch et al. 1991, 54). Hybrid corn, writes Jack Kloppenburg, "set the technological treadmill turning at an unprecedented pace…Mechanization and chemical technology associated with the new corn varieties further accelerated the vicious cycle of innovation, increased production, depressed prices, further innovation" (Kloppenburg 2004, 119). Between 1935 and 1960, the number of farms in the greater Corn Belt plummeted by 35%.

"Deskilling"

A second harm has been hybrid corn's impact on how farmers acquire knowledge and skill, undermining farmer self-sufficiency. Prior to the spread of commercial hybrid corn, many extension agents had been teaching farmers ways to *reduce* their reliance on external inputs and expertise. Many had preached a gospel of self-help throughout the 1920s, including how to identify and detassel diseased seed corn in the fields. In the early days of Mendelian breeding some public breeders had worked to demystify the scientific components of corn growing. But "hybrid corn rendered these hard-won lessons pointless" as farmers were increasingly "locked out from an understanding of their own operations without the aid of experts" (Fitzgerald 1993, 130,343). "It matters little that farmers acquiesced in the shift," writes Deborah Fitzgerald; "what did matter was that their authority and knowledge were thereby delegated to geneticists and seed dealers" (Fitzgerald 1993, 343).

What was happening as hybrids spread was *agricultural deskilling*. Observers of factory industrialization have written about a deskilling process whereby skilled work is replaced by machines and/or simpler, less skilled, tasks that can be performed by lower-paid and less empowered workers (Braverman 1974). Thus textile production by skilled weavers was replaced by mills where low-skilled workers ran power looms, butchers were replaced by meat fabrication plants, and so on. In agriculture deskilling can fit this description in some ways: hybrid corn did indeed eliminate the skilled craft of corn breeding that many farmers practiced (Ziegenhorn 2000, 136). But agricultural deskilling is also different: unlike the weaver or the butcher, the farmer is still there, but operating with less and less ability to understand the details of the technology being used (Stone 2007).

Hybrids deskilled not only because they eroded the teaching of self-reliance but because they were "illegible." Farmers could easily recognize OPVs like Reid's Yellow Dent from Western Plowman and know what to expect from the crop. But hybrid seeds all looked pretty much the same, and seed companies were loath to disclose any information other than what would promote their products. (Catalogs and advertisements were quick to throw out figures but these were based on test plots and often were exaggerated.) We know that breeders including Henry A. Wallace were adamant about keeping pedigree information secret (Ziegenhorn 2000, 138), and even seed salesmen were perplexed by "the invisibility of crucial properties of hybrids" (Fitzgerald 1993, 340).

Hybrids also deskilled through brand proliferation. With the public sector soldiering away at the research and development role to which it had been relegated, and private seed companies making their own hybrids and also slapping their own proprietary names on public lines, farmers quickly found themselves facing an alarming assemblage of difficult-to-distinguish brands. By 1937 the breeders at the University of Illinois alone were offering farmers 100 hybrid combinations; in 1938 the Funk Brothers seed catalog listed 65 hybrids (36 from the company and 29 public). Within a few years there would be over 600 hybrid corn brands on the market in Minnesota, many of them publicly developed hybrids sold many "aliases" (Kloppenburg 2004, 107). Many of these hybrids varied little from one to another, and their profusion convinced farmers that their experience was of little use in the new world of seed selection. The Federal Seed Act was intended to check this source of profusion and confusion, but it went largely unenforced.

Nothing summed up the deskilling quote as succinctly as the message to farmers that began to appear in the Funk Brothers seed catalog in 1935: "You may not know which strain to order. Just order FUNK'S HYBRID CORN" and the company would pick your seed for you. It hadn't taken long for farmers to be pushed out of any role in even choosing seeds.[19] And as seed industries have grown and the commercial logic of seeds has become increasingly entrenched, the deskilling has expanded far beyond row crop agriculture to even include gardeners (as Gilbert 2013 discovered when studying allotment gardeners in the UK).

It is not hard to envision a very different world for farmers today if the Mendelians had not won their struggle with selection breeders in the early 20th century – which brings us to our third case of harm from hybrids: the demise of what had been a network of lively and productive OPV breeding.

The Opportunity Cost.

The final harm to consider can only be speculative: what did we lose by reorienting so much of the public breeding system to background research for hybrid seed companies? What if that effort, expertise, and funding had gone to breeding more oriented to benefiting farmers and consumers rather than the seed industry?

To be sure, some have maintained that public breeding's shift to hybrid research has been enormously beneficial to society. An oft-cited estimate is that the returns to society by investment in hybrid corn are around 700%, making it "one of the most dramatic breakthroughs in agricultural technology within our country" (Kloppenburg 2004, 297). Interestingly enough, the 700% figure came from Griliches (1958, 419) around the same time he was publishing the famous articles attributing hybrid adoption to economic benefits to farmers. Societal benefits were based on increased corn production, which we now know to not be entirely (or even mostly) due to hybrids; but more to the point, it is perverse to count increased production as a societal benefit when the government was paying farmers to idle their land in a desperate attempt to *tame* overproduction. Moreover corn yields were poised to really take off just as Griliches was calculating the societal benefits of hybrids. The "Big Corn Yields" that Funk Brothers would be boasting a few years later were for real; the takeoff shown in Table 5.1 was the last thing American farmers or the economy needed. Societal benefit indeed.

But even if all the increased overproduction was a societal good, Griliches himself acknowledges that this reckoning of costs and benefits is rather like gauging the returns to oil well drilling without considering the costs of all the "dry holes" (Griliches 1958, 426). What might agricultural research have accomplished had it not prioritized the gushers for industry? We will never know what directions public breeding would have taken, but we know for sure what happened to progress in the time-tested strategy of population improvement. Public funding *had been* supporting research, development, and infrastructure that benefited both food producers and food consumers with open-pollinated corn, and there were corn surpluses when hybrids came along. And when the public breeding establishment put its thumb – or its whole fist – on the scale, it hurt OPV breeding just as much as it helped hybrids.

We will never know what sort of crop innovations and improvements we might have today if breeders had kept working with OPVs (Wise 2019, 121). It is plausible that in the US, corn fields would be more biodiverse and farms would be less indebted and dependent on government support. Might the crop even be just as productive as it is today? Richard Lewontin thinks so, writing that since the 1930s, "virtually no one has tried to improve the OPV's, although scientific evidence shows that if the same effort had been put into such varieties, they would be as good or better than hybrids by now" (1982, 16). I am not sure that "scientific evidence" can show what would have happened, but it is a plausible speculation. It is even echoed in breeder Norman Simmonds' classic text *Principles of Crop Improvement* (1979), which points out that the enormous effort that has been thrown behind hybrid corn has been at the expense of population-based breeding which "is evidently capable of rates of advance which are at least comparable and may well be achieved more cheaply" (Simmonds 1979, 162).[20]

Notes

1 Edward Murray East, a key figure in the history of crop breeding who we will meet shortly, wrote a popular book just at the moment he was rewriting the rules of who benefited from breeding. His (co-authored) 1919 book *Inbreeding and Outbreeding* presented the crop breeder as like a force of natural selection, choosing the "prese types for survival and propagation. He dodged the question of who got to decide what was "types and what their interests were, "conveniently hiding all the historical contingencies, the political economic sticks and carrots...that had made one particular strain of plant 'better' than the next," notes historian Theodore Varno (2011, 116).
2 It is also known as recurrent selection.
3 However none of these facts prevented agricultural leaders from predicting the usual eminent Malthusian disaster. In 1910 the USDA's Office of Experiment Stations wrote:

> It has been shown that production of the staples in this country is not keeping pace with the increased home demand, and that without a change in the methods of farming and the establishment of a permanent, self -sustaining agriculture, such as has not yet been established in any country, the food supply of the future will not be adequate to meet the needs of the teeming millions.

4 Some have pondered how the world scientific community could have been so oblivious (Mayr 1982, 722–726, Moore 2001). Part of the problem was that Mendel did not "sell" the work very well; he did not give further presentations and did not publish again. The offprints he sent to the major Swiss botanist Carl Nägeli led to a disastrous correspondence in which Nägeli, rather than encouraging Mendel or helping get his work into a top scientific journal, sent Mendel down a blind alley. Nägeli persuaded Mendel to test his theories in a different plant: hawkweed, one of the few plants that were completely incompatible with Mendel's theories because it reproduces by the unusual process of apomixis (self-cloning). Nägeli apparently believed that Mendel's work would refute the theories that he himself was developing, which he finally published in a 1884 book that does not even mention Mendel. Mendel's vengeance would come posthumously: today

if you look up Nägeli you will see that he was a minor scientist known mainly as the man who discouraged Gregor Mendel and helped keep him "hidden."

5 They "wanted to be something more than fertilizer analysts," and complained bitterly that the farmers' demands constrained their activities as scientists (Kloppenburg 2004, 76).

6 This precept was codified in the law that opened the floodgates of eugenic sterilization: Virginia's Sterilization Act of 1924 – which led to the landmark Supreme Court decision *Buck v. Bell* – required that sterilizations only be performed if the hospital superintendent deemed the procedure to be in the patient's interests. But the superintendents were enthusiastic eugenicists; Joseph DeJarnette, superintendent of an asylum in Staunton, VA, lamented in 1934 "Hitler is beating us at our own game" (Black 2003, 7).

7 Approximately 5% of plants use the C4 pathway. The only other major C4 crop plants are sugarcane and sorghum.

8 Dioecious species have male and female plants. This is true of many tree species but only a few food crops, such as asparagus and spinach.

9 Precisely why inbreeding depression occurs was not understood in the early 20th century and is not completely understood today. At least part of the answer lies in the stock of maladaptive recessive alleles present in all plants and animals. Such alleles may have the potential to reduce a plant's reproductive fitness, but they are not under evolutionary pressure because their effects are normally masked by dominant alleles. Inbred plants may be homozygous for these alleles, allowing them to express. However it is clear that the phenomenon is more complex than this, and plant geneticists continue to debate its causes (Carr and Dudash 2003).

10 Shull worked under Davenport at the Carnegie Institution's Station for Experimental Evolution.

11 East himself had moved from the public breeding sector to Harvard's Bussey Institute.

12 This was understood from the beginning of Mendelian breeding; in fact Erich von Tschermak – one of the three scientists who simultaneously rediscovered Mendelian heredity –stressed as early as 1901 that breeders would have to plant huge numbers of hybrids to find the rare offspring with superior performance.

13 The original name was the Hi-Bred Corn Company.

14 A very small number of companies were able to commandeer most of the benefits of government largesse and grow to dominant positions. Funk Brothers and Wallace's Pioneer Hi-Bred were joined by the DeKalb Agricultural Association (later the DeKalb Genetic Corporation) in establishing special relationships with the USDA, AESs, and LGUs, which gave them preferential access to the techniques and breeding lines developed at these public research agencies (Kloppenburg 2004, 106).

15 One farmer wrote to Wallace:

> It seems unfortunate that producers cannot get pedigrees just the same as livestock producers can at this time...I am writing to you especially to learn about this matter of keeping us in the dark on pedigrees"
>
> *(Ziegenhorn 2000, 140)*

16 Data from Iowa Corn Yield Tests show that except for the drought year 1936, hybrids outyielded OPVs by 6–15% during the years of adoption in Iowa — despite breeding resources being poured into hybrids at the expense of OPVs (Zuber and Robinson 1941).

17 Griliches failed to take these developments into account. He based his analysis of hybrid adoption patterns on a geography dissertation that clearly stated that hybrid seed was only one of many technologies adopted between 1935 and 1955 that contributed to the rise of corn productivity (Grotewold 1955).

18 Sociologist Howard Becker provides a glimpse into how lucrative hybrid corn selling was by the 1940s. He describes how when he was playing piano in Chicago strip joints during World War II, "Guys would come in from the hybrid-seed-corn convention and spend three or four thousand dollars buying drinks for the girls" (Gopnik 2015).

19 The Indian cotton farmers we met in Chapter 4 were an extreme example of the same process.

20 Even breeder David Duvick, who provided the neo-Malthusian quote about early breeders feeding growing populations with their new methods, has shown us something of what we have missed by throwing earlier breeding philosophies under the bus. He describes a controlled multi-year comparison of recurrent selection (population improvement) and hybrid breeding carried out in Iowa: the hybrids showed a bit less improvement (Duvick 1977, 2005, 121).

References

20th Century Time Machine. 2016. Norman Borlaug: The Man Who Saved the World from Hunger (online documentary). https://www.youtube.com/watch?v=699T-8aF7Yg

Allen, Garland E. 2000. "The Reception of Mendelism in the United States, 1900–1930." *Comptes Rendus de l'Académie des Sciences – Series III* 323:1081–1088.

Bateson, William. 1902. "Practical Aspects of the New Discoveries in Heredity." In *Proceedings of the International Conference on Plant Breeding and Hybridization*. New York: Horticultural Soc of New York.

Berlan, Jean-Pierre, and Robert C. Lewontin. 1986. "The Political Economy of Hybrid Corn." *Monthly Review* 38:35–47.

Black, Edwin. 2003. *War against the Weak: Eugenics and America's Campaign to Create a Master Race.* Washington, DC: Dialog Press.

Bogue, Allan G. 1983. "Changes in Mechanical and Plant Technology: The Corn Belt, 1910–1940." *The Journal of Economic History* 43 (1):1–25.

Borlaug, Norman E. 1970. "Acceptance Speech." Nobel Prize, 10 December. Oslo. http://www.nobelprize.org/nobel_prizes/peace/laureates/1970/borlaug-acceptance.html.

Braverman, Harry. 1974. *Labor and Monopoly Capital*. New York: Monthly Review Press.

Brummer, E Charles, Wesley T Barber, Sarah M Collier, Thomas S Cox, Randy Johnson, Seth C Murray, Richard T Olsen, Richard C Pratt, and Ann Marie Thro. 2011. "Plant Breeding for Harmony between Agriculture and the Environment." *Frontiers in Ecology and the Environment* 9 (10):561–568.

Busch, Lawrence, W.B. Lacy, J. Burkhardt, and L.R. Lacy. 1991. *Plants, Power, and Profit: Social, Economic, and Ethical Consequences of the New Biotechnologies.* Cambridge: Blackwell.

Carr, David E., and Michele R. Dudash. 2003. "Recent Approaches into the Genetic Basis of Inbreeding Depression in Plants." *Philosophical Transactions: Biological Sciences* 358 (1434):1071–1084.

Cochrane, Willard W. 1993. *The Development of American Agriculture: A Historical Analysis, 2nd ed.* Minneapolis: Univ. of Minnesota.

Crabb, A. Richard. 1947. *The Hybrid Corn Makers: Prophets of Plenty.* New Brunswick, NJ: Ruthers Univ. Press.

Culver, John C., and John Hyde. 2000. *American Dreamer: The Life and Times of Henry A. Wallace.* New York and London: W.W. Norton.

Danbom, David B. 1979. *The Resisted Revolution: Urban America and the Industrialization of Agriculture 1900–1930.* Ames: Iowa State Univ.

Darwin, Charles. 1876. *The Effects of Cross and Self Fertilization in the Vegetable Kingdom.* London: Murray.

Davenport, Charles Benedict. 1906. *Inheritance in Poultry.* Washington, DC: Carnegie Institution of Washington.

Davenport, Charles Benedict. 1911. *Heredity in Relation to Eugenics.* New York: Henry Holt and Co.

Davis, Donald R., Melvin D. Epp, and Hugh D. Riordan. 2004. "Changes in USDA Food Composition Data for 43 Garden Crops, 1950 to 1999." *Journal of the American College of Nutrition* 23 (6):1–14.

Duvick, David N. 1977. "Genetic Rates of Gain in Hybrid Maize Yields during the Past 40 years." *Maydica* 22:187–196.

Duvick, Donald N. 2001. "Biotechnology in the 1930s: The Development of Hybrid Maize." *Nature Reviews Genetics* 2 (1):69–74.

Duvick, Donald N. 2005. "The Contribution of Breeding to Yield Advances in maize (Zea mays L.)." *Advances in Agronomy* 86:83–145.

East, Edward Murray. 1906. "The Improvement of Corn in Connecticut." *Connecticut AES Bulletin* 152:6.

East, Edward Murray. 1923. *Mankind at the Crossroads.* New York: Scribner.

East, Edward Murray, and Donald F. Jones. 1919. *Inbreeding and Outbreeding: Their Genetic and Sociological Significance.* Philadelphia: J.B. Lippincott.

Egan, J. Franklin, M. Barlow Kathryn, and A. Mortensen David. 2014. "A Meta-Analysis on the Effects of 2,4-D and Dicamba Drift on Soybean and Cotton." *Weed Science* 62 (1):193–206. doi: 10.1614/WS-D-13–00025.1.

Estabrook, Barry. 2011. *Tomatoland: How Modern Industrial Agriculture Destroyed Our Most Alluring Fruit.* Kansas City: Andrews McMeel Publishing.

Fernandez-Cornejo, J. 2004. The Seed Industry in U.S. Agriculture: An Exploration of Data and Information on Crop Seed Markets, Regulation, Industry Structure, and Research and Development. *Agriculture Information Bulletin No. (AIB-786).*

Fitzgerald, Deborah. 1990. *The Business of Breeding: Hybrid Corn in Illinois 1890–1940.* Ithaca, NY: Cornell Univ. Press.

Fitzgerald, Deborah. 1993. "Farmers Deskilled: Hybrid Corn and Farmers Work." *Technology and Culture* 34:324–43.

Garvin, D.F., R.M. Welch, and J.W. Finley. 2006. "Historical Shifts in the Seed Mineral Micronutrient Concentration of US Hard Red Winter Wheat Germplasm." *Journal of the Science of Food and Agriculture* 86:2213–2220.

Giesen, James C., and Mark Hersey. 2010. "The New Environmental Politics and its Antecedents: Lessons from the Early Twentieth Century South." *The Historian* 72 (2) Summer:271–98.

Gilbert, Paul Robert. 2013. "Deskilling, Agrodiversity, and the Seed Trade: A View from Contemporary British Allotments." *Agriculture and Human Values* 30 (1):101–114.

Gopnik, Adam. 2015. "The Outside Game: How the sociologist Howard Becker studies the conventions of the unconventional." *New Yorker* 12 January. http://www.newyorker.com/magazine/2015/01/12/outside-game

Griliches, Zvi. 1957. "Hybrid Corn: An Exploration in the Economics of Technological Change." *Econometrica* 25:501–523.

Griliches, Zvi. 1958. "Research Costs and Social Returns: Hybrid Corn and Related Innovations." *Journal of Political Economy* 66 (5):419–431.

Griliches, Zvi. 1960. "Hybrid corn and Economics of Innovation." *Science* 132:275–280.

Grotewold, Andreas. 1955. "Regional Changes in Corn Production in the United States from 1909 to 1949." PhD, Geography, Univ. of Chicago.

Harpstead, D. D. 1975. "Man-Molded Cereal: Hybrid Corn's Story." In *The 1975 Yearbook of Agriculture: That We May Eat*, edited by J. Hayes, 213–224. Washington, DC: US Govn Printing Office.

Harwood, Jonathan. 2015. "Did Mendelism Transform Plant Breeding? Genetic Theory and Breeding Practice, 1900–1945." In *New Perspectives on the History of Life Sciences and Agriculture*, edited by Denise Phillips and Sharon Kingsland, 345–370. Cham: Springer International Publishing.

Henrich, Joseph. 2001. "Cultural Transmission and the Diffusion of Innovations: Adoption Dynamics Indicate That Biased Cultural Transmission Is the Predominate Force in Behavioral Change." *American Anthropologist* 103 (4):992–1013.

Hogg, Dominic. 2000. *Technological Change in Agriculture: Locking in to Genetic Uniformity.* London: Palgrave Macmillan UK.

Holmes, Nigel. 1992. "1,000 years at a glance." *Time* 140:25–27.

Iowa Corn and Small Grain Growers' Association. 1924. Iowa Corn Yield Test, Results of 1924 Tests, Plans for 1925 Tests.

Jenkins, Merle T. 1936. "Corn Improvement." In *Yearbook of Agriculture, 1936* Washington, DC: US Govn Printing Office.

Jenkins, Merle T. 1951. "Genetic Improvement of Food Plants for Increased Yield." *Proceedings of the American Philosophical Society* 95 (1):84–91.

Kimmelman, Barbara A. 1983. "The American Breeders' Association: Genetics and Eugenics in an Agricultural Context, 1903–13." *Social Studies of Science* 13 (2):163–204.

Kloppenburg, Jack Ralph, Jr. 2004. *First the Seed: The Political Economy of Plant Biotechnology, 1492–2000, 2nd edition.* Madison: Univ. Wisconsin Press.

Kunze, Joel P. 1988. "The Purnell Act and Agricultural Economics." *Agricultural History* 62 (2):131–149.

Lake, David A. 1989. "Export, Die, or Subsidize: The International Political Economy of American Agriculture, 1875–1940." *Comparative Studies in Society and History* 31 (1):81–105.

Leary, Warren E. 1994 "Cigarette Company Developed Tobacco With Stronger Nicotine; Head of F.D.A. Tells of Chemical Manipulation." *New York Times* 22 June, 1. https://www.nytimes.com/1994/06/22/us/cigarette-company-developed-tobacco-with-stronger-nicotine-head-fda-tells.html.

Lewontin, Richard. 1982. "Agricultural Research and the Penetration of Capital." *Science for the People* Jan-Feb:12–17.

Makoi, Joachim H. J.R., Samson B.M. Chimphango, and Felix D. Dakora. 2009. "Effect of Legume Plant Density and Mixed Culture on Symbiotic N2 Fixation in Five Cowpea (Vigna unguiculata L. Walp.) Genotypes in South Africa." *Symbiosis* 48 (1):57–67. doi: 10.1007/bf03179985.

Manning, Richard. 2004. *Against the Grain: How Agriculture Has Hijacked Civilization.* New York: North Point Press.

Marcus, Alan I. 1986. "The Ivory Silo: Farmer-Agricultural College Tensions in the 1870s and 1880s." *Agricultural History* 60 (2):22–36.

Mayr, Ernst. 1982. *The Growth of Biological Thought.* Cambridge, MA: Belknap Press.

Moore, Randy. 2001. "The "Rediscover" of Mendel's Work." *Bioscience* 27 (2):13–24.

NASS. 2016. *Crop Production Historical Track Records.* Washington, DC: Nat Agric Statistics Service, USDA.

Office of Experiment Stations. 1910. *Experiment Station Record, Volume 22.* Washington, DC.

Pioneer. 2019. "Innovators in the Advent of Hybrid Corn." https://www.pioneer.com/home/site/us/agronomy/hybrid-corn-innovators/.

Porter, Jane M. 1979. "Experiment Stations in the South, 1877–1940." *Agricultural History* 53 (1):84–101.

Richey, Frederick D. 1922. "The Experimental Basis for the Present Status of Corn Breeding." *Journal of the American Society of Agronomy* 14 (1&2):1–17.

Robinson, Joseph L., and Oliver A. Knott. 1963. *The story of the Iowa Crop Improvement Association and its Predecessors.* Ames: Iowa Crop Improvement Association.

Ruttan, Vernon W. 1996. "What Happened to Technology Adoption—Diffusion Research?" *Sociologia Ruralis* 36:51–73.

Ryan, Bryce, and Neal C. Gross. 1943. "The Diffusion of Hybrid Seed Corn in Two Iowa Communities." *Rural Sociology* 8:15–24.

Shewry, Peter R., Till K. Pellny, and Alison Lovegrove. 2016. "Is Modern Wheat Bad for Health?" *Nature: Plants* 2:16097. doi: 10.1038/nplants.2016.97.

Shull, George H. 1908. "The Composition of a Field of Maize." *Proceedings of the American Breeders' Association* 4:296–301.

Shull, George H. 1909. "A Pure-Line Method in Corn Breeding." *Journal of Heredity* os-5 (1):51–58. doi: 10.1093/jhered/os-5.1.51.

Shull, George H. 1946. "Hybrid Seed Corn." *Science* 103:547–550.

Simmonds, Norman W. 1979. *Principles of Crop Improvement.* New York: Longman.

Steele, Leon. 1978. "The Hybrid Corn Industry in the United States." In *Maize Breeding and Genetics,* edited by David B. Walden, 29–40. New York: John Wiley.

Stone, Glenn Davis. 2007. "Agricultural Deskilling and the Spread of Genetically Modified Cotton in Warangal." *Current Anthropology* 48:67–103.

Stone, Glenn Davis. 2011. "Field versus Farm in Warangal: Bt Cotton, Higher Yields, and Larger Questions." *World Development* 39 (3):387–398. doi: 10.1016/j.worlddev.2010.09.008.

Stone, Glenn Davis. 2018. "Agriculture as Spectacle." *Journal of Political Ecology* 25 (1):656–685. doi: 10.2458/v25i1.22385.

Stone, Glenn Davis, and Andrew Flachs. 2017. "The Ox Fall Down: Path Breaking and Technology Treadmills in Indian Cotton Agriculture." *Journal of Peasant Studies* 45:1272–1296. doi: 10.1080/03066150.2017.1291505.

Sutch, Richard. 2011. "The Impact of the 1936 Corn Belt Drought on American Farmers' Adoption of Hybrid Corn." In *The Economics of Climate Change: Adaptations Past and Present*, edited by Gary D. Libecap and Richard H. Steckel, 195–223. Chicago, IL: University of Chicago Press.

Sutch, Richard C. 2008. "Henry Agard Wallace, the Iowa Corn Yield Tests, and the Adoption of Hybrid Corn." National Bureau of Economic Research, Working Paper 14141. http://www.nber.org/papers/w14141.pdf

US Census Bureau. 1950. United States Census of Agriculture– 1950 – Volume V, Part VI. edited by United States Census Bureau.

van der Ploeg, Jan Douwe. 1993. "Potatoes and Knowledge." In *The Growth of Ignorance: An Anthropological Critique of Development*, edited by M. Hobart, 209–227. London: Routledge.

Varno, Theodore James. 2011. "The Nature of Tomorrow: Inbreeding in Industrial Agriculture and Evolutionary Thought in Britain and the United States, 1859–1925." PhD, History, Univ. of California - Berkeley.

Wallace, Henry A. 1934. "The Year in Agriculture: Secretary's Report to the President." In *Yearbook of Agriculture*, edited by Milton Eisenhower, 1–99. Washington, DC: US Govn Printing Office.

Wallace, Henry A. 1936. *Yearbook of Agriculture, 1936*. Washington, DC: US Government Printing Office.

Watson, James D., and Francis H.C. Crick. 1953. "A Structure for Deoxyribose Nucleic Acid." *Nature* 171 (4356):737–738.

Weber, Margaret. 2018. "The American Way of Farming: Pioneer Hi-Bred and Power in Postwar America." *Agricultural History* 92 (3):380–403.

Wilson, Alexandra. 2015. Heroes of the Harvest: Breeding Program Brings Better, Safer Corn to South. In *USGA Blog* 29 October. https://www.usda.gov/media/blog/2015/10/29/heroes-harvest-breeding-program-brings-better-safer-corn-south.

Wise, Timothy A. 2019. *Eating Tomorrow: Agribusiness, Family Farmers, and the Battle for the Future of Food*. New York: The New Press.

Wood, Phillip J. 1986. *Southern Capitalism: The Political Economy of North Carolina, 1880–1980*. Durham, NC: Duke Univ. Press.

Ziegenhorn, Randy. 2000. "The Commodification of Hybrid Corn: What Farmers Know." In *Commodities and Globalization: Anthropological Approaches*, edited by Angelique Haugerud, M. Priscilla Stone and Peter D. Little, 135–150. Lanham, MD: Rowman & Littlefield.

Zuber, Marcus S., and Joe L. Robinson. 1941. "The 1940 Iowa Corn Yield Test." *Iowa Agricultural Experiment Station Bulletin* P19 (NS):519–93.

6

THE GREEN REVOLUTION AND INDUSTRIALIZING DEVELOPING WORLD FARMS

Jed Bartlett, the fictional US President in the TV drama The West Wing, was relaxing with his staff and reflecting on agriculture in the developing world. "Did you ever read The Population Bomb?...Ehrlich said it was a fantasy that India would ever feed itself," he explained.

> Then Norman Borlaug comes along. See the problem was wheat is top-heavy. It was falling over on itself and it took up too much space. The dwarf wheat... guys, it was an agricultural revolution that was credited with saving one billion lives.

Screenwriter Aaron Sorkin's forte is smart people, and the Bartlett character was his smartest – a Nobel laureate in economics and a big thinker able to "see the whole board," as he put it in another episode. In this scene he was marveling at how some of most revolutionary solutions are the simplest: wheat was top-heavy, along comes Norman Borlaug to fix the plant, prove Ehrlich wrong, and save a billion lives – or "billions" as some would say (Njoroge 2020). Borlaug went on to win a Nobel Peace Prize and be hailed as the greatest man in history (Vidal 2014).

Sorkin invented the dialog but not this account of the Green Revolution: it is a mainstay of discussions of food and population. The Green Revolution – referring to introduction of "high-yielding" dwarf wheat (bred by Borlaug) and rice (bred in the Philippines) in the late 1960s – is often credited with revolutionizing food production in the Global South. Borlaug's seeds are credited with wondrous traits: they were "a hardier strain of wheat" that was "impervious to pests, bad weather and poor soil" (The Times 2009) that inspired scientists to engineer "healthier" foods (Fung 2012) and "enable[d] the world to support a far greater human population than many thought possible" (The Times 2009).

But it is specifically India that is supposed to have been on the edge of Malthusian catastrophe (as we saw in Chapter 1), India that became ground zero for the seed revolution, and India that emerged as proof of the neo-Malthusian creed just as Ireland had "proved" the original Malthusian creed. Thanks to those "high-yield dwarf varieties," we read in *Science*, India went from dependence on shiploads of food aid to being a wheat exporter (Bagla

DOI: 10.4324/9781003286257-6

and Stone 2013). A parallel story of marvelous seeds unfolded in the Philippines, where breeders had also used dwarfing genes to "fix" rice. Green Revolution rice was greeted by press reports that the "Miracle Rice" was "a breath-taking breakthrough is that its productivity is not induced through new expensive farm tools or novel farming techniques…[t]he miracle is lodged in the grain itself – a built-in productivity" (Rama 1966, 5).

President Bartlett faithfully recounted the legend, but far from seeing the whole board, he had missed how the Green Revolution actually worked. We will see that, contrary to what has been written repeatedly, the "revolution" *did not speed up India's food production at all*. Wheat production did climb after Borlaug's seeds were adopted, but only at the expense of other crops – and even then the rise was not because of the dwarf wheat itself. The local Indian wheat was not "falling over on itself" and Borlaug's dwarf wheat was not "hardier," "healthier," or "impervious" to much – least of all to pests and poor soil. Nor were the seeds hybrids, as some scientists seem to think (Stewart, Richards, and Halfhill 2000). The dwarf crops were just responsive to high doses of fertilizer and water, and they led to farmers needing more fertilizer and water for each ton they grew. The seeds did not power a Green Revolution any more than the gas pump powers your car or the ATM generates money. The actual work of selectively boosting crop productivity came from the resources the seeds funneled – including fossil fuels, wells, fertilizer factories – and from changes in state policies – including paying farmers more and not undercutting them with cheap imports. The Green Revolution is not just the story of how the core industrial agricultural appropriations of seed and fertilizer pushed their way into the developing world, it is the classic tale of how we find a way to attribute productivity to a piece of technology in the farmer's field rather than to the external resources and policies that actually cause change.

The Green Revolution is also important to us because of our focus on the gap between how agriculture actually works and how it is understood, and this gap is bigger when it comes to the Green Revolution than any other story in agriculture. The halo on the Green Revolution is even bigger than the halos on fertilizer and seeds. After all, it combines both fertilizer and seeds, it features a telegenic hero, and it throws in the specter of averted massive for good measure. Question the legend and you are accused of "preferring mass starvation" (Harwood 2012, xv). But question the legend I will, not only because it is false – Borlaug's handiwork did not actually raise food production – but because it obscures the real story of industrial agricultural appropriatipushing their way into the developing world.

Let us begin by looking at the Green Revolution's roots in Mexico. Borlaug himself cited the Mexican wheat regime as a model for India, saying "What Mexico did, your country can also do, except that yours should do it in half the time" (Baranski 2015a, 92). But just what had Mexico done?

What Mexico Did

One of the ironies of the Green Revolution is that this program of input-intensive agriculture was inspired by the idea of small farmer self-sufficiency and independence from purchased inputs. But that is not part of the standard telling of the program's origins, which begins with a road trip through Mexico by Vice President-elect Henry A. Wallace in December 1940 (Figure 5.4). Wallace was dismayed by the sight of low-yielding food crops on marginal lands (Wallace 1941, Perkins 1997, 106), and he supposedly persuaded Rockefeller Foundation (RF) President Raymond Fosdick to start an agricultural program there.

The alternative history of the program's origin is laid out in the award winning book *Agrarian Crossings* by Tore Olsson (2017). Olsson traces the impetus of the Mexican Agricultural Program to physician John Ferrell and newspaper man Josephus Daniels, both of whom had seen the grinding poverty of tenant cotton farmers in the early 20th century US South, and had been deeply impressed by the impact of farmer programs run by a forerunner of the RF. Those programs had preached independence from the market and creditors through use of manure, legumes, crop rotation, and production of subsistence crops. When Ferrell and Daniels both wound up in Mexico – Ferrell as a public health worker and Daniels as an ambassador – they were struck by parallels between rural poverty in Mexico and US cotton country, and together urged the RF to mount a similar program to help Mexican farmers prosper through non-industrial practices.[1] (It was only after they lobbied Fosdick that he reached out to Wallace for advice.)

In 1941 Fosdick sent a team of three experts to assess Mexican agriculture, resulting in a report urging the RF to send a scientific commission to advise the Mexican Department of Agriculture. Thus in 1943 began the RF's Mexican Agriculture Program (MAP), headed by Elvin Stakman (one of the expert trio) and with an initial charge of breeding maize and wheat varieties resistant to the wicked disease of stem rust. Stakman offered the job of running the wheat program to his former PhD advisee in plant pathology who was then working in a DuPont factory developing a napalm precursor. This was Norman Borlaug (Figure 6.1).

Borlaug was well cast for the role of Green Revolution hero. He was a handsome, earnest, and driven 29-year-old from a farm in Iowa. A budding neo-Malthusian, he had gone to study under Stakman after being impressed by plant pathologist's views on the role of science in averting a looming world crisis (Cullather 2010, 49). In Mexico he proved to be an impatient workaholic. He quickly instituted his signature strategy of "shuttle breeding"

FIGURE 6.1   Norman Borlaug in Mexico, holding strains of wheat claimed to have "provided food for starving people" (Phillips 2013). But it is a mystery just who would have starved without this wheat. Photo credit: Art Rickerby/The LIFE Collection/ Shutterstock.

which involved planting two crops a year: summer crops were grown in the highlands near Mexico City, the harvested seeds being taken up to the Sonoran desert for a winter crop. The system brought down the ire of his superiors as it clashed with the orthodox (and sensible) view that seeds should be bred where they would be grown. When the MAP brass ordered him to stop shuttle breeding, he resigned, but was quickly rehired and allowed to continue. He made good progress in breeding rust-resistant wheat and began releasing varieties by 1948 (Perkins 1997, 228).

Up to this point, there is little about the story that points to industrialization of agriculture in Mexico or beyond. The MAP still prioritized peasant-friendly farming, and other MAP scientists were working on nonindustrial farming methods such as "green manure" crops and organic methods for farmers who could not afford fertilizer (Harwood 2009, 404).[2] This was about to change. To understand the change we need to look at the thinking underlying the intervention into peasant farming.

Rockefeller at Mid-Century

If industrialization allows agriculture to be consumed by the vested interests connected to external inputs, we should ask what interests drove the RF at mid-century? It was a major philanthropy but one that has been "fairly characterized as a guardian of corporate interests and a scientific auxiliary of the federal government" particularly with respect to technology (Cullather 2010, 25); it was a "mouthpiece for US interests" (Patel 2013, 10, Ross 1998, 161) that worked where official US involvement might arouse suspicion and an agent for fostering conditions for US corporate profits abroad.[3] However foundation staff were keen not to be seen as tools of Washington; their aim was to be aligned with US government policy yet not under Washington's control (Perkins 1990, 9).[4]

The priorities of the Foundation (and their friends in government) were also strongly shaped by contemporary theories about peasant economies. Particularly important was the dominant "theory of surplus labor:" peasant agriculture was assumed to be unproductive and wasteful of human labor, the countryside deemed "overpopulated" because of both the crowding and the backwardness of traditional agriculture. Economists saw getting people out of the countryside and into the factories as a win-win (Rosenstein-Rodan 1944, 160). The RF confirmed this perspective for itself by sending a team of plant scientists and an engineer to investigate population, culture, and agriculture in India. The resulting 1952 report showcases the scornful mid-century perspective, explaining that the "villages are as uniform as so many ant hills...[having] the appearance of structures built by creatures motivated by inherited animal instincts, and devoid of any inclination to depart from a fixed hereditary pattern" (quoted in Dowie 2001, 110). It added that "millions are enslaved by centuries of tradition" (Perkins 1990, 12). (In Chapter 7 we will see a dramatically different perspective on peasant innovativeness.)

As the Cold War ramped up, thinking on population and agriculture took on an increasingly geopolitical cast to observers in government and major foundations like Rockefeller, and concerns about stagnant agriculture and rural poverty were compounded by anxiety over hunger feeding Communist insurgency. "If one sees another culture as overabundant, hungry insects," John Perkins writes,

> one might well conclude that the only issue is how much food does it take to keep
> them alive and tranquil...the RF's heavy emphasis on overpopulation as the cause

of hunger created a situation in which Foundation staff could not see and appreciate other dimensions of hunger, especially distribution to people without access to land or money.

(1997, 17)

Mid-century thinkers agreed on the solution: reconfigure rural peasants as capitalist producers, thereby raising yields, filling bellies, and reorienting attitudes toward producing for the market and buying modern manufactured inputs.[5] Despite its original brief of improving farming in Mexico, the RF increasingly saw the MAP as a handy laboratory for devising technologies to promote these changes, especially in Asia (Cullather 2010, 44, Gray 1950). This explains why the MAP became increasingly focused on the productivist goal of technologies to raise yields, despite Mexico being a food exporter of cattle, vegetables, fruit, and coffee (Haggerty 1945).

Alongside the mid-century dogmas on surplus labor and productivism was another belief that would animate the Green Revolution: the shock doctrine. One of its originators was economist Paul Rosenstein-Rodan, who coined the term "big push" in 1943 to describe the large investments needed for poor countries to break free from their "low-level equilibrium trap." Agricultural progress would require not just yield-boosting technology but a radical transformation of peasant attitudes on consumption and work (Harrar, Mangelsdorf, and Weaver 1952). No one was a more avid devotee of the shock doctrine than Borlaug, who dreamed of seeds that could "destroy in one stroke the built-in conservatism or resistance to change that has been passed on from father to son for many generations in a system of traditional agriculture" (Borlaug et al. 1969, 11). The trick, as he saw it, was to "provoke shock" with yields "so big that everything they've believed in comes down in shambles all around them" (Cullather 2010, 201–202). This conviction was more important than most writers have appreciated. The Green Revolution would not be designed to maximize food production (Harwood 2019) and, as we will see, it didn't. It was to be a spectacle that would shock and awe (Stone 2018).

Shock, Fertilizer, and Japanese Seeds

The seeds that would provoke such shock would be fertilizer-intensive wheats. Borlaug knew that fertilizer would be plentiful in the postwar world and had begun experiments with fertilizer-intensive wheats in the late 1940s (Baranski 2015a, 88). But his plants had problems with lodging – growing too tall and falling over. But with exquisite timing he would come upon a dwarf variety that would open the door to his fertilizer-intensive wheat.

Dwarf wheat had been around for a long time,[6] particularly in Japan. In 1873, an American agricultural advisor in Japan wrote that "Japanese farmers have brought the art of dwarfing to perfection" with wheat that "seldom grows higher than 2 feet...no matter how much manure is used it will not grow longer, but rather the length of the wheat-head is increased" (Dalrymple 1978, 11). The Japanese pioneering such wheat was a classic example of *induced innovation*, the principle that inventions are driven not by flashes of inventor insight but by economic factors making certain inventions valuable (Binswanger and Ruttan 1978). Therefore while 19th century Americans were inventing labor-saving agricultural machinery in the land-rich labor-short Midwest, the Japanese were developing fertilizer-intensive grains for a crowded island.

In the 1920s breeders at Japan's Norin station crossed a native dwarf wheat with American varieties, resulting in a bushy wheat with a tendency to tiller (produce multiple stalks) (Reitz and Salmon 1968). It was released in 1935 and named Norin 10.[7] In 1946 the agricultural advisor to the US Occupation Army helped himself to seed samples and brought them back to US breeders. Norin 10 itself grew poorly in North America but it was spectacular at parenting dwarf wheats. Borlaug got seeds of a Norin 10 progeny in 1953 and was able to breed varieties that directed a rich nutrient diet toward producing grain rather than stalk, avoiding the problem of lodging. By 1961 the program began to release short fertilizer-intensive wheats to Mexican farmers.

But not just any farmers. The timing of the arrival of these new wheat varieties meshed perfectly with developments in Mexican politics. The 1940 election of President Avila Camacho ended years of government support for small-scale farming and semi-communal *ejidos* and brought policies that set the stage for a dress rehearsal for the Indian Green Revolution. Camacho diverted funds from *ejidos* to large-scale irrigation works, leading to an agricultural gold rush in which most land was steered into the hands of the largest and best-capitalized farmers (Pearse 1980, 35). The impact was particularly strong in northwestern state of Sonora, where there already were numerous large irrigated commercial wheat farms. These farmers did not need to be shocked into using fertilizer, especially since it was government subsidized and since canal irrigation replaced flood irrigation that recycled nutrients through alluvia. The final elements of the government subsidy of industrializing agriculture were price supports and subsidized transport from the northwest to the mills to the south (Pearse 1980, 35).

With the irrigation and subsidies in place by the mid-1940s, commercial wheat production was booming even before Borlaug got his hands on the Norin 10 seeds. Between 1945 and 1956 average wheat yields rose by 83% (Borlaug 1988, 25); by 1955 Mexico was a wheat exporter. The dwarf wheat varieties that the MAP began to release in 1961 could theoretically raise yields a further 50% if fertilized heavily.

These developments in Mexican agriculture are not referred to as "Green Revolution" as are the subsequent developments in Asia, which is interesting because of the MAP's role as a crucible for developing technologies for Asia. So when Borlaug refers to "what Mexico did," it is important to be clear that what Mexico really did was to industrialize its agriculture, providing seeds that thrived under heavily irrigated and fertilized conditions that the government had subsidized for its best capitalized farmers, producing wheat for urban consumers or export (Harwood 2009, 405). The wheat boom drove the rise of a new rural elite with a style of agriculture that was similar to the agriculture of the US (Perkins 1997, 115). What Mexico did was conspicuously unconnected to the problems of farmer welfare and food supply that originally inspired the MAP.[8] By the 1970s, analysts had begun to note that the program's effects in Mexico included "narrowing the genetic base; supplanting indigenous, sustainable practices; and displacing small and communal farming with commercial agribusiness, pushing millions of peasants into urban slums or across the border" (Cullather 2010, 68). The food-producing smallholders that were supposed to be the beneficiaries of the MAP were its victims.

All of these developments were being rehearsed before the curtain went up in Asia.

"Ship to Mouth"

In the Green Revolution legend, perpetually underfed India entered desperate straits in the 1960s as population raced far beyond food production. Kept afloat only by US food aid, the country was supposedly already careening toward catastrophe when 1966 brought severe drought and headlines about famine. Borlaug's high-yielding wheat arrived just in time and saved a billion lives (dwarf rice arrived from the Philippines around the same time, although this is less commonly credited with saving lives). The go-to phrase for describing the country's dependence on American grain shipments is "ship to mouth":

> During the 1960s, India was the largest importer of food aid, mainly under the PL480 programme of the U.S. In fact, during 1966, over 10 million tonnes of wheat was imported, leading to India being labelled as a nation surviving on a ship-to-mouth basis.
> *(Swaminathan 2012)*

But while wheat imports did spike in 1966–1967, the underlying causes had little to do with population. After over a century of colonial rule, British India split into the independent nations of India and Pakistan in 1947. The partition devastated India's wheat production. Wheat, consumed mainly as chapatis, was only India's third largest food crop (well behind rice and sorghum), but it was politically important because of its role in elite and urban diets (Kumar 2019, Subramanian 2015, 48). The Punjab was the highest producing province in British India, with an abundance of rivers and ancient irrigation works that the British had upgraded for export wheat production. But the Radcliffe Line separating India and Pakistan left the lion's share of the province to Pakistan (Figure 6.2) – including most of the most developed canals and agricultural research facilities (Perkins 1997, 161–162). From its beginning, independent India was operating with this serious handicap in wheat production.

But Indian food production could soon suffer an even more serious blow that again had little to do with population and everything to do with the designs of the developmental state. During its long reign there, Britain had suppressed development of industry and forced the colony to produce raw materials; with independence came a fundamental struggle over the path economic development should take. India was a heavily agrarian country and Mahatma Gandhi, who had led the independence movement, wanted to keep it agrarian and self-sufficient (Fox 1989). But Prime Minister Jawaharlal Nehru prioritized building heavy industry such as steel, chemicals, and tools – not agriculture. (Fertilizer factories were "heavy industry" but were low on the list of priorities.) Building industry was expensive and the food production sector was forced to underwrite it, as mandatory procurement of foodgrains at low prices kept food for urban workers cheap but stifled rural economies (Perkins 1997, 171). Nehru's calculus was also partly political, with subsidized food seen as helping manage unrest in the cities (Mooij 1998, 85).

What farmers were incentivized to grow were industrial cash crops, and so they planted more cotton, sugarcane, and jute. Jute is a fibrous crop used to produce burlap, rope, rugs, clothing, and packaging, and India is the world's largest producer. Jute exports accounted for a full third of India's foreign exchange earnings in the 1950s (Cullather 2010, 180–181). But still, most farmers grew foodgrains and they suffered under Nehru.

Many Indians were fiercely critical of the anti-agrarian policies (Saha 2013b, 202), and there certainly were other routes to an industrialized economy. In contrast, when the newly formed Soviet Union set about developing an industrial economy in the 1920s, it began with agriculture, bringing in equipment and expertise to boost farm output (Fitzgerald 1996, 474). But Nehru's urban-centric approach was encouraged by US advisors (Cullather 2010, 199) – at least at first – and rural India lost its champion when Gandhi was assassinated in January of 1948. India had set itself up to need food imports.

PL 480

Meanwhile the US was developing reasons for wanting to send India grain. One reason was geopolitical: the Cold War was heating up with the USSR, the US, and China all eyeing India as a potential client, and in Spring 1951 India was importing grain from all three. At the same time the US's old domestic problem of agricultural overproduction was roaring back with a vengeance (Chapter 4). Acreage reduction programs barely slowed the runaway train of increasingly fertilizer-intensive agriculture, and by 1954, with storage costs for government-purchased farm products topping $700,000/day (Graves 1954), it was actually cheaper to ship grain to distant shores than to store it. That year, farm state senators pushed through Public Law 480 ("Agricultural Trade Development and Assistance Act"),[9] formalizing the policy of disposing of US agricultural surplus where it would further US foreign interests.[10] By 1958 the program had swollen to over $6 billion, with the largest shipments – mainly wheat – bound for India; by 1966, it had spent $22.3 billion shipping food (Harwood 1967).

PL 480 seemed like a win for both the US and India. The US saw it as helping to prevent hunger and thus revolution, while propping up the US hyperproducing industrial agricultural system. The American agrifood system would eventually get much better at soaking up the gusher of surplus farm produce: factory farms would spread, high-fructose corn syrup would be invented, corn would be turned into ethanol, and the public would be swayed to eat more and sweeter foods (Pollan 2006). But in the 1950s, the main way to get rid of surpluses was to dump them on developing countries.[11] In India, the program allowed government monies to go toward heavy industry while helping to feed the urban workforce. Much of the grain flowed through government-run "Fair Price Shops" that proliferated in the 1950s (Mooij 1998, 101). By 1965 there were over 100,000 of these shops, including many in affluent suburbs, and the wheat was being made not just into chapatis but white bread in plastic bags that reinforced a sense of modernity (Cullather 2010, 140, 144). The instantly popular product *Modern Bread* appeared in 1965, made in part from American wheat. The spigot of free grain also gave Indian regulators an invaluable tool for managing prices and public opinion.[12]

But major problems were festering on both ends of the spigot. In the US, the ramped up procurement of farm produce stimulated production in the countryside, exacerbating the surplus problem it was designed to solve. India faced two different problems. The first was the growing sense of vulnerability and dependence among leaders, intellectuals, and the public. When new Prime Minister Indira Gandhi visited the US in 1966, one headline waiting for her was "New Indian Leader Comes Begging" – still remembered in India 50 years later (IndiaToday 2007). When President Lyndon Johnson adopted a "short-tether policy" to force policy changes in India before releasing wheat, embarrassment turned to deep resentment among Indians who knew the food transfers benefited the US as much as India (Goldsmith 1988, 183). The second problem caused by PL 480 was in the impact of cheap grain imports on indigenous agriculture. Food imports are always a double-edged sword: emergency food may save lives when local farming has been disrupted, but large-scale and prolonged imports always undermine local farming. PL 480 food had this effect in various developing countries,[13] but nowhere as much as in India, where over 50 million tons of American grain poured into markets at cut-rate prices, punishing farmers already being squeezed by domestic agricultural policies (Mooij 1998, 83). The flow of American grain accomplished Nehru's goal of keeping Indian grain prices down (Perkins 1997, 175), but this undercut Indian farmers who were "lowballed, mortgaged, and taxed to the point of resignation" (Cullather 2010, 206). In short, importing cheap grain deepened dependence on imported cheap grain, and India's food deficit grew alarmingly as the shipments progressed (Mooij 1998, Perkins 1997, 164). By 1964 the US was sending India 600,000 tons per month and both ends of the international grain conduit were on the verge of crisis.

Famine?

Meanwhile the US was escalating its war in Viet Nam, propelled in part by the fear that a Communist victory would set off a domino effect in Asia. India would be the largest domino and the White House saw it as a particularly wobbly one, especially after the charismatic Nehru, dead of a heart attack in May 1964, was replaced by the weaker Lal Bahadur Shastri. But to President Johnson's frustration, Congress did not share his enthusiasm for aiding India; it was busy slashing foreign aid. Johnson turned to a classic weapon in the neo-Malthusian arsenal: claims of famine. In July 1964 he asked the Indian ambassador to help convince Congress that increased food aid was needed to fight the ongoing famine, leaving a startled ambassador to deny the existence of a famine (Cullather 2010, 217). But, conveniently for Johnson (and, as we will see, for Norman Borlaug as well), the Fall brought the start of a rare weather catastrophe that would bolster the claims of famine.

India divides its agricultural year into two seasons. *Kharif* crops are planted in Spring, watered by monsoons harvested in the Fall; *rabi* crops are planted in Fall, watered by residual moisture and harvested in Spring; either crop may also be irrigated. A major El Niño event in 1965 caused one of the worst droughts of the century, followed by a highly unusual second year of drought. The effects on agriculture were serious; foodgrain production dropped by 19% and US food shipments jumped to over 14 million metric tons. At one point in 1967 grain ships were leaving for India every 10 minutes (Das 2000, 129).

Most affected was the state of Bihar (Figure 6.2), where very little land was protected by irrigation.[14] Predictably, some saw Bihar's situation in starkly Malthusian terms. US government economists and the CIA predicted food shortages and starvation; Nobel laureates and public intellectuals predicted people would soon be feeding on each other and LBJ claimed that "people were being hauled away dead in trucks" (Cullather 2010, 171, 223). In 1966 alone the *New York Times* ran 16 headlines about *famine* in India, and in the Netherlands, schoolchildren fasted to raise relief funds (Reuters 1966).

"Inconveniently," writes Nick Cullather, "Indian officials declared the famine a sham" (2010, 223). Prime Minister Indira Gandhi said that despite a difficult food situation, there was no famine (Dunn 1966), and agriculture minister Chidambaram Subramaniam called it scaremongering. British journalists more familiar with India were also skeptical. India hand Cyril Dunn published "Indian Famine Situation Is Unclear: No Starvation Deaths" (Dunn 1966), and a *London Times* headline read "Food ships streaming into famine-free India" (Times 1966). Later analyses would show there has been no famine at all (more below). Nevertheless, the perception of crisis was timed perfectly to pave the way for Borlaug's seeds.

FIGURE 6.2 Part of north-central India and Pakistan discussed in the text. The hatched area shows the pre-partition state of Punjab.

Seeds

There are no miracles in agriculture, Norman Borlaug wrote in 1970; no single grain can "serve as an elixir to cure all ills of a stagnant, traditional agriculture." Yet the Green Revolution is indeed presented as a triumph of breeding "miracle grains" (Paddock 1970) and Borlaug did credit his seeds with catalyzing a miraculous change in agricultural systems that had been "stagnant" – the term he repeatedly applied to farming systems that he had not fixed yet (Borlaug 1970). Fellow Green Revolutionary MS Swaminathan shared this view and many years later was still claiming that "agriculture growth in India was practically stagnant until the onset of the Green Revolution" (Kulkarni 2019). Actually pre-Green Revolution Indian agriculture was growing surprisingly well considering how it was being undercut (as we will see), and the lineup of seeds in Indian wheat fields was adapted to consumer preferences and economic realities. They were also being constantly improved.

Rice was a much bigger crop in India and the seed lineup was even stronger. Over time rice growers had developed varieties suitable to specific soil types, topographies, and agronomic practices (Saha 2013b, 213.) Moreover, unlike the stagnant food production system in the Green Revolution legend, rice cultivation in India had enjoyed what one historian calls a revolution since the 1940s (Subramanian 2015, 37). During the 1950s, rice yields were rising 5% per year on average – a faster rate of growth than during the Green Revolution years, as we will see.

But US interests had been trying to push Indian scientists and planners toward more input-intensive technologies for years. In the mid-1950s both the RF and the US government began bringing Indian scientists by the thousands for graduate training in US land-grant schools where chemical-intensive agricultural research was booming (Lele and Goldsmith 1989, 318). It is no accident that by 1962 some Indian wheat breeders had begun to breed for stiffer-stalked varieties adapted to high levels of fertilizer (Smale et al. 2008, 421). Plant geneticist M.S. Swaminathan emerged as a leader of the fertilizer-oriented agronomists, and he began a long-term partnership with Borlaug. At Swaminathan's urging, Borlaug toured India in Spring 1963 and then sent Mexican seeds to test, demonstrate, and multiply; Swaminathan reported dramatically superior performance (Perkins 1997, 237).

But it is possible that none of this would have mattered much without the death of Nehru in May 1964. Under Nehru's successor Shastri, a rural Brahmin much less committed to the urban-industry bias, the priority of heavy industry at the expense of domestic agriculture was being rethought. Shastri named the food situation as his top priority and proclaimed a new direction. His new Agriculture Minister, Chidambaram Subramaniam, moved to adjust the financial incentives for farmers to grow more food crops, and by late 1965 he had established higher prices and subsidies for fertilizer (Subramanian 2015, 169). The area planted to wheat, which had been declining, jumped by 17% in 1968 and within five years it was up almost 50%. Many writers believe that it was this policy change more than the new seeds that accounted for the surge in wheat production, but the two were entangled; the seeds were a powerful fetish, and when Shastri announced the change in agricultural strategy he lauded the new seeds. Subramaniam wanted to buy more Mexican seeds in Spring 1965, but lacked the precious foreign exchange; the RF stepped in, buying the 250 tons of seed (Perkins 1997, 241). Then in summer of 1966, India bought 18,000 tons of RF-subsidized Mexican wheat in the largest single seed transaction in history.

Arriving just in time for the *rabi* planting, the seeds were enough to plant just over a half million hectares, almost all in Punjab and some in Haryana and Uttar Pradesh (the states that grew most of India's wheat (Patel 2013)). At the time, 64% of the farmland in this area was irrigated, as compared to 38% for the rest of India (Subramanian 2015, 48). Most of the farms were owned and operated by members of the Sikh ethnic group, and were large, heavily capitalized, and mechanized – among the most prosperous in India. The strategy of directing resources to the wealthiest farmers was called "targeting" and its merits were hotly debated. Meanwhile, dozens of "seed villages" were busy growing enough wheat seed to plant almost 3 million hectares in Fall 1967.[15] Simultaneously, fertilizer-intensive dwarf rice was on its way from the Philippines.

By January of 1968 reports of miracle wheat (and rice) crops began to appear; a *New York Times* headline read "Bumper Crops to Feed More Millions" (McLaughlin 1968). Harvests in the Philippines and Pakistan were mentioned, but it was the 1968 wheat crop in India that became the most storied harvest in history and would launch the Green Revolution legend. The *rabi* wheat harvest came in at 16.5 million tons, a full 45% jump over the preceding drought year. The contrast to the earlier articles about famine and "ship to mouth" existence in India was dramatic. By June headlines announced that India had more grain than it could even store (New York Times 1968a).

Awkwardly for Ehrlich, his *Population Bomb* had just appeared in bookshops.

The Green Revolution Brand Hero

This turnabout was dubbed the "Green Revolution" in an address by US AID[16] administrator William Gaud in March 1968. It was a political speech that included an explicit contrast to the "violent red revolution" of the Soviets (Gaud 1968). The speech was important both for the name it coined and for framing what was happening in India as a humanitarian intervention by Western science led by new "high yielding seeds," claims that would immediately become cornerstones in the Green Revolution legend.

Borlaug quickly emerged as a public figure and the "brand hero" of the Green Revolution (Sumberg, Keeney, and Dempsey 2012). In summer 1968 he took a victory lap in a conference presentation featuring a misleading graph that emphasized the rise in wheat yields while obscuring that farmers had also planted more wheat (which accounted for much of the bumper crop). Convinced that he had achieved the "shock" the farmers needed, he beamed that the "revolution in wheat production which is now well advanced is provoking rapid changes in rice, sorghum, maize and millet production" (Borlaug 1968, 19) – which was patently false. He also began to roll out the narrative that he had saved the world. Scientists and politicians had been "predicting doom for the human race because of the growing imbalance between food production and population growth," he explained, and he himself had been pessimistic that "hungry nations" could even temporarily manage their food production challenges. But now,

> I am optimistic about the outlook of food production in the emerging countries for the next two to three decades. We have demonstrated the feasibility of short cuts to increased production, if such attempts are properly organized and executed by skillful and courageous scientists.
>
> *(1968, 11)*

Borlaug followed up his reference to himself as a skillful and courageous scientist with the remarkable article "A Green Revolution Yields a Golden Harvest" which made a series of breath-taking claims. The Green Revolution was the result of "a spectacular breakthrough in wheat, rice and maize production" that would jump yields from 700 to 5,000 kg/ha and destroy peasant conservatism in one stroke. The Green Revolution, he explained, was already spreading beyond Asia to Africa, generating "new hope for a better life among hundreds of millions of rural people" and injecting "a new rhythm of business activity into formerly stagnant economies." The US press found the story irresistible, and that summer a *New York Times* editorial gushed about the "miracle seeds" behind a "revolution in world agriculture that has begun to produce record crops in a growing number of desperately hungry lands" including the Philippines (suddenly self-sufficient in rice!), Iran (now a wheat exporter!), and Ceylon (record rice harvest!) (New York Times 1968b). All of Borlaug's claims about Africa and yield increases were whoppers, as was almost everything in the Times article. In the Philippines some dwarf seeds had been planted but the country's gap between production and consumption had not changed and President Marcos's announcement of rice self-sufficiency was fraudulent – he was exporting token quantities with great fanfare while secretly importing larger quantities from Hong Kong (Cullather 2010, 170–171). And neither Iran nor Ceylon (Sri Lanka) had planted any dwarf grains at all. Communist China was not mentioned, but it too had bumper harvests in 1968 – indeed one of its best growing seasons ever (McLaughlin 1968) – with no Green Revolution seeds of any kind.

But Mexican seeds were steadily adopted in India's wheat-growing areas during the 1970s as subsidized fertilizer continued to flow and private tube wells were drilled. Many farmers switched back from Mexican wheats to local varieties because of input shortages and better prices for the local wheat and straw (Baranski 2022), but as the local seeds were increasingly displaced this became impossible. The wheat side of the Green Revolution would remain primarily an Indian affair; by 1976, India was still planting half again as much as all other countries combined. The adoption of dwarf rice was much less striking in India (Dalrymple 1978), and reported adoption rates were also greatly padded by extension workers (Subramanian 2015).

Were the Improved Seeds Really Improved?

Although the new seeds are still referred to as "improved," "high yielding," and "modern," it is debatable whether the seeds were really any of these things. India's pre-revolution wheat and rice varieties were not "pre-modern"; they were already quite good in their own way, and Indian breeders were busily developing new varieties, notably wheats that tolerated drought and poor soils and still delivered excellent cooking qualities (Pal 1966). Indian breeders had nothing against fertilizer-intensive crops, but the country had no fertilizer industry to speak of, its fertilizer prices were the highest in the world, and only a small fraction of its farmers were well capitalized enough to want input-intensive seeds. They had developed their own fertilizer-intensive dwarf wheats but did not release them because other varieties were better suited to actual conditions; the Indian variety C-306, released the same year that Borlaug's seeds were approved (1965), outyielded all of the Mexican seeds (Subramanian 2015, 54). Rice seeds were extremely diverse: the head of a rice research institute argued against government promotion of the dwarf seeds on the grounds that they would endanger the variety represented by his institute's collection of 19,000 landraces adapted to a range of local growing conditions (Saha 2013a, 309). Diversity of seeds, rather than a very small number of "improved" seeds, is generally a key element in sustainability for small farmers (e.g., Zimmerer 1998).

In fact, the work of Indian breeders was one reason that before the 1965 drought, Indian agriculture had been growing faster than Indian population. This fact has been carefully scrubbed from the Green Revolution legend of a country "ravaged by overpopulation," but in the past it actually appeared in high-profile forums. When an economist presiding over a 1970 conference on the "revolution" claimed Indian agriculture had been stagnant before 1965, a major Indian magazine pointed out that his own data showed something totally different: between 1949 and 1964, Indian foodgrain production had grown at 3% yearly while population growth had averaged just over 2%. *Scientific American* published a major article in 1967 showing food production beating population growth across the Near East (Pirie 1967), and then one in 1976 – by the chief economist of AID – showing that Indian foodgrain production had climbed slightly faster than population ever since independence (Mellor 1976, 159). Given the impediments to foodgrain production discussed above, these are remarkable facts, and it is shameful that Indian breeders who were adapting wheat and rice seeds to diverse regions and low inputs have been relegated to the dustbin of history by the self-serving myth-makers of the Green Revolution.

It is not even clear that the indigenous wheats were bested by Borlaug's varieties in the India trials. B. Sivaraman, the Secretary of Agriculture, convinced Minister Subramaniam to promote the Mexican wheats after seeing results from two test plots in which the Mexican seeds shone. When Sivaraman later learned that there had been 12 other trials in which local varieties had bested the Mexican seeds, he wrote off those outcomes as the result of sloppy standards and had the field records seized (Sivaraman 1991, 304).

There has also been controversy on how the Mexican seeds performed when not heavily fertilized. Borlaug had pioneered the concept of "wide adaptation" in crops, reversing the established practice of breeding crops in the environment where they would be grown so they would be adapted to local conditions (Baranski 2015b). Borlaug's shuttle breeding selected for the more generalized performers able to grow in both Toluca and Sonora, although not optimal for either setting.[17] Borlaug and his associates lauded wide adaptation as an improvement over local breeding, and this ideal would work its way into breeding ideology in India and elsewhere. Breeders may define wide adaptation as the ability to "excel under any condition" (Baranski 2022), and in 1965 Borlaug and Swaminathan insisted that the Mexican seeds were highly productive even without substantial chemical fertilizing and irrigation. But this was a dubious claim, supported only by a series of trails in which the non-fertilized controls were still planted on carefully managed, fertile research plots (Baranski 2015a, 149). Moreover, while the Mexican dwarf varieties turned in the highest *average* yields, the highest yielders in many tests were tall Indian varieties (Krull et al. 1967, 10). The technicians who actually ran the Indian wheat tests were explicit that "the Mexican varieties show their potential only under very high fertility levels" (Baranski 2015a, 152). In the first years of the "revolution" the Mexican seeds were planted almost entirely on well fertilized and watered fields, and it is unknown how the seeds performed in less fertilized fields where they were later planted. But a RF-funded study of Punjab wheat production in 1967–1968 year found, surprisingly, that the marginal product of fertilizer application to old wheat was three times as high as on the Mexican wheats. This was explained away as an "unreasonable" finding (Subramanian 2015, 176).

The seeds' actual performance under varying levels of fertilizing was a touchy sociopolitical issue. While it is true that Cold War tensions were tearing at its political fabric, India was not simply a pawn in a Cold War tug-of-war; it was struggling in its own distinctive way to balance economic development and social equity. These concerns reverberated through Indian agricultural research, and scientists had to convince economic planners that the technologies they were developing contributed to social equality. "The doctrine of wide adaptation," writes historian of science Marci Baranski, "was a rhetorical lynchpin in these efforts" (2015b, 44); seeds that were known to benefit only the small percentage of farmers who could afford chemical fertilizers would have faced gale force political headwinds. The headwinds would have been even stronger if it was understood who would be subsidizing the fertilizer.

"Fertilizer, Fertilizer, Fertilizer"

Chemical fertilizer is the cornerstone of industrial agriculture and the Indian Green Revolution is very much a story of chemical fertilizer. The story of the US subsidizing its fertilizer industry just when agriculturalists were advocating farm-produced fertilizers echoes in India's Green Revolution but with an ironic twist: the big event for moving subsidized fertilizer-intensive agriculture into the Global South unfolded in a country unusually rich in organic fertilizer. Legumes like black gram, lentils, mung beans, and chick peas feature prominently in Indian foodways and were widely grown, and they were nitrogen fixers that gave soil a long-lasting boost in fertility (Saha 2013a, 300). But the richest source of fertilizer was India's abundant bovines – the buffalo and "sacred cows."

That India's cows went mostly uneaten when the country was importing so much food was galling to many Americans. As a boy in the mid-1960s, India first entered my consciousness as an upside-down country where people starved while cows wandered freely. *The Washington Post* editorialized that even as it faced famine, "India's sacred cows eat food and divert resources that could keep humans alive," a sobering clash between "traditional culture and modern progress" (1967). Americans' exasperation was a product of the times: the US had set off on a hamburger-eating binge that coincided with the rising food shipments to where cows roamed free. The surge in American beef consumption in the 1950s – the first McDonald's opened in 1955 – was an indirect result of the US corn overproduction, as cheap corn poured into the proliferating cattle feedlots.

But India's large national herd was providing a bigger contribution to the food supply alive than it would have as hamburgers. Cattle provided milk, pulled plows, threshed grain, and converted grass and crop stubble into fuel and fertilizer for a population that sensibly ate lower on the food chain. The manure was free and, unlike on those US feedlots, had virtually no environmental or public health cost. On the contrary, Indian residential courtyards are often coated regularly with cow dung slurry, to which many attribute antiseptic properties. (Surprise: some studies have indeed found evidence for Indian cow manure having anti-viral, anti-bacterial, anti-fungal, and mosquito-repelling properties (Girija et al. 2013, Mandavgane, Pattalwar, and Kalambe 2005).)

Years later when recounting the Green Revolution legend, the former Agriculture Minister Subramaniam struggled to explain why chemical fertilizers were superior to this wealth of organic ones.[18] Like Borlaug, he argued that there was not enough manure, and even if there were, so much would have to be applied to the fertilizer-intensive grains that it would "drown the crop" (Subramaniam 1979, 79). But this was a specious argument, notes historian Kapil Subramanian; countries with a lower density of animals like China and Japan had managed impressive production increases with organic fertilizer without drowning crops (2015, 168). There was ample room for Indian farmers to have increased and improved their use of manure; one reason those Chinese farmers got good results was they spent more time than Indians on manure fertilizing (Nair 1983, Subramanian 2015, 181). After the Green Revolution the Indian government would try several schemes for encouraging manure use but the dwarf crops and chemical fertilizer had left less fodder in the fields for cattle and so reduced the amount of manure.

The cost of turning agriculture away from free manure to purchased industrial chemicals was exorbitant. In 1965 India's fertilizer production capacity was low, the quality was poor, and the price was the highest in the world (Cullather 2010, 208). Both importing fertilizer and building plants would take much precious foreign exchange. But despite the rhetoric about "new seeds," the real change the Green Revolutionaries were pushing for was in fertilizer, and Borlaug knew this better than anyone. In a 1967 talk he said "I wish I were now a member of India's Congress; I would stand up out-of-order every few minutes and shout in a loud voice: What India needs now is fertilizer, fertilizer, fertilizer..." (Hesser 2006, 76).

Borlaug may have seen fertilizer simply as a tool in the neo-Malthusian struggle against overpopulation, but anthropologist Eric Ross points out that it was more of a tool for opening markets for American products (1998, 191). For years US companies, with government backing, had been trying to export fertilizer into India and to invest in fertilizer factories there. In 1960 the US had tried to build a fertilizer plant in Bombay with the understanding that six other fertilizer projects would be opened up to American investors (Goldsmith 1988, 184). When this failed to bear fruit for investors, in 1963 the US lobbied India to let the Bechtel Corporation build a group of fertilizer plants, with the Indians buying oil from Bechtel's partners, Gulf and Texaco – a scheme rejected as an infiltration of the Indian food system (Cullather 2010, 208–210, Goldsmith 1988, 184).

The US financial interests were also on display in William Gaud's "Green Revolution" address. After praising the "excellent chance of achieving self-sufficiency in food grains" due to the new seeds, Gaud pointed happily to the extraordinary new dependence by Green Revolution countries on American loans and American fertilizer. Gaud was clearly pleased that Pakistan's fertilizer use had climbed from 30,000 to 430,000 tons since 1960, and

> only foreign assistance can satisfy this need. The Agency for International Development (A.I.D.), which over the past three years has made over $70 million in Development Loans available for fertilizer exports in Pakistan, proposes to lend Pakistan $60 million for this purpose in 1969 alone.
>
> *(Gaud 1968)*

Gaud also delighted in reporting that India was now spending 20% of its foreign exchange to import fertilizer and oil to make it, and that AID was loaning India $200 million to buy more (Gaud 1968).

The TVA, which had grown more enthusiastic about promoting the fertilizer industry than promoting the Tennessee Valley Watershed, became a key actor in this process. The TVA contained the National Fertilizer Development Center, which worked closely with the USAID to provide developing nations with technical assistance. Today this center estimates that the majority of fertilizers in use worldwide – as much as 75% of them – owe their existence to research performed in Muscle Shoals by TVA staff (IFDC 2008, Johnson 2016).

With his own Swaminathan- and Borlaug-inspired visions of high-producing Punjabi wheat fields, Minister Subramaniam emerged as the government point man for the agricultural input industries. In December 1965, with the drought on and concerns about food shortages running high, Subramaniam met with US Agriculture Secretary Orville Freeman and with US fertilizer companies. He announced that the Indian cabinet had approved a series of policies to open up the closely regulated fertilizer market, encourage foreign investment, and subsidize the fertilizer industry. Prices would be largely deregulated, the government would procure fertilizer at favorable prices, and US firms could be majority owners of plants and repatriate their profits. The Indian cabinet allocated $60 million in precious foreign exchange to buy US fertilizer.

The US press reported the arrangements in impressively neo-Malthusian terms. *The Washington Post* explained that fertilizer "was the absolute prerequisite if India ever is to grow enough food from her neglected soil to feed ever-multiplying mouths," and that foreign businesses finally had profit incentives to build fertilizer plants there (Unna 1965). The plan was being withheld from the Indian public to avert "outcry that India has sold itself out to the West" – which "local leftists" were saying anyway – but *The Post* insisted that India had looked out for its own interests – for instance by rejecting the greedy demand from US corporations that India commit to buying all fertilizer they couldn't sell on the open market. But it was later revealed that the Indian government had agreed to precisely that: Subramaniam had met with Freeman the month before and signed a secret treaty stipulating that India would "announce a plan before January 1, 1966 to purchase any fertilizer produced in excess of market demand at world market prices" (Freeman 1965). It seems the "local leftists" had a point. The US fertilizer industry, which had grown by milking the US government for the previous four decades, had a new cash cow.

The Indian government's subsidies for fertilizer companies wouldn't get the stuff into the fields where it was needed for dwarf wheat to yield well; the farmers still had to buy it. Only a small fraction of Indian farmers could buy fertilizer and even the heavily capitalized farmers in the Punjab wanted to be subsidized. The government quickly rolled out a subsidy scheme that gave each farmer a 202 rupees subsidy for every acre cultivated with chemical fertilizers. For the Punjab alone this amounted to credits worth 50.5 million INR to get 27.5 million kg of nitrogen, phosphate, and potassium onto crops (Saha 2013a, 308). But this was just the beginning. Ten years after the Green Revolution's 1967–1968 debut, India's fertilizer consumption had tripled, and within 30 years it was up tenfold.

In 1977, with Green Revolution varieties being planted on half of the wheat fields and one third of the rice fields, India formalized the fertilizer subsidy system with a set of policies that allowed manufacturers to charge high prices and farmers to pay low prices, with the government making up the difference (Shamrao 2011). The government also guaranteed manufacturers a comfortable 12% profit. Eager to board the gravy train, fertilizer companies sprang up quickly, with some entering the ranks of the most profitable companies. Imported fertilizers too were provided to farmers at subsidized prices (Johl 2013, 256). The government budget includes an explicit amount for fertilizer subsidy but this is a highly incomplete figure conducive to "gold plating" – padding expense claims submitted to the government (Johl 2013, 256). Nevertheless the official fertilizer subsidy climbed to 966 billion INR by 2008 before the government finally had some small success in roping in the largesse. For 2017–2018 the amount was 700 billion INR, or around $10.5 billion. The "targeting" with which the Green Revolution began – focusing subsidized inputs on the largest and wealthiest farmers – remains in place, with an estimated 8% of all subsidy going to Punjabi farmers who comprise 2.5% of the farmed area (Johl 2013, 256).

At the end of the day, the result was that while the Green Revolution did not actually produce more food (as we will see), it produced food with a lot more subsidized fertilizer.

Other Industrial Inputs

We have focused on the seeds and fertilizer aspects of the Green Revolution, but industrial inputs in agriculture tend to pave the way for other industrial inputs, and this was particularly true of the Green Revolution. Borlaug's "out of order" rant was not just about "fertilizer, fertilizer, fertilizer" but also about "credit, credit, credit!" (Hesser 2006, 76). His wheats also needed irrigation, irrigation, irrigation, and also pesticide, pesticide, pesticide, since increased irrigation and fertilizer improve habitats for insects and weeds. The jump in insecticide use was particularly unfortunate in the targeted northern states, where DDT and other organochlorines began to appear in wells (Kaushik, Sharma, and Kaushik 2012), breast milk (Sharma et al. 2014), and 100% of wheat samples (Chawla and Kalra 1983). With dwarf rice, pesticide use is estimated to have increased sevenfold (Subramanian, Ramamoorthy, and Varadarajan 1973), although losses to insects remained unchanged as the dwarf varieties were more vulnerable to insects (Pimentel and Pimentel 1990, 330). Borlaug became a combative proponent of pesticides, for which he used the marketing euphemism of "crop protection chemicals" (Borlaug and Dowswell 1995, 123). In 1971, with a consensus forming on the banning of DDT, he took to the stage at the FAO convention and to the op-ed pages of the *New York Times* to insist that pesticides were essential to the Green Revolution. His tirade attacked the "vicious, hysterical propaganda campaign … by fear provoking, irresponsible environmentalists" that was "brainwashing the general public" with "scare tactics" (Borlaug 1971). He expressed special contempt for the "diabolic, vitriolic, bitter, one-sided attack on the use of pesticides" in Rachel Carson's *Silent Spring* (Howe 1971).

But the other major input, irrigation, was more important yet. In late February 1969, one year after William Gaud had proclaimed a "Green Revolution," agricultural economist Wolf Ladejinsky went to the Punjab to report on the new agriculture there. Ladejinsky was a well-known figure in agricultural development circles and hardly a skeptic on agricultural technology; his *New York Times* obituary would praise him as "a prominent voice among Americans engaged in the precarious task of imposing modern agricultural practice on an unyielding Asian tradition" (Montgomery 1975). Yet he gave the Green Revolution a decidedly mixed review. He first questioned the enormous inequity he saw, as "owner-farmers with irrigated land are making money hand over fist, and the bigger the farm the more they make" (Ladejinsky 1969, A73). He then called out the narrative attributing surging wheat production to "miracle seeds." The new varieties had taken over, he wrote, but

> As between them and tube-wells, it is not a case of the chicken or the egg coming first. The tube-wells determine the rhythm of the new technology and, having increased in number from 7,500 in 1960–61 to 110,000 in 1968–69, they are the core of the agricultural transformation of the State…
>
> *(Ladejinsky 1969, A73)*

Historian Kapil Subramanian (2015) shows that Green Revolution seeds had indeed seized credit for production increases that were primarily due to new irrigation facilities. In 1965, a World Bank mission had convinced India to adopt an irrigation policy based on privately owned tube wells.[19] The goal was not simply to produce more food – more irrigation from dams or public tube wells probably would have been better at that – but to promote "high-input, high-output" agriculture (Subramanian 2015, 192, 210–211). With World Bank aid, India mounted a program of subsidizing the spread of private tube wells, which soon became the most important form of irrigation in India. With 5.5 billion INR government spent on loans, subsidies, and rural electrification (in part to run the tube well pumps), by 1969 there were almost a quarter of a million private tube wells operating. Farmer adoption of the new seeds and increased fertilizer hinged on whether they had tube wells (Subramanian 2015, 192–200).

The tube wells were also key to rice production, which boomed in the mid-1970s when wells proliferated on rice farms. The wells not only provided more water but buffered farmers from the monsoon cycle. As with wheat, the role of the dwarf rice seeds has been overstated. Subramanian marvels that the Green Revolution's fans and critics alike have agreed on a "seed-centric narrative," even if they took opposite positions on the seeds' impacts (Subramanian 2015, 38). His analysis negates the seed narrative as well as the obsession with agri-scientific innovation in general: irrigation after all is an ancient agricultural practice, and the spread of tube wells was not prompted by any breakthrough in technology but by a change in state policy (Subramanian 2015, 12).

In His Hands?

President Bartlett's soliloquy on Norman Borlaug followed a press conference in which one President Nimbala of a fictive African republic had gushed about the man who had been able "to make miracles in the world." "In his hands," Nimbala explained, India's "wheat crop increased from 11 million tons to 60 million tons annually." Did India's wheat production really rise that much, and if so was it because the seeds became more than five times as productive in Borlaug's hands? Did this actually constitute a miracle in India's food supply?

The first question is easily checked because agricultural statistics from the quantitative-minded Indian government are readily available. India's wheat harvest in 1968 – the first big harvest of Mexican seeds – was 11.4 million tons and the 60 million figure apparently pertains to 1994 when total production was 59.8 million tons. A 425% increase over 27 years is impressive, but the statistics also show that the contribution of Borlaug's "high yield" breeding was much more modest. Yields per hectare climbed 168% (from 887 to 2380 kg/ha) during these years; the rest of the production increase came from the area farmers in wheat climbing by 97% (from 12.8 mh to 25.2 mh). And the increased wheat planting was not due to Borlaug's hands but to policy changes.

Before 1965 Indian food price policies discouraged wheat production because output above what the government procured at fixed rates offered little profit to the farmer. Market-oriented farmers grew whatever paid well, which often meant export crops that the government incentivized. But Shastri formed two new agencies in early 1965 that would dramatically change farm production. The Agricultural Prices Commission would set more favorable agricultural prices, and the Food Corporation of India (FCI) would procure foodgrains from farmers. Now instead of price ceilings, there would be price floors; farmers could get a good price for as much as they could produce because the FCI would buy unlimited grain at a support price. The procured foodgrain went to government *godowns* (storage facilities) where it could serve as a buffer stock against price fluctuations and be sold at subsidized prices at Fair Price Shops (Mooij 1998, 101). The general policy of unlimited procurement would remain in place and grow into one of the world's largest logistical operations (Subramanian 2015, 165). The overflowing granaries that made my "strange evening in Hyderabad" so memorable were run by the FCI.

The impact of the new policies was dramatic. The prices for a 100 kg of wheat immediately jumped by one third (Perkins 1997, 184) and the area planted in wheat began the climb noted above. For large farmers it was a windfall: in the Punjab average income rose by 70% within two years, while land values doubled or tripled (Frankel 1971, 24–26). Even outside of Punjab, farmers jumping aboard the government gravy train contributed to the start of a wheat boom (Patel 2014). The wheat boom that Borlaug attributed to "skillful and courageous scientists" like himself raising yields was in large part due to Indian farmers growing more wheat because the state paid them more for their wheat. Even William Gaud, who had framed the revolution as a triumph of the "new seeds," later admitted that the price policies deserved primary credit (Cullather 2010, 234).

So was there a miracle in India's *food production*? We have been looking at the Green Revolution crops and especially wheat, but obviously the real issue at stake was food, not any particular grain. India did not specifically need wheat; on the contrary, wheat is less nutritious than the pulses that are important in Indian cuisine. To see how the Green Revolution affected overall food production, let us compare the production trajectories before and after the agricultural seasons of 1965–1966 and 1966–1967 which brought both drought and the first Green Revolution harvest. Figure 6.3 shows what is always swept under the Green Revolution rug: despite the policies that undercut domestic production, Indian food production had been growing fairly rapidly ever since independence. Pre-revolution agricultural growth had actually been "higher than that in other countries during the corresponding stage of their economic development" (Economic & Political Weekly 1971, 88). One good reasons for this was that after 0% growth in colonial-period agriculture between 1900 and 1947, farmers were relieved of punitive land revenue demands and taxes on digging wells and other improvements (Kumar 2016).

Figure 6.3 also depicts the brutal fact that the Green Revolution did not increase the pace of growth of *foodgrain* production at all. The farming system that Borlaug derided as "stagnant, traditional agriculture" was averaging 4.4% growth per year in the 15 years before the drought – despite government disincentives and the undercutting by US wheat – and 3.0% growth per year in the 15 years after the "revolution." What did rise dramatically was not foodgrain production but *fertilizer use*: by 1980 the amount of subsidized fertilizer used to produce a ton of foodgrain had risen almost sixfold from the last pre-drought year of 1965. India experienced a "revolution" in wheat production but farmers devoted less land, labor, and resources to the less subsidized crops.[20] The Green Revolution's increases in wheat, as

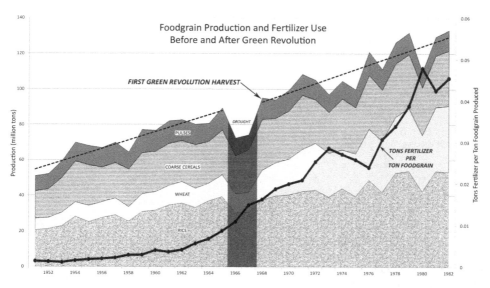

FIGURE 6.3 Trends in India's foodgrain production before and after the 1965-1967 drought and first Green Revolution harvest of Spring 1968. Data on crops are from Directorate of Economics and Statistics; data on fertilizer use are from the Fertiliser Association of India.

Jonathan Harwood puts it, were "purchased at the expense of grain production overall" (2019, 6).

Figure 6.4 shows what happened to the production trajectories for the Green Revolution and other crops. Like Sarma and Gandhi (1990), Subramanian (2015), I omit figures for the drought years of 1965–1967 and followed trends through 1985.[21] Agricultural conditions in India vary enormously from year to year so the production figures do not form neat linear patterns. Still the comparison of trends before and after the arrival of new seeds, subsidies, and incentives is telling. The surge in wheat production is obvious; had overall wheat production kept growing at the pre-drought pace, the 1985 harvest would have been up by 200% from the baseline whereas in reality it up by 582%. But for other crops, production increases *slowed* after the Green Revolution. Especially unfortunate was the slowdown in production of pulses, which were a key source of protein in the Indian diet and hard to import as they were not a widely traded international commodity (Subramanian 2015, 43); they also offer the agronomic benefit of fixing soil nitrogen. Pulses had accounted for 15% of India's foodgrain before the Green Revolution, but dropped to less than half of that in

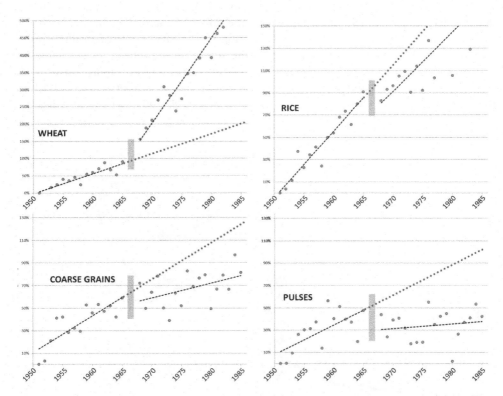

FIGURE 6.4 Yearly production totals before and after the two-year drought and start of the Green Revolution, expressed as percentage change from the 1950 baseline. Dashed lines show actual pre- and post-revolution production trends; dotted lines show how production would have grown if pre-revolution linear trends had continued. Wheat is shown on a different scale than the other food crops. Data are from the India Directorate of Economics and Statistics.

the 1980s. Perhaps most damning to the Green Revolution legend is that production of rice – the other revolutionary dwarf crop – grew *more slowly* after the revolution. Between 1950 and 1965 India's rice harvest was growing at an average of 5.2% per year; if this had continued the national harvest would have been 63.2 million tons by 1985, but with the Green Revolution the growth *slowed* to 4.7% per year and the harvest was 58.3 million tons. Growth of coarse grains also slowed dramatically.

In the years since, wheat production has continued to grow rapidly. India was producing 31% as much wheat as rice in 1950; the figure had jumped to 61% by 1971, to 85% by the end of the millennium, to 93% today. India has turned itself into an industrial wheat-eating nation.

Self-Sufficient?

The last element of the legend to examine is the frequent claim that the dwarf crops delivered India from food dependence to being "self-sufficient in the production of all cereals" (Singh 2011). Despite early claims that the Green Revolution would keep poor countries from running short on food (*Washington Post* 1972), periodic drought-related food shortages and food imports continued. Intermittent food emergencies are probably unavoidable where poverty is rampant, and by September 1971 famine conditions recurred in Pakistan, the second largest adopter of Green Revolution wheat. The next year famine loomed again in India, and a *Washington Post* editorial lamented that the "ostensible purpose of the 'green revolution' was to liberate governments and their citizens from the inevitable caprices of weather" but that it was "like so many other new things – oversold." "The real causes of famine," *The Post* noted in a moment of surprising lucidity, involve social inequities and government unresponsiveness (*Washington Post* 1972).

But the fickle nature of the monsoon is also a cause, as the region was soon reminded. In 1974 the Yale economist Robert Evenson wrote bluntly about the Green Revolution's belly flop, noting that the "optimism that existed three years ago has all but vanished… [t]he adoption of high yielding varieties has fallen short of expectations, and the abnormally poor weather of the past two years has produced serious food shortages throughout the world" (Evenson 1974, 387). As Borlaug basked in the praise for ending India's foodgrain dependency, the country's 1975 imports of 10 million tons of wheat and rice almost equaled the imports during the 1965–1967 crisis, and they were higher than any other year during the PL 480 years. India still imports grain when the monsoons falter, including 6.7 and 5.9 million tons of wheat in 2006 and 2016, respectively (https://www.indexmundi.com/agriculture).

The truth is that India was and is a large country with fickle weather and fluctuating food production. Since independence its food production has tended to grow faster than its population despite agriculture being undercut by pricing policies and wheat imports, but when the monsoons are weak it does what most countries do regularly: import food. The Green Revolution did not change these basic facts of India's situation, although it did make India a ravenous consumer of fertilizer; indeed food shortages stopped being blamed on overpopulation and started being blamed on supply problems in the oil for making fertilizer (Associated Press 1974). These facts are not mentioned by the Green Revolution fetishizers, but they were being recognized within a few years of the first "miracle" harvests. A 1973 US-AID report concluded that the Green Revolution had not impacted the availability of cereal grains per person, and even the RF staff wrote that "India has made no real progress in improving her people-food equation in the decade of the "revolution" (Baranski 2015a, 16). The same year, in *The Death of the Green Revolution* (Bhagavan 1973), a group of academics concluded that the Green Revolution was a piece of defunct propaganda.

Overproduction?

So the Green Revolution did not produce any more food but it greatly accelerated the use of external inputs. Now recall that in our analysis of the basic drivers of industrial agriculture, one was the inexorable tendency to overproduce. So does India today suffer from over-production? On this I tipped my hand in Chapter 1: in some senses, yes. The overflowing granaries described in Chapter 1 were the indirect result of the pricing policies set in place in the 1960s – the same pricing policies that did much more to boost grain production than any "miracle seeds."

The unlimited foodgrains that the FCI procures is supposed to be sold cheaply to the poor, but today less than half of it reaches the poor (Johl 2013, 254); the rest rots, finds its way onto the open market, or is released to grain traders below its acquisition cost (Stone 2002, 615). In recent years the FCI has usually procured 25–35% of the rice and wheat harvest (Saini and Kozicka 2014, 19), an enormous amount of foodgrain that routinely exceeds the FCI's storage capacity of around 90 million tons. When I first came to India in summer 2000 the FCI godowns were bulging with 18 million tons of foodgrain over the norm levels and rapidly climbing. The overage would reach 41.2 million tons by 2002 – ironically, just when a debate was raging about whether genetically modified crops could help India feed its hungry. At the time I wrote that neo-Malthusian observers "need to explain why crop genetic modification will feed hungry Indians when 41.2 million tons of excess grain will not" (2002, 616). The question remains unanswered, and the overage grew to 53.6 million tons by 2012 (Figure 6.5).

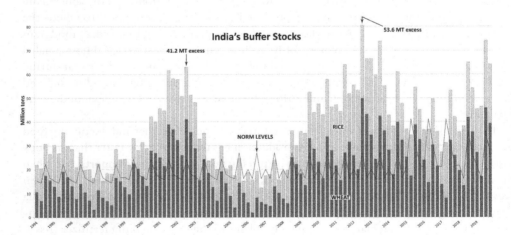

FIGURE 6.5 Trends in wheat and rice stored in the Food Corporation of India's buffer stocks. The jagged line indicates the "norm levels," above which is surplus. The norm levels vary with the season, and they are reset periodically.

Of course whether or not India suffers from "overproduction" is not a simple quantitative question and the phenomenal overages in the buffer stocks are only one indicator. But they do fulfill the criterion of overproduction discussed before: they have high costs and negative consequences. There are crippling costs for maintaining the surplus stocks: the equivalent of $2 billion/year to store the 41.2 million tons overstock (Stone 2002, 615). Of course there are also the financial costs for the government to subsidize the inputs and procure the grain and the environmental costs of the chemical fertilizer, pesticide, and irrigation. "Farmers in Punjab, Haryana and Maharashtra," the BBC observed in 2020, "need to be weaned away from producing an excess of subsidised, water-guzzling crops such as wheat, paddy and sugarcane that deplete groundwater" (Biswas 2020).

Indian agricultural overproduction is not as much of a problem as it has been in the US because Indian agriculture is nowhere near as mechanized and subsidized as US agriculture. But even if we are unlikely to see anything approximating the hyperproducing mega-farms of industrialized US agriculture, we can expect foodgrain production to continue to outpace demand enough to cause serious problems. A careful analysis by agricultural economists projected that by 2025 India would face rice surpluses of 26.9–60.9 million tons; wheat was projected at somewhere between 8 million tons short and 28 million tons surplus. "Managing surpluses," note the authors, "rather than deficits is likely to be the bigger policy challenge for India in the future" (Ganesh-Kumar et al. 2012, vii).

Taking Stock

India's Green Revolution is such a dominant legend in the history of agriculture, and the legend is so starkly at odds with what the numbers actually show, that we need to take a step back and ask what to make of the episode and what it tells us about agriculture.

As noted, the legend has resonated over the years in part because it is such a good story. It has everything. It has India, supposedly careening toward a Malthusian catastrophe; a hero in the person of the telegenic humanitarian breeder; villains including the "monster" of population growth and also the tradition-bound, nay-saying economists and Indian agricultural scientists; and a stirring conclusion, with a food-independent India, a billion lives saved, peasants' "built-in resistance to change" demolished (Borlaug et al. 1969, 11), and a Nobel Peace Prize won.

What this legend gets right is that what happened in Asian agriculture in the 1960s had widespread and lasting effects. What it gets wrong is everything else:

- India was not importing US grain because it couldn't feed itself, but rather allowing the US to dump surplus wheat while India prioritized its heavy industry. Undercut by the cheap imports, Indian farmers were taking land out of food production, not losing a Malthusian battle to feed their country.
- No Malthusian famine was averted. It is true that Indian food imports spiked during the highly unusual 1965–1967 drought, but no major famine occurred. Then the rains returned and the Green Revolution started. If there was no famine during the drought, just what famine was averted? Vandana Shiva (1991) actually makes a plausible case that it *cost* lives by leading to intensified competition over water resources that underwrote waves of violence.

• The Green Revolution itself had virtually no impact on the growth of India's actual food production. Even with wheat imports undercutting its farmers, India's foodgrain production had been growing slightly *faster* than population before the Green Revolution and it slowed slightly after. Farmers grew more input-intensive wheat and less of other crops that were less input-intensive (and more nutritious).

What, then, was the point of it all?

What Was the Point?

Norman Borlaug's fervent speeches and writings tell us much about the actual purpose of the Green Revolution. We know that he was driven by the stark neo-Malthusian dogma of external inputs to agriculture being the only solution to overpopulation. Moreover he was convinced that peasant farmers were backward and stubbornly resistant to change, and that there was no time for their ignorance to be "overcome by massive extension exercises" (Farmer 1986, 184) as others advocated; farmers needed a spectacle to be "shocked" into buying external inputs. Hence the dwarf seed, the genius of which was "to create a cultivar that was at once so spectacularly productive and so needy of the kind of inputs only government could provide" (Cullather 2010, 267). And provide it did. The real "miracle" was not the harvest of wheat but the harvest of government subsidy, in manufacturing fertilizer in factories supported by the government, using fossil fuels subsidized by the government, and making environmental messes that the government allowed. Borlaug was fine with US corporations getting their noses deep into the trough. Once he got peasant farmers "clamoring for fertilizers" he "strongly advocated that the fertilizer industry, specifically ESSO [oil company] representatives, should play an 'enormous role' in the upcoming revolutionary changes" (Saha 2012, 147).[22]

We have seen that replacements of on-farm practices with industrial inputs lead to replacement of smaller farmers with larger farmers who are better input customers. We saw how American agricultural engineers wished to replace farmers with factory workers making labor-saving equipment, and in 1948 RF President Chester Barnard advocated a revolution of agriculture in developing countries, in which "agricultural personnel are taken off the land and out to work in factories to make farm machinery" (Cullather 2010, 67). No one was as enthusiastic about this replacement as Borlaug, who gushed about the promise of his Green Revolution package to not just made more wheat but to "*free farmers from the land*" (Mann 2018, 159). He had nurtured a dim view of farm life and farm work from his youth on a struggling Iowa farm, and when he referred to smallholders he always tacked on adjectives such as backward, stagnant, and obsolete. He knew nothing about the productiveness of Boserupian intensification or the innovativeness of smallholders that Netting showed (Chapter 7). He wanted to get as many of them as possible off the farm, leaving behind just the ones who had been "shocked" into buying fertilizer and pesticides.[23]

But given that the vast majority of India's 100+ million farmers were much smaller and poorer than the Punjabis, Borlaug's strategy of targeting for spectacle and shock would seem ill-fitted and unsustainable, and it was. Policy-makers quickly realized the need to change course, and by 1971 India was starting to redirect resources to integrated rural development programs focused on smaller farms and the UN and the International Labour Office were calling for more labor-intensive technologies and local materials (Harwood 2019, 8). Even the RF, stung by criticism of its programs having neglected the needs of both Mexican and Indian smallholders, set up a project to look at social and political impacts of their technologies and announced that future programs would focus more on unfavorable growing conditions occupied by the rural poor (Harwood 2019). World Bank policy under Robert McNamara shifted attention toward alleviating poverty and devoting more resources to small farms (Harwood 2019).

These efforts are all essentially trying to undo Borlaug's obsession with the large well-capitalized farmers who made for such good customers for input industries – which makes it all the more ironic that boosters of the Green Revolution legend today credit Borlaug not only with saving a billion lives, but with bringing beneficial technology to the small farmer.

But as great as the Green Revolution has been for the industrial agriculture's bottom line, it has been an even bigger win for the field of rhetoric. Propped up by its own "regime of truth," the legend of 1960s India forms the national anthem, the poster child, and the sacred text of neo-Malthusianism (Patel 2013, 7,25). If 1840s Ireland supposedly proved the Malthusian dogma of positive checks on the poor, 1960s India supposedly proved that Malthusian positive checks can be averted if we are willing to hand the reins to Western agricultural technology.

In the early 2000s I attended a lecture by Norman Borlaug at a biotechnology research center in St. Louis. Borlaug was then in his late 80s, but was as combative as ever, heaping scorn on a range of people who diverged from his views on agricultural growth. When the floor was opened after the lecture, one of the first questions came from an Indian biologist who preceded his question with an emotional announcement: "I am one of the billion lives you saved, and I want to thank you." The auditorium was full of highly educated scientists, almost all of whom knew perfectly well that even without Borlaug this young man would have not only lived but eaten the same diet, differing only in perhaps a slightly lower percentage of American surplus wheat. Yet there was a sustained round of heartfelt applause and head nodding. Although Borlaug admirers claim he demurred when credited with saving a billion lives (Mann 2018, 102), he seemed to always accept the praise, as he did, "modestly," in the auditorium that evening.

Notes

1 Daniels' recommendations were explicitly aligned with the policies of left-leaning Mexican President Lázaro Cárdenas, who had enacted land reform and supported the semi-communal peasant ejidos (Olsson 2017, 122).

2 Although it is best to keep "peasant-friendly" in quotes because, as Aaron Eddens (2019) has pointed out, the MAP scientists maintained a condescending and racialized view of peasants and their farming.

3 The US government even funded interventions started by Rockefeller: a case in point was the breeding program started by Rockefeller in the 1940s and funded by the US Department of Agriculture in the 1950s (Patel 2013, 12).

4 There certainly was an economic interest in protecting the Rockefeller family's oil assets in Mexico. In the 1930s the Cardenas regime had nationalized Standard Oil's assets. After 1940 the Camacho regime had abandoned the program and the Rockefellers wanted to prevent the "instability that results from a hungry populace" (Dowie 2001, 107).

5 On the Green Revolution as a Cold War project, see Patel (2013); Perkins (1997, 1990); Cullather (2010).

6 Wheat plants common in the US before mid-century were generally 110–150 cm in height. The "Green Revolution" varieties tended to stand a little more than half as tall. I do not distinguish among dwarf, semi-dwarf, and double-dwarf.

7 "Norin" is an acronym made up of the first letter of each word in the Romanized title of the Japanese Agricultural Experiment Station (Reitz and Salmon 1968). In an ironic twist, one of those American parents of Norin 10 was Turkey Red, which had been famous in the American heartland after Mennonites introduced it in the 1870s. Turkey Red is still sold as a "heirloom" variety, often billed as a "pre-Green Revolution" wheat.

8 By the 1950s the thrust of the program was a crop grown by less than 3% of the number of Mexican farmers who grew maize for subsistence (Harwood 2009, 405).

9 The program would be extended in 1959, renamed "Food for Peace" in 1961, revised in 1966, and reconfigured in 1990 and 2008, but throughout it has generally been known as PL 480 and it is still with us.

10 In theory the grain was not free but sold at a discounted price and paid for in local currency. But this was a ruse to protect government officials from being accused of giving away too much to foreigners; it was understood that the funds would never be used (Das 2000, 128–129).

11 The dumping program was also managed by the Commodity Credit Corporation, an agency insulated from Capitol Hill where foreign aid bills faced headwinds. The CCC representatives assured Indian officials that they could count on the grain shipments for as long as they wanted (Cullather 2010, 143).

12 PL 480 wheat soon became the cornerstone of India's food policy, undercutting Indian wheat. Government officials were especially fond of the free US wheat because it all came through their hands, avoiding the markets that affected Indian-grown grain.

13 In South Korea, for example, wheat imports quadrupled between 1966 and 1977, allowing industrial wages to stay low while depressing farm prices. But the effect can be seen in wealthy countries as well. In the 1870s, changes in trade patterns and transport costs led to Britain being flooded with food imports – mainly grain from the US and refrigerated meat from Australia (Brock 2008, 375). The result was Britain's Agricultural Depression, during which prices for livestock and agricultural products plummeted, arable farmland was abandoned, and rural population left for the city.

14 Adding insult to injury, Bihar suffered a series of destructive floods during the monsoon season.

15 Simultaneously, Green Revolution rice was on its way from the Philippines. Both crops were fertilizer-intensive dwarfs, but they also had their differences. The Mexican wheat breeding started well before there was a formal breeding institute, although by 1963 the International Maize and Wheat Improvement Center (CIMMYT) had come into being to carry on breeding of maize and wheat. With rice, the institute preceded the revolution: the International Rice Research Institute (IRRI) was founded in 1960 and released its first dwarf variety, IR-8, in 1966. IR-8 debuted in the Philippines with much fanfare and claims of revolutionary high yields (Stone and Glover 2017), and by the late 1960s this and other dwarf varieties were being planted in India.

16 The Agency for International Development.

17 The most important factor in wide adaptation was insensitivity to photoperiod, i.e. day length (Baranski 2022).

18 I am drawing on work by Kapil Subramanian (2015), no relation to the Agriculture Minister Subramaniam.

19 A tube well consists of a pipe, usually around 6″ wide, sunk down into an aquifer from which water is pumped by an electric motor. Unlike irrigation canals, tube wells are normally privately owned and managed.

20 An analysis of agricultural trends in India between 1950 and 1989 showed the steady replacement of "coarse grains" (such as maize, sorghum, millet, and barley) by rice and wheat (Byerlee 1992). By the 1980s yields of coarse grains were growing at only 1.1%/year (compared to 2.8% and 2.7% for wheat and rice, respectively) and production of coarse grains was only growing by 0.2%/year (compared to 3.4% and 2.9% for wheat and rice, respectively).

21 However I have lumped the years 1968–1985, rather than separating out the years 1968–1976 as the "Green Revolution" period; the dwarf crops continued to be planted after their adoption in the mid-late 1960s.

22 The windfalls for oil companies followed the Green Revolution into many countries. Colombia borrowed 44 million pesos to invest in chemical fertilizer plants (Hall 1985, 142), most of which were controlled by the Rockefeller Corporation and Exxon (Ross 1998, 186).

23 Resource-poor farmers would not be good customers, and Borlaug consistently fought efforts to send seeds or fertilizers away from capitalist farmers of the Punjab. Even before Borlaug showed

up, some Indian leaders had been garlanding input-intensive farmers, honoring some with the title of "master farmer" (Siegal 2017, 65). With the Green Revolution this class expanded to include
a new population of prosperous mid-sized farmers, well capitalized enough to take full advantage
of the new wave of subsidized inputs, derisively called bullock capitalists (Siegal 2017).

References

Associated Press. 1974. "India Envoy Moynihan Sees '75 Famine There." *Washington Post*, 30 Jan.

Bagla, Pallava, and Richard Stone. 2013. "Science for All." *Science* 340 (6136):1032–1036. doi: 10.1126/science.340.6136.1032.

Baranski, Marci R. 2015a. "The Wide Adaptation of Green Revolution Wheat." PhD, Biology & Society, Arizona State Univ.

Baranski, Marci R. 2015b. "Wide Adaptation of Green Revolution Wheat: International Roots and the Indian Context of a New Plant Breeding Ideal, 1960–1970." *Studies in History and Philosophy of Biological and Biomedical Sciences* 50:41–50.

Baranski, Marci R. 2022. *The Globalization of Wheat: A Critical History of the Green Revolution.* Pittsburgh: Univ. of Pittsburgh Press.

Bhagavan, M. R. 1973. *The Death of the Green Revolution.* London: Third World First.

Binswanger, Hans P., and Vernon W. Ruttan, eds. 1978 *Induced Innovation: Technology, Institutions, and Development.* Baltimore, MD: Johns Hopkins Univ. Press.

Biswas, Soutik. 2020. "What Has Brought India's Farmers to the Streets?" *BBC News*, 3 Dec. https://www.bbc.com/news/world-asia-india-55157574.

Borlaug, Norman E. 1968. "Wheat Breeding and Its Impact on World Food Supply." In *Proceedings of the Third International Wheat Genetics Symposium.* Canberra: Australian Academy of Science.

Borlaug, Norman E. 1999 [1970] The Green Revolution, peace, and humanity. In *Nobel Lectures in Peace 1951–1970.* F.W. Haberman, ed., pp.445–480. Singapore: World Scientific Publishing.

Borlaug, Norman E. 1971. "DDT, the First Domino." *New York Times*, 21 Nov, 13.

Borlaug, Norman E. 1988. "Challenges for Global Food and Fiber Production." *Journal of the Royal Swedish Academy of Agriculture and Forestry Supplement* 21:15–55.

Borlaug, Norman E., and C. Dowswell. 1995. "Mobilising Science and Technology to Get Agriculture Moving in Africa." *Development Policy Review* 13 (2):115–129.

Borlaug, Norman E., Ignacio Navarez, Oddvar Aresvik, and R. Glenn Anderson. 1969. "A Green Revolution Yields a Golden Harvest." *Columbia Journal of World Business* 5:9–19.

Brock, William H. 2008. *William Crookes (1832–1919) and the Commercialization of Science.* Aldershot and Burlington: Ashgate.

Byerlee, Derek. 1992. "Technical Change, Productivity, and Sustainability in Irrigated Cropping Systems of South Asia: Emerging Issues in the Post-Green Revolution Era." *Journal of International Development* 4 (5):477–496.

Chawla, R.P., and R.L. Kalra. 1983. "Harvest Time Residues of DDT and HCH in the Punjab Wheat Crop Untreated with These Chemicals." *Agro-Ecosystems* 8 (3):255–257. doi: 10.1016/0304-3746(83)90008-2.

Cullather, Nick. 2010. *The Hungry World: America's Cold War Battle against Poverty in Asia.* Cambridge, MA: Harvard Univ. Press.

Dalrymple, Dana G. 1978. *Development and Spread of High-yielding Varieties of Wheat and Rice in the Less Developed Nations, 6th edition (Foreign Agricultural Economic Report 95).* Washington, DC: USDA.

Das, Gurcharan. 2000. *India Unbound: The Social and Economic Revolution from Independence to the Global Information Age.* New York: Anchor Books.

Dowie, Mark. 2001. *American Foundations: An Investigative History.* Cambridge, MA: The MIT Press.

Dunn, Cyril. 1966. "Indian Famine Situation Is Unclear." *The Washington Post*, 7 Apr.

Economic & Political Weekly. 1971. "How Green Is the Green Revolution?" *Economic and Political Weekly* 6 (2):88–90.

Eddens, Aaron 2019 "White Science and Indigenous Maize: The Racial Logics of the Green Revolution." *The Journal of Peasant Studies* 46(3):653–673. doi: 10.1080/03066150.2017.1395857

Evenson, Robert. 1974. "The "Green Revolution" in Recent Development Experience." *American Journal of Agricultural Economics* 56 (2):387–394. doi: 10.2307/1238772.

Farmer, B. H. 1986. "Perspectives on the 'Green Revolution' in South Asia." *Modern Asian Studies* 20 (1):175–199.

Fitzgerald, Deborah. 1996. "Blinded by Technology: American Agriculture in the Soviet Union, 1928–1932." *Agricultural History* 70 (3):459–486.

Fox, Richard G. 1989. *Gandhian Utopia: Experiments with Culture.* Boston, MA: Beacon.

Frankel, Francine R. 1971. *India's Green Revolution: Economic Gains and Political Costs.* Princeton, NJ: Princeton Univ. Press.

Freeman, Orville L. 1965. Telegram from the Embassy in Italy to the Department of State. U.S. State Dept., Office of the Historian, https://history.state.gov/historicaldocuments/frus1964-68v25/d253

Fung, Brian. 2012. "Engineering a More Nutritious Banana." *The Atlantic* 17 May. http://www.theatlantic.com/health/archive/2012/05/engineering-a-more-nutritious-banana/257331/

Ganesh-Kumar, A., Rajesh Mehta, Hemant Pullabhotla, Sanjay Prasad, Kavery Ganguly, and Ashok Gulati. 2012. "Demand and Supply of Cereals in India: 2010–2025." *IFPRI Discussion Papers* 01158:Jan.

Gaud, William. 1968. "The Green Revolution: Accomplishments and Apprehensions." Address to the Society for International Development. http://www.agbioworld.org/biotech-info/topics/borlaug/borlaug-green.html

Giesen, James C., and Mark Hersey. 2010. "The New Environmental Politics and Its Antecedents: Lessons from the Early Twentieth Century South." *The Historian* 72 (2) Summer:271–298.

Girija, D, K Deepa, Francis Xavier, Irin Antony, and PR Shidhi. 2013. "Analysis of Cow Dung Microbiota-A Metagenomic Approach." *Indian Journal of Biotechnology* 12 (3):372–378.

Goldsmith, Arthur A. 1988. "Policy Dialogue, Conditionality, and Agricultural Development: Implications of India's Green Revolution." *The Journal of Developing Areas* 22 (2):179–198.

Graves, Aubrey. 1954. "Farm Price Support Debate Gets Hotter." *The Washington Post and Times Herald*, 6 Aug.

Gray, George W. 1950. "Blueprint for Hungry Nations." *New York Times*, 1 Jan.

Haggerty, John J. 1945. "Wartime Shifts in Latin American Agriculture." *Foreign Agriculture* 9 (5):75–81.

Hall, Lana L. 1985. "United States Food Aid and the Agricultural Development of Brazil and Colombia, 1954–73." In *Food, Politics, and Society in Latin America*, edited by J. Super and T. Wright, 133–149. Lincoln: Univ. of Nebraska Press.

Harrar, J.G., Paul C. Mangelsdorf, and Warren Weaver. 1952. Notes on Indian Agriculture. Rockefeller Foundation Archives, RG 6.7, Box 10cl8.

Harwood, Jonathan. 2009. "Peasant Friendly Plant Breeding and the Early Years of the Green Revolution in Mexico." *Agricultural History* 83 (3):384–410.

Harwood, Jonathan. 2012. *Europe's Green Revolution and its Successors: The Rise and Fall of Peasant-Friendly Plant Breeding.* London: Routledge.

Harwood, Jonathan. 2019. "Was the Green Revolution Intended to Maximise Food Production?" *International Journal of Agricultural Sustainability.* doi: 10.1080/14735903.2019.1637236.

Harwood, Richard. 1967. "LBJ Cites World Risk of Famine." *The Washington Post*, 7 Nov.

Hesser, Leon. 2006. *The Man Who Fed the World: Nobel Peace Prize Laureate Norman Borlaug and His Battle to End World Hunger.* Dallas: Durban House.

Howe, Marvine. 1971. "DDT's Use Backed by Nobel Winner." *New York Times*, 9 Nov. https://www.nytimes.com/1971/11/09/archives/ddts-use-backed-by-nobel-winner-borlaug-denounces-efforts-to-ban.html.

IFDC. 2008. TVA Fertilizer Technology Used Worldwide – But Few New Products since 1970s In *AAAS EurekAlert*. https://www.eurekalert.org/news-releases/618391

IndiaToday. 2007. 1966: No Confidence. *IndiaToday*, 2 July. http://indiatoday.intoday.in/story/1966-indira-gandhi-became-the-prime-minister/1/155559.html

Johl, S.S. 2013. "Economics and Politics of Farm Subsidies in India." In *Agricultural Sustainability: Progress and Prospects in Crop Research*, edited by Gurbir S. Bhullar and Navreet K. Bhullar, 253–261. London: Elsevier.

Johnson, Timothy. 2016. "Growth Industry: The Political Economy of Fertilizer in America, 1865–1947." PhD, History, Univ. of Georgia.

Kaushik, C.P., H.R. Sharma, and A. Kaushik. 2012. "Organochlorine Pesticide Residues in Drinking Water in the Rural Areas of Haryana, India." *Environmental Monitoring and Assessment* 184 (1):-103–112. doi: 10.1007/s10661-011-1950-9.

Krull, C.F., I. Narvaez, N.E. Borlaug, J. Ortega, G. Vasquez, R. Rodriguez, and C. Meza. 1967. *Results of the Fourth Inter-American Spring Wheat Yield Nursery, 1963–1964. CIMMYT Research Bulletin No. 7.* Mexico, D.F.: CIMMYT.

Kulkarni, Vishwanath. 2019. Towards a Hunger-free India. *The Hindu (Business Line)* 27 January. https://www.thehindubusinessline.com/specials/businessline-25/towards-a-hunger-free-india/article26103979.ece

Kumar, Richa. 2016. Putting Wheat in Its Place, Or Why the Green Revolution Wasn't Quite What It's Made Out to Be. *The Wire,* 31 October. https://thewire.in/76956/green-revolution-borlaug-food-security/

Kumar, Richa. 2019. "Visioning Agrarian Futures on Selective Readings of Agrarian Pasts: India's Green Revolution and Beyond." *Economic and Political Weekly* 54(34). https://www.epw.in/journal/2019/34/technology-and-society/indias-green-revolution-and-beyond.html

Ladejinsky, Wolf. 1969. "The Green Revolution in Punjab: A Field Trip." *Economic and Political Weekly* 4 (26):A73–A82.

Lele, Uma, and Arthur A. Goldsmith. 1989. "The Development of National Agricultural Research Capacity: India's Experience with the Rockefeller Foundation and Its Significance for Africa." *Economic Development and Cultural Change* 37 (2):305–343. doi: 10.2307/1153832.

Mandavgane, S.A., V.V. Pattalwar, and A.R. Kalambe. 2005. "Development of Cow Dung Based Herbal Mosquito Repellent." *Indian Journal of Natural Products and Resources (IJNPR)* 4 (4):270–273.

Mann, Charles C. 2018. *The Wizard and the Prophet, Two Remarkable Scientists and Their Dueling Visions to Shape Tomorrow's World.* New York: Alfred A. Knopf.

McLaughlin, Kathleen. 1968. "Bumper Crops to Feed More Millions." *New York Times*, 19 Jan.

Mellor, John W. 1976. "The Agriculture of India." *Scientific American* 235 (3):155–163.

Montgomery, Paul. 1975. "Wolf Ladejinsky, Land Reformer, Dies; Helped to Break Feudal System in Japan." *New York Times*, 4 July. https://www.nytimes.com/1975/07/04/archives/wolf-ladejinsky-land-reformer-dies-helped-to-break-feudal-system-in.html.

Mooij, Jos. 1998. "Food Policy and Politics: The Political Economy of the Public Distribution System in India." *The Journal of Peasant Studies* 25 (2):77–101. doi: 10.1080/03066159808438667.

Nair, Kusum. 1983. *Transforming Traditionally: Land and Labor in Agriculture in Asia and Africa.* New Delhi: Allied Publishers.

New York Times. 1968a. "India Has Problem in a Bumper Crop: She Lacks Storage Space after Period of Drought." *New York Times*, 23 June.

New York Times. 1968b. "Save the Good Revolution." *New York Times*, 18 July.

Njoroge, James. 2020. NGOs & Foundations Want to Dictate Africa's Agricultural Destiny. *European Scientist*, 28 October. https://www.europeanscientist.com/en/features/ngos-foundations-want-to-dictate-africas-agricultural-destiny/

Olsson, Tore C. 2017. *Agrarian Crossings: Reformers and the Remaking of the US and Mexican Countryside.* Princeton, NJ and Oxford: Princeton Univ. Press.

Paddock, William. 1970. "How Green Is the Green Revolution?" *Bioscience* 20 (16):897–902.

Pal, B.P. 1966. *Wheat.* New Delhi: Indian Council of Agricultural Research.

Patel, Raj. 2013. "The Long Green Revolution." *The Journal of Peasant Studies* 40 (1):1–63. doi: 10.1080/03066150.2012.719224.

Patel, Raj. 2014. "How to be Curious about the Green Revolution." 29 August. http://rajpatel.org/2014/08/29/every-factoid-is-a-mystery-how-to-think-more-clearly-about-the-green-revolution-and-other-agricultural-claims/

Pearse, Andrew. 1980. *Seeds of Plenty, Seeds of Want: Social and Economic Implications of the Green Revolution*. Oxford: Clarendon Press.

Perkins, John H. 1990. "The Rockefeller Foundation and the Green Revolution, 1941–1956." *Agriculture and Human Values* 7 (3):6–18. doi: 10.1007/bf01557305.

Perkins, John H. 1997. *Geopolitics and the Green Revolution: Wheat, Genes, and the Cold War*. New York: Oxford Univ. Press.

Phillips, Ronald l. 2013. "Norman Ernest Borlaug." *Biographical Memoirs of Fellows of the Royal Society* 59:59–72.

Pimentel, David, and Marcia Pimentel. 1990. "Comment: Adverse Environmental Consequences of the Green Revolution." *Population and Development Review* 16:329–332. doi: 10.2307/2808081.

Pirie, N.W. 1967. "Orthodox and Unorthodox Methods of Meeting World Food Needs." *Scientific American* 216 (2):3–11.

Pollan, Michael. 2006. *The Omnivore's Dilemma: A Natural History of Four Meals*. New York: Penguin.

Rama, Napolean G. 1966. "Miracle Rice – Instant Increase!" *Philippines Free Press*, 6 Aug, 5, 70–71.

Reitz, L.P., and S.C. Salmon. 1968. "Origin, History, and Use of Norin 10 Wheat." *Crop Science* 8 (6):686–689. doi: 10.2135/cropsci1968.0011183X000800060014x.

Reuters. 1966. "Pupils Fast to Give Aid." *Washington Post*, 10 Feb.

Rosenstein-Rodan, P. N. 1944. "The International Development of Economically Backward Areas." *International Affairs (Royal Institute of International Affairs 1944-)* 20 (2):157–165. doi: 10.2307/3018093.

Ross, Eric B. 1998. *The Malthus Factor: Population, Poverty, and Politics in Capitalist Development*. London: Zed Books.

Saha, Madhumita. 2012. "State Policy, Agricultural Research and Transformation of Indian Agriculture with reference to Basic Food Crops, 1947–1975." PhD, History of Technology and Science, Iowa State Univ.

Saha, Madhumita. 2013a. "Food for Soil, Food for People: Research on Food Crops, Fertilizers, and the Making of "Modern" Indian Agriculture." *Technology and Culture* 54 (2):289–316.

Saha, Madhumita. 2013b. "The State, Scientists, and Staple Crops: Agricultural "Modernization" in Pre-Green Revolution India." *Agricultural History* 87 (2):201–223. doi: 10.3098/ah.2013.87.2.201.

Saini, Shweta, and Marta Kozicka. 2014. Evolution and Critique of Buffer Stocking Policy of India. Indian Council for Research on International Economic Relations.

Sarma, J.S., and Vasant P. Gandhi. 1990. *Production and Consumption of Foodgrains in India: Implications of Accelerated Economic Growth and Poverty Alleviation*. Washington, DC: IFPRI.

Shamrao, Tanpure Sambhaji. 2011. "A Study of Fertilizer Policy in India." *International Journal of Agriculture Sciences* 3 (3):145–149.

Sharma, A., J.P. Gill, J.S. Bedi, and P.A. Pooni. 2014. "Monitoring of Pesticide Residues in Human Breast Milk from Punjab, India and Its Correlation with Health Associated Parameters." *Bulletin of Environmental Contamination and Toxicology* 93 (4):465–471. doi: 10.1007/s00128-014-1326-2.

Shiva, Vandana. 1991. *The Violence of the Green Revolution*. London: Zed Books.

Siegal, Benjamin. 2017. "Modernizing Peasants and 'Master Farmers': Progressive Agriculture in Early Independent India." *Comparative Studies of South Asia, Africa, and the Middle East* 37 (1):64–85. doi: 10.1215/1089201x-3821309.

Singh, Salil. 2011. "Norman Borlaug: A Billion Lives Saved." *AgBioWorld*. http://www.agbioworld.org/biotech-info/topics/borlaug/special.html.

Sivaraman, B. 1991. *Bitter Sweet: Governance of India in Transition*. New Delhi: South Asia Books.

Smale, Melinda, Joginder Singh, Salvatore Di Falco, and Patricia Zambrano. 2008. "Wheat Breeding, Productivity and Slow Variety Change: Evidence from the Punjab of India after the Green Revolution*." *Australian Journal of Agricultural and Resource Economics* 52 (4):419–432. doi: 10.1111/j.1467–8489.2008.00435.x.

Stewart Jr., C. Neal, Harold A. Richards IV, and Matthew D. Halfhill. 2000. "Transgenic Plants and Biosafety: Science, Misconceptions and Public Perceptions." *BioTechniques* 29:832–843.

Stone, Glenn Davis. 2002. "Both Sides Now: Fallacies in the Genetic-Modification Wars, Implications for Developing Countries, and Anthropological Perspectives." *Current Anthropology* 43:611–630.

Stone, Glenn Davis. 2018. "Agriculture as Spectacle." *Journal of Political Ecology* 25 (1): 656–685. doi: 10.2458/v25i1.22385

Stone, Glenn Davis, and Dominic Glover. 2017. "Disembedding Grain: Golden Rice, the Green Revolution, and Heirloom Seeds in the Philippines." *Agriculture and Human Values* 34 (1):87–102. doi: 10.1007/s10460-016-9696-1.

Subramaniam, Chidambaram. 1979. *New Strategy in Indian Agriculture: The First Decade and After.* New Delhi: Vikas.

Subramanian, Kapil. 2015. "Revisiting the Green Revolution: Irrigation and Food Production in 20th Century India." PhD, History, Kings College London.

Subramanian, S.R., K. Ramamoorthy, and S. Varadarajan. 1973. "Economics of IR-8 paddy-a Case Study." *Madras Agricultural Journal* 60:192–195.

Sumberg, James, Dennis Keeney, and Benedict Dempsey. 2012. "Public Agronomy: Norman Borlaug as 'Brand Hero' for the Green Revolution." *Journal of Development Studies* 48 (11):1587–1600.

Swaminathan, M. S. 2012. "Food as People's Right." *The Hindu*, 3 Jan. http://www.thehindu.com/opinion/lead/food-as-peoples-right/article2769348.ece.

The Times. 2009. "Norman Borlaug: Agronomist and 'Grandfather of the Green Revolution'." *The Times*, 14 Sept. https://www.thetimes.co.uk/article/norman-borlaug-agronomist-and-grandfather-of-the-green-revolution-bt0qx2btpsf.

Times, London. 1966. "Food Ships Streaming into Famine-free India." *London Times*, 29 Feb, 8.

Unna, Warren. 1965. "Profit Motive May Spur Indian Fertilizer Output: Profit Incentive May Increase Indian Fertilizer Output." *The Washington Post*, 15 Dec.

Vidal, John. 2014. "Norman Borlaug: Humanitarian Hero or Menace to Society?" *The Guardian*, 1 April. https://www.theguardian.com/global-development/poverty-matters/2014/apr/01/norman-borlaug-humanitarian-hero-menace-society.

Wallace, Henry A. 1941. "Wallace in Mexico." *Wallace's Farmer*, 22 Feb.

Washington Post. 1967. "India's Cow Crisis." *Washington Post*, 21 May.

Washington Post. 1972. "India: Wheat, Famine and Domestic Policy." *The Washington Post, Times Herald*, 16 Dec.

Zimmerer, Karl. S. 1998. "The Ecogeography of Andean Potatoes." *Bioscience* 48 (6):445–454.

7

THE THIRD AGRICULTURE

Before turning to the "third" (intensive) agriculture let's address the elephant in the room: is there even any point in discussing alternatives to industrial agriculture? Whatever problems there may have been on the industrial agricultural road we have been traveling, you will certainly hear that we must face "things as they are," to quote Malthus, and admit that realistically we have no choice. If industrial agriculture really is the only way to feed the world today and in the future, then it doesn't matter that much if its appropriative technologies pollute, externalize costs, inexorably overproduce, and are only made viable by lavish government subsidy.

We have seen that chemical fertilizer in particular is at the heart of industrial agriculture, and even questioning it will get you accused of promoting mass starvation; the claim that industrially fixed nitrogen from the Haber-Bosch process feeds the planet is presented as an argument-stopping fact. But then Norman Borlaug's wheat saving a billion lives is also presented as a fact, and we have seen this claim dissolve when compared to actual numbers on growth of Indian food production. Does the claim about nitrogen stand up to scrutiny? Is it possible that we don't need the endless gusher of fertilizer (even if *industrial agriculture* does)?

The claim is often supported by the influential technology writer Vaclav Smil (2001, xiii), who writes that the world's "expansion from 1.6 billion people in 1900 to today's 6 billion would not have been possible without the synthesis of ammonia." This certainly sounds like we would still be at 1.6 billion people if not for Haber. Smil actually points out that we could get by with much less fertilizer, but he is still cited as proof of our desperate need for Haber-Bosch nitrogen. For instance a recent article in the prestigious journal *Nature:Geosciences* cites Smil among other sources to supposedly prove that by 2000, Haber-Bosch nitrogen fertilizer was "responsible for feeding 44% of the world's population" (Erisman et al. 2008). The article includes a chart showing the world population booming after World War II right along with the percentage of the world "fed by Haber-Bosch nitrogen," and a line suggesting there would be more than 3 billion fewer people without this technology.

DOI: 10.4324/9781003286257-7

When I showed the graph to my colleague, demographer Geoff Childs, he laughed. Unlike the chemists who wrote the article, he actually studies causes of population change, and he recognized this a classic case of spurious association. He explained:

> Post WWII global population growth was propelled primarily by baby booms the US, Europe and Japan, areas that constituted a much larger share of global population than they do today. The secondary cause was improved healthcare and sanitation in poorer countries which led to what we call the epidemiological transition: child mortality dropped quickly and fertility rates dropped more slowly. It would be very difficult to credit fertilizers for the decrease in infectious diseases. Could fertilizer have led to more food as an inducement to have more kids? Actually fertility rates were dropping in Asia, Latin America and the Middle East in the 1960s-70s (Bongaarts and Watkins 1996), just when fertilizer use was going up in those areas, especially where Green Revolution crops were adopted.

Conveniently, the FAO issued a major report on the state of food and agriculture in 1955, which was just after the *Nature:Geosciences* authors claim Haber-Bosch nitrogen let world population take off (FAO 1955). The report shows that the same areas that were using the most fertilizer before WWII – Europe, North America, and Japan – were using 90% of global fertilizers in 1954. This means that all except 10% of the fertilizers that supposedly let population grow to new levels were actually being used in areas with *no food shortages*. On the contrary, "the most disquieting feature of the food and agricultural situation in recent years," said the FAO, was the emerging problem of surpluses: "the accumulation of large unsold stocks of grain and other agricultural products, which clearly means that not all the increase in production has gone to raise the world's inadequate levels of nutrition and clothing" (FAO 1955, 90).

So in the Global North, industrial agriculture became even more industrialized and overproductive – especially in the US after World War II, as we have seen. We have also seen that the world would have been a better place had this not happened, and it is fanciful to assume that food shortages would have blocked population from rising above the dashed line.

So is there another form of high-producing agriculture that can keep us fed? Yes: there is a third agriculture. The first agriculture was based on Malthus's dogma that agriculture only grows by putting more land under the plow, and that two ears of grain could never grow where only one had grown before; the second agriculture is industrialized and it grows *eight* ears of corn where one grew before, but only by inexorably overproducing, externalizing costs, and sucking subsidies from government like a gargantuan leach. The third agriculture is what captivated the attention of Robert Netting under the mango tree in Chapter 1. It takes diverse forms, but it is distinctive in that production can – and does – grow *without* major dependence on industrial technologies. Instead it grows by changing practices, labor, and local technology: people do things differently, work more, and devise local technologies. Such agricultural growth has been documented and analyzed by scientists from many perspectives and we tend to agree on many of its key features, but not on its name: it has been called ecological agriculture, peasant agriculture, labor-driven intensification, Boserupian intensification, and intensive sustainable smallholder agriculture (Robert Netting's term).[1] For simplicity's sake I will use the term most common in the scientific studies of it: intensive agriculture (as distinguished from industrial agriculture). The term to avoid is "subsistence farming," which is misleading even though intensive agriculturalists do produce much of their own food; virtually all intensive farmers sell some produce. The common assumption in agricultural development circles that "smallholders live outside the market and must be assisted into it" is misinformed, notes Michael Dove; on the contrary, the real problem for smallholders "is not how to get into the market, but how to stay –partly – out of it" (Dove 2011, 6, Stoll 2017, 72).

Industrial agriculture fans will insist that the idea of highly productive agriculture based on labor and local technology is unrealistic, romantic, even crunchy, but it is not; it has been well described, analyzed, and fit into a general theory. Just as Malthus insisted on going to the first principles of agricultural growth – even though he got the principles wrong – we can peel back the layers of what makes intensification work. The Nigerian Kofyar from Chapter 1 were a classic case of intensive agriculture, and they still offer us an excellent window into how it works and changes. They are also interesting because they are in sub-Saharan Africa, which is routinely described as an agricultural backwater with hopeless soils in dire need of external scientific technology. Yet their agriculture is highly productive and in most ways more sustainable than the industrial agriculture that many outsiders would send their way. Let's explore this case and what it tells us about intensive agriculture, and then turn attention to the intensive agriculture scene today.

The Kofyar Homeland: Sustainable Intensive Farming

The Kofyar homeland (Figure 7.1) has long been crowded by rural African standards, with close to 500 people per km^2 in many areas (Stone 1996, 60).[2] The main reason for the crowding was protection. For centuries the small, militarily vulnerable groups in the Middle Belt of Nigeria had been preyed on by the more powerful empires to the north, whose cavalries threatening to steal livestock and capture slaves. The Jos Plateau had a steep and jagged southern escarpment that was impenetrable to cavalry. The Kofyar did not choose their location on aesthetic grounds, but the location certainly paid aesthetic dividends; the valleys and peaks offered striking scenery and the promontories provided enchanting panoramic views of the plains below. Their word for home, *koepang*, literally meant "of the mountain," although by the early 20th century they had also spread into a band of settlement at the escarpment base, where Netting first encountered them in Doemak village.

Most of the Kofyar lived in individual farmsteads with a residential compound of adobe huts surrounded by an annually cultivated infield. Infields were planted in intercrop mixtures, most commonly a combination of sorghum, pearl millet, and cowpeas (black-eyed peas). Crop mixes were strategic: the millet ripened early and the sorghum late, so that families could work their fields steadily throughout the season. Most households also had outfield plots on the edges of settled areas, which were usually cropped intermittently and allowed to fallow part of the time. Outfield plots were planted in grains like corn and acha, vegetables like green beans, legumes like peanut and Bambara nut, and root crops like cocoyam and sweet potato.

Late in the dry season, Kofyar planted seeds in irrigated nurseries so that transplantable seedlings would be ready as soon as the rains arrived. Fields had long since been cleared of rocks, and they were tilled with large Sudanic hoes, with the soil being arranged in waffle ridges that checked runoff and erosion (Figure 7.2). Within villages, most of the trees were

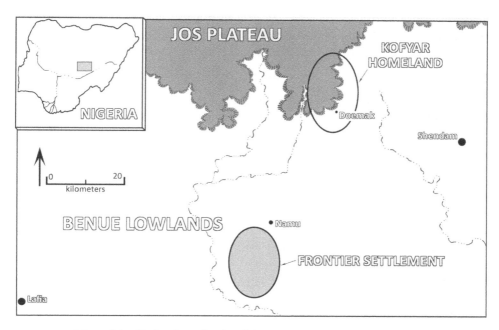

FIGURE 7.1 Map of the Kofyar homeland and frontier settlement area, central Nigeria.

FIGURE 7.2 Left: A work group in a Kofyar hill village tills the land, forming waffle ridges for planting. Right: The Sudanic hoes that are the only tool needed. Photos by G. D. Stone.

economic, with the mango trees providing fruit and shade while the palm and canarium trees provided flavorful cooking oils which were both consumed and sold in local markets. Between villages, wooded areas were left in part to provide firewood and habitat for game animals.

For fields cultivated year in and year out, soil fertility is obviously crucial. Commentaries on African farming like to lament the continent's infertile soils (Smil 2001, 146) and assume, in good neo-Malthusian fashion, that Africans will be lost until they can buy industrial fertilizers:

> Exhaustion of the soil caused by the lack of fertilizers is depressing yields and pushing agriculture onto more erodable soils. Organic agriculture is nearly always nitrogen starved unless land is set aside for the sole purpose of producing green manures, a luxury the poor can ill afford. Agriculture as it is practiced now in much of sub-Saharan Africa is environmentally unsustainable and a new approach that will require considerable investment in agricultural research is needed.
>
> *(Chrispeels 2000, 3)*

The Bill and Melinda Gates Foundation, which is zealous about trying to industrialize African agriculture, claims that more fertilizer shops are crucial because farmers have to walk "50 kilometers or more" to get fertilizer (Gates Foundation 2014).

Seriously? Actually the Kofyars' verdant fields of grains, vegetables, and root crops were well fertilized without sacrificing land for green manure or depending on "investment in agricultural research." Each household kept a small herd of goats and sheep in a corral during much of the year; by spring the animal wastes and uneaten leaves had composted into what the Kofyar called *zuk* – rich compost, often six feet deep. The *zuk* was heaped into baskets and spread on the fields, where it was augmented by hearth ashes and other organic household refuse (Figure 7.3). The nitrogen-fixing action of cowpeas further boosted soil fertility. Where these measures were not sufficient, nightsoil was collected and composted

FIGURE 7.3   A homeland infield after compost had been distributed but before it was tilled with hoes. Photo by G. D. Stone.

in small structures at some distance from residences. The combined effect was a productive landscape that was well fertilized and nitrogen-rich.

Many writers have claimed over the years that too much nutrient value is lost in manuring for it to be sustainable, that population expansion leads to "writing check after check against the land's nitrogen account while making wholly insufficient deposits to replenish those stores" (Charles 2005, Loc 1107). But we saw no indications that crop yields were on the decline. In fact, the Kofyar had *improved* the landscape in terms of productivity and fertility.

Kofyar livestock not only provided fertilizer, but they could be eaten or would walk themselves to the market to be sold. Except for the purchased steel hoes that would last an adult a lifetime, the Kofyar relied on virtually no external technologies, loans, or hired services. Their agriculture was powered entirely by human labor, from the construction of terrace walls and stone corrals to the tilling, fertilizing, planting, weeding, harvesting, and animal husbandry. It was all developed indigenously, with no input from agricultural extension, government programs, farmer field schools, or NGO interventions.

The Kofyar were harvesting an average of 0.5 tons/acre of threshed grain and legumes from their infield plots in the 1960s, which was close to the 0.5-0.7 tons/acre US corn farmers were getting a few decades before – and this did not count the unmeasured tubers, sauce crops, and vegetables scattered in the infields (Netting 1968, 97). Contemporary production on US industrial farms was in the process of climbing to much higher levels, after decades of heavily government-supported seeds and fertilizers, but let us not forget that much of that production was problematic surplus attained at enormous environmental and public health cost. Coupled with produce from outfield plots, trees, hunting, and the occasional livestock slaughter, the dense population managed to keep itself normally well fed using entirely indigenous methods with virtually no external dependencies. The picture of sub-Saharan farming that was widely accepted at the time – and that is still surprisingly common – was that it was unproductive, destructive, and unable to improve or change without coaching and external technology. The Kofyar showed this to be an ignorant caricature.

Agricultural Change and Surplus Production

Farming in the homeland was highly productive but it produced little marketable surplus, and the Kofyar had been probing other areas for market opportunities. In the 1950s some Kofyar began to clear bush farms in the Benue Valley a day's walk to the south beyond the small town of Namu. Netting visited the frontier settlement area in 1961, finding that the Kofyar here had promptly abandoned their intensive farming practices for "slash and burn" cultivation. They used fire to clear trees and then planted in the ashes for several years before turning to a fresh patch of forest. Here was another myth exploded: slash and burn, or "swidden farming," was widely seen as the practice of backward wastrels who didn't know any better, certainly not farmers coming from a tradition of highly productive systems of annual cultivation. The swidden fields were highly productive, and to their previous roster of crops the Kofyar added cassava, rice, and yams to sell in local markets. (This was the white-fleshed African yam, a staple in Nigerian cuisine, not the sweet potato that is often called yam in the US.)

In the mid-1980s a group of us began a new round of research on the Kofyar frontier (Netting, Stone, and Stone 1993, Stone 1996, Stone, Netting, and Stone 1990). We were particularly interested in the processes of agricultural change and movement into the cash economy. Had the slash and burn practices proved unsustainable? Had the Kofyar readopted intensive methods? How much food were they contributing to the growing Nigerian cities? Had their new semi-cash economy upended the social conventions that had worked so well in the homeland?

One of the takeaways from our research was that the same people who had provided such a striking case of sustainable mainly-subsistence farming were now thriving as cash croppers. While the Kofyar had become more deeply enmeshed in the market economy, they had worked out their own careful balance of cash and noncash transactions and dependencies. All households provided for most of their own staple foods and all households raised a surplus for the market, with many selling impressive amounts of yams, rice, peanut, and millet. They were providing for the majority of the labor on their farms and also participated in communal labor arrangements; many households also hired some wage laborers for peak times. Consumer goods had begun to appear in Kofyar households but mostly of a practical nature such as bicycles, motorcycles, aluminum roofs, clothing, and radios.

Slash and burn methods had largely disappeared; the tree cover was greatly reduced and many of the trees were ones the Kofyar had planted for shade and fruit. Farming indeed had been re-intensified, running largely on human labor with little external technology beyond the ubiquitous hoes (Figure 7.2). Chemical fertilizers were available intermittently and were bought by some farmers, but given the cash expense and the unreliability of supply, most were making manure compost again, now from pigs as well as the sheep and goats. No Kofyar owned agricultural machines, although they would occasionally hire tractors from town for specific jobs.

The physical technology may have been simple but the social technologies for mobilizing human labor and expertise was anything but. There now was a densely packed agricultural calendar that produced sorghum, pearl millet, cowpeas, maize, yams, rice, peanuts, and sesame, along with several minor crops. There was a complex interlocking schedule with an intricate balance among each crop's ecology and the timing of its labor demands (Stone, Netting, and Stone 1990).

The frontier farmers had adapted homeland social institutions for organizing work and had developed new ones as well. Household labor was the most important and also the most flexible and skilled. But also crucial were festive labor parties called *mar muos* – literally "beer farming" – which would attract up to 100 community members to work and then socialize over a large batch of millet beer. Neighborhood work exchange groups called *wuk* were also useful for certain agricultural tasks; the work was compensated only with reciprocity, which was important at times when millet for beer brewing was in short supply. Church groups would hire themselves out to raise money for the church; groups of young men would hire themselves out for particularly arduous tasks in exchange for a meal of pork or mutton.

"Innovation" does not only refer to technology. Some of the Kofyars' most effective innovations involved farming strategies and uses of local labor. Let me illustrate with two inventive practices that had appeared on the frontier.

The first was "advance heaping." On the frontier Kofyar often rotate fields between yams (planted in knee-high heaps) and grains (the millet-sorghum-cowpea mix). But in grain fields, after the millet is harvested the remaining sorghum plants are invaded by *striga* weeds that can greatly lower sorghum production. The Kofyars' innovation was to make the heaps for the *next year's* yams in *this year's* grain field, working around the still-ripening sorghum plants (Figure 7.4). This doesn't only uproot the striga: it also eliminates what would be a serious labor bottleneck the next Spring when preparation of grain fields competes with the time-consuming job of making the yam heaps.

The second innovation was "wuk selling." The wuk reciprocal labor groups involved 10–20 workers from nearby households, meeting several times each week to work in turn on each participant's farm on whatever task the farm owner put them to. But with market transactions playing an increasing role in household economies, the person hosting the wuk could need cash more than farm work. This led to the innovation of selling the wuk labor to a neighbor: instead of directing the group to a task on the host's own farm, the host would direct the group to the farm of a neighbor, who would then pay the wuk host.

The Kofyar frontier farm system looked nothing like the neo-Malthusian vision in which Western technologies are bestowed on hapless African peasants with their infertile soils and inferior seeds, allowing them to buy more external inputs and become commercial farmers. But it was a more realistic and sustainable situation. These farmers were feeding themselves and also producing an impressive surplus for the market: the average farm in the main settlement area south of Namu was 5.5 ha in size and responsible for over 1,000 yams and nine 90-pound bags of grain, along with smaller quantities of legumes, vegetables, and meat (both chicken and pork). The system was innovative, dynamic, and self-supporting with no state subsidized inputs. It was also sustainable by any reasonable definition of that term. It was not depleting aquifers or degrading soils. Farmers were dependent on no external inputs, although they did occasionally buy a bag of fertilizer or hire a tractor.

FIGURE 7.4 A field after a work party for advance heaping. The stalks on the ground are from pearl millet harvested several weeks before; the man points to where a quick crop of sesame has been planted in the heaps. Photo by G. Stone.

A Unique Case?

African farmers living under crowded conditions but farming productively and sustainably – and with little reliance on external technology – are certainly a surprise, given what we are used to hearing. Was this a freak case?

Hardly. Without even leaving Nigeria we can find many well-described examples of highly productive intensive farming. In the south, Ibos raised yams and cassava and oil palms with fertilizers made from local resources (Morgan 1957, Udo 1965) and ingenious simple water harvesting systems; in the north, Hausas in peri-urban areas grew grains with manure from their own farms and from the city (Mortimore 1993). Some of the very first European descriptions of West African farming were of intensive systems. European slave traders were amazed at the intensive farming in densely populated Whydah (today, Nigeria's neighbor, Benin):

> European visitors wrote of agriculture in Whydah in rapturous terms. William Smith noted that "the natives were so industrious that no place that was thought fertile could escape being planted, though even within the hedges that enclose their villages and dwelling places, and they were so very anxious in this particular, that the next day after they had reaped they always sowed again without allowing the land any time to rest." In this way they managed to get three or even four harvests in a single year. Although they did not let the land lie fallow, they preserved the fertility of the soil by a system of crop rotation: peas, rice, millet, maize, potatoes, and yams were planted in strict succession. The areas near hedges and walls were used for planting melons and vegetables… not an inch of land was wasted.
>
> *(Harms 2002, 159)*

While the crops and tactics varied, what these farming systems had in common is that they all developed under conditions of high population density. Throughout much of the 20th century, when sub-Saharan Africa was colonized by European powers, colonial officers took for granted that high populations meant environmental destruction. But this too proved a myth. An instructive case comes from across the continent in Kenya's Machakos District. In the early 20th century the British colonial regime confined Akamba herder-farmers to the Machakos native reserve – in some ways analogous to an American Indian reservation. In 1937 a colonial soil conservation officer lamented that the Akamba were over-populating because they were "free from the checks of war and…disease, under benevolent British rule." Some areas were showing signs of soil erosion and the Akamba, the official explained, "are rapidly drifting to a state of hopeless and miserable poverty and their land to a parching desert of rocks, stones and sand" (Tiffen, Mortimore, and Gichuki 1994, 3). In 1990 the World Bank engaged a team of Africanist geographers to reconstruct what had happened in Machakos following these dire predictions. The researchers found that population had climbed sixfold since the 1930s, but the agricultural system that had arisen was intensive, sustainable, and profitable. Steep hillsides were terraced and most farmers were getting two crops of maize and minor crops each year from fields well fertilized with manure and compost. Aside from providing for their own food sufficiency farmers were earning income from coffee. The takeaway from the study gave the name to the remarkable book *More People Less Erosion* (Tiffen, Mortimore, and Gichuki 1994).

Intensive smallholder farming by Africans is particularly interesting because these are the farmers that are so often depicted as destitute bumpkins desperate for just about *anyone* to tell them how to farm and give them a bag of fertilizer. Nobody batted an eyelash when PBS ran a news story about a young American man with no agricultural experience who visited Kenya and decided to "use his new MBA skills" to help smallholders there, buying them some seeds and fertilizer which immediately gave them "the best harvest of their entire lives" (PBS Newshour 2012). But worldwide there are an estimated 2.5 billion smallholders (defined as owning under two hectares) (Zimmerer, Carney, and Vanek 2015) and they manage to grow most of the food eaten in the developing world and, as we will see, there are substantial and growing populations of neo-smallholders in Europe and North America. But we have highlighted Malthus's insistence on going back to first principles to ask what really drives agricultural systems. We took a hard look at Malthus's own first principles and then at the drivers of industrial agriculture. Let us explore the first principles of intensive farming before we consider the promise of smallholders today.

Boserup and the Science of Intensive Agriculture

Ten years before Paul Ehrlich's ride in a Delhi taxi, Ester Boserup (Figure 7.5) took her own ride in rural India. Her ride also generated an insight into population, but it was a starkly different one from Ehrlich's, and it would revolutionize scientific understanding of nonindustrial agriculture.

An expert in the economics of agricultural policies, Boserup came to India in 1957 as part of a multi-country study of agriculture in Asia (Myrdal 1968). We know that during this time the theory of "labor surplus in agriculture" was widely accepted (Chapter 6). As the influential economist Paul Rosenstein-Rodan wrote about the developing world,

> there is a tremendous waste of labour, because a very considerable number of the people living on the land are, in fact, either totally or partially unemployed. They are the sons, cousins, uncles and aunts, who live on a farm and pretend to do something…It

FIGURE 7.5 Economist Ester Boserup circa 1978. Drawing by Mia Villani.

is an instance of what economists call "disguised unemployment," and all the agrarian economists of the world agree that if those people were removed from the land agricultural output, far from falling, would increase.

(1944, 160)

Mid-century thinkers essentially agreed with Malthus that once land is put under the plow, little more can be done, and further population growth could lead only to poverty. But while there may have been a consensus on this point, there was no evidence to back it up; none of the economists had actually looked closely at agricultural work in the developing world. But Boserup did, and she saw that intensity of land use was quite variable. Some fields were planted only once per year even though the environment allowed for double cropping; those farmers didn't raise a second crop because they had good-paying work in nearby coal mines (Boserup 1999, 17–18). Yet when population grew and more local labor became available, farmers changed their whole approach to the landscape:

> a forested landscape becomes a landscape of fields with shorter and shorter fallow, dry land becomes irrigated, hilly land terraced, etc. The larger population need not go hungry, as the classical economists assumed, and with them the neo-Malthusians. Instead, the increasing population gradually transformed the environment, and this led to a different diet and new techniques of cultivation.
>
> *(Boserup 1999, 20)*

Jettisoning the theory of labor surplus in agriculture, Boserup placed farming practices on a continuum that included long fallowing, short fallowing, annual cultivation, and multi-cropping (more than one harvest per year). Virtually any piece of land could be cultivated well below its productive capacity with long periods of rest or it could be productive year in and year out without fallowing. Less fallowing meant more productivity in the long run, and this was what generally happened as landscapes became more crowded. This pattern was striking in rural India, and subsequent research showed her that the more and less intensive agricultural systems, ranging from long fallow systems to multi-cropping systems around the world, "were adaptations not to differences in environment and culture, but to differences in population densities" (Boserup 1999, 18). Her 1965 book *The Conditions of Agricultural Growth: The Economics of Agrarian Change under Population Pressure* formulated a general theory of agricultural practice based on the heretical observation that "agricultural developments are caused by population trends rather than the other way around" (Boserup 1965, 12). Malthus had gotten it not just wrong, but backward.

Boserup also had something startling to say about technology. Recall that neo-Malthusians replace Malthus's original view of inelastic agriculture with the insistence that agriculture only grows by new external inputs being sold to farmers. This idea was crystallized in the influential book *Transforming Traditional Agriculture*, in which economist Theodore Schultz (later a Nobel laureate) described peasant farmers as "poor but efficient" and only able to grow their agriculture with external inputs and technologies. Boserup's examples showed that demography drives agricultural change more than technology does; intensification does not require external technology and technology may change little. Sometimes a new technology or crop may prompt a change in farming, but the much more common pattern is that smallholder farmers figure out how to intensify when they have to, adjusting their practices

and technologies as need be. Her theory was revolutionary, and it released what one economist called the "stranglehold which the Malthusian logic had on the thought patterns of the
orthodox economists" (Wolfe 1936, 243).[3]

Boserup also stressed that the potential for intensification contradicted contemporary
Cold War fears about an overpopulated Third World (Cullather 2010). As she later wrote,

> my conclusion was the opposite of the general opinion at that time, when it was
> believed that the carrying capacity of the globe was nearly exhausted and that the
> ongoing demographic transition in developing countries would result in soaring food
> prices and mass starvation.
>
> *(Boserup 1999, 21)*

It bluntly countered the modern environmental movement's views of agricultural growth
that became popular soon after its publication. (*Conditions* appeared three years before Ehrlich's *Population Bomb*, but he clearly had not read it.)

Boserup's release of the stranglehold hinged on the details of agroecology.

Agroecology and Agricultural Intensity

The variation in farming practices – the different ways a plot could be cultivated – that were
unimportant to Malthus is at the heart of Boserup's theory. The key are the differences in
agro-ecology along the continuum of intensive and extensive agriculture.

Extensive farming is also known as *long fallowing, shifting cultivation, swidden farming* (which
means fire-based), or *slash and burn*; all refer to a system in which trees or bushes are burned
off and the plot is cultivated for a limited period of time and then left to fallow. The magic
of extensive farming is its built-in efficiency: it lets fire and fallow do most of the work.
To turn a patch of forest into a farm plot, you have to (1) clear enough of the canopy for
light to get through, (2) boost the soil fertility, and (3) reduce the populations of weeds and
insects. Fire does all three jobs. Swidden farmers usually cut some trees or bushes to dry
in place and serve as fodder in a controlled burn. The cutting and burning open the field
to sunlight; the heat kills weeds and insects; the leftover ash boosts soil fertility. Seeds are
then usually planted in holes made with a "dibble stick." Swidden plots are rarely weeded
much. After a period of cultivation, the farmer shifts to a new field and leaves the old one
to become a fallow.

Fallows allow the soil to regain fertility; as ecological succession occurs and grasses are
replaced by bushes and eventually by trees, "the forest manures itself" as organic farming
pioneer Sir Albert Howard (1940, 25) put it. The return to forest also provides fodder for
the next time the field is burned for cultivation. But we now know that fallow fields contain
dozens or even hundreds of plant species useful for construction, medicine, animal fodder,
spicing, food, or sale (Cairns 2007). Fallows are also resources for providing animal foods,
and landscapes with fallows at different stages of succession provide a mosaic of habitats that
makes for something of a supermarket for hunting.

The many advantages of extensive farming explain why this type of agriculture was discovered and used by almost all farming cultures where population density was low. Even studies
in the early US find shifting cultivation over and over again, from Scandinavians in the Del-
aware Valley (Jordan and Kaups 1989) to Britons in the Virginia piedmont (Nelson 2007).

As Netting (1989, 223) points out, the US Midwest was settled by shifting cultivators including Abe Lincoln's father, who "went from one wilderness clearing to another, blaming bad luck but getting crops with a minimum of effort and moving when the hunting declined." And contrary to the image of slash and burn as the height of environmental irresponsibility, most cultivation done by this method throughout history has been sustainable. Today the Amazon rainforest provides alarming images of destruction by slash and burn farming, but slash and burn had been practiced there for at least 6,000 years before state policies from the 1970s on encouraged deforestation (Hecht and Cockburn 1989).[4]

However swidden farming has one key limitation: it requires a large land base and fairly low population density. If population density rises, there is little choice but to shorten fallow times. Instead of allowing plots to return to forest, farmers must recultivate plots with bush cover and then those with grass cover, and then fields are put under no-fallow annual cultivation and finally under multi-cropping regimes. Fallow shortening means less and less fodder to burn, so less effective control of pests and less fertilizing ash at the same time that farmers need better pest control and more of a fertility boost. Other problems arise as well; for instance grassy fields may leave a dense root mat that the firing does not break down, making it harder to plant and weed. As fallows shorten, farmers have to take over more and more of the work that was done by fire and fallow. They have to adopt more time-consuming and laborious ways to manage the soil and control pests. They may eventually even have to adopt the plow – which, although you may think of it as a "labor saving" device, means a lot more work than burning and fallowing. As the benefits of fire and fallowing are sacrificed, farmers not only work more hours, but *proportionately* more hours for each unit of output: their labor gives diminishing *marginal returns* and is less *efficient* in terms of energy put in and taken out. To Boserup this is the key to agricultural variability, because farmers generally prioritize production per hour worked, not production per acre. This is precisely why Boserup said we should not expect intensification except where it was forced by population.

But intensification surely does squeeze more food from the land: cultivating fields more and fallowing less raises the yield per unit of area over time. A swidden plot can be productive when it is being cultivated, but its long-term productivity is low because it spends much of its time in fallow. Technically, then, intensification can be defined as raising production per unit of area over time by accepting lower labor efficiency, and in Boserup's theory movement along the continuum is driven by population density. But to understand why intensification both raises production and also lowers labor efficiency, we need to take a look at what intensive farmers actually do any why they do it.

What Intensive Farmers Actually Do

There is much local variation in intensive agriculture, but there are also some key patterns in the farmer's toolbox. Let us look at some of the salient aspects of intensive cultivation.

The most pervasive single problem intensive farmers confront is soil fertility, and they use an astonishing variety of materials for fertilizer – compost, legumes, cakes of sesame and turnip seeds, straw, ash, cinders, bonemeal, fish meal, animal urine, mollusk shells, marl, and pond muck. But animal manure has always been the king of fertilizers, and farmers often become connoisseurs of the stuff. Second century BC Roman writers evaluated various types of dung for fertilizing meadows, gardens, and field crops (Cato 160 BC); in the first century AD they compared the dung of birds, humans, and all major forms of livestock. For the Kofyar, goats and sheep were the key manure producers; indigenous Andean farmers used bird guano if they lived on the coast and llama and alpaca manure in the mountains (Cushman 2013, 7); for farmers in eastern China the source was pigs, fed a special diet to improve the fertilizing quality of their output. The benefits of manuring are both immediate and long term. In a study in England, researchers applied dung to a field for 20 years and then stopped; a full century later, the field was found to retain higher level of fertility than grounds never fertilized (Stoll 2002, 51).

On-farm livestock have long been the preferred source of manure, not only because of their proximity but because the animals could also be eaten, sold, used for traction, or deployed for social status. Operations that combine the synergies of crops and livestock are practicing *farm-level metabolism* but for millennia farmers have also relied on *town-country metabolism* whereby urban manure is moved to farmland, removing pollution while helping to feed the town. Manure was sold out of Athens and Rome, and Jerusalem even had a "Dung Gate" through which manure was hauled (Semple 1932). In Canton, China, farmers had city stable manure shipped to their farms where they mixed it with fertile mud from canals and nitrogen-fixing clover to ferment for a month before being applied to their rice crop (King 1911). The earliest evidence for town-country metabolism comes from scatters of broken pot sherds around ancient cities in the Near East, showing where urban street detritus had been swept up with animal manure and brought out to farmers (Wilkinson 1982). I saw the same process in 1984 in the countryside surrounding the Nigerian city of Kano, in which thousands of goats and sheep roamed free producing copious amounts of *taki* (manure). Collectors transported the taki, along with street detritus, out to the farms in the "Close Settled Zone" where it was sold or traded for agricultural products.[5]

Some areas of the world also have developed organized trade in human manure, or night soil. Detailed accounts from 13th century Han-cho, China, describe a highly organized trade in night soil collected from residences and brought to surrounding farms, allowing an urban life without sewers and a farming system dependent on recycling valuable organic material, "an ecologically symbiotic relationship unmatched in the Western world" (Netting 1993, 48). Heavily fertilized farmland extended outward from Chinese cities to the distance a hauler could travel in a day's round trip. Chinese farmers were connoisseurs of these organic fertilizers and would sometimes travel to particular towns to procure animal or human dung with particular qualities. In some places night soil from foreign settlements within Chinese cities fetched a premium, as the farmers found it to be richer due to more varied diets (Vogt 1948, 221).

Town-country nightsoil metabolism not only contributed to intensive sustainable farming, but kept cities cleaner than where there were "modern" sewage systems. For much of the 19th century Tokyo had a system of daily removal or nightsoil to peri-urban fields. Water quality tests in the 1870s found that Tokyo, a crowded pre-modern city with a population of more than a million, had cleaner water than London, the largest city in Europe's first industrial nation, which used the latest metal pipe technology. In parts of China, Korea, and Japan the metabolism has continued well into the 20th century (Tarr 1975, 598–599).

Tillage (land preparation) is another ubiquitous feature of intensive farming because roots of grasses and shrubs impede planting. For the Kofyar the Sudanic hoe was an ideal tool for loosening and turning the soil, uprooting weeds, and creating the waffle ridges that controlled water flow. The animal-drawn plow also turns the soil and uproots weeds, and it is obviously one of humanity's great inventions. Yet it is not used by swidden farmers, who do not have to till soil, and it is also useless in many productive intensive systems including root crop systems and intercropped systems like the Kofyars'. Even when the plow is adopted, its labor savings in the field itself come at a substantial cost for acquiring, training, feeding, and housing the draft animals (Netting 1993, 132–133). Moreover the field must be cleared of stumps and roots, which is difficult and time consuming.[6] This is why even farmers who are well aware of the plow historically have not adopted it unless they are obliged to farm intensively (Pryor 1985).

Stepped-up weed management is another element in intensive systems. Swiddeners rely on a hot fire to kill but without a good burn the time demands for weeding can climb sharply; in the case of the re-intensifying frontier Kofyar, 30% of a full work schedule went to weeding (Stone, Stone, and Netting 1995).

Fertilizing, tilling, and weeding are the three biggest demands on farmers' time and energy as fallows shorten, but techniques and tactics adopted in intensive systems are almost infinitely variable; agriculture is elastic because it can be stretched in so many different ways. Some of Malthus's own specific examples of the inelasticity of agriculture turn out to be superb examples of its elasticity. Of mountain pastures, Malthus wrote:

> The limits to the population of a country strictly pastoral are strikingly obvious. There are no grounds less susceptible of improvement than mountainous pastures. They must necessarily be left chiefly to nature; and when they have been adequately stocked with cattle, little more can be done.
>
> *(1826, 123)*

However a study of agriculture and population in alpine Switzerland showed how much more can be done after the pastures are stocked with cattle: the creative Swiss farmers boosted both hay production and herd size by digging irrigation ditches, using fertilizer, and manually moving soil top check topsoil erosion (Netting 1981).

We now know that, ironically, Malthus's book – with its conviction that farmers can do little to raise production – was published in the middle of a century of intensification and the fastest yield growth in Britain's history (Bennett 1935, 28). But smallholder intensification was happening long before that. The Anglo-Saxons who populated England in the 5th century AD initially mostly farmed extensively and grazed livestock, but by the 8th century expanding populations in many areas led to more labor-intensive cultivation, with moldboard plows, manuring, and ridge-and-furrow fields similar to those of the Kofyar (Banham and Faith 2014, 74-76, 294). Accounts from the 16th century show English farmers to have become connoisseurs of soil fertility management:

> The best manures were, for general purposes, dung from sheep and corned horses; for dry grassland, from pigeons and poultry; and for dry soils, from pigs. In warm soils, well-rotted composts of short dung were preferred, and in cold, long dung that opened the land and decomposed in it. For composting, vegetable matter was readily available. Old thatch, offal straw, rushes, bracken, thistles, fallen leaves and other things were soaked in ponds...Near the coast, seaweed (ore) was much used.
>
> *(Kerridge 1967)[7]*

In "Low Country" (in today's Netherlands and Belgium), as early as early as the 13th century high-density populations had practiced a textbook Boserupian system of cultivation with high yields per acre and virtual elimination of fallow. This was made possible by heavy fertilization and cultivation of crops on fallows. Writes historian Bruce Campbell,

> The agricultural system which resulted from these developments was remarkably intensive and reached its fullest fruition on small and medium-sized farms with less than 10 acres of arable land. On these holdings productivity per capita was sacrificed to productivity per unit area, and economic viability was maintained only by employing labour-intensive techniques-spade cultivation, careful weeding, and heavy fertilization-and by cultivating high value crops.
>
> *(1983, 26–27)*

The common denominator is all of these farming systems are high levels of work and low levels of external inputs. To Malthus, hard "exertions" in agriculture were a Godly virtue in a human race that was "inert, sluggish, and averse from labor, unless compelled by necessity" (Levin 1966, 94). There actually is a small sliver of agreement with this in Boserup's intensification theory: farmers **don't** put in the added work of intensification unless compelled (or incentivized). But this was not because humans are loafers but because down deep they are economists; intensive farming really is less labor-efficient.

The inherent laziness that obsessed Malthus – he even categorized the different ways in which the Irish, native Americans, and others were lazy (Levin 1966, 94) – was nowhere to be found among the Kofyar. They were putting in long hours, with much of the work being physically demanding, and they had no major breaks in the schedule; they had carefully chosen some cropping strategies to fill in relative slack times and to extend the season (Stone, Netting, and Stone 1990, 15–20). Yet I never once heard a Kofyar complain about the work of farming.[8] Bob Netting was also struck with the Kofyar's unflagging enthusiasm for work in their fields (1968, 182–183); he believed that intensive farmers generally cultivated such a work ethic. Like practitioners of any trade, if a technology offers to save them work and has no serious downside, they are likely to adopt it, but this doesn't mean they dreaded the work they were doing before. When you hear outsiders bemoaning the horrible toil of farming, it is probably not empathy you are hearing, but a self-serving pitch from people with interests in external inputs.

The Lessons of Intensive Agriculture

The cases touched on here are only the tip of an iceberg of research on intensification. Boserup's *Conditions of Agricultural Growth* (1965) and Netting's *Smallholders Householders* (1993) are key sources, but the scientific literature has dozens of case studies, controlled comparisons, and cross-cultural statistical studies (for summaries see Stone 1996, 203).

There have also been arguments on particular aspects of Boserup's theory. Most challenges have concerned simplifications and factors the theory holds constant. All general theories make simplifications, and this one is no different (Stone 2001, Stone and Downum 1999). In particular it holds constant factors of culture, ecology, and politics:

- *Culture.* In Boserup's theory, farmer responses to population pressure are determined by the energetics of agricultural ecology, not by culture. The causal arrow runs from population density to agricultural practices and from there to other cultural institutions like land tenure (Boserup 1965, 79).[9] But actually cultural institutions can affect how farmers respond to population pressure. On the Namu frontier, alongside the Kofyar were Tiv who migrated up from a homeland where they were known for the use of aggressive tactics to elbow other farmers out of the way, keeping population density down and agriculture extensive. Kofyar and Tiv had the same crops and tools, but they responded differently to population pressure. The Kofyar, for the most part, intensified their agriculture as Boserup predicted; the Tiv put more energy into seeking fresh land or driving away other populations (Stone 1997).

- *Ecology.* Boserup writes that the process of intensification cross-cuts environments and types of crops, but her agro-ecological dynamics do not really apply to all environments. There are "non-Boserupian" ecological conditions where farmers cannot raise productivity by investing more labor; our example was ancient Puebloan farmers in the Wupatki area of Arizona, where production was limited more by water than land (Stone and Downum 1999). There are also some crops for which high-input cultivation is as (or even more) efficient as low-input cultivation; the best example is paddy ("wet") rice which actually tends to be more efficient than upland ("dry") rice (Padoch 1985, Stone 2001). This is an enormous exception to the model.

- *Politics.* Boserup describes farmers as free to adjust their practices, but they may lack access and control over the resources necessary to intensify. They may not own the land or may not be able to enforce their ownership rights, they may be denied access to materials they need to devise new technology, and they may have inescapable demands on their labor. For instance, after *More People Less Erosion* was published, scholars pointed out that Machakos land holdings had become polarized over the years, with larger farmers prospering and many poorer farmers having to rely on nonfarm work and struggling financially. Agricultural innovation had been led by wealthier farmers (Murton 1999, Siedenburg 2006). Boserup's focus on how farmers can and do intensify agriculture holds constant the fact that some cannot.

But while recognizing these simplifications, the theory does provide a sound economic and ecological explanation for how and why ***agricultural productivity can and does rise as a result of population growth.*** Netting's *Smallholders* offers a trove of cases and statistics on what intensive agriculture productivity offers.

Agricultural intensification is not dependent on external inputs or instruction. New external technologies can boost production in some situations, especially if and when propelled by state subsidy, but agricultural growth has never been purely dependent on external technology and the neo-Malthusian dogma that the world can only be fed with more external technologies is certainly false. Agricultural growth can occur without external scientific interventions, and it may not even require technological change at all, as the Kofyar show. And the more extreme neo-Malthusian positions such as the belief that "smallholder farmers in Africa are poor – like their parents and grandparents before them – because the productivity of their labor in farming has not yet been enhanced by any of the modern applications of science" (Paarlberg 2008) are possible only through a breathtaking ignorance of a vast scientific literature on agricultural growth.

The third form of agricultural growth is real, scientific, and unromantic. But how much promise does it hold today?

Intensive Agriculture Today

We have looked at a classic case of intensive agriculture and at the ecological and economic logic of this type of agriculture in general. Let's now turn to the practical questions of how widespread intensive agriculture is today, and how adaptable can it be going forward. We will take those two questions in turn.

How Widespread?

Agricultural growth with little reliance on industrial inputs is common around the world. Recent examples come from the Ecuadorian Andes (Oyarzun et al. 2013), Europe (van Vliet et al. 2015), Bolivia (Zimmerer 2013), Brazil (Petersen and Silveira 2017), Burkina Faso (Gray 2005), and Madagascar (Laney 2002). A meta-study of 91 cases of agricultural growth in the tropics found the most common contributors to be Boserup's classic factor of fallow shortening (Keys and McConnell 2005, 325), changes in crop mixes, and increased labor inputs – all being more common than the industrial inputs of chemicals and machinery. Even where swidden farming is still practiced, there is usually intensive farming alongside it.

Highly productive agriculture with little reliance on purchased inputs is widespread indeed, but providing precise numbers is difficult for several reasons. One is that by its nature intensive agriculture is harder to monitor and measure than industrial agriculture; recall that one of the key reasons that governments have been so enthusiastic about subsidizing input industries is that industrialized agriculture is more "legible" to bureaucracies. Rowcrop monocultures in large fields are easy to measure; not so the mixed fields common on intensive farms. Intensive farmers also keep a significant portion of their economy on a nonmarket basis.

But if farms are defined simply on size, a common cutoff for "smallholders" is two hectares, and estimates by academic and FAO analysts converge on a number somewhat over 500 million of the planet's 570 million farms, representing roughly 2.5 billion people (FAO 2014, Graeub et al. 2016, 1–2, Zimmerer, Carney, and Vanek 2015). Estimates of how much of the world's food is produced on these farms are as high as 80% and as low as 30% (Ricciardi et al. 2018) although the latter figure is definitely an underestimate due to the difficulty of measuring subsistence production. Farms smaller than five hectares produce between 50% and 75% of the food calories consumed globally (Ricciardi et al. 2018, Samberg et al. 2016). Small farms also provide jobs and livelihoods in rural communities and play an important role in sustaining agricultural biodiversity (D'souza and Ikerd 1996, Rivera et al. 2020, Rosset 2000). In Latin America small farms produce 50% of the maize, 60% of the potatoes, 70% of root crops (Herrero et al. 2017, 36) and nearly 80% of the beans consumed domestically; in Asia the vast majority of rice is produced on small farms.

But whether a farm is under two hectares or is worked by a family is not the real issue as we have defined intensive agriculture. It is true that intensive farms are small (indeed they enjoy advantages to the economy of *small* scales) and rely on household labor and management (Netting 1993), but the key to the promise of third agriculture is its low dependence on the external inputs that define industrial agriculture. Moreover the bought inputs they do use mostly come from local informal markets; a comprehensive analysis of where smallholders in six countries got their seeds found that 40% were saved or gotten from relatives and friends and 51% were bought in local markets (McGuire and Sperling 2016).

There has been one major analysis of the scale and promise of farms defined in this way. A team of scientists (mainly ecologists) estimated the productive capacity for 293 specific types of intensive and industrial food production, finding intensive systems to be 82–106% as productive as comparable industrial production systems (Badgley et al. 2006).[10] The overall average was 92% – more than enough to feed the world, considering the high level of industrial agricultural overproduction – and the estimate of total amount of food that could be produced by intensive agriculture was 50% higher than current produce. Tellingly, the overall average yield for developing countries was 180% of industrial agricultural production there, which is not surprising considering that industrial agriculture depends heavily on subsidies that developing countries are less able to afford. These scientists also stress that they *underestimate* the productivity per hectare of intensive agriculture since they had no way to capture the output of multiple crops often planted together (Badgley et al. 2006, 94).

The High Level Panel of Experts on Food Security and Nutrition, a science-policy interface of the United Nations, also writes that "the permanence of smallholders, and their numbers" challenges the claims that "smallholders are romanticized 'relics' from the past or about to disappear" (Committee on World Food Security 2012, 33). In fact, their numbers are growing if we consider the important movements of neo-agrarians that are putting a new twist on intensive farming as I have described it.

Neo-agrarians

New types of intensive farmers called neo-agrarians and New Peasants don't look like the Kofyar, but then the Kofyar themselves were a moving target, reconfiguring their farm practices and economic strategies as conditions changed. Intensive small farmers today tend to sort out into two types, write Almekinders et al. (2019, 120). Most farmers in the Global South – certainly including the Kofyar – fall into the "indigenous" category. In contrast, neo-agrarians are the farmers who have established farms in recent decades. They favor humane, sustainable, and biodiverse production methods with greatly limited reliance on purchased inputs. Farms matching this description number well into the tens of thousands, with most located in North America and Western Europe but with rising numbers near large urban areas in parts of the Global South.

The best publicized farmer in the US is neo-agrarian Joel Salatin, whose Polyface Farm in central Virginia is a classic intensive operation producing copious amounts of food with almost no eternal inputs. Salatin himself has described his operation in various forums (Salatin 2007), and Michael Pollan's *Omnivore's Dilemma* showcased the farm as exemplifying the "organic ideal" in agriculture, in contrast to input-intensive "industrial organic" agriculture. Salatin may be unique in the outsized profit he turns from food sales, books, and workshops (Stone 2018), but in other ways he is typical of neo-agrarians who are intensive farmers who rely on skilled labor, purchase very limited industrial inputs, and usually aim to capture a premium by marketing farm products through short commodity chains (such as farmers' markets). They virtually all share – and many are primarily motivated by – a deep-seated aversion to industrial agriculture. We have examined how excess is inherent in industrial agriculture; it is driven by profits for input industries and profit is something no one ever has enough of. But in excess lie the seeds of more sustainable and equitable practices (Robbins 2019, 77). There are anti-industrial farming movements in many parts of the world, but it is no accident that American neo-agrarianism is the world's largest, given the leading role the US has played in industrializing agriculture. (I have interviewed over 100 US neo-agrarians and have not found a single exception to the deep hostility, which is striking because they vary on every other scale: they are old and young, wealthy and poor, from urban or rural backgrounds, conservative and liberal, religious and atheist, they have PhDs and high school diplomas. In short, they are not only nonindustrial, but committedly anti-industrial.)

There are no precise numbers on the scale of neo-agrarian farming in the US but there are some interesting indirect indicators.[11] The number of farmers' markets several in the US has grown to over 8,600, with 72% of counties having at least one farmers' market in 2018. There were 144,530 farms that sold $1.3 billion in fresh foods directly to consumers in 2012,[12] the vast majority of which would meet our definition of neo-agrarian operations.

Contemporary intensive farmers take on different characteristics in different parts of the world. Sociologist Jan Douwe van der Ploeg, a leading analyst of agriculture, describes "New Peasants"– farmers with shared characteristics in such diverse areas as Peru, the wealthy Parma region of Italy, and the northern Netherlands. The salient features of New Peasants are clearly those of the third agriculture: these are highly productive, largely labor-based smallholders who participate in market economies but find ways to maintain some control over their own resource base and a partly nonmonetized farm economy. They are not averse to using external inputs but carefully avoid becoming heavily dependent on them. While they share these features with neo-agrarians, they are driven less by a reformist philosophy than by a reaction to the squeezes imposed by industrial agriculture, with its ever-growing input costs and stagnating prices due in part to overproduction.

For instance, van der Ploeg's long-term research in the high-end food producing area of Parma, Italy, found the dairy farmers to sort out into capital-intensive, highly commercial "entrepreneurial" operations and labor-intensive semi-commercial "peasant" or smallholder operations. The peasants do much more of the farm work themselves (instead of hiring laborers); own more of their land (instead of renting it); raise cattle, feed and fodder (instead of buying); spend much less on machines; and borrow much less money (van der Ploeg 2008, 116). The peasant farms were more productive and more profitable, and were actually pulling farther ahead of the more commercial farms. Van der Ploeg also documents new peasants in northern Netherlands, finding remarkable similarities with the shared values he saw in his studies of peasants in Peru.

In response, writes van der Ploeg, "European farmers are enlarging the peasantness of their farms, and reconstituting themselves as new peasants – not as 'yesterday's peasants', but as peasants located at the beginning of the third millennium" (van der Ploeg 2008, 151).

Adaptable to the Future?

If we are seriously considering our agricultural future, the most important aspect of intensive agriculture today probably is its dynamism and ability to change. We know the stereotypes of nonindustrial farming, encapsulated by Norman Borlaug ("tradition-bound" and "stagnant") and Theodore Schultz (tied to the past by their static technology). Some writers today actually attribute all African poverty to the lack of agricultural inputs from Western science (Paarlberg 2008), and the young man we met before who claimed to have dropped into Kenya and given farmers the "best harvest of their entire lives" went on to explain that hunger stems from farmers still using "tools that literally date to the Bronze Age" (PBS Newshour 2012). Intensive farmers seem to be hapless, slack-jawed relics.

"Blatantly wrong" writes van der Ploeg (2008, 122), and Robert Netting would go even farther. In years of collaboration with Netting, I heard much from him on his admiration for intensive sustainable farmers, but when I asked him once what he thought was their most important single feature, he didn't have to stop and think: "their innovation!" And it is true that when you set aside the technological fetish that agricultural growth and improvement only come from external technologies, you can see a whole world of creative invention in their practices and strategies. We saw the new Kofyar farm practices and methods of balancing market and nonmarket transactions, innovations that were as important as technological changes. Similarly, Michael Dove, a leading agricultural anthropologist, marvels at the innovations of Indonesian smallholders, and not just changing strategies for managing crops but "the development of mechanisms for rationalizing the combination of market-oriented cash-cropping and subsistence-oriented food production" (Dove 2011, 6).

The same inventiveness in agricultural practices marks the neo-agrarians. Virtually all of the innovation at Polyface Farm concerns new practices and strategies, sometimes backed up with locally devised technology. In the winter barn where cattle are fed, he adds wood chips and corn kernels to the accumulating manure, letting pigs root through and aerate which keeps the pigs happy and accelerates decomposition, which keeps the barn warm. Cattle are moved among paddocks, leaving behind manure in which flies lay eggs, providing high-protein snacks for laying hens that are let in after a few days. The farm abounds with other such "inventions."

These innovations are not primarily technological, but intensive farmers can be highly inventive with technology – usually relatively inexpensive, locally adapted, and often ingenious (van der Ploeg 2008, 169). Polyface Farm offers examples such as the movable poultry cages, hare pens, scalable farm infrastructures, and machines with colorful names like the Eggmobile, Gobbledygo, or Shademobile. Salatin commands a lot of attention but my own interviews with neo-agrarians in the central Virginia region show similar technological ingenuity. I have seen farmer-designed duck-feeding apparatuses, various different types of poultry cages, customized watering systems, tool carts, and customized vehicles.

Some of the most interesting innovations are to be found in the two core industrial agricultural technologies of fertilizers and seeds. Van der Ploeg's "new peasants" provide some more recent examples, including new types of fertilizers that could be applied to plant leaves in Peru (van der Ploeg 2008, 68) and forms of manure with improved nutrient ratios and new ways of surface distribution in the Netherlands (van der Ploeg 2008, 192). With seed breeding the most impressive successes have come not from farmers breeding on their own but by collaborating with professional breeders in what is called participatory seed breeding. Here the farmers' knowledge, creativity, and seeds combine with the breeders' facilities and seed collections (Chambers, Pacey, and Thrupp 1989, Cleveland and Soleri 2002). But there are also many striking cases of innovative breeding by farmers themselves. Two species of rice – African-originated *Oryza glaberrima* and Asia-originated *O. sativa* – have grown in West Africa for centuries. Creation of fertile hybrids of the two species has long been a goal of breeders, but due to genetic incompatibilities this elusive goal was only achieved in the late 1990s with the announcement of NERICA (New Rice for Africa). A decade later, a team led by agricultural anthropologist Paul Richards stunned the scientific world by showing that peasant farmers had created their own crosses well before NERICA was announced, and adding the crosses to their repertoire of crops had helped farmers adjust to climate change and war-related displacement (Nuijten et al. 2009, 8).

Lastly it is important to note that sometimes agricultural innovation does not mean adopting new technology, but devising ways to avoid it. In 1954 Everett Rogers, the late sociologist often cited as the dean of technology adoption research, interviewed Iowa farmers about their adoption of "agricultural innovations." Agricultural scientists were strongly recommending pesticides and most farmers were going along, but one refused because they killed earthworms and songbirds in his fields. Automatically accepting the scientists' advice, Rogers classified the farmer as a "laggard" and even concluded that he was being "irrational." But the 1960–1970s brought research showing the environmental and public health toll of pesticides, and by 1980 the USDA reversed its opposition to organic farming. The rising number of organic farmers after that were not "hippies" but instead showed the classic characteristics of "innovators." Looking back, Rogers later wrote that by present-day standards, the "laggard" was actually "a superinnovator" (2003, 181–183).

Repurposing older technologies can also be highly innovative. Consider the retro-tractor movement. The latest wave of externally developed agri-technology is the suite of equipment, software, and service plans known as digital agriculture (or "Big Data"). Most new tractors have onboard computer systems and sensors that drive up the cost of tractors and also make repairs a nightmare. In contrast, "the old tractors work really well, are cheaper, and farmers can just replace a part themselves when they break down" (Gault 2020). Farmers have established YesterdaysTractors, a lively online forum to disseminate information, facilitate sales, and resist the continual push of appropriative technology.

Actually bucking globalization to produce food for local consumers on small non-input-dependent farms is deeply innovative, even if as it recalls those features of past food regimes (Stuiver 2006, 148). But there is little nostalgic about it, and most neo-agrarians, writes anthropologist Megan Larmer (2016, 95), "groan at the mention of agrarian nostalgia" with its connotation that their farming is impractical and unscientific. It is true: for everything you see on a neo-agrarian farm that reminds you of what went before, you will see innovations.

My aim is not to make third agriculture out to be idyllic or downplay the headwinds faced by intensive farmers today. Many struggle with resource scarcity, especially since they are usually disempowered and frowned up on by governments (for reasons detailed in Chapter 3). Even Robert Netting, whose *Smallholders Householders* presents the most laudatory picture of intensive smallholders, recognizes the common conflicts within households and over land (1993), and Piers Blaikie's influential *Political Economy of Soil Erosion in Developing Countries* (1985) details how the pressures on smallholders can push them into environmentally destructive practices. Jan Douwe van der Ploeg's *New Peasantries* (2008) shows that along with "repeasantization" there are also many cases of smallholders giving up on farming (which he terms "deactivation").

But it is remarkable – and crucially important to the world's agricultural situation today – that this branch of farming has been obscured, marginalized, misunderstood, and caricatured so relentlessly and for so long. Most people in the public, the media, and government don't bat an eyelash at claims that farmers are poor because they lack external input technologies (Paarlberg 2008) and that the world will starve without more external input technologies (McGloughlin 1999), even as hundreds of millions of third agriculturalists produce an enormous portion of the world food supply. The hiding, marginalizing, and misrepresenting this world of intensive farming is not an accident, and before wrapping up our exploration of this crucial alternative to industrial agriculture, let us ask why.

Why Is It Invisible?

Intensive smallholders are omnipresent, notes van der Ploeg (2008, xiv), but somehow "invisible." Why does the widespread and well-documented process of intensification remain largely unknown or misconstrued by policy-makers, the public, and even many scientists, who seem convinced that agricultural growth comes only from capital-intensive technologies? This is an alarming blind spot in a world that is so concerned about the issue of food and population. Why is this a story that is not told? It certainly is not because no one is interested; there has been keen public interest in and debate on sustainable farming in recent decades. I will point to two reasons.

First is that the scientists who study intensification have done a poor job of getting this story out. No scientists understood smallholder intensification in Malthus's time; when his intensification-denying book appeared in the middle of a century of intensification (Bennett 1935, 28), no one called him on it. The importance and underlying dynamics of intensification came to light in the mid-20th century, but most knowledge on it has remained largely locked up in the academic writing of the scholars who study it. Intensive high-population farming has never been brought to wider audiences by a skilled and thoughtful journalist, as Michael Pollan has done with best-sellers on organic farming and other topics. Boserup's *Conditions* was short and direct, Netting's *Smallholders* and van der Ploeg's *New Peasantries* were long and heavily footnoted, but all were clearly written for social scientists and development officials, not for a wider public. And I am guilty as well − which is one of the reasons for this book!

The second reason that intensification remains little known and misunderstood is because of the persuasive power of those who have vested interests in misrepresenting it. Appreciation for agriculture that runs on labor and locally generated resources is consistent with the interests of few and contrary to the interests of many in power. For government officials in developing countries, being credited with technology-heavy "agricultural development" is career-enhancing; NGOs often find agricultural interventions based on external technologies to be fundable and press-worthy, even when they are unsustainable (Stone 2011). But the main credit for intensive farming's vanishing act goes to the inputs industries and their allies in academia. The Green Revolution was entirely an exercise in replacing intensive techniques and indigenous knowledge with external technology and expertise, and we have already encountered Norman Borlaug's scorn and ignorance of nonindustrial agricultural growth. "In our experience," he and his aide-de-camp Christopher Dowswell (1995, 123) wrote, only "modern agricultural inputs, such as improved seed-fertiliser and crop-protection chemicals" (pesticides) could prevent "human drudgery and the risk of hunger and misery."

In this way neo-Malthusians have made it their business to denigrate not just intensive agriculture but the anthropologists and others who study and advocate it. For Africa, the critique goes like this:

> Agroecology [intensive agriculture] is being foisted upon unsuspecting African farmers from the outside − by wealthy NGOs that romanticize peasant lifestyles. Claims

of the benefits of agroecology are not well grounded in science. What farmers really need ...[are] technological packages, and agroecology is dangerous and immoral for serving as an impediment to this.

(AGRA Watch 2020, 16)

Timothy Wise is correct that "criticisms of agroecology have been well-orchestrated and scripted, invoking underdevelopment and backwardness and extolling the virtues of industrial agriculture" (2021). Monsanto (now a division of Bayer Cropscience), one of the world's largest input producers, has been especially zealous in promoting this narrative. They depict Asian small farmers as "exhausted serfs, 'shackled to their fields' and oppressed by the demands of their own time-consuming 'intensive farming practices', which drained the soil of its health and fertility"; the company and its partners hold up their products as an alternative enabling "extraordinary improvements in ... yields, incomes, quality of life and environmental impacts" (Glover 2007). Industrial agriculturalists' go-to phrase for intensive farm work is "back-breaking": nonindustrial farming is an "endless cycle of back-breaking labor and low-yield production" (Njoroge 2020, Wise 2021) and a program director for the Alliance for a Green Revolution in Africa (which promotes external technologies) bemoans the "back-breaking labour in the field," adding that "We should banish the hoe in Africa" (Reuters 2017). The African hoe – the only tool the Kofyar need to practice productive sustainable intensive farming – is even called "unsustainable" in a Monsanto publication that touts genetically modified sweet potatoes as an example of a sustainable technology (Monsanto Corporation 2000). But the "sustainable" genetically modified sweet potato never worked and was never released, while the hoe still works just fine for many farmers.[13]

Moreover, despite the extensive documentation of indigenous agricultural knowledge, smallholders are repeatedly depicted as clueless about the basics of farming. Here is Monsanto, seller of the world's most widely used herbicide (Roundup®), depicting Indian farmers as slack-jawed cretins unaware of weeds:

Weeds...are responsible for 30–60% of the damage to our agriculture yields. But there is very little awareness of this among Indian farmers, while those who are aware, lack knowledge of the appropriate solutions. The penetration level of chemical herbicides is also very low, ranging from 17% in rice to less than 1% in maize.

(Monsanto India 2000)

The arrival of GM seeds in the mid-1990s led to an orgy of belittling nonindustrial agriculture. Largely in response to backlash and opposition by environmentalists and (especially European) consumers, around 2000 the biotech industry launched a sustained campaign centered on the conceit that GM seeds could save the developing world from the poverty and hunger caused by its backward agriculture (Glover 2010, Stone 2002). Scientists funded by biotechnology industries cited farmers' supposed inability to learn anything new as grounds for selling them GM crops. "For years people have tried to change cultural practices of these farmers, and it just hasn't worked," explained the head of a biotechnology lab; "but with biotech...all you have to do is give them the seed" (McGloughlin 2000). "Genetic farming is the easiest way to cultivate crops," writes a particularly clueless industry-supported academic biotechnologist; "all that farmers have to do is to plant the seeds and water them regularly" (Thaindian News 2008). Borlaug and the Green Revolution feature prominently in these arguments, and a Google Books Ngram shows that mentions of "Borlaug" began a major surge in 2000 that was obviously connected to the biotech industry's new narrative.

Speak highly of smallholder intensification and you will be branded an anti-science "romantic":

> the romantics have portrayed the food crisis as demonstrating the failure of scientific commercial agriculture, which they have long found distasteful…
>
> *(Collier 2008)*

> Advances in modern science tend to diminish both unspoiled nature and unquestioned faith, prompting those with a strong romantic or spiritual side to register their objections by seeking foods that incorporate less modern science.
>
> *(Paarlberg 2008, 71)*

> However much they may respect traditional farming practices, agricultural scientists must resist the temptation to romanticise them. They must not succumb to the illusion that, confronted with explosive population growth, Africa's food needs can be met through the improved 'low-input sustainable' systems that are based largely on traditional practices but require much more from farmers in terms of labour, knowledge, and skill.
>
> *(Borlaug and Dowswell 1995, 123)*

I have not romanticized the lives of intensive farmers; they have problems with inequality and conflict just like everyone else. Many are poor by standard measures and they can rarely count on lavish government subsidy like so many industrial farmers. But they do give the lie to the neo-Malthusian fiction that agriculture can only grow by developing new technologies for farmers to buy. And if anyone suggests that the research on agricultural intensification is romantic or unscientific, remind them that of the scientists who have led the study of intensive agriculture, economist Ester Boserup and anthropologist Robert Netting were both elected to the US National Academy of Sciences. Both were honored for work in an area in which they, unlike Norman Borlaug and friends, were actual experts: the third agriculture.

Yes We Have a Problem

This book has not been a how-to guide to fixing our agrifood system. Instead it has been about the underlying principles of what drives agricultural growth. But unless we understand these underlying principles, how-to guides won't make much sense.

You have surely heard about how much more food the world needs to make to feed itself in the future. These claims like to cite the year 2050 and factual-sounding statistics on how much more food we will need to produce – although they disagree on whether we will need 50% or 100% more (Lal 2016). But they agree that we have a serious problem and they always promote solutions – sometimes cleaning up our individual diets, but usually new agricultural technologies. Occasionally the solutions are the technologies we have focused on – more and better crop breeding and fertilizers (e.g., Hickey et al. 2019) – but in recent years the most common "solution" has been genetically modified seeds ("GMO Scientists

Could Save the World From Hunger, If We Let Them" proclaims *Newsweek* (Parrett 2015), easing regulation on which will start "a new Green Revolution, one that would make Dr. Borlaug proud" (Erwin and Glennon 2020, 388–389).[14]

They say the first step for alcoholics is to admit you have a problem, but if you are an alcoholic there is no question what the problem is: you drink too much. But the first step for an agricultural world pondering its future is to admit that we don't have the problem we think we have. All of those claims about how to feed the world rest on the beliefs that (a) population outracing food supply is a dire problem, that (b) it may be solved by – and only by – new technology. ***But that's not the problem.*** The problem is deeper, more complicated, and more interesting. The real point of this book has been to take the first step and show what our dilemma really is. And the only way to understand it is to the three agricultures. Let's sum up the three and the essential relationships between them.

Malthusian agriculture hinges on the first principles that population tends inexorably to grow faster than food production, which is largely inelastic: agricultural growth comes only from bringing more land into production. It follows that food supply checks population, and it does so less by outright starvation than by poverty, sickness, and degraded living conditions. The theory was an invaluable political tool that sanitized the poverty, sickness, and degraded living conditions running rampant among the factory workers of the early Industrial Revolution. Malthus was right about the importance of indirect problems caused by food:population imbalances, although he was tragically wrong on what he attributed to shortages. He was also patently wrong about the inelasticity of food production. Malthus's was a theory of population and agriculture that got the population part and the agriculture part wrong. Malthus himself soon realized that the population part was wrong. He never did realize how far off he was on the agriculture part; industrial agriculture did not even begin to rear its head until around the time he died, and intensive agriculture was not understood and recognized for 167 years – although it had been going on since before Malthus was born. But he left this idea embedded well enough in popular thought to make industrial agriculture seem necessary and inevitable; after all, if the underlying principle is that agriculture is forever scrambling to keep pace with population, then scramble it must.

But however embedded that notion is, it is simply not true when industrial agriculture enters the scene. The first glimmers of industrial agriculture – industry appropriating parts of farm production and selling them back as inputs – were being born just as Malthus was dying. Industrial agriculture changes the drivers of agriculture. Input industries quickly found that they enjoyed a special access into public coffers and resources. Technologies that were not inherently cost-effective on the farm and that polluted the environment off the farm were made cost-effective and allowed to pollute by public subsidy; they were even promoted by the state. This changed the underlying principle of what drove agriculture: input industries wanted to sell as much product as they could, and as overproduction became endemic to the system the same state that had midwifed the input industries paid to protect the industries and the farmers from the costs of overproduction.

As industrial agriculture grew beyond the core technologies of fertilizer and seed, with proliferating forms of mechanization, chemicals, biotechnology, and digital information services, a lot of work needed to be done to justify the growth in public and policy minds, with neo-Malthusian dogma serving as the most persuasive tool in the box.

Input industries widely used their wealth and influence to bolster the public misunderstanding of the underlying principles of agriculture. Just as the early 19th century British power structures had instantly promoted Robert Malthus to a prestigious position as a thought leader, 20th Century input industries cultivated and created high-profile agricultural experts to propagate the philosophy of neo-Malthusianism. None were more prominent than Norman Borlaug, whose industrial wheats didn't cause any more food to be produced, but who spent his post-Nobel years on neo-Malthusian tirades against critics of just about any industrial agricultural technology.

But population growth is not an unstoppable runaway train, inherently faster-growing than agriculture and ultimately checked by food supply. Agricultural intensification based on labor and local technology was here long before Malthus, was going on around Malthus, and is still here. Meanwhile, industrial agriculture is the real runaway train, with fields producing far more than anyone could ever eat as state-subsidized inputs pour onto farms and externalized costs roll off, damaging environment, public health, and farmers in the Global South. Industrial agriculture is a conglomeration of separate appropriative technologies, always publicly subsidized and never as "efficient" as they claim unless you wear blinders that keep you from seeing the delayed, distant, and diffuse external costs. And yet we obsess over how we need more industrial agricultural technologies. We are letting our house wash away in a flood because we are willingly convinced that we may run out of water.

Epilogue

In the years following publication of *The Population Bomb*, Paul Ehrlich was asked several times why his Malthusian predictions had not come true. When asked about this in 2004 by *Grist Magazine* he insisted that "we never made 'predictions,' even though idiots think we have" (Grist 2004). But "In the 1970s and 1980s hundreds of millions of people will starve to death in spite of any crash programs embarked upon now" is clearly a prediction, and Ehrlich was also explicit that the cause was a Malthusian population:food imbalance, pure and simple:

> the underdeveloped countries of the world face an inevitable population-food crisis. Each year food production in these countries falls a bit further behind burgeoning population growth … it now seems inevitable that it will continue to its logical conclusion: mass starvation…Of these poor, a minimum of ten million people, most of them children, will starve to death during each year of the 1970s.
>
> *(Ehrlich 1968, 3)*

Ehrlich then passed the buck on his "non-prediction," explaining that "starvation has been less extensive than I (or rather the agriculturalists I consulted) expected…[b]ut it's still horrific, with some 600 million people very hungry and billions under- or malnourished." But we have seen that blaming systemic hunger on agricultural failure is slight of hand. Recall that in India, by far the world's hungriest country (as measured by the sheer number of food-short people), foodgrain had been growing much faster than population for decades; India was a major food exporter and domestically its buffer stocks were climbing toward a record 53.6 million tons over what it was even equipped to store.

But even more central to this book is the question of who those "agriculturalists" were. That word does not appear in the 1968 edition of *The Population Bomb*, and my suspicion is that he did not consult any experts in agriculture. This would have been very much in keeping with the *first agriculture*; after all, Robert Malthus himself based his famous pronouncements about agricultural growth on nothing more than the dreary world he imagined as he stewed in his rented room in Okewood. If Ehrlich had wanted to consult with agriculturalists, he might have tried Norman Borlaug, who brought the *second agriculture* to the Global South and then militantly defended it for the rest of his life. Borlaug's claim in 1968 that the poor nations of the world would be able to feed themselves for the foreseeable future was quite correct, even if his high-input seeds wouldn't lead to any more food being produced. Or he might have consulted with Robert Netting, who was years from election to the National Academy of Sciences but who that year published his book *Hill Farmers of Nigeria*. It described Kofyar food production, which had intensified as population rose, as happens with the *third agriculture*.

Notes

1 Other terms with substantial overlap in meaning are "Boserupian intensification," "sustainable intensification," "ecological intensification," "smallholder intensification," and "peasant intensification."

2 The people described here call themselves, and have been called, by various names. On the ethnonym Kofyar, see Netting (1968, 35–43) and Stone (1996, 68). In 1989 a new local government area called Qua'an Pan was established, encompassing the Kofyar homeland along with a neighboring area; since then many of the people in this area self-identify as Pan or Qua'an Pan.

3 Big ideas like this always have forerunners, and flickers of Boserup's theory had been seen before. Malthus himself had made a small nod in this direction when he pointed out that even when land was fully occupied there could be "amelioration." Some writers had already noticed the tendency for fallows to shorten and workloads to rise under population pressure. But it was Boserup who put together a general theory of population and agricultural change and framed it as a reversal of the Malthusian orthodoxy of inelastic agriculture. When Malthus (and the classical economists like Ricardo) had mentioned that under pressure farmers might try to squeeze some extra produce from their field, they treated this possibility as just a footnote to the real story of food production capacity being fixed, with more population necessarily meaning less food per person.

4 In fact much of the Amazon rainforest that we hear is being destroyed was shaped by millennia of slash and burn farming prior to the 1970s (Denevan 1992, 373–374). Of course when conditions are wrong, swidden farming can be unsustainable and destructive, such as when settlement schemes lead to burning of vast contiguous areas and when economic policies encourage clearing for cattle and ranching to claim ownership of land (Hecht and Cockburn 1989).

5 Early 19th century New York City had its own version of town-country manure metabolism. The city's streets in the 1820s were notoriously filthy and in some areas awash in organic refuse which people simply threw out into the street given the lack of municipal garbage collection. In poorer areas many people ran hogs in the streets as street cleaners; these became the subject of heated dispute and even "hog riots" when city officials tried to banish them in the 1830s. The hogs turned organic trash into dung, which mixed with the tons of manure from horses to create "street dirt" of considerable value to peri-urban farmers (McNeur 2014).

6 In the early US farms were commonly cultivated for many decades using hoes before it was worth the extra work of switching to the plow (Nelson 2007, 45–46).

7 In Eastern Norfolk, where 13th century population densities rose as high as $500/mi^2$, fallows were shortened and in some cases eliminated. Farmers fertilized field and relied on repeated plowings to destroy weed growth. "The transforming effect that such unstinting use of labour could have upon medieval agriculture has rarely been recognized," writes Campbell (1983, 38), "but it was plainly fundamental to the high level of productivity attained in eastern Norfolk in the early fourteenth century."

8 Note that they were shy about complaining; Kofyar vented, sometimes bitterly, about government corruption, about a game park taking land, about Tivs stealing their yams, and about other frustrations.

9 Students of anthropology will recognize this framework as very similar to Julian Steward's cultural ecology (1955). However Steward treated food production technologies as an independent variable, whereas technological change is a key dependent variable to Boserup.

10 The study focused on "farming practices that may be called agroecological, sustainable, or ecological; utilize natural (non-synthetic) nutrient-cycling processes; exclude or rarely use synthetic pesticides; and sustain or regenerate soil quality"– essentially what I label intensive agriculture. Rather misleadingly, it claimed to be on "organic" agriculture, but their definition had nothing to do with "certified" organic agriculture – which includes enormous highly industrial farms that substitute inputs for pesticides and fertilizers.

11 Reliable figures on the number of farmers markets are surprisingly elusive, but a recent guestimate puts the number in the US at around 9,000.

12 https://farmersmarketcoalition.org/wp-content/uploads/2015/06/Farmers_Market_Week_Fact_Sheet_small.pdf

13 When someone actually does despise the work of farming, it is usually not because the work is inherently onerous but because that person is not being compensated for their work. For instance, when the work of slaves on sugar plantations is characterized as back-breaking, it is more convincing.

14 Well before it was fashionable to cite the world of 2050, similar claims were made for fertilizers and hybrid seed. The National Fertilizer Association insisted that fertilizer was needed to "feed the world" when most fertilizer was actually being used in areas growing inedible crops (Johnson 2016, 108). Hybrid corn has been credited with delaying Malthus's "dire predictions" for two centuries (Harpstead 1975).

References

AGRA Watch. 2020. *Messengers of Gates' Agenda: A Case Study of the Cornell Alliance for Science Global Leadership Fellows Program*. Seattle, WA: Community Alliance for Global Justice.

Almekinders, Conny J. M., Glenn Davis Stone, Marci Baranski, Judith A. Carney, Jan Hanspach, Vijesh V. Krishna, Julian Ramirez-Villegas, Jacob van Etten, and Karl S. Zimmerer. 2019. "Socio-ecological Interactions amid Global Change." In *Agrobiodiversity: Integrating Knowledge for a Sustainable Future*, edited by Karl S. Zimmerer and Stef de Haan, 117–143. Cambridge, MA: MIT Press.

Badgley, Catherine, Jeremy Moghtader, Eileen Quintero, Emily Zakem, M. Jahi Chappell, Katia Aviles-Vazquez, Andrea Samulon, and Ivette Perfecto. 2006. "Organic Agriculture and the Global Food Supply" *Renewable Agriculture and Food Systems* 22 (2):86–108. doi: 10.1017/S1742170507001640.

Banham, Debby, and Rosamond Faith. 2014. *Anglo-Saxon Farms and Farming*. Oxford: Oxford Univ. Press.

Bennett, M.K. 1935. "British Wheat Yield for Seven Centuries." *Economic History* 3(10):12–29.

Blaikie, Piers. 1985. *The Political Economy of Soil Erosion in Developing Countries*. London: Longman.

Bongaarts, John, and Susan C. Watkins. 1996. "Social Interactions and Contemporary Fertility Transitions." *Population and Development Review* 22:639–682.

Borlaug, Norman E., and C. Dowswell. 1995. "Mobilising Science and Technology to Get Agriculture Moving in Africa." *Development Policy Review* 13 (2):115–129.

Boserup, Ester. 1965. *The Conditions of Agricultural Growth: The Economics of Agrarian Change under Population Pressure*. New York: Aldine.

Boserup, Ester. 1999. *My Professional Life and Publications, 1929–1998*. Copenhagen: Museum Tusculanem Press.

Cairns, Malcolm, ed. 2007. *Voices from the Forest: Integrating Indigenous Knowledge into Sustainable Upland Farming*. Washington, DC: Routledge.

Campbell, Bruce M.S. 1983. "Agricultural Progress in Medieval England: Some Evidence from Eastern Norfolk." *The Economic History Review* 36 (1):26–46. doi: 10.2307/2598896.

Cato, Marcus. 160 BC. *On Agriculture*. https://penelope.uchicago.edu/Thayer/E/Roman/Texts/Cato/De_Agricultura/A*.html

Chambers, Robert, Arnold Pacey, and Lori Ann Thrupp, eds. 1989. *Farmer First: Farmer Innovation and Agricultural Research*. London: Intermediate Technology.

Charles, Daniel. 2005. *Master Mind: The Rise and Fall of Fritz Haber, the Nobel Laureate Who Launched the Age of Chemical Warfare*. New York: HarperCollins.

Chrispeels, Maarten J. 2000. "Biotechnology and the Poor." *Plant Physiology* 124 (1):3–6.

Cleveland, David A., and Daniela Soleri, eds. 2002. *Farmers, Scientists and Plant Breeding: Integrating Knowledge and Practice.* Oxon: CAB International.

Collier, Paul. 2008. "The Politics of Hunger: How Illusion and Greed Fan the Food Crisis." *Foreign Affairs* Nov-Dec. https://www.foreignaffairs.com/articles/2008-11-01/politics-hunger

Committee on World Food Security. 2012. *Investing in Smallholder Agriculture for Food and Nutrition Security.* Rome: FAO.

Cullather, Nick. 2010. *The Hungry World: America's Cold War Battle against Poverty in Asia.* Cambridge, MA: Harvard Univ. Press.

Cushman, Gregory T. 2013. *Guano and the Opening of the Pacific World: A Global Ecological History.* New York: Cambridge Univ. Press.

D'souza, G., and J. Ikerd. 1996. "Small Farms and Sustainable Development: Is Small More Sustainable?" *Journal of Agricultural and Applied Economics* 28 (1):73–83.

Denevan, William M. 1992. "The Pristine Myth: The Landscape of the Americas in 1492". *Annals of the Association of American Geographers* 83 (3):369–385.

Dove, Michael R. 2011. *The Banana Tree at the Gate: A History of Marginal Peoples and Global Markets in Borneo.* New Haven, CT: Yale Univ. Press.

Ehrlich, Paul R. 1968. *The Population Bomb.* New York: Sierra Club/Ballantine Book.

Erisman, Jan Willem, Mark A. Sutton, James Galloway, Zbigniew Klimont, and Wilfried Winiwarter. 2008. "How a Century of Ammonia Synthesis Changed the World." *Nature Geoscience* 1 (10):636–639.

Erwin, John A., and Robert Glennon. 2020. "Feeding the World: How Changes in Biotech Regulation Can Jump-Start the Second Green Revolution and Diversify the Jump-Start the Second Green Revolution and Diversify the Agricultural Industry Agricultural Industry" *William. & Mary Environmental Law & Policy Review* 44:327–389.

FAO. 1955. *The State of Food and Agriculture.* Rome: Food and Agriculture Organization.

FAO. 2014. *The State of Food and Agriculture 2014: Innovation in Family Farming.* Rome: Food and Agriculture Organization.

Gates Foundation. 2014. "Alliance for a Green Revolution in Africa: How We Work." https://www.gatesfoundation.org/How-We-Work/Resources/Grantee-Profiles/Grantee-Profile-Alliance-for-a-Green-Revolution-in-Africa-AGRA.

Gault, Matthew. 2020. Farmers Are Buying 40-Year-Old Tractors Because They're Actually Repairable. *Vice* 7 January. https://www.vice.com/en/article/bvgx9w/farmers-are-buying-40-year-old-tractors-because-theyre-actually-repairable.

Glover, Dominic. 2007. "Monsanto and Smallholder Farmers: A Case Study in Corporate Social Responsibility." *Third World Quarterly* 28 (4):851–867. doi: 10.1080/01436590701336739.

Glover, Dominic. 2010. "The Corporate Shaping of GM Crops as a Technology for the Poor." *Journal of Peasant Studies* 37:67–90.

Graeub, Benjamin E., M. Jahi Chappell, Hannah Wittman, Samuel Ledermann, Rachel Bezner Kerr, and Barbara Gemmill-Herren. 2016. "The State of Family Farms in the World." *World Development* 87:1–15. doi: 10.1016/j.worlddev.2015.05.012.

Gray, Leslie C. 2005. "What Kind of Intensification? Agricultural Practice, Soil Fertility and Socioeconomic Differentiation in Rural Burkina Faso." *The Geographical Journal* 171 (1):70–82.

Grist. 2004. "When Paul's Said and Done." *Grist Magazine* 13 August. https://web.archive.org/web/20041115081108/http://www.grist.org/comments/interactivist/2004/08/09/ehrlich/index1.html

Harms, Robert. 2002. *The Diligent: A Voyage through the Worlds of the Slave Trade.* New York: Basic Books.

Harpstead, D.D. 1975. "Man-Molded Cereal: Hybrid Corn's Story." In *The 1975 Yearbook of Agriculture: That We May Eat,* edited by J. Hayes, 213–224. Washington, DC: US Govn Printing Office.

Hecht, Susanna, and Alexander Cockburn. 1989. *Fate of the Forest: Developers, Destroyers, and Defenders of the Amazon.* London: Verso.

Herrero, Mario, Philip K. Thornton, Brendan Power, Jessica R. Bogard, Roseline Remans, Steffen Fritz, James S. Gerber, Gerald Nelson, Linda See, Katharina Waha, Reg A. Watson, Paul C. West, Leah H. Samberg, Jeannette van de Steeg, Eloise Stephenson, Mark van Wijk, and Petr Havlík.

2017. "Farming and the Geography of Nutrient Production for Human Use: A Transdisciplinary Analysis." *The Lancet Planetary Health* 1 (1):e33–e42. doi: 10.1016/S2542-5196(17)30007-4.

Hickey, Lee T., Amber N. Hafeez, Hannah Robinson, Scott A. Jackson, Soraya C. M. Leal-Bertioli, Mark Tester, Caixia Gao, Ian D. Godwin, Ben J. Hayes, and Brande B.H. Wulff. 2019. "Breeding Crops to Feed 10 billion." *Nature Biotechnology* 37 (7):744–754. doi: 10.1038/s41587-019-0152-9.

Howard, Albert. 1940. *An Agricultural Testament.* New York and London: Oxford Univ. Press.

Johnson, Timothy. 2016. "Growth Industry: The Political Economy of Fertilizer in America, 1865–1947." PhD, History, Univ. of Georgia.

Jordan, Terry G., and Matti Kaups. 1989. *The American Backwoods Frontier: An Ethnic and Ecological Interpretation.* Baltimore, MD: The Johns Hopkins Univ. Press.

Kerridge, Eric. 1967. *The Agricultural Revolution.* London: George Allen & Unwin.

Keys, Eric, and William J. McConnell. 2005. "Global Change and the Intensification of Agriculture in the Tropics." *Global Environmental Change* 15 (4):320–337. doi: 10.1016/j.gloenvcha.2005.04.004.

King, F.H. 1911. *Farmers of Forty Centuries: Permanent Agriculture in China.* Madison, WI: Mrs. FH King.

Lal, Rattan. 2016. "Feeding 11 billion on 0.5 billion Hectare of Area under Cereal Crops." *Food and Energy Security* 5 (4):239–251. doi: 10.1002/fes3.99.

Laney, Rheyna M. 2002. "Disaggregating Induced Intensification for Land-Change Analysis: A Case Study from Madagascar." *Annals of the Association of American Geographers* 92 (4):702–726.

Larmer, Megan. 2016. "Cultivating the Edge: An Ethnography of First-generation Women Farmers in the American Midwest." *Feminist Review* 114 (1):91–111.

Levin, Samuel M. 1966. "Malthus and the Idea of Progress." *Journal of the History of Ideas* 27 (1):-92–108. doi: 10.2307/2708310.

Malthus, Thomas Robert. 1803. *An Essay on the Principle of Population, or, A View of its Past and Present Effects on Human Happiness with an Inquiry into Our Prospects Respecting the Future Removal or Mitigation of the Evils Which it Occasions* (2nd edition of Population). London: J. Johnson.

Malthus, Thomas Robert. 1826. *An Essay on the Principle of Population, or a View of its Past and Present Effects on Human Happiness; with an Inquiry into our Prospects Respecting the Future Removal or Mitigation of the Evils Which it Occasions* (6th edition of Population). London: John Murray.

McGloughlin, Martina. 1999. "Without Biotechnology, We'll Starve." *Los Angeles Times*, 1 Nov. http://articles.latimes.com/1999/nov/01/local/me-28638.

McGloughlin, Martina. 2000. "Interview." PBS. http://www.pbs.org/wgbh/harvest/interviews/mcgloughlin.html.

McGuire, Shawn, and Louise Sperling. 2016. "Seed Systems Smallholder Farmers Use." *Food Security* 8. doi: 10.1007/s12571-015-0528-8.

McNeur, Catherine. 2014. *Taming Manhattan: Environmental Battles in the Antebellum City.* Cambridge, MA: Harvard Univ. Press.

Monsanto Corporation. 2000. *Biotechnology: Solutions for Tomorrow's World.* St. Louis, MO: Monsanto Corporation.

Monsanto India. 2000. Investors Annual Report. MonsantoIndia.com https://bit.ly/36iHMWa.

Morgan, W.B. 1957. "The 'Grassland Towns' of the Eastern Region of Nigeria." *Transactions of the Institute of British Geographers* 23:213–224.

Mortimore, Michael J. 1993. "The Intensification of Peri-urban Agriculture: The Kano Close-Settled Zone, 1964-1986." In *Population Growth and Agricultural Change in Africa*, edited by B.L. Turner II, G. Hyden, and R.W. Kates, 358–400. Gainesville: Univ. of Florida Press.

Murton, John. 1999. "Population Growth and Poverty in Machakos District, Kenya." *The Geographical Journal* 165 (1):37–46. doi: 10.2307/3060509.

Myrdal, Gunnar. 1968. *Asian Drama: An Inquiry into the Poverty of Nations.* New York: Pantheon.

Nelson, Lynn A. 2007. *Pharsalia: An Environmental Biography of a Southern Plantation, 1780–1880.* Athens: Univ. of Georgia Press.

Netting, Robert McC. 1968. *Hill Farmers of Nigeria: Cultural Ecology of the Kofyar of the Jos Plateau.* Seattle: Univ. of Washington Press.

Netting, Robert McC. 1981. *Balancing on an Alp: Ecological Change and Continuity in a Swiss Mountain Community*. Cambridge: Cambridge Univ. Press.

Netting, Robert McC. 1989. "Smallholders, Householders, Freeholders: Why the Family Farm Works Well Worldwide." In *The Household Economy: Reconsidering the Domestic Mode of Production*, edited by Richard R. Wilk, 221–244. Boulder, CO: Westview.

Netting, Robert McC. 1993. *Smallholders, Householders: Farm Families and the Ecology of Intensive, Sustainable Agriculture*. Stanford, CA: Stanford Univ. Press.

Netting, Robert McC., Glenn Davis Stone, and M. Priscilla Stone. 1993. "Agricultural expansion, intensification, and market participation among the Kofyar, Jos Plateau, Nigeria." In *Population Growth and Agricultural Change in Africa*, edited by B.L. Turner II, G. Hyden, and R. Kates, 206–249. Gainesville: Univ. of Florida Press.

Njoroge, James. 2020. NGOs & Foundations Want to Dictate Africa's Agricultural Destiny. *European Scientist* 28 October. https://www.europeanscientist.com/en/features/ngos-foundations-want-to-dictate-africas-agricultural-destiny/

Nuijten, Edwin, Robbert van Treuren, Paul C. Struik, Alfred Mokuwa, Florent Okry, Béla Teeken, and Paul Richards. 2009. "Evidence for the Emergence of New Rice Types of Interspecific Hybrid Origin in West African Farmers' Fields." *PLoS One* 4 (10):e7335.

Oyarzun, Pedro J., Ross Mary Borja, Stephen Sherwood, and Vicente Parra. 2013. "Making Sense of Agrobiodiversity, Diet, and Intensification of Smallholder Family Farming in the Highland Andes of Ecuador." *Ecology of Food and Nutrition* 52 (6):515–541. doi: 10.1080/03670244.2013.769099.

Paarlberg, Robert. 2008. *Starved for Science: How Biotechnology Is Being Kept Out of Africa*. Cambridge, MA and London: Harvard Univ. Press.

Padoch, Christine. 1985. "Labor Efficiency and Intensity of Land Use in Rice Production: An Example from Kalimantan." *Human Ecology* 13:271–289.

Parrett, Tom. 2015. "GMO Scientists Could Save the World From Hunger, If We Let Them." *Newsweek*, 21 May. http://www.newsweek.com/2015/05/29/gmo-scientists-could-save-world-hunger-if-we-let-them-334119.html

PBS Newshour. 2012. Business Fund Puts African Farmers on Road to Market. 3 April. https://www.pbs.org/newshour/show/business-fund-puts-african-farmers-on-road-to-market

Petersen, Paulo F., and Luciano M. Silveira. 2017. "Agroecology, Public Policies and Labor-Driven Intensification: Alternative Development Trajectories in the Brazilian Semi-Arid Region." *Sustainability* 9 (4):535.

Pryor, Frederic L. 1985. "The Invention of the Plow." *Comparative Studies in Society and History* 27 (4):727–743.

Reuters. 2017. "Agriculture Needs a Makeover to Lure Young People Back to Farming." *Reuters. com* 21 August. http://www.reuters.com/article/africa-farming-food/feature-agriculture-needs-a-makeover-to-lure-young-people-back-to-farming-idUSL8N1AR4WS

Ricciardi, Vincent, Navin Ramankutty, Zia Mehrabi, Larissa Jarvis, and Brenton Chookolingo. 2018. "How Much of the World's Food Do Smallholders Produce?" *Global Food Security* 17:64–72. doi: 10.1016/j.gfs.2018.05.002.

Rivera, María, Alejandro Guarín, Teresa Pinto-Correia, Henrik Almaas, Laura Arnalte Mur, Vanessa Burns, Marta Czekaj, Rowan Ellis, Francesca Galli, Mikelis Grivins, Paola Hernández, Pavlos Karanikolas, Paolo Prosperi, and Pedro Sánchez Zamora. 2020. "Assessing the Role of Small Farms in Regional Food Systems in Europe: Evidence d:\research\reads\from a Comparative Study." *Global Food Security* 26:100417. doi: 10.1016/j.gfs.2020.100417.

Robbins, Paul. 2019. *Political Ecology: A Critical Introduction, 3rd Edition*. Oxford: Wiley Blackwell.

Rogers, Everett M. 2003. *Diffusion of Innovations*, 5th Edition. New York: Free Press.

Rosenstein-Rodan, P.N. 1944. "The International Development of Economically Backward Areas." *International Affairs (Royal Institute of International Affairs 1944-)* 20 (2):157–165. doi: 10.2307/3018093.

Rosset, Peter. 2000. "The Multiple Functions and Benefits of Small Farm Agriculture in the Context of Global Trade Negotiations." *Development* 43 (2):77–82.

Salatin, Joel. 2007. *Everything I Want To Do Is Illegal: War Stories From the Local Food Front*. Swoope, VA: Polyface, Inc.

Samberg, L.H., J.S. Gerber, N. Ramankutty, M. Herrero, and P.C. West. 2016. "Subnational Distribution of Average Farm Size and Smallholder Contributions to Global Food Production." *Environmental Research Letters* 11 (12). doi: 10.1088/1748–9326/11/12/124010.

Semple, Ellen C. 1932. *The Geography of the Mediterranean Region: Its Relation to Ancient History*. London: Constable & Co.

Siedenburg, Jules. 2006. "The Machakos Case Study: Solid Outcomes, Unhelpful Hyperbole." *Development Policy Review* 24 (1):75–85. doi: 10.1111/j.1467–7679.2006.00314.x.

Smil, Vaclav. 2001. *Enriching the Earth: Fritz Haber, Carl Bosch, and the Transformation of World Food Production*. Cambridge, MA: The MIT Press.

Steward, Julian H. 1955. "The Concept and Method of Cultural Ecology." In *Theory of Culture Change*, edited by H. Steward Julian, 30–42. Urbana: Univ. of Illinois Press.

Stoll, Steven. 2002. *Larding the Lean Earth: Soil and Society in Nineteenth-century America*. New York: Hill & Wang.

Stoll, Steven. 2017. *Ramp Hollow: The Ordeal of Appalachia*. New York: Hill and Wang.

Stone, Glenn Davis. 1996. *Settlement Ecology: The Social and Spatial Organization of Kofyar Agriculture*. Tucson: Univ. of Arizona Press.

Stone, Glenn Davis. 1997. "Predatory Sedentism: Intimidation and Intensification in the Nigerian Savanna." *Human Ecology* 25:223–242.

Stone, Glenn Davis. 2001. "Theory of the Square Chicken: Advances in Agricultural Intensification Theory." *Asia Pacific Viewpoint* 42:163–180.

Stone, Glenn Davis. 2002. "Both Sides Now: Fallacies in the Genetic-Modification Wars, Implications for Developing Countries, and Anthropological Perspectives." *Current Anthropology* 43:611–630.

Stone, Glenn Davis. 2011. "Contradictions in the Last Mile: Suicide, Culture, and E-Agriculture in Rural India." *Science, Technology and Human Values* 36:759–790.

Stone, Glenn Davis. 2018. "Agriculture as Spectacle." *Journal of Political Ecology* 25 25(1):656–685. doi: 10.2458/v25i1.22385

Stone, Glenn Davis, and Christian E. Downum. 1999. "Non-Boserupian Ecology and Agricultural Risk: Ethnic Politics and Land Control in the Arid Southwest." *American Anthropologist* 101:113–128.

Stone, Glenn Davis, Robert McC. Netting, and M. Priscilla Stone. 1990. "Seasonality, Labor Scheduling and Agricultural Intensification in the Nigerian Savanna." *American Anthropologist* 92:7–24.

Stone, M. Priscilla, Glenn Davis Stone, and Robert McC Netting. 1995. "The Sexual Division of Labor in Kofyar Agriculture." *American Ethnologist* 22:165–186.

Stuiver, Marian. 2006. "Highlighting the Retro Side of Innovation and Its Potential for Regime Change in Agriculture." In *Between the Local and the Global, Confronting Complexity in the Contemporary Agri-food Sector*, edited by T. Marsden and J. Murdoch, 147–173. Oxford: Elsevier.

Tarr, Joel A. 1975. "From City to Farm: Urban Wastes and the American Farmer." *Agricultural History* 49 (4):598–612.

Thaindian News. 2008. Genetic Engineering Can Help Solve Food Crisis: US Expert. GMOFoodForThought 30 July. https://bit.ly/3u3MU8V

Tiffen, Mary, Michael Mortimore, and Francis Gichuki. 1994. *More People, Less Erosion: Environmental Recovery in Kenya*. Chichester: John Wiley and Sons.

Udo, Reuben K. 1965. "Disintegration of Nucleated Settlement in Eastern Nigeria." *Geographical Review* 55:53–67.

van der Ploeg, Jan Douwe. 2008. *The New Peasantries: Struggles for Autonomy and Sustainability in an Era of Empire and Globalization*. London and Sterling: Earthscan.

van Vliet, Jasper, Henri L. F. de Groot, Piet Rietveld, and Peter H. Verburg. 2015. "Manifestations and Underlying Drivers of Agricultural Land Use Change in Europe." *Landscape and Urban Planning* 133 (Supplement C):24–36. doi: 10.1016/j.landurbplan.2014.09.001.

Vogt, William. 1948. *Road to Survival*. New York: William Sloane.

Wilkinson, T. J. 1982. "The Definition of Ancient Manured Zones by Means of Extensive Sherd-sampling Techniques." *Journal of Field Archaeology* 9:323–333.

Wise, Timothy A. 2021. Old Fertilizer in New Bottles: Selling the Past as Innovation in Africa's Green Revolution. In *Global Development and Environment Institute Working Paper No.21-01*. Global Development and Environment Institute, Tufts Univ.

Wolfe, A.B. 1936. "The Theory of Optimum Population." *The Annals of the American Academy of Political and Social Science* 188:243–249.

Zimmerer, Karl S. 2013. "The Compatibility of Agricultural Intensification in a Global Hotspot of Smallholder Agrobiodiversity (Bolivia)." *Proceedings of the National Academy of Sciences* 110 (8):2769–2774. doi: 10.1073/pnas.1216294110.

Zimmerer, Karl S., Judith Carney, and Steven Vanek. 2015. "Sustainable Smallholder Intensification in Global Change? Pivotal Spatial Interactions, Gendered Livelihoods, and Agrobiodiversity." *Current Opinions in Environmental Sustainability* 14:49–60.

INDEX